The Armature of Conquest

*Spanish Accounts of the
Discovery of America,
1492–1589*

Beatriz Pastor Bodmer

The Armature of Conquest

Spanish Accounts of the
Discovery of America,
1492–1589

Translated by
Lydia Longstreth Hunt

Stanford University Press
Stanford, California
1992

Stanford University Press
Stanford, California
© 1992 by the Board of Trustees of the
Leland Stanford Junior University

Printed in the United States of America

CIP data are at the end of the book

The Armature of Conquest
was originally published in Spanish
in 1983 under the title
El discurso narrativo de la conquista de América,
© Colección Premio Casa de las Américas,
Havana, Cuba.
The second, revised edition appeared
in 1988 under the title
Discursos narrativos de la conquista de América,
© Ediciones del Norte, Hanover, NH.

Published with the assistance of the
Piñon Charitable Trust

To my mother, of course.

Acknowledgments

I want to thank all those who offered support, encouragement, and suggestions while I was writing this book, and, in a very special way, I want to thank Fernando Alegría, Jaime Concha, Alban Forcione, and Herbert Lindenberger for their comments and for the encouragement they gave after reading the first version of this manuscript, way back in 1983. I am also most grateful indeed to my dear friend and colleague Irene Vegas García who, with her characteristic enthusiasm, persuaded me to submit the manuscript for the Casa de las Américas Prize, and to John D. Wirth who encouraged me to prepare an English edition of the Spanish version.

I want to acknowledge as well my debt of gratitude to David T. McLaughlin for his unfailing support of my work while he was president of Dartmouth College, and to Pat and John Rosenwald, Jr., for their generous support of my research through the endowed professorship that I hold.

I am also grateful to my colleague Robert H. Russell who suggested the English title; to Teresa Thurston who typed the first Macintosh copy of the manuscript; to the Interlibrary Loan librarians at Baker Library, Dartmouth College, who facilitated my research enormously by helping me locate all sorts of hard-to-find documents; and to Nancy Lerer, from Stanford University Press, for her help in editing and preparing the English manuscript.

I am indebted to the Fundación Biblioteca Ayacucho, the American Antiquarian Society, the Dumbarton Oaks Research Library, and the Library of Dartmouth College for generously allowing me to reproduce all the graphic materials included in this volume.

Dwight Lahr helped me through the labyrinth of doubts and rewrites I faced when revising the translation. How can I thank him? There is no question that without his active participation in these revisions this English version never would have seen the light of day.

B.P.B.

Contents

Contents

The Armature of Conquest

*Spanish Accounts of the
Discovery of America,
1492–1589*

Introduction

No analysis of that elusive, mysterious, shifting object that I have called the "armature of conquest" can be undertaken or accomplished by merely sharpening the bright tools of criticism. It must first evoke a world fascinating and remote; invent a form of complicity that would allow us to share the chimeras, revive the legends, sense the disappointments felt by people living more than four hundred years ago. It must advance like an imaginary voyage, coming upon places never before discovered, experiencing the solitude of vast wildernesses, recognizing the faces of the dead, pushing back the boundaries of oblivion. Such is the endeavor at the root of this book's exploration, its written pursuit of a journey from fantasy to reality, from complicity to rejection, from mythification to criticism.

The period covered by this study was not chosen arbitrarily. It was determined, rather, by its object. It focuses on narratives of the Spanish conquest, and its beginning and end are clearly defined. The period starts in 1492 with the narrative discourse of Christopher Columbus, where we find the first verbal representation ever conveyed of America perceived in terms of the imaginary coordinates of a European worldview. It ends in 1589, the year of publication of the third part of Alonso de Ercilla's great epic poem *La Araucana*, the first deliberately literary expression of a new consciousness, and an irreplaceable testimony of the central contradictions that dynamized the conquest, while gradually undermining the prevailing conception of the world.

Situated between these two poles and spanning a little under one hundred years of history, the narrative discourses of the Spanish conquest of America are defined primarily by a shared stated objective: to provide a direct account of the concrete facts of the discovery, exploration, and conquest of the New World's lands and cultures. But when I refer here to the "narrative discourses of the conquest" I am not speaking of the reconstruction of the events written by the historiographical chroniclers, who based their narratives on the oral accounts and tales collected from the participants in the action. Unlike the historiographical discourse of the great chroniclers, these discourses of conquest were shaped by the voices of men who both participated directly in the discovery and conquest of America and shared a determination to become a part of history through the written testimony of their personal experience.

This testimony, preserved in various journals, letters, and other accounts, is not a mere narrative of the facts or the action. For overarching their self-proclaimed objectives and lying beneath the objectivity and veracity that their voluminous sworn statements so ostensibly presume to certify (such sworn statements having been drawn up constantly in support of the documentary character of the accounts), the texts present a set of personal and collective issues that project their significance well beyond that of a simple relating of the events, toward an inquiry into the nature of the interaction between the New World and its discoverers. The narratives of the Spanish conquistadors trace symbolically the internal dynamics of the exploration and colonization of America. Grounded in their representations, however, and drawing all the various texts together, there develops a signifying process that focuses on the transformation of the conquistador, his perception of America, and his view of the world.

The transformation of the conquistador's worldview that gradually unfolds in the texts of the narrative discourses of the Spanish conquest is related to another development, and it is the conjunction of these two processes that makes this discourse of conquest so fundamentally important. The concerns of this second development are aesthetic, not ideological; for the way in which textual strategies unfold shaping the presentation and transformation of the narrative material traces the beginnings of a new literature in the making. Gradually the aesthetic requirements and canons of Europe are left behind as this new literature begins to convey the new realities of early colonial Spanish America, haltingly and clumsily at first, but then with increasing clarity and conviction until it achieves the complex poetics informing Ercilla's *La Araucana*.

This book does not claim to represent an exhaustive study of all the texts, as numerous as they are diverse, that shape the various narrative discourses of the Spanish conquest. Rather, it offers an analysis of the armature of that conquest, based on a selection of key texts I believe to be representative of the main narrative discourses. For the fact is that the armature that shaped the conquest and transformation of an unknown world was articulated by many voices, which often conveyed conflicting representations of a complex reality, opposite points of perception and radically different modes of conceptualization. For analytical purposes, these different narrative voices can be grouped in three fundamental narrative modes or discourses. The first I have called the "discourse of mythification." It is defined by a conception of the world and certain representational strategies that lead to the creation and perpetuation of a set of myths and models that can hardly be taken to convey accurately the concrete reality they purport to reveal and describe. Up against this discourse, two major forms of "discourse of demythification" develop progressively throughout the period of the conquest. Shaped by different strategies both will, nevertheless, question the validity of the myths and models formulated by the former discourse, as they develop a representation of the conquest that gradually demythifies the reality of the New World and the process of the conquest itself. The first of these forms, in terms of its chronology, is the "narrative discourse of failure"; the second, the "narrative discourse of rebellion."

The first part of this study deals with an analysis of the first narrative mode, the discourse of mythification. This discourse shapes a set of representations that distort New World realities and idealize the nature and meaning of the conquest. Chapter 1 focuses on Christopher Columbus and on his formulation of a model of representation in which America would be conceived of as booty. Rather than revealing American reality, this model conceals the specific character of the New World and of its inhabitants, systematically distorting and instrumentalizing them. Chapter 2 focuses on the letters of Hernán Cortés and analyzes the author's use of fictional structures and narrative strategies to create a mythical representation of the conquistador and the conquest.

The second part of the book centers on the manner in which two major demythifying discourses question and increasingly challenge the models formulated by the discourse of mythification exemplified by Columbus and Cortés. It also analyzes the literary aspects of these demythifying discourses. Chapter 3 examines the mythical objectives formulated during the exploration and conquest of the northern regions of the American continent, focusing on the conquistadors' growing disillusionment and on the development of a critical distance from the models created by the discourse of mythification. The discussion concludes with an analysis of Alvar Núñez Cabeza de Vaca's *Naufragios* as a literary expression of the process of critical demythification already apparent in various earlier reports on failed expeditions. Chapter 4 begins with an analysis of the dynamics of formulation of mythical objectives during the course of the exploration of the South American continent; it concludes with an examination of the accounts of Pedro de Ursúa's expedition to El Dorado, in an attempt to show the ideological crisis and the symbolic elimination of prevalent myths and models as they unfold in the narrative discourse of rebellion.

Chapter 5 provides a synthesis of a set of essential points that express the progressive transformation of the conquistador's worldview and perception of America, throughout the different narrative discourses that articulate the armature of the conquest. And finally, the analysis focuses on the question of the unfolding of a Spanish American consciousness and its aesthetic expression in the form of literature. The basic text studied in this last section is *La Araucana*, which is examined both as a critical overview of the entire process of the discovery and conquest of the New World and as the first literary expression of a new consciousness.

The discussion of the origins of a Spanish American consciousness undertaken in this study is grounded on the analysis of how this new consciousness begins to unfold in the writings of the conquistadors themselves. The focus here is on the dynamics of transformation of the Spanish component of the new emerging consciousness, that is, on the metamorphoses of the conquistador, his worldview, and his perception of the new reality. Only marginal reference is made to that other version of the facts and their meaning that Miguel León-Portilla has called "the other side of the conquest"; or to the view of the nature of the conquest held by the conquered, a view that likewise underwent a transformation parallel and complementary to the one examined in this study. The fact is that any analysis of this second transformation—which culminated in the contradictory, nostalgic discourse of the Inca Garcilaso de la Vega rather than in the critical, disillusioned poetry of Ercilla—would go beyond the compass of this work. Such an analysis could not by any means be conceived of as simply another section of the present work: for historical, cultural, and linguistic reasons, its material would require a separate study of great scope and complexity.

Nonetheless, I do not wish to conclude here without stressing the point that any truly complete analysis of the origins and development of a

Spanish American consciousness would have to include an evaluation of multiple cultural traditions, the native and the Spanish, and an assessment of all the converging developments that contributed in equivalent measure to a new conception of the world and to the birth of a Spanish American historical and cultural reality.

Part One

The Discourse of Mythification

Chapter One

Christopher Columbus and the Definition of America as Booty

Images of an Unknown World

It was October 12, 1492. From one of the caravels in the fleet commanded by Christopher Columbus—a Genoese navigator, adventurer, and trader now soon to become Admiral of the Ocean Sea—someone sighted land: the Caribbean island of Guanahani. Neither Columbus nor any of his men could have guessed that this mere sighting was in fact the very first instant of the discovery of a new world, that it foreshadowed the first contact between two different cultures whose crossing would bring them very different destinies. Paradoxically, it was also the first step in a process that would reach more than four centuries into the future, in which American reality would be conquered, exploited, and destroyed.

Columbus's arrival in the Caribbean marks the beginning of a process of destruction of American reality. That process involved many forms of abuse and depredation. It caused a sharp, general decline in the size of the indigenous population within a few years,[1] devastating and culturally impoverishing areas that, until the Spaniards came to America, had been relatively well balanced and prosperous.[2]

But the form, instruments, and methods of this process of destruction were neither casual nor arbitrary. Nor can they be analyzed in ethical or philosophical terms that would separate them from the specific ideological and historical context within which the enterprise of the conquest was conceived and developed. This ideological and historical context lay at the very roots of a perception of concrete reality that must be examined, if there is to be any accurate understanding of the inner dynamics of the process of destruction condemned by Bartolomé de las Casas.[3]

At that first instant of sighting land, the discovery would appear to be inseparable from an innocence that never in fact existed. Not even in that first moment of their encounter can Christopher Columbus be thought of solely as a discoverer, or America as an unknown continent. Although these attributes pertained, Columbus and America were so much more than "discoverer" and "unknown" that to describe them thus, without clear reference to their specific historical context, would simply misrepresent the actual nature of Columbus's discovery.

When Columbus first sighted the New World, he was the great navigator of the Sea of Shadows. But he was also the prophet who had preached in vain for almost twenty years the viability of a western route to the fabulous wealth of Asia; a prophet chosen by God for the glorious venture of crossing the Sea of Shadows, a mission that he believed to have been reserved for him by Providence since the beginning of time.[4] Finally, it should not be forgotten that Columbus was a Genoese trader who was absolutely determined to make his dreams come true and to turn them into a solid, lucrative enterprise.[5] As for America, far more than being an unknown land barely discernible from the top of a mast, she was the sum of the knowledge, legend, and myth current at the time concerning all the strange places imagined to lie beyond the Sea of Shadows.[6]

It is essential that the terms of this first encounter between Christopher Columbus and America be thus specified, because they hold implications for the meaning and function of Columbus's account of the discovery. An analysis of his narrative discourse will reveal a fundamental shift in the literal meaning of his accounts. From the very beginning, rather than discovering, he confirms and identifies. The central meaning of the term "to discover," that is, to unveil or to make known, does not describe the actions and conceptualizations of Columbus, whose method of inquiry, informed by his need to identify the newly discovered lands with preexisting sources and models, was a mixture of invention, misrepresentation, and concealment.[7] Columbus's own calculations and knowledge of geography and cosmography long prevented him from suspecting that the lands he was exploring were a new continent.[8] For years he insisted on making these lands correspond to the cast coast of Asia and to what his historical, geographical, and cosmographical sources claimed about the little-known territories of the Far East.

Las Casas devotes entire chapters of his *Historia de las Indias* to an overview of the geographical knowledge available to the ancient world that Columbus could have used to support his project.[9] Aristotle, Plato, Albertus Magnus, Saint Anselm, Avicenna, and Ptolemy authorize the most varied theories of the circumference of the earth, the proportion of land and water on the Earth's surface, the habitability of the torrid zone, the breadth of the Sea of Shadows, and the existence of mythical islands somewhere in the midst of its unexplored waters. Pierre d'Ailly speaks of "extremely devout" people who inhabit "the farthest reaches of the earth where it is night six months of the year and day the other six; their lives can go on forever and they only die when, tired of living, they throw themselves from the top of a rock into the sea."[10] Aristotle and Saint Anselm claim that there are many islands in the Ocean Sea, and they refer particularly to the island called "Perdita," the greenest and most fertile of them all, and to how it would appear when not looked for and would vanish when sought.[11] Both Las Casas and Ferdinand Columbus refer at length to Plato and Aristotle's description of Atlantis, the island presumed to lie somewhere in the Atlantic Ocean. The version summarized by Las Casas, based on the Platonic and Aristotelian texts, goes into extraordinary detail:

> Plato speaks of this island's fertility, happiness, and abundance of resources; its rivers, springs, plains, countryside, woodlands, hills, glades, orchards, fruits, cities, buildings, ports, temples, royal households, politics, organizations and government, livestock, horses, elephants, precious metals of all types except for gold; its immense power, strength, and authority on land and at sea . . . but after their corrupt habits and ambitions made them forget the careful practice of virtue, this great and prosperous happy island, with all its kingdoms, cities, and people, was swallowed up by a flood and a dreadful earthquake in a single day and night, without a sign or trace of anything remaining except that the sea became hindered by mud and impassable to navigation for a long time thereafter.[12]

Las Casas's detailed summary contains several features common to a great many mythical representations of unknown places and fantastic accounts of travels and explorations, which circulated widely at the time. A series of motifs related to the lushness of nature, the presence of boundless wealth, and complex, sophisticated forms of social organization were repeated constantly, almost obsessively, in many medieval and Renaissance descriptions of faraway lands and countries. What is most relevant, however, is that out of all that fabric of truth and error, fact and fantasy, geographic data and fabulous accounts, there gradually emerged a complex characterization of what was referred to then as "the unknown." The vast region through which Christopher Columbus proposed to sail had never before been explored,[13] hence the name the Sea of Shadows. But Columbus had a very clear notion of what he expected to find there, and this notion was to play a decisive role in the development of his perception of the New World and in his subsequent exploration of it.

Columbus's image of the unknown lands and islands, which he identified with the easternmost islands and coastlines of Asia, was based on the same models mentioned above in reference to the description offered by Las Casas. These models provided the source at the time of an archetype of the nature and characteristics of the countries and lands to be found beyond the limits of the Western world. There are, however, four main texts that Columbus appears to have used consistently in his search for material to organize his understanding of the unknown regions of the earth: first, Cardinal Pierre d'Ailly's *Imago Mundi*, published between 1480 and 1483; second, the 1489 Italian version of Pliny the Elder's *Historia Naturalis*; next, a copy of Aeneas Sylvius's *Historia Rerum Ubique Gestarum*;[14] and, finally, a 1485 Latin version of *The Travels of Marco Polo*. The copies of these books used by Columbus have been preserved, showing all the handwritten annotations made as he read them carefully over and over again.[15] A number of these annotations refer to cosmographical and geographical questions and indicate the direction followed by Columbus until he reached his final—and mistaken—conclusions regarding the breadth of the Sea of Shadows and the disposition and proportion of land in relation to water on the surface of the globe. Other annotations, however, refer to the specific character of those lands, associating them with kingdoms either known in antiquity, mentioned in the Bible, or described in recent travel accounts such as Marco Polo's. Tarshish, Ophir, and Sheba, together with Cathay, Mangi, and Cipangu, are reference points to which Columbus returned constantly, first in his readings and then in practice as he attempted to identify the unexplored territory.

Notions held at that time about the nature of those lands were fabulous, as were Columbus's expectations regarding his journey. Some of the descriptions available were taken from Greek authors—mainly Ptolemy, Marino of Tyre, Aristotle, and Posidonius—those works had begun to circulate again in the thirteenth century. Other descriptions came from more recent scientific works such as Roger Bacon's *Opus Majus*, published in 1269, and the rest were to be found in travel accounts like those of Odorick of Pordenone, Sir John Mandeville, and, especially, Marco Polo.[16] These accounts were doubtless the main sources of information on Asia for the people of the time, and they provided Columbus with constant references as he formulated his project and developed his plans.

The image of the unexplored lands faraway that emerges from all these works taken together is complex and often contradictory. Pierre d'Ailly refers in his *Imago* to an Asia without bounds, spreading beyond the limits estimated by Ptolemy, its wonderful regions covered by lush vegetation and irrigated by immense rivers. He mentions countless islands in the proximity of India, abounding in pearls, gold, silver, and precious stones. He speaks of a fauna consisting of exotic animals like elephants, parrots, and monkeys, coexisting with an entire gallery of monsters and mythical animals—griffons, dragons, and so on—typical of any bestiary current at the time. And he speaks of the island of Taprobane, with its mountains of inaccessible gold defended by griffons, dragons, and anthropomorphic monsters. According to Las Casas, d'Ailly was consistent with Ptolemy, Solinus, Pomponius, and Saint Anselm when he claimed that ants larger than dogs watched over the treasures of Taprobane which was called the land of gold because of its mountains. Drawing on the Book of Kings, both Columbus and Las Casas maintained that on this mythical island lay the region of Ophir. There the vessels of King Solomon used to journey in ancient times, returning after almost two years laden with pearls, ivory, amber, precious stones and woods, and gold and silver mined for them by griffons and other monstrous creatures.

Aeneas Sylvius, on the other hand, provided in his *Historia* information that complemented that of the *Imago Mundi*. He incorporated in his work the main aspects of Ptolemy's thinking and ideas on geography, but disagreed about the enormous size attributed to Eastern Asia. He presumed the lands discussed to be inhabited by civilized, peace-loving people, and he contributed to the persistence of fantastic notions about those regions, held by people in the West, with his descriptions of cannibals and Amazons. Aeneas Sylvius claimed that it was impossible to live in the torrid zone but possible to sail around Africa, and repeated some of Odorick of Pordenone's most extraordinary descriptions of the Orient.

However, the most direct and detailed information on the distant lands of Eastern Asia was unquestionably provided by Marco Polo in his account of his travels. Moreover, this account enjoyed the credibility given to it by the fact that, rather than being the fruit of theoretical speculation, it was the result of direct, personal observations made by Niccolo and Maffeo Polo on their 1256 expedition, and by Marco Polo himself when he joined them to make the same voyage again in 1271.

Marco Polo's account was not an isolated case. From the thirteenth century on information was available concerning other journeys made toward Asia by noblemen and friars, such as William of Rusbruck, Andrew of Perugia, and Jordan Severac.[17] But what made Marco Polo's account special was the exceptional way in which it combined a great deal of practical information with extraordinary imaginative and enthusiastic descriptions. The author himself points out that a distinction should be made between speculative or theoretical works and his own, in which he states "distinctly what he saw and what he heard from others." On the basis of this distinction, he maintains the implicit credibility of what he presents, however fantastic it may appear: "For this book will be a truthful one."[18]

Culturally, the dissemination of this work was extremely important. Marco Polo's experience stretched the bounds of civilization to the limits of the Tartar Empire. His account provided a detailed description of the political, commercial, and social organization of a large number of kingdoms lying beyond the habitual reaches of the Western world. It describes one kingdom after another (Mosul, Kierman, the eight kingdoms of Persia, Kashcar), followed by the fabulous cities of Balach, Kobiam, Yasdi, and many others. The objectivity and accuracy of Marco Polo's observations on the matter of trade—the various types of merchandise to be found, the commercial potential of the places he visited, the practical viability of possible routes toward different points in the East—are complemented by the fantastic nature of the tales he relates from hearsay. The tale of the Old Man is a good example. The Old Man built a garden in a valley between two mountains, which was like the Paradise of Mohammed and believed by the Saracens to be so. In that garden, the Old Man deceived unwary boys into believing that he was the Prophet himself, and, training them in the skills of evil, he converted them into horrible assassins forcing them to carry out all his designs. Another example is the tale about the travelers lost in the desert of Lop, lured on by mysterious voices. But none of these fantastic stories is more fabulous than Polo's description of the Tartar Empire and the Great Khan. He presents in extraordinary detail all the social, political, cultural, and physical aspects of the court of the Great Khan, whose grandeur, luxury, and refinement surpassed anything imaginable in any kingdom of the period. In a setting of flowers, jewels, precious stones, magnificently decked animals, garments of silk embroidered in gold, walls covered with precious metals and surrounded by beautiful trees, lived a fairy tale king guarded over by twelve thousand men on horseback and surrounded by twelve thousand barons wearing costumes of gold, pearls, and precious stones which they changed on each of the thirteen most solemn feast days of the court.[19]

Marco Polo's account is filled with wonder and astonishment, but there is a consistent line of thought from which he never strays. Underlying his obvious sense of wonderment and fascination is the alert analytical and pragmatic attitude of the merchant—an attitude often present in Columbus. Read from this perspective, Polo's account provides the most complete guide to the commercial opportunities the fantastic kingdoms he describes offered to Europe at that time. Wherever he goes, he makes a careful inventory of the raw materials, crafts, and commercially interesting products available. Turkomania has cloth and tapestry; there is silk in Georgia; coal in Cathay; pepper, nutmeg, and other spices in Java; gold and precious stones in Mangi and Cathay; pink and white pearls in Cipangu.

Besides making a record of the local merchandise, Marco Polo always includes an analysis of its market value and often mentions the likely drop in value when a product's source is far from the main trade routes. He says, for example, that in the province of Kangigu "gold is found . . . in large quantities . . . but being an inland country, distant from the sea, there is little opportunity of vending" it.[20] This is why he pays such insistent attention to geographic conditions and possible access routes to all the centers of trade. Hard-to-cross deserts, narrow defiles, and mountain passes that make communication among different commercial centers easier or more difficult, navigable rivers that can compensate for the disadvantage of being far from the sea, ports, and so on, are carefully recorded, described, and evaluated. Marco Polo also discusses the hospitality of the inhabitants, the comfort a merchant can expect to find in inns and hostels, and difficulties in relaying or changing horses. He is constantly amazed at the advantages offered by the Tartar Empire, with its land communication system, its postal service, its royal network of inns and relay stations, making it ideal for organizing productive trade routes between the East and Europe. Lastly, he refers to two basic questions in the mind of any trader wishing to start a business: profit and risk. The first can be ensured by the establishment of transportation networks that will make it possible to pour into Europe's high-demand markets the oversupply of desirable merchandise stored in the East. The second can be minimized if, when routes are put down, the findings of preliminary studies such as those made by Marco Polo are taken into account, to identify potential problems related to geography, politics, or culture, and if the places chosen along these routes to serve as trade centers are safe, inhabited by people favorable to trade, and easily connected by land or sea with other points along the trade routes.

It would be impossible to find a more informative text for any would-be trader, colonizer, or discoverer than the account in the *Travels*, and it is in no way surprising that Columbus should have read it and carefully annotated his copy, or that it should have persistently influenced him throughout his voyages. Complemented by the *Imago Mundi*, the *Historia Rerum*, and the *Historia Naturalis*, an indispensable reference for anything connected with geography, botany, or zoology, Marco Polo's book completed the scholarly sources Columbus used to make his plans, and to which he constantly returned to compare his subsequent experiences as a discoverer and colonizer. Drawing on these essential sources, Columbus organized his material, selected qualities, eliminated differences and contradictions, and eventually succeeded in forming a general image of the object of his future journeys, to which he attributed certain archetypical characteristics that may be summarized as follows.

Asia was so enormous that her eastern shores were quite close to Europe. The Sea of Shadows was much smaller than what had been assumed by the ancients, and it could be sailed across easily in a few days, if the winds were favorable.[21] In that sea, some fifteen hundred miles off the China coast, lay the fabulous island of Cipangu. Between Cipangu and the Asian mainland there was a multitude of islands. The inhabitants of all those lands were light-skinned, peace-loving, cultured, and civilized, and both the islands and the mainland contained incalculable wealth in the form of gold, silver, pearls, precious stones, spices, silk, and all the other merchandise considered valuable in the Western markets.

These vast, unexplored lands—whose inhabitants "have fair complexions, are well built, and are civilized in their manners" and who have gold in great abundance, "its sources being inexhaustible . . . which nobody is exploiting yet"—had the advantage of being located beyond the range reached by the commercial expeditions of the Italian merchants; according to Marco Polo, "as the king does not allow of [the gold's] being exported, few merchants visit the country, nor is it frequented by much shipping from other parts."[22] The lands would therefore belong to the first man to reach them, in accordance with the rules of the imperialistic pattern of appropriation current at the time.

But not everything was so positive, in Columbus's conception, about those fabulous lands "awaiting him" somewhere in the Ocean Sea.[23] According to his sources there was also something uncanny and sinister about them, embodied in the monsters referred to by several authorities from Pliny on: griffons with the body of a dragon and the wings of an eagle; dragons that spat fire and strangled elephants with their tails; sirens, in the form of a woman and a bird or a fish and a woman, who sang sailors to sleep and then tore them to bits.[24]

Christopher Columbus was not alone in this view of the Far East of Asia. Around the same time Fernan Martins, a canon from Lisbon who had traveled to the Far East, was trying to promote the reestablishment of contact between the West and China, a contact that had been almost entirely severed after Marco Polo returned to Venice. Canon Martins attended the ecclesiastical council held in Florence between 1438 and 1445,[25] and there a meeting took place that was to have a great impact on the cosmographical aspects of Columbus's plan. Martins met a Florentine physicist named Paolo da Pozzi Toscanelli, with whom he exchanged information on astrology, astronomy, and cosmography; subsequently they apparently maintained a correspondence on these same subjects. Las Casas claims that while Columbus was in Portugal developing the plans he proposed to present to the court of Alphonse V, "he became very friendly with Canon Martins, to the point of discussing his plans with him."[26] It appears that Martins advised him to get in touch with Toscanelli and assured him that the latter would be able to provide scientific support for his plan to sail a western route to Asia. Columbus wrote to Toscanelli toward 1480 and received in reply a letter that included a copy of another, written to Canon Martins by Toscanelli, dated 1474. The letter refers to Columbus's plan to go "where spice is born." From a cosmographic perspective, Toscanelli corroborates two fundamental points contained in Columbus's plan. The first has to do with the size of Eurasia toward the east. Following the opinion of Marco Polo, who had extended it by 30 degrees, and opposing most scholars of the day, Toscanelli estimated it to be very much larger than it in fact was. The second point refers to the breadth of the Ocean Sea between Europe and Asia, toward the west. Toscanelli imagined the distance involved to be equivalent to a total of 4,500 miles divided into two sections by Cipangu, that is, 3,000 miles from the Canaries to Cipangu (as compared to Martin Behaim's 3,080), and 1,500 from Cipangu to Cathay. Columbus's plan would show an even smaller distance—some 3,500 nautical miles as against the real distance of 11,766.

It is not surprising that, given such mistaken calculations, Toscanelli should have recommended to the king of Portugal through his friend Martins "a shorter way of going by sea to the land of spices, than that which you are making by Guinea."[27] The introductory note Toscanelli wrote to Columbus refers to a sea chart, now unfortunately lost, that shows "whereunto you ought to come, and how much you ought to decline from the pole or from the equinoctial line, and through how much space, i.e. through how many miles you ought to arrive at the places most fertile in all spices and gems."[28]

In his second letter to Columbus, Toscanelli again argues that Columbus's navigational plan is viable and insists that the route he has indicated is true and sure. After outlining the essential cosmographic information Columbus will need, Toscanelli describes several places in Far East Asia. There are evident echoes of Marco Polo in his account, especially in regard to the description of Cipangu and its palaces, with their walls and ceilings lined with gold. In fact, Toscanelli's imaginary descriptions often overlap Columbus's. Both men imagined lands rich beyond anything ever before encountered, inhabited by peace-loving people inclined toward commerce and trade who, subject to no foreign sovereign, would welcome the first man who discovered them. Toscanelli tells Columbus that he must visit all these lands with their powerful kingdoms and rich, densely populated cities, for "that will be agreeable to those kings and princes, who are most anxious to communicate and treat with the Christians in our countries because they have a great desire to be instructed in our Catholic religion and in all the sciences that we possess."[29]

This optimistic prediction is especially interesting because it brings together for the first time two ideas that were to characterize from then on the philosophy underlying the conquest of the New World: first, a more or less explicit commercial interest in the potential treasure and booty lying in store in the lands to be discovered; and second, a religious justification resting both on a perceived obligation of the Christian monarchs and their vassals to extend the Christian empire and on a presumed need of the infidels to adopt the Christian faith. Toscanelli's remarks must be considered in the context of the early chapters of *The Travels of Marco Polo*, in which Polo describes his visit to the Great Khan and discusses the latter's request for Christian emissaries to give him and his people religious instruction. But the importance of the model formulated by Polo and Toscanelli goes beyond the literary, for it established one of the main ideological parameters that was to govern most expeditions to America. It shaped the perception of the West's initial encounter with the Americas. Once the roles and relationship of each group were irrevocably defined within the framework of the model, it was irrelevant that the inhabitants of the New World did not appear to have a particular interest in changing their faith. Within the ideological context thus created, the legitimacy of the conquest was not in question: as a movement designed for the propagation of the faith, its validity was absolutely consistent with the Christian worldview. It was thus logical to think of the Christian conquistador as a man chosen by God to subject the newly discovered cultures to the Christian West, represented by the Spanish monarchs, with all that this entailed economically and politically. And any material property acquired was considered to be legitimate compensation for the effort of propagating the faith.

The role of religion in the contacts between East and West, alluded to by Toscanelli, was certainly not a new issue. It belonged to a long tradition dating back to the Middle Ages, associated with the Crusades and the *Reconquista.** The ideological patterns emanating from this tradition were comparatively subdued for Columbus, as a result of his own particular cultural and class origins, for he was not a medieval knight but a Genoese merchant. But they would manifest themselves to an extraordinary degree with the first generation of great conquistadors, as they shaped the first century of the conquest.

It is difficult to find a more controversial subject in the documents on the life of Columbus than his correspondence with Toscanelli.[30] The authenticity of this correspondence, taken here at face value, is however of only secondary importance when it comes to analyzing and evaluating the origins and development of Columbus's plan, if we consider how numerous were the sources that informed it. Toscanelli's letters and the maps they describe do not really change the information assembled by Columbus from his readings of the *Imago Mundi*, the *Historia Rerum*, and *The Travels of Marco Polo*. Toscanelli's cosmographic calculations did little more than provide a scientific base for Polo's estimates. Moreover, these calculations were not entirely consistent with those eventually prepared by Columbus.

In any event, neither the cosmography nor the descriptions offered by this controversial source appear to have had much individual importance. They did, however, provide a point of reference for the practical aspects of Columbus's journeys. And they especially appear to have confirmed the elements of the archetype he had created for himself, based on his long years of reading and on the strange tales and objects he had heard about, such as mysterious pieces of carved wood or the bodies of pale-faced, exotic-looking men and women pushed eastward by the sea toward Galway Bay or the Madeira Islands in stormy winter weather. Columbus had an image of what those remote lands were like and what they promised as they awaited him, the man chosen by Providence, on the other side of

---

*The series of campaigns fought by the Christian states between the eighth and the fifteenth centuries to recapture territory after the occupation of the Iberian Peninsula by the Moors. By the mid-thirteenth century the latter retained their hegemony only in the south, which they lost with the fall of Granada to the Spanish monarchs in 1492.—TRANS.

a sea that had almost lost its shadows, that had almost ceased to be unnavigable as he shortened its breadth degree by degree with each new calculation.

A Real World Disregarded

This archetype, which invested Columbus's knowledge of the lands he proposed to discover with imagination and conjecture, influenced him considerably as he conceived and developed the plans for his venture. But, paradoxically, it became even more important during his four voyages as he explored the New World and formulated his conceptualization of its reality. Contact with this New World should have led Columbus to correct his model, and the experience of discovery and exploration should have initiated a new period of practical learning. But, instead of approaching the exploration of new territories as the means to discovery, he relied on his own preconceived ideas about the new lands as the mechanism for reducing reality, distorting it, and ignoring what was actually there.

There are several reasons why Columbus's archetype survived in the face of so much evidence to the contrary. First, the cultural and scientific context of the period was such that it could easily absorb theoretical formulations inconsistent with the new empirical findings. Certain cosmographic theories, for example, continued to hold sway long after the explorations undertaken by Portuguese navigators had proved them to be false. One such theory was that the land below the equator was uninhabitable, which continued to be believed several years after the Portuguese had reached the Cape of Good Hope. Second, Columbus's worldview, reflected consistently in all his writing, demonstrates an irrationality involved in his own particular messianism that prevented him from altering his model.

Las Casas exhaustively discusses the notion that Columbus and his mission as a discoverer and evangelizer were part of a divine plan determined long before his birth. Throughout the *Historia de las Indias*, Las Casas supports his opinions with scholarly references in an attempt to prove beyond question that Columbus was no less than God's envoy, sent to discover the New World and convert it to Christianity. With a zeal informed more by passion than by objectivity, Las Casas unearths prophecies and commentaries on the Scriptures and the classics, which he claims clearly predict Columbus's discovery of America.[31] His arguments would be merely of anecdotal interest were it not for the fact that they reinforce the line of reasoning running throughout Columbus's own discourse, from the *Journal* of his first voyage to the *Lettera Rarissima* written to the king and queen from Jamaica in 1503. In the *Journal* Columbus refers from the very outset to God as working through his agent Columbus and attributes to God actions that range from running the ships aground at Nativity Island to locating the Babeque gold mines.[32]

It might appear that God's role reduces the Admiral to the level of a mere instrument, diminishing much of the merit of Columbus's choices and deeds. But this is to judge from a modern perspective and not in the religious context of the times. In Columbus's day, to be an instrument of Divine Providence did not mean that a man lost honor or merit; on the contrary, his prestige and credibility increased to the point of making him nearly infallible. Any potential loss of responsibility or initiative was more than outweighed by an authority that virtually eliminated the possibility of error, guaranteeing the success of actions that appeared to be directly inspired by God.[33]

It is clear from his own statements that Columbus saw himself as an instrument of divine will and believed everything he did to be guided and protected by God. At the beginning of his letter to Santangel he refers to the discovery as the "great victory with which Our Lord has crowned my voyage." Only at the end of the letter does he include the sovereigns in his partnership with God, making them as it were honorary members: "Our Redeemer has given the victory to our most illustrious King and Queen."[34] On his second voyage, his confidence in divine support takes the form of repeated appeals to God in his mercy to alleviate his problems, sorrows, and disappointments. The fact that now his relationship with God is reduced to an appeal for divine mercy implies that his messianic optimism has been temporarily suspended, and constitutes a sign pointing, within the context of his narrative discourse, to a referent that is never explicitly uttered. This referent is failure, unmentionable by definition within the ideological parameters that guarantee the success of any project inspired and guided by God. The appeals to divine mercy that appear so frequently in Columbus's account of his second voyage allude over and over again to the elliptical, albeit specific, terms of a discouraging problematic reality that make God's protection especially necessary. However, his hesitation and vulnerability are over by the third voyage, when he again claims himself to be a man chosen and protected by God who "led him miraculously to Isabella island" and "always brought him victory."[35] He is so confident that, when accused of incompetence in the administration of the enterprise by Roldán, he places himself explicitly on the side of God and implies that anyone accusing him of anything is committing a sin. "They brought a thousand false accusations against me, and this has persisted until today. But Our Lord, who knows my intention and the truth of all things, will save me as he has thus far; for until now, no one who has done malice against me has gone unpunished by Him."[36] Columbus's alliance with God seems sounder than ever, allowing him to threaten with divine vengeance a "them" who can easily be made to include the monarchs, according to whether they side with God and Columbus or with their enemies.

Columbus's messianic conception of himself and his deeds as the work of Divine Providence reaches a climax during his fourth voyage when, in the course of a hallucinatory vision, he hears voices assuring him of his special relationship with God and of God's loyalty toward his messengers so evidently in contrast to the ingratitude of the monarchs. The secret meaning of his tribulations as part of the eternally unfathomable designs of Providence is revealed to him, and the vision ends with an explicit promise of assistance and better times to come.[37]

The main problem with this kind of providentially supported ideology is the extent to which it weakens the role of reason as an instrument of knowledge. If actions are perceived as having been predetermined since the beginning of time and performed by a man illuminated and guided by God, intuition is tantamount to prophecy, and personal interpretation amounts to objective truth. This helps explain why Columbus held to his original imaginary conception of what the new lands were like even in the face of the most contrary realities.

His very persistence is an indication of the degree of blindness affecting his perception of America and of how distorted his written accounts are. Too often he presented reality in terms of what it was not, or turned it into fiction to make it fit previously conceived models. Within his narrative discourse, the fictionalized version of American reality conveyed by letters and journals was shaped by the substitution of a rational, analytical approach with a mere process of identification and association. From the outset, rather than observing and acquainting himself with the concrete realities of the New World before him, he chose to interpret each of its components in a manner that would allow him to identify it with his imaginary model of the land he felt destined to discover. This determination to identify the New World with the mythical lands described by d'Ailly, Marco Polo, and others is evident in everything he wrote in connection with his great venture: from the account of his first voyage in the *Journal* and the letter to Santangel to his last description of America in his letter to the king and queen written in Jamaica at the end of his fourth voyage.

There is reasonable agreement now regarding Columbus's itinerary on each of his four voyages. Furnished with his journals, S. E. Morison set out from the Canary Islands in 1939 to follow his route. The Admiral touched land at San Salvador and then continued on to Santa María de la Concepción, Fernandina, Isabella, Juana, and Hispaniola, after which he returned to Spain.[38] His first response to San Salvador was not overly enthusiastic, according to the journal entries on October 11 and 12. He makes a summary note of the appearance of the land with its "green trees and much water and fruit of various kinds" and mentions a paltry booty of "parrots and cotton thread in bales, and spears and many other things" that he says would be too tedious to describe.[39] He then hastens to mention that, although there are signs of gold, the Indians have told him that he must go toward the southeast to find both gold and precious stones. He concludes that he is northwest of the lands he is seeking, mentioning incidentally that there is gold in San Salvador as well (there never was, but according to his notions there should have been), and he proposes to go toward the island of Cipangu, which he assumes to be very near.

From then on, Columbus has a very clear sense of where he believes himself to be: in waters near Cipangu. He must therefore explore all the islands in the vicinity and ascertain whether they are what he expects to find—especially Cipangu. Discovery thus becomes a process of elimination: Columbus briefly inventories each island in regard to the fertility of the land, the level of civilization, the dress habits of the people, the signs of precious metals, before moving on. Impatient over what he finds on Fernandina, he trusts in God to guide him toward his goal: "and it is gold because I showed them some pieces of gold which I have; I cannot fail with the aid of Our Lord, to find the place whence it comes."[40] At Isabella he is encouraged by what he learns from the natives, who appear to be telling him that he is getting close to what he seeks:

> I shall presently set out to go round the island, until I have had speech with this king and have seen whether I can obtain from him the gold which I hear that he wears. After that I wish to leave for another very large island, which I believe must be Cipangu, according to the signs which these indians whom I have with me make; they call it "Colba" . . . and according to whether I shall find a quantity of gold or spices, I shall decide what is to be done. But I am still determined to proceed to the mainland and to the city of Quisay and to give the letters of Your Highnesses to the Grand Khan.[41]

He repeats this the following day, in words implicitly confirming that what he is doing involves a process of elimination:

> I wished to-day to set out for the island of Cuba, which I believe must be Cipangu, according to the indications which these people give me concerning its size and riches. I did not delay longer here or . . . round this island to go

to the village, as I had determined, to have speech with this king or lord, in order not to delay too long, since I see that here there is no gold mine . . . and since it is well to go where there is much business. I say that it is not right to delay, but to go on our way and to discover much land, until a very profitable land is reached.[42]

All the land between him and his goal is no more than "land drawn" en route, and its only interest lies in the fact that it may be indicating the proximity of Polo's fabulous islands.

On October 30, 1492, after having been on Cuba for two days, Columbus changes his mind about it being Cipangu. This does not mean however that he recognizes the island's real identity. Rather, he simply replaces his earlier conclusion with another, identifying Cuba as Cathay. On November 1 he changes his mind again: Cuba now becomes the mainland and Quisay. "It is certain," says the Admiral, "that this is the mainland, and that I am before Zayto and Quisay, a hundred leagues." He accordingly decides to send an ambassador ashore to contact the Great Khan and present him with a letter of introduction, signed by the Monarchs and brought along for the occasion.[43] He is now so sure that he is in the Great Khan's territory that he writes with great optimism about "the cities of the Grand Khan, which will doubtless be discovered, and . . . many other cities of other lords who will delight to serve Your Highnesses."[44] This confidence is particularly revealing of the way Columbus functioned. It should be recalled that at the time—a month after reaching San Salvador— he had found *nothing* of what he expected. This did not concern him, however, because once he had decided to equate what he discovered with what he expected to discover, the fulfillment of his desire was only a matter of time, hence the conviction expressed in his account that what he is seeking "will no doubt be found."

Contrary winds keep him from sailing around Cuba, and Columbus leaves the island persuaded that his identification of Cuba with the Asian mainland is accurate. When he reaches the last island he is to discover on this first voyage, Hispaniola, he decides that now indeed he has found Cipangu. So great is his need to identify his findings with his imaginary model that besides leading him to systematically disregard most of the concrete aspects of the New World, it persuades him that Cipangu may after all be near Cathay (i.e., Cuba), despite the fact that, like Marco Polo before him, he had estimated Cipangu to be some 1,500 miles from the Asian mainland. Moreover, he thinks he hears the natives refer to Cibao, a region in the interior of Hispaniola, and although the names are quite different there is no question in his mind that Cibao is the same as Cipangu and that the Indians simply do not know how to pronounce the name of their own island.

On January 4, 1493, after exploring Hispaniola for two weeks, Columbus decides that he is right in thinking that the island is Cipangu. In his transcription of the *Journal*, Las Casas says that Columbus "concludes that Cipangu is on that island and that there is much gold and spice and mastic and rhubarb."[45] The mechanism of Columbus's reasoning is clear, and the conclusions he arrived at are logical: if Cibao *was* in fact Cipangu it was *bound* to contain such treasures. But the premise was false. No gold or spices were to be found in Hispaniola. Blinded by his own needs and preconceptions, however, Columbus misrepresented the identity and nature of the new lands. In listing these products, he was creating a fiction instead of providing accurate information about realities he was unable to perceive objectively.

After convincing himself of the accuracy of his extraordinary identification of Hispaniola with Cipangu, Columbus concludes the fabulous discoveries of his first voyage by associating a particular region of the island with the mythical islands of Tarshish and Ophir. Pedro Mártir de Anghiera says in his first *Decade* that Columbus told him he had found the island of Ophir, which he identified with Hispaniola.[46] And Las Casas confirms this by referring to a letter from Columbus to the king and queen: "The Admiral says here that the island of Ophir or Mount Sopora (where King Solomon's vessels sailed in search of treasure) is this island of Hispaniola, which is already your property." Columbus returns to this point later in the summary of his discoveries sent to the sovereigns from Seville in 1498. There he speaks of "Solomon who sent . . . from Jerusalem to the farthest Orient to see Mount Sopora, where the ships remained three years, which now belongs to Your Highnesses on the island of Hispaniola."[47]

Columbus returned to Spain with a version of Hispaniola consisting far more of invention than of description. He had either assumed San Salvador, Concepción, and many other islands to be unimportant signs or transit points on the way to his real objective or misrepresented them in an attempt to identify them with his archetype of the unknown lands beyond the Sea of Shadows. The true natural and cultural identity of the islands in the Caribbean remained unknown after his long journey, during which he had simply "recognized" Cipangu, Cathay, Quisay, the kingdom of the Great Khan, Mangi, and the mythical islands of Tarshish and Ophir. But his sense of triumph over what he had "found" was to be short-lived, for it would prove increasingly difficult to make reality fit his schemes and intuitions and turn his fantastic notions into facts.

Throughout his second voyage, during which he visited Jamaica and the islands lying between Dominica and Cuba, none of his efforts provided him with adequate proof of the validity of his claims. Consequently, the language of the report sent with Antonio Torres to the king and queen would be very different from that of the letters and journals of his first voyage. Gone is the triumphant tone of the letter to Santangel:

> God has been pleased to manifest such favour toward their service, that not only has *nothing hitherto occurred to diminish* the importance of what I have formally written or said to their Highnesses; but on the contrary *I hope*, by God's grace, shortly to *prove* it more clearly by facts; because we have found upon the sea shore, without penetrating into the interior of the country, some spots showing *so many traces and indications* of various spices, as naturally to *suggest the hope* of the best results for the future. The same holds good with respect to the gold mines; for two parties only, who were sent out in different directions to discover them . . . found . . . a great number of rivers whose sands contained this precious metal in such quantity, that each man took up a sample of it in his hand; so that our two messengers returned so joyous, and boasted so much of the abundance of gold, that I fear I should weary the attention of their Highnesses, were I to repeat all that *they* said. But as Gorbalán, who was one of the persons who went on the discovery, is returning to Spain, he will be able to relate all that he has seen and observed; although there remains here another individual . . . who without doubt discovered, beyond all comparison, more than the other, judging by the account of the rivers he had seen, for he reported, that each of them contained things that appeared incredible. It results from all this that their Highnesses ought to return thanks to God, for the favour which He thus accords to all their Highness's enterprises.[48]

What is most noteworthy about this paragraph is its extreme ambiguity, the vagueness of the data it provides, and the way it delegates responsibility. From the outset, rather than using an affirmative mode of expression consistent with his earlier promises and with what the monarchs expect of him ("I have found more"), he switches to the negative mode ("I have not found less"). Treasure is referred to without specification or detail. There are "traces," "indications" of spices. At the same time, there is cause for optimism since he has not really been able to stop to explore beyond the shoreline. It is reasonable "to hope" for (or expect) much better things, not because of any immediate evidence, but because of the remarks of people who have seen gold in many of the area's rivers. Columbus, whose narrative "I" had performed every noteworthy action during the first voyage, suddenly relinquishes this role and with it, accountability for any mistakes. Responsibility is now shifted to other members of the crew like

Gorbalán, who describes what *he* saw, or Hojeda, who claims that he has seen so much gold in the rivers that Columbus himself finds this "incredible."

The style and structure of the *Memorial* show that the Admiral's confidence in his earlier identifications was being shaken by the real nature of the new lands before him. Two documents reveal, however, that the inconsistency between what he "knew" he was sure to find and what he was in fact finding had not destroyed Columbus's faith in his model, no matter how problematical this inconsistency may have seemed to him. The first document is a letter written in October 1495 by Michele de Cuneo to Hieronymo Annari describing the second voyage, in which Cuneo took part. He refers to the identification of a Caribbean island with the fabulous Kingdom of Sheba: "before we landed on the great island Columbus spoke these words: 'Gentlemen, I want to lead you now to the very place whence departed the three kings who went to worship Christ. The name of the place is Saba.' "[49] The "great island" the Admiral associates immediately with the Kingdom of Sheba seems to have been Jamaica, as has been demonstrated at length by Juan Manzano. The second document is even more revealing. It consists of a sworn statement signed by almost the entire crew, to the effect that they "could now see that the land turned toward the south southwest and the southwest and the east; and that not only did he not doubt that it was the mainland and not an island but would affirm and defend the fact that this was so and that, sailing along the coastline, within a few leagues' journey land would be found with people who were urbane, informed, and knowledgeable about the world."[50]

This statement was signed upon completion of Columbus's partial exploration of the Cuban coastline. Evidently not only geography but the judgment of a goodly number of the crew was in conflict with Columbus's interpretation. Cuneo, for example, is quite skeptical about identifying Cuba with Cathay and reports that most of the crew agreed with Abbot Lucena that Cuba was an island. In any event, however, the sworn statement indicates that Columbus was even then determined to be guided by his imaginary model and was prepared to go to any length to make the facts of reality and the perception of others abide by it. The mainland alluded to in Michele de Cuneo's letter is not just any mainland but the mainland of Cathay, Mangi, or Far East Asia, "the point nearest to the Indies [from where he was], or the point farthest away from the Indies over land from Spain."[51]

During his third voyage, Columbus's preposterous identifications reach their limit. These are carefully recorded in texts that provide a magnificent example of the literature of the fantastic, even though their author offered them as objective descriptions of the South American continent. The islands off the coast of Venezuela are taken to be the pearl producing islands of Asia described by d'Ailly in his *Imago Mundi*;[52] Monte Christi is Solomon's Mount Sopora;[53] and, what is especially remarkable, the Gulf of Paria and the Venezuelan coastline become the site of the Terrestrial Paradise or the Garden of Eden.

The procedure is simple: Columbus is faced with certain unexpected phenomena he cannot ignore, such as the turbulence in the sea caused by the flow of fresh water from the mouth of the Orinoco, the unexpected habitability of an area presumed to be largely unfit for human life, the light skin of the natives, the movement of water that appears to be flowing from Paria toward the Azores. This situation presents him with two possible alternatives: either explore the mouth of the river and the mainland to find out what really is there or resort to some of his literary models for an explanation. He decides on the latter and uses his habitual sources, from the Bible to the *Imago Mundi*, to prove that: (1) the earth is shaped not like a sphere but like a pear or the breast of a woman, (2) the nipple of the breast is in the region of Paria, and (3) the Terrestrial Paradise is on the nipple, together with the original sources of the Tigris, Euphrates, Ganges, and Nile. Using the same line of reasoning, he attributes the gentleness of the climate, the kindness of the people, and the lushness of the landscape to the proximity of the mythical garden. He believes that the whirlpools produced in the bay by the Orinoco are the original source of fresh water for the four great rivers. These, according to d'Ailly, start in Paradise and rush down a high mountain (the nipple), making a great commotion. Columbus attributes the din to the meeting of the salt water and the fresh water at the mouth of the Orinoco: a great lake is formed there containing fresh water that cannot easily mix with the salt water outside the bay.[54]

Here again, Columbus imposes a preexisting literary model on the realities he is discovering and exploring. Concrete reality is replaced by fiction, and the appearance of the New World is distorted to make it fit his preconceptions. Two years later, after the disappointments and tribulations experienced at the end of his third voyage, Columbus reviewed his success as a discoverer in a letter to Doña Juana de Torres, (quondam) nurse of the prince Don Juan. He by then no longer had the will to insist on his extraordinary associations except through a veiled allusion, implicit in his reference to "the new heaven and the new earth."[55] He had first used these words in his letter to the king and queen, written in Paria on October 15, 1498, to describe the lands where the Terrestrial Paradise lay.

When he finally had what he needed for his last voyage, Columbus decided to look for something very different from his fantastic Garden of Eden: a strait between the oceans. In the process, however, he made several new false identifications. Central America was identified generally with Asia, and the inhabitants of Cariay with those in Aeneas Sylvius's *Historia*. He identified Quiriquetana, the Indian name for the region to the interior of Admiral's Bay, with Ciamba, Marco Polo's name for Cochin China. He soon decided, however, using information provided by the natives, that Ciamba was the province of Ciguare, also in the interior. Finally, believing himself to be sailing along the coast of Asia, he identified the coastline with that of Quersoneso Aureo and the Malay Peninsula. Expecting to find the fabulous mines from which King Solomon obtained great quantities of gold for his treasury, he willed them to be—despite their nonexistence—the most recent fantastic acquisition of the Spanish crown: "The Aurea mines are the same as those at Veragua," he would triumphantly announce to the queen and king.

Columbus's substitution of an objective apprehension of reality by his identification of the New World with preexisting literary models is reflected by the elements that organize the modes of description and characterization in his discourse. The mode of description consists fundamentally of "descriptive confirmation," which is inseparable from a process of selecting data whose logical, inevitable consequence was the distortion of reality through the elimination of a whole array of concrete elements. Reality as it emerges from the descriptions in these texts is both fictionalized by identification and deformed by reduction. The mode of characterization reveals a form of selective perception whose purpose is to acknowledge only those features that are consistent with the need to identify America with Asia. Accordingly, the resulting representation coincides with the terms of the representational code implicit in Columbus's first theoretical formulation of his geographical objective: the lands in East Asia described by his literary sources.

What Columbus came upon first in the New World was nature, and it is not surprising that we find detailed descriptions of the new lands in the journal of his first voyage. A careful analysis of these descriptions reveals that they may be associated over and over again with a long tradition of representations of the Garden of Eden. Often they consist of no more than a simplified version of familiar Paradisiacal images of the mythical garden. With few exceptions, characterization is limited to the use of a series of set motifs and adjectival constants whose primary function is to link the material with the earlier literary models.

Columbus refers frequently to the air, always associating it with two of its qualities: balminess and warmth. Many other possible attributes such as luminosity, transparency, dryness, humidity, and so on, are just as frequently ignored. This is not because they were not present, but rather because only the balminess and warmth of the atmosphere provided support for Columbus's contentions, in opposition to those of others, who claimed that the lands in the torrid zone across the Atlantic were uninhabitable. Reducing the quality of the air to its temperature and breathability offered a foundation for Columbus's convictions to the contrary.

The land in Columbus's account of his first voyage appears to be characterized only by its size, fertility, and topography. The islands are "large," "spacious," "extremely spacious," "extremely large," "green," and "extremely fertile." Seldom will his descriptions omit these adjectives. As to topography, there is constant reference to whether there are any mountains on the land. Until he reaches Hispaniola, Columbus remarks that all the islands are flat, adding in some cases "very flat, without any mountains."[56] Here again, the repeated reference to topography and the natural richness of the soil by means of a very limited, repetitive list of adjectives, far from being arbitrary, reflects the specific components of his imaginary model. The natural richness and lushness of the land are referred to constantly by Columbus's sources in describing Far East Asia. And the presence or absence of mountains has to do with the identification of the Caribbean islands with islands in Asia, full of fabulous quantities of gold, according to d'Ailly; with Mount Sopora in the mythical regions of Tarshish and Ophir; and with Marco Polo's mountainous Cipangu.

Water is described by Columbus solely with regard to its abundance: there are deep rivers, large lakes, "a great deal of water," and so on. The effect of this description is twofold: it establishes a connection with d'Ailly's account of large amounts of water in East Asia; and it reinforces the notion of lushness and fertility, thus suggesting an association with the natural richness of the land in Asia described by Marco Polo.

American fauna is merely described as exotic. The Admiral refers briefly to misshapen parrots, monkeys, and fish, stressing their difference from those in the West and imbuing them with a strangeness that brings to mind the flora and fauna described in Pliny's *Historia Naturalis* and several medieval bestiaries.

Last, there is the vegetation in America, an astonishing, overwhelming reality for any European new to the tropics. Unlike Morison, for whom

Columbus's description of tropical nature are sometimes filled with poetical inspiration and resonance, I believe these descriptions to be singularly poor, limited to repeated allusions to a few typical attributes through an even more limited use of adjectives. In Columbus's perception, tropical vegetation possesses only two qualities. The first, lushness, is described by two sets of adjectives related to the categories of fertility (the obsessive repetition of the word "greenness," the implicit equivalence between "green" and "beautiful") and abundance (constant mention of the words "thick," "large," "numerous," "countless," and so on). The second quality, material value, involves the potential for producing spices. Columbus's mental reaction to every unknown tree he finds—meaning almost all of them—is always the same. He either identifies it, often mistakenly, as a highly prized species such as the mastic tree or the aloe;[57] or he avoids describing it, referring only to its greenness or the lushness of its leaves and fruit. Any specific features are usually replaced by attributes associated with the potential for producing valuable spices in high demand such as nutmeg, cloves, and pepper.[58] Once again, the process is not arbitrary: when it came to identifying what Columbus was seeing with what he was trying to confirm, both lushness and the potential for producing spices were essential attributes.

Gold, precious stones, and pearls deserve special mention in the context of this examination of Columbus's attitude toward the gifts of nature. Holding a special place in his estimation, they were central to the way his method functioned. This is not to imply that his description or characterization of them was unique or more precise. But their existence was essential to the validity of his confirmation process, and the identification of America with his Asian model depended on his success in finding them. Their value was therefore not only material but symbolic. They were the key to the validity of his interpretations and the good fortune of his enterprise: without them he could sustain neither. It was fundamental that the mythical treasures described by Marco Polo, predicted by d'Ailly and Aeneas Sylvius, and promised by Columbus at the outset of his venture become materialized in the New World in the form of gold and precious stones. Hence the urgency of the search for such treasures above all else from the point of view of the Admiral, who "only sought gold."[59] Columbus's repeated claims concerning fabulous amounts of gold, silver, and precious stones are based on a prior knowledge rather than on exploration. In Columbus's reasoning, it was not that America was Asia because the plenty predicted by the model had been found there. Rather, that plenty *had to be* somewhere in the new lands, since, as far as the Admiral was concerned, the lands were unquestionably part of Asia.

In the summary that introduces the January 30, 1494, *Memorial*, Columbus refers to only three of the many components of American reality highlighted in his first journal: spices, of which he now finds only signs ("traces," "indications"); gold, remarked on solely in terms of its abundance ("*a great number* of rivers . . . contained this precious metal *in such quantity*"); and land, described only with regard to its fertility or potential for production: "We are very certain, as the fact has shown, that wheat and grapes will grow very well in this country . . . everything is so wonderful, that there is no country on which the sun sheds his beams that can present such an appearance, together with so productive a soil."[60] And the progressive establishment in the text of an equivalence between "productive" and "beautiful," to the point where the terms practically become synonymous, affords a perfect illustration of the ideology underlying Columbus's aesthetic and descriptive criteria.

Columbus continues to use this method of descriptive confirmation during his third and fourth voyages, with adjustments suited to their respective purposes. Thus, in his account of the islands off the coast of Paria, the mouth of the Orinoco, and the South American coastline, he notes in particular only those aspects that will allow him to argue in favor of identifying the newly found lands with the pearl islands of the Orient described by Polo or with the Terrestrial Paradise as portrayed in the *Imago Mundi*. Gold, which is central to his being able to identify Central American with Quersoneso Aureo, takes absolute precedence in the texts on his fourth voyage.

The use of this method, which simultaneously distorts and reduces the specific attributes of American realities, is not limited to the descriptive confirmation of the elements of nature. It also structures Columbus's characterization of the most important aspect of American reality, its people. From the first voyage on, he negatively views the inhabitants of the New World. Again he takes his model from *The Travels of Marco Polo*. But unlike the people described by Polo, the natives of the Caribbean are "poor," and they neither wear clothes, possess weapons, nor engage in trade. Thus characterized, they are reduced to the exact opposite of the Polo model. Everything about this initial perception may be taken to refer to two main attributes: the material worth of the Caribbeans, reflected by their level of civilization, culture, and wealth; and their potential for being used by the Western economies, represented in the text by comments on their disinclination for trade, their inability to defend themselves, and their indisposition to attack others. On subsequent voyages, Columbus characterizes the inhabitants of the New World according to his need to make what he finds conform to his models. His representation of the people in America as "gentle savages," developed briefly in his account of the second voyage, provides a basis for his fable concerning the alternative model of a factory as opposed to outright plunder. His report on the people he sees during his third voyage, however, with its stress on their light skin and the silky quality of their clothing, associates them with the people described by Polo and reinforces the identification of South America with Asia and d'Ailly's Terrestrial Paradise.[61] This association continues in the account of the fourth voyage, which again echoes Polo's portrayal of the Asians, referring to several important items in the lives of the inhabitants of Central America. First, there is their *clothing*: the people "go clothed" and "they wear rich clothes"; next, their *wealth*: besides "rich clothing" they have "good things" and their "chairs and chests are inlayed with gold"; then, *trade*: the "natives have markets, and they trade in merchandise"; and, finally, *weapons*: "they have wars" and "carry bombards, bows and arrows, swords, and armor."

These four items taken together are for Columbus tantamount to civilization. Their association with the people he describes warrants the claim that they are civilized and that Ciguare and Cariay are Marco Polo's Ciamba or Cochin China.[62] Having depicted the natives of the Caribbean islands as naked, poor, ignorant of trade or war and therefore as savages on his first voyage, Columbus would subsequently have to view the inhabitants of Central America positively, if the identification of the mainland with Polo's advanced cultures were to obtain.

In basing his characterization on literary models, Columbus produces an account informed by myth and fiction rather than by any objective historiographical material. Facts and attributes are adjusted to fit certain imaginary parameters of perception and representation, based on the presumption that Asia and the New World are identical. At the same time, the repeated use of descriptive confirmation as a means of apprehending and characterizing reality brings up a fundamental question concerning language and communication. As he describes his discoveries, Columbus selects or evades, interprets and transforms, creating a verbal representation of American reality in which the imaginary and the fictitious tend to be predominant. He offers a carefully reasoned explanation for each of his identifications and introduces whatever changes are needed to make the realities he discovers confirm his perception and provide evidence for the validity of his judgment. Nature, the land, the sea, the inhabitants, the flora and fauna are described in words appropriately chosen to transform them and to prove the accuracy and validity of his model and his cosmographical calculations. Especially interesting is that this approach is made to encompass a particularly irreducible aspect of the New World: the language of its inhabitants.

Columbus was not alone in the New World. America was inhabited by people who—unlike himself—had become familiar with her nature over a long period of collective history and personal experience. They knew, for example, whether there were pearls, spices, and gold; they knew whether the islands they lived on were large or small; they knew the customs of their people, and whether, how, and with whom they traded; they knew whether they fought wars, and how. These people talked to one another, even though—contrary to the Admiral's simplistically optimistic claims in his account of the first voyage—they did not all share the same language. Moreover, they talked to Columbus and to the other Spaniards. Columbus asked questions, and the natives answered them. He showed them samples of the merchandise he was seeking and used them as informants and guides. Yet the information they possessed about their own land and culture either never reached the pages of his account or always managed to be consistent with his fantasies. It always seems to have corroborated his associations, distorting the essence of each of his discoveries in flagrant contradiction with a reality with which the natives were of course well acquainted.

The reason for this is that what was presumably a dialogue between interlocutors appears in Columbus's discourse as a monologue in which one of the real interlocutors has been reinterpreted and transformed to the point of becoming a mere sign confirming the Admiral's perceptions. The way Columbus used what the natives told him, interpreting it systematically as it suited him best, involved such flagrant distortions that even Las Casas, who generally went beyond reason in defending the Admiral, comments humorously on the ease with which Columbus allowed himself to be convinced that what he heard and was told was precisely what he wanted to hear and be told: "He had already persuaded himself of this, and so everything the Indians told him by signs, which was as remote . . . as the sky is from the earth, he would adjust and attribute to what he wanted."[63]

Columbus's presentation of native speech varies throughout his writings. In the *Journal* of his first voyage, most of the information presumably provided by the natives—always corroborating his own identifications—is preceded by veiled or explicit caveats: "he understood that," "he believed they said," "it seemed to him that," "he believed that," "I understood him to be telling me," "as far as I could tell." This makes the truth of what is described relative, subordinating the validity of the information to the narrator's ability to understand it. This ability was in fact very limited, because Columbus could not speak the native languages. Nonetheless, the impression given by his narrative is quite different, for however cautiously he presents his information, there is nothing hesitant about the conclusions he draws from native reports. Columbus believed, for example, that he had understood Juana to be part of the mainland, and from this he concluded that he was sure to be in Cathay and Mangi. The inconsistency between his subjective interpretation of the facts and the objective conclusions into which he transformed them indicates the true function of his reservations: they are merely rhetorical formulas, with no effect on the ultimate message.

Later the Admiral made no effort whatsoever to use rhetoric to temper his categorical statements. He provides interpretations, pronouncements, and assertions based on signs and gestures whose real meaning he does not understand, without the least reference to his own ignorance of the verbal and nonverbal forms of communication used by the people he quotes with so much assumed authority. He becomes more obstinate toward the end of his accounts, especially in the *Lettera Rarissima*, when describing the third and fourth voyages—particularly the latter. Using the collocation "they say" he introduces a long series of statements claiming that there is trade among the natives, and gold, silver, pearls, and precious stones; that the natives possess weapons like those of the Europeans; that they use gold to cover their tables and chairs, and so on. Rather than being discouraged by the information provided by the natives, he subordinates it to his purposes, reinterpreting it and using it to corroborate the validity and accuracy of his identifications. When the discrepancy between what the natives say and what he wants them to say is too obvious to be ignored, Columbus simply makes a correction. This is particularly apparent where proper names are concerned. When he arrives at Hispaniola and decides that Cipangu is bound to be there, he must find a way to explain why the inhabitants call the region Cibao. The same problem arises when he reaches the "great island" referred to by Michele de Cuneo in his letter to Annari. He has promised his crew to take them to Sheba, whence the three kings traveled to adore the Christ child. Upon disembarking, Columbus and his men ask the inhabitants what the name of the island is, and the answer they are given is Sobo. At this, says Cuneo, "the

Admiral said that the word was the same, but that the natives *did not know how to pronounce it.*"⁶⁴

Thus not only is the specific information provided by the natives disqualified but also their authority as speakers of their own language. Their message, which becomes fainter with each successive distortion, is erased altogether once their verbal competence itself is made to appear doubtful. The implication of Columbus's corrections is now not only that the inhabitants of the New World cannot be understood because they speak different languages from those of the Europeans, but they are unintelligible because they do not know how to speak their own languages. The native viewpoint, initially ignored, is subsequently rejected, generally and explicitly, based on his new appraisal of their capacity. And the step from questioning the natives' ability to speak their own language to questioning the natives' ability to speak at all is, for Columbus, amazingly short and easy. He says in his first journal that he intends to take some Indians back with him to Spain "that they may learn to talk."⁶⁵ In his January 1494 *Memorial* to the king and queen, he remarks that the natives need to learn Spanish, but he never calls Spanish "our language" or "the Spanish language"; rather, he repeats over and over that the natives must learn "language," as if they had none of their own. Needless to say, the possibility of the Spaniards learning the language of the natives is never even suggested.

Columbus's extension of his method of descriptive confirmation to the native language—distorting, amending, and inventing it, and ultimately questioning its very existence—has important implications. Denying the natives their possession of speech, the Admiral appropriates language and with it all linguistic representation of the new reality, to the exclusion of any alternative interpretation. In consequence, the first portrayal of America—the representation contained in Columbus's writings—is presented as objective and comprehensive rather than as subjective and biased. Columbus grants himself the exclusive right to *create* America where its inhabitants are concerned, following the parameters of his literary model, and he presents the resulting fiction as if its accuracy were undeniable. Further, the implicit denial in his narrative of the natives' capacity for speech amounts to a denial of any form of cultural pluralism. Just as the language spoken by Columbus is presented as *language itself* versus the silence imposed on the natives, Western culture is presented as *culture* in opposition to the natives' implied cultural vacuum. Because he speaks *language* and represents *culture*, it is he who is entitled to conceive of, formulate, and define language, culture, and humankind; he who may select the forms of exchange and relations between Spain as the representative of

Western civilization and America as a future economic and cultural appendage of Europe. Columbus's complete appropriation of language throughout the narrative discourse constituted by his letters and journals, in a manner that because of its insidiousness and subtlety gives an impression of innocence, marks the beginning of a relationship of power and exploitation between two continents: Europe and America. At the same time, it marks the beginning of a long historiographical, philosophical, and literary tradition in the representation and analysis of American reality, which was to be characterized by an exclusively European historicocultural perspective and by the systematic elimination of the natives' perception of that reality.

The Instrumentalization of Reality

The fictionalization of America through the use of literary models is neither the single nor the most important process of distortion that shapes the Admiral's narrative discourse. It represents a secondary aspect of another process of transformation. Its drive is economic rather than literary as it seeks, discreetly at first but ever more explicitly later on, to define the New World strictly for commercial purposes. Rather than being mutually exclusive, these two forms of distortion complement each other and appear to be rooted in the same archetype. The literary sources of Columbus's imaginary model often described lands they had never seen, combining the fantastic theories of the ancient with legends, myths, hearsay, tales culled from bestiaries, and a large dose of imagination. If they are to be classified at all, these studies of the world were no doubt far more literary than scientific. Marco Polo built upon his sound, lucid, commercial inventory a fabulous fiction of East Asia, mixing the direct account of his experience—often inextricably—with complementary legends and tales, thus giving it a dimension of fiction and the fantastic. Even Pliny's *Historia Naturalis* included, notwithstanding its scientific title, an array of mythical, fabulous elements inconsistent with natural reality but faithfully illustrative of the contemporary worldview.

Columbus's imaginary model was a selective amalgamation of the material drawn from these sources rather than an imitation of any one of them. He based his selection on European commercial criteria, with an emphasis on utilitarian concerns current at the time, and the selective criteria implied in the choice of specific elements provides an initial insight into the ideological structures underlying the discovery and the subsequent development of the conquest of America.

In spite of the mythical image that emerges from many traditional, well-meaning, but not particularly accurate, critical and biographical accounts of the life of Columbus, his writings reveal a man who was far from being merely a dreamer. He was no doubt unusually imaginative, for otherwise he could have neither conceived nor executed his plans. But this is not to ignore that he was not exactly a selfless poet, or that his talents were directed toward satisfying certain concrete material and social interests. Columbus's messianic conception of the divine foundations of his role and venture was complemented by his notion of the precise economic and entrepreneurial aspects of his mission and the material benefits he could expect from its success.[66] It is therefore not surprising that the specific elements that we find in his imaginary model of the New World should have had more to do with the symbolic representation of the commercial designs of a merchant than with the musings of a dreamer. Pearls, gold, precious stones, silk, and spices were certainly meant to stir people's imaginations with their dreamlike magnificent qualities, but they also constituted a shopping list that happened to include the most valuable commodities on the European market.

The image of vast expanses of unknown lands, inhabited by prosperous, civilized, peace-loving people with a long tradition as tradesmen not only corresponded to Marco Polo's version of Asia but reflected the need for trade and new markets that Columbus's project promised to satisfy. The notes he made on the margins of the *Imago Mundi* and *The Travels of Marco Polo* provide an early indication of the specific elements that would address Europe's commercial needs and that, once incorporated into the final composition of Columbus's archetype of the New World, would shape his perception of America through his repeatedly mistaken identifications. But although his model reflected the mentality of a European tradesman, the commercial implications of this venture went much further. After obtaining the support of the king and queen, he signed a contract under which he was granted important privileges but which also committed him to the achievement of certain results.[67] The idea had been his, but its execution depended on the money contributed by a number of investors. At first voyages to the the Indies were financed almost exclusively by the Crown, with the exception of certain funds provided by a few Genoese tradesmen and private citizens living in the south of Spain. It was only when success appeared certain that the Castillian merchants became an important source of funding.[68] By accepting vessels and provisions from such investors, Columbus committed himself to finding in the Indies or any other lands he discovered everything he had promised.

This commitment was very considerable indeed, and it throws light on an important aspect of Columbus's determination to characterize things as he did, during his subsequent voyages. His identification of the New World with his imaginary model of the islands and other lands in Eastern Asia served two basic functions. The first was personal, for it allowed him to validate his cosmographical theories, prove the accuracy of his plan and the ideas and calculations on which it was founded, and confirm in his own estimation that he was God's chosen agent. The second function was economic, serving to justify his venture commercially and establish his prestige in the eyes of his investors. Thus his obsession for identifying things was not merely a question of irrationality or boundless imagination, for it also had to do with the obligation to fulfill his financial commitments. The growing pressure he was under explains his repeated insistence on certain apparently arbitrary identifications, which would otherwise make him seem unreasonable in the extreme. The irrational, messianic conception he had of his mission was an important factor in allowing him to hold on to the validity of his model in the face of the relentless contradictions of reality. But it was only one factor among others, for his dogged defense of his claims also reflected specific obligations involving certain very real promises and contracts.

Columbus's mercantile ideology together with his economic commitments to the Crown are at the foundation of a process involving the fictionalization of American reality for commercial purposes. In Columbus's writings, the first code of representation portrayed America in terms of his literary models. This code of representation was complemented by another, which made her a function of the commercial requirements of Europe. The New World was thus redefined, transformed, and instrumentalized to meet the demands of both the imaginary model and the European economy.

The process of gradual instrumentalization that we find in Columbus's writings starts with an inventory. The order of priorities is always the same: gold, precious stones, spices, and then the rest. His route is largely determined by the need to find gold. During the first voyage he barely stops along the way as he follows the real or perceived indications of the natives toward its source. He looks for pearls on his third voyage, gold again on the second and fourth. During the latter he abandons his plan to find a strait between the two oceans and returns to Veragua because he thinks he has seen significant indications of gold there and associates the area with Quersoneso Aureo and King Solomon's mines. The need to find spices, however, becomes more and more pressing and, as a result, the vegetation in America is likewise transformed by his increasingly utilitarian perception. In one particularly striking instance, he loads ten quintals of worthless agave plants into one of his vessels, convinced that what he has found is the extremely valuable aloe. The unfamiliar trees he sees—meaning most of them—present his fancy with a number of possibilities and become in his imagination the source of pepper, resin, and aloe. He sees a tree that was probably full of parasites as a sample of a bizarre species:

> Many of them had many branches of different kinds, and all coming from one root; one branch is of one kind and one of another, and they are so unlike each other that it is the greatest wonder in the world. . . . How great is the difference between one and another! For example: one branch has leaves like those of a cane and another leaves like those of a mastic tree, and thus, on a single tree, there are five or six different kinds all so diverse from each other. They are not grafted, for it might be said that it is the result of grafting; on the contrary, they are wild.

Here again Columbus's will outweighs the evidence before him, and he remarks that the trees he finds, albeit unfamiliar, are no doubt "useful"; he has "smelled" a strong scent of musk even though he has not seen it; the region is full of nutmeg although "it was not ripe and its use was unknown"; he and his men have found many mastic trees but could not gather samples because "it should be gathered at the due season."[69]

Having found, or rather invented, the two things he considers most important—precious metals and spices—Columbus makes an inventory of everything else. Anything that cannot be associated specifically with these two items is evaluated economically for its agricultural or commercial potential in Europe. Anything that cannot be processed or made use of there is simply omitted from Columbus's considerations. He has two projects particularly in mind, one involving factories or trading centers for which he proposes to study the potential for producing mainly wheat, barley, rice, almonds, olives, and grapes; and another for the establishment of regular commercial networks between Europe and America. The tropical lands of the New World are thus fictitiously transformed into Mediterranean orchards, as America duplicates the landscape of Andalusia and Sicily (as in his 1494 *Memorial*) or the countryside in Córdoba and Seville (as in the *Journal* of the first voyage).[70]

The goal of establishing trade routes for the transportation and sale of agricultural and mineral products to Europe shapes some aspects of Columbus's narrative. His descriptions are oriented toward identifying, selecting, and classifying natural resources in terms of commercial strategies. Mountains mentioned earlier to identify the new lands with Eastern Asia are now referred to in the context of this commercial code of representation regarding the difficulties they may represent for establishing communication and transportation networks. The deep, wide rivers, initially associated with d'Ailly's Terrestrial Paradise, signify according to this second code that the land can be used for agriculture and that river navigation routes can be established to carry its products.[71] Columbus refers to deep rivers and potential seaports constantly: rivers are "good" if they are "large," "beautiful" when they are "deep";[72] ports are "marvelous" if they are "useful," "perfect" if they are "ample," their beauty and perfection being determined by the number and type of commercial vessels they can accommodate. The most "marvelous" port is therefore the one able to contain the greatest number of carracks.[73] The adjectives Columbus uses do not reflect much lyrical enthusiasm for the natural beauty of the New World. The beauty of the rivers, coastline, bays, and other natural accidents of the terrain is secondary to their potential for either of his two economic projects. His consistent subordination of the perception and representation of every single discovery to his economic goals becomes increasingly clear: "He went to a creek . . . that the largest carrack in the world could lie alongside the land, and there was a place or corner where six ships might lie without anchors as in a hall. It seemed to him that a fort could be made there at a small cost, if any considerable trade should develop at any time in that sea of islands."[74] Beauty is evidently secondary to utility—breadth and depth—and the description of the ports is directly related to the acquisition and trading of merchandise.

The most complex aspect of Columbus's intrumentalization of the New World involves the characterization of the natives and their gradual transformation into potential merchandise. His first explicit proposal in this connection appears in his 1494 *Memorial,* but the perception and ideology underlying it are clear as early as the first day of the discovery. There is no qualitative change in attitude from that time on, through the *Lettera Rarissima.* Morison, whose biographical portrait of the Admiral is very positive and yet quite accurate, is forced to admit this in the light of the documentary evidence: "Even the Admiral's humanity seems to have been merely political, as a means of eventual enslavement and exploitation . . . and it is clear from the concluding sentences of Columbus's Journal for October 12 that on the very day of discovery the dark thought crossed his mind that these people could be easily enslaved." Morison is probably referring to Columbus's entry for October 14: "when your Highnesses so command, they can all be carried off to Castile or held captive in the island itself, since with fifty men they would all be kept in subjection and forced to do whatever may be wished."[75] It seems likely that having achieved nothing tangible on his second voyage, especially with regard to the treasures that he had anticipated with such confidence in his letter to Santangel, Columbus felt obliged to offer an alternative to gold, precious stones, and spices as a means of compensating his investors. He accordingly designed a practical way of making commercial use of the native population.

Columbus's characterization of the inhabitants of the new lands involves three main representational codes: an identification code, a commercial code, and an evangelical conversion code. The first two apply in the characterization of all aspects of American reality and are related respectively to his imaginary model and his commercial projects, whereas the third refers exclusively to his human representations. The relation among the three codes is not uniform but changes with each stage of the characterization. At first the identification code is the most evident one in his characterization of the natives, and is used until toward the middle of the first voyage. It reappears briefly in his description of the inhabitants of regions presumed to lie near the Garden of Eden, during the third voyage, and finally in his secondhand account of the people living in the interior of Ciguare and Veragua.

The second code appears a few days after the initial discovery, once Columbus recognizes the primitive nature of the natives. From then on both the second or commercial code and the third or evangelical conversion code are present, the second remaining throughout more or less openly subordinate to the third, and the third functioning as a justification for Columbus's commercial proposals.

During the last stage of Columbus's characterizations, which become gradually more defined in the period between his 1494 *Memorial* and his blatant proposals in the letter from Jamaica, the natives appear to be represented solely in terms of the commercial code. In the process of transformation that takes place gradually between the first stage and the last, human beings in the New World will first be metamorphosed into *beasts* in Columbus's discourse and, subsequently, into *things*.

The first stage is the shortest. The actual degree of civilization of the Tainos encountered by Columbus was very clear right from the start, and they could hardly be mystified or identified with the people described by Marco Polo. Still, this first representation of humankind in America is characterized precisely by a systematic inversion of the terms of Polo's model, meaning that the identification code is implicitly present.

In his *Journal* of his first voyage, the Admiral presents the natives as being naked/poor/cowardly/generous. They are neither aggressive nor do they have weapons, and each of these character traits is an inversion of one of the central aspects of Polo's characterization of the inhabitants of Eastern Asia. What is interesting is how Columbus combines these "negative" aspects to form a human type far more revealing of his ideology than of the actual nature of the Tainos. The first three features of Marco Polo's model in their inverted version—nakedness, poverty, and lack of weapons—support in combination Columbus's first judgment concerning the natives. The conclusion he draws from this first perception is recorded in his entry for October 12. Columbus remarks there briefly that "they should be good servants." The fourth quality, generosity, becomes another negative quality in terms of the Polo model, in the sense that it reveals the natives' lack of civilization resulting from their ignorance in the matters and laws of trade. But this semantic shift, which transforms generosity into an emblem of bestiality, takes place very gradually. On October 17 Columbus says, "They give what they have for whatever is given to them," and on December 3, "Whatever they have they give at once for anything that may be given to them, without saying that it is little, and I believe that they would do so with spices and gold, if they had any." On December 21:

> and they brought us all that they had in the world. . . . They did this all with such a generosity of heart and such joy that it was wonderful. And it is not to be said that because what they gave was of little value, they therefore gave it liberally, for they did the same and as freely when they gave pieces of gold as when they gave a gourd of water. . . . [They are] so generous with what they possess, that no one who had not seen it would believe it.[76]

But even as early as his letter to Santangel, Columbus expresses his twofold conclusions in relation to such generosity in a few devastating words: "They never refuse anything that is asked for. They even offer it themselves, and show so much love that they would give their very hearts . . . they gave in return what they had, like animals."[77]

According to the first code of identification, Columbus had classified the natives as *savages* and *servants*, and as *beasts*, because they were unprepared for trade in terms of European rules of commerce. Their other characteristics—they were gentle, hospitable, lacking in aggression, and bore no weapons—likewise led Columbus to characterize them in a particular way. "They do not bear arms or know them," he says of the Tainos on October 12. "They were good people and did harm to no one" is his entry for November 1, and he adds on December 24, "all display the most extraordinarily gentle behavior and have soft voices." It does not take long for him to reach a conclusion regarding so much gentleness and vulnerability. As early as October 14 he had remarked in his report to the sovereigns on how easily the Caribbean people might be made slaves, claiming that "with fifty men they would be all kept in subjection and forced to do whatever may be wished." On December 3 he insists on this even more explicitly: "ten men would make ten thousand take flight; so cowardly and fearful are they, that they do not bear arms except some spears, at the end of which there is a sharp stick, hardened by fire."

Thus appears the first portrait of the people of America, in the context of Columbus's first representational code. Perceived as defenseless, savage, and cowardly, their function is clear to Columbus. Rather than being traded with, as would be the subjects of the Great Khan, the natives are to be deprived of their property and employed as serfs. Because they are "loving, unselfish, agreeable to anything," this is the only role for which they seem qualified. And Columbus held on to this notion until the end of his fourth voyage. In his letter from Jamaica, he claims that he has seen in Veragua greater indications of gold during his first two days there than in Hispaniola in four years; "the land in the area could not be more beautiful or well tilled, nor the people more cowardly." Throughout the *Journal* and the letters of his last voyage, Columbus's inventory of the booty he finds will consistently be followed by a "green light" regarding the hospitable, nonaggressive nature of the natives, and what this gentle nature implies for him and his future fellow discoverers in terms of their exploitation.

Columbus's portrait of the natives and his interpretation of what it signifies provides by implication a summary of what for him makes a person civilized. This involves two essential attributes: aggressiveness and the capacity and desire for trade. Absence of the latter he considers to be tantamount to a loss of humanity, nontrading people being for him the equivalent of beasts, while its presence is what defines people as people and as civilized beings. In turn, aggressiveness is presented throughout his discourse as the second civilizing attribute. For example, referring, in his entry for December 5, to the attacks by the people of Hispaniola on those of Cuba, he establishes the following equivalence between aggressiveness and ingenuity: "the people of that island of Bohio must be *more astute* and have *greater intelligence* than they to capture them, because these men are very faint-hearted." And he implies a further equivalency, between weapons and reason, when he writes on November 23 that "since they were armed, they must be endowed with reason."

Columbus's characterization of the natives in terms of the reverse values of his first code is soon followed by another gradually rising from his second and having to do with the natives' evangelical conversion. Just as the identification code was inspired by his first explicit objective (the discovery of land in East Asia), the evangelical code is now inspired by the second objective (the dissemination of the Christian faith and the conversion of the infidels). And the use of the evangelical code to characterize the natives serves to reinforce two claims made under the first code: their primitive, savage nature is consistent with their lack of religion— "they had no creed" in the Admiral's words—and their meekness will make them easy to convert and manipulate.[78] But what is really interesting about this evangelical-representational code is that it provides an introductory bridge toward Columbus's commercial proposals, which he later developed to their final consequences in the form of his commercial code. Thus, the first proposal he makes to the sovereigns concerning the possibility of making the natives slaves is rationalized by his plan to convert them to Christianity. These are people, reasons the Admiral, who worship idols and behave like beasts, and most of them do not know "language." It would therefore be easier to spread the faith if they were sent to Castile as slaves where they could "learn language" and with it, the teachings of the holy faith: "they may one day be led to abandon their barbarous custom of eating their fellow creatures. By learning the Spanish language in Spain, they will much earlier receive baptism and ensure the salvation of their souls."[79] The proposal appears in the 1494 *Memorial,* but this is not the first time Columbus establishes a connection between the conversion of the natives and profit. As early as November 12, 1492, he writes:

> So Your Highnesses should resolve to make them Christians, for I believe that, if you begin, in a little while you will achieve the conversion of a great number of peoples to our holy faith, with the acquisition of great lordships and riches. . . . For without a doubt there is a very great amount of gold in these lands . . . and . . . there are very large bracelets, pearls of great value and an infinite amount of spices.[80]

This paragraph establishes an unequivocal link between the tenets of the evangelical conversion code and those of the commercial code: the very same quality that makes a man easy to convert—his primitive, vulnerable nature—will make it easy for him to be controlled and exploited. These two aspects complement each other, preparing the way for a characterization shaped by a commercial code of representation that will gradually transform humans into merchandise.

The focus of the commercial code has to do with the third major objective of Columbus's initial plan: material gain. Here, the perception and characterization of America as a warehouse of goods to be absorbed by the European market leads logically to the perception and characterization of

people in America as dehumanized merchandise.[81] This last characterization develops gradually and involves a series of semantic shifts and changes
leading to the establishment of certain basic equivalencies. The first of
these appears in the *Journal* of the first voyage, as part of the entry for
November 12. Here Columbus says that "they brought seven head of
women, small and large." (The word "head" was used this way at the time
exclusively with reference to cattle, just as it is today.) The equivalency
between *women* and *cattle* is directly related to another to be found in
Columbus's letter to Santangel, where he explicitly identifies *men* with
beasts. He again repeats this notion, expressing it differently, in his letter
to the king and queen written at the end of 1495 where he speaks of
"charging 1,500 maravedis the piece for the slaves." Here again, as sharply
criticized by Las Casas, the Admiral uses a term the implicit effect of
which is to reduce the inhabitants of the New World to the category of
beasts "as if they were *pieces*, or goats from a herd, as he calls them."[82]

Subsequently, in Columbus's mind and writings *natives* will gradually
become equivalent to *things*. For example, in the letter just cited he says:
"so there are slaves here, and from all appearances live brazilwood; . . .
and all that is needed in order to obtain the income I have mentioned is
for the vessels to come and carry away the things I have described."[83]
Placed on the same level as brazilwood and reduced to the status of
merchandise, the natives are turned into objects. Their nonhuman characterization, however, is a reflection not only of Columbus's perception
and ideology but of his commercial strategy as well, for it is no doubt
related to a rather thorny problem he would have to solve if he were to
propose to his very Catholic Queen Isabella the establishment of a trade
in slaves: how to justify on ethical and moral grounds the need to sell the
natives instead of—or besides—converting them to Christianity. There are
two parts to his strategy here: first, the enslavement of the natives is
presented in the 1494 *Memorial* as a condition of their conversion, a
means toward getting them to "learn to talk," "abandon their barbarous
custom," and hence their sinful ways. Second, the natives are characterized
in such a way as to deprive them of all humanity, either explicitly or
implicitly. If the people living in the New World are beasts or things, their
reduction to the status of merchandise and their sale like that of any other
item of trade should present no problem.

This transformation of human beings into merchandise takes place in
two distinct stages. First, there is the implicit equivalency drawn between
native and *servant* and between *native* and *slave*, to be found respectively
in the journal of the first voyage (entry for October 13) and the letter to

Santangel (which contains the following religious justification, "as many slaves as you should desire to be loaded, who shall be chosen from among those who worship idols").[84] In the second stage, Columbus becomes more explicit on the subject. In his 1494 *Memorial* he refers for the first time to the "unloading and reloading of all kinds of merchandise" and to "the traffic of slaves," thus making an absolutely clear statement about the reduction of women and men in America to the category of an appropriate item of trade.[85] Having defined the natives as merchandise, Columbus estimates their potential price on the European market and concludes, after comparing his "product" with those of other countries, that the American native is more valuable: "one of these is evidently worth three [from Guinea]." Next, he refers to the last factor that will make the natives valuable as merchandise, the demand for slaves in the West, remarking that "a large number of slaves are used in Castile, Portugal, Aragon, Italy, Sicily, the islands of Portugal and Aragon, and the Canary Islands—and I believe that there are no longer very many coming from Guinea." In view of the quality of the merchandise and the existing demand, Columbus decides that he will be able to sell the natives at "1,500 maravedis per piece,"[86] an excellent business proposition for himself, his investors, and the crown.

In my analysis of the strategies that shape, within Columbus's narrative discourse, a distorted representation of America, the term "fictionalization" can be used to refer to this overall process. This is not an arbitrary choice, for his characterizations in terms of the codes reviewed above produced an account much closer to fiction than to the reality it presumed to represent faithfully.

Throughout his letters and diaries, Columbus claims to be discovering when he confirms or verifies, revealing when he conceals, and describing when he invents. The context of Columbus's discourse is defined by his personal and social need to identify America with his models and to characterize it in terms of the demands and expectations of the European market. Within this context, the descriptive techniques he applied allowed him to replace what he saw by a fiction reflecting his dreams of personal and economic achievement. Anything considered irrelevant was excluded, as complex realities were reduced to whatever could be of commercial interest. This involved a systematic stressing of certain equivalencies and the substitution of "what things were" by "what things should be." These equivalencies linked his mode of representation to an ideology that went beyond him, and made it possible for him to define everything in the New

World in terms of its commercial potential. The fact that the criteria underlying Columbus's transformation of reality are not primarily aesthetic does not make the result any the less fictitious. His discourse draws on a literary tradition derived especially from d'Ailly, Aeneas Sylvius, and Marco Polo; the structures of his own imagination, enriched by his readings; and the particular economic and ideological demands of Europe during its period of expansion in the fifteenth and sixteenth centuries. None of these occur in isolation nor are they mutually exclusive: on the contrary, it is their dialectical relationship that shapes the fictional structure of the account they articulate.

Columbus's representation of American reality projected an image of the New World that would provide a basis, in the realm of the imagination, for developing a system designed for plunder, exploitation, and degradation—a system that inevitably led to what Las Casas called "the destruction of the Indies" without in any way exaggerating its scope or significance. But it would be a mistake to think of this image as the product of a single, particularly perverse imagination. Columbus was a man of his time, and the model he developed was consistent with the ideological structures at the foundation of the expansionist, predatory culture then prevailing in Europe. When his account is compared with the accounts of some of his companions, it is his that appears more sensitive and humane. His portrayal of the Tainos is considerably less degrading and offensive than those by Dr. Chanca and Michele de Cuneo. Praise such as his for the beauty of nature in the tropics is nowhere to be found in the writings of Cuneo, Chanca, or even Diego Méndez.[87] Columbus was more human, imaginative, and tolerant than most European merchants living at the end of the fifteenth century. But he identified with the prevailing ideology, hence his despair when he found himself rejected by the society whose worldview he had merely applied in practice. The profound disappointment and devastating loneliness expressed in some of the passages of the *Lettera Rarissima* must be understood in the light of this apparent contradiction.

Questioned by his investors upon returning from his second voyage, humiliated by imprisonment at the end of the third, divested of prestige as a consequence of administrative practices less unscrupulous than those of the Bobadillas who were sent to replace him, Columbus did not appear to understand that what was involved was merely the strategy of an absolute authority that did not want to share its power. By the end of his fourth voyage he had come to think of his enterprise as a failure and his rejection as a foretaste of death. In July 1503 he wrote from Jamaica:

I am indeed in as ruined a condition as I have related; hitherto I have wept over others;—may Heaven now have mercy upon me, and may the earth weep for me. With regard to temporal things, I have not even a *blanca* for an offering; and in spiritual things, I have ceased here in the Indies from observing the prescribed forms of religion. Solitary in my trouble, sick, and in daily expectation of death, surrounded by millions of hostile savages full of cruelty, and thus separated from the blessed sacraments of our holy Church, how will my soul be forgotten if it be separated from the body in this foreign land? Weep for me, whoever has charity, truth, and justice![88]

The Admiral's isolation in his exile on the island of Jamaica at a time when the general criticism of his prestige and achievements that had been steadily growing since the end of his second journey had become explicit and acute reflects his increasing isolation from the political and social context in Spain. Yet his perception of the New World as represented in his narrative discourse was perfectly consistent with the prevailing ideology and, far from being rejected along with its author, it became more and more deeply rooted as the conquest and colonization of America continued. And with the very notable exception of Las Casas and a small number of other dissidents, no one denounced the profound significance and implications of this perception, which shaped the succession of exploitative and abusive practices that became inseparable from what has come to be called—in the official version of History—"the civilizing of America."

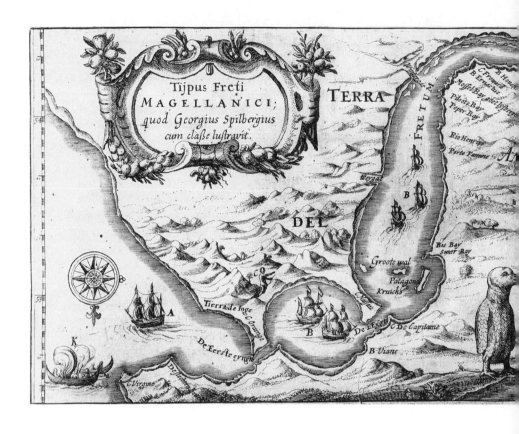

Tijpus Freti MAGELLANICI; quod Georgius Spilbergius cum classe lustravit.

TERRA

FRETUM

DEL

An

B Houtt
C Fraguer?
B Ernatbas
Mossel Bay of Isspering
Pilotte Bay
Peper Bay

Rio Hent go
Porte Famine

Bos Bay
Somer Bay

Groote wal

Patagons
Kruicks

Weygat

A

Tierra de fuge

C Orange

B Nassaw

De Eerste eyngh

De Fyet

C De Capitane

B Viane

B

K

Distachia

C Virgine

Map of the Strait of Magellan. From *Speculum Orientalis Occidentalisque Indiae*, by Georgius Spilbergius, 1619. Courtesy of the American Antiquarian Society, Worcester, Mass.

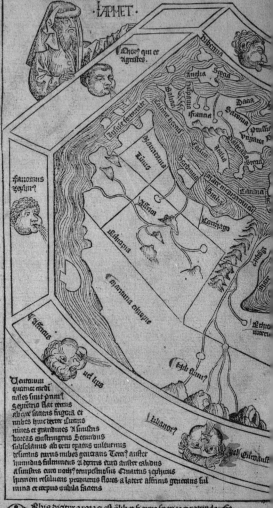

Uentorum
quattuor cardi
nales sunt primus
septetrio stat cornus
ab axe sumens frigora et
nubes hunc terre siccus
mites et grandines A sinistris
boreas constringens secundus
subsolanus ab ortu spatis vulturnus
vrientis euros nubes generans Tertius auster
humidus fulmineus A dextris euro auster calidus
A sinistris euro nothus tempestuosus Quartus zephirus
humerem resoluens prouintus flores a latere affricus generans ful
mina et corpus nubila faciens

Rbis dicitur a rota τ est qlibet figura sperica τ rotunda. Et
ideo mudus orbis dr. qz rotudus est; τ dz orbz terre vl orbisterra
ru. Sicut at bm vince. filij sem obtinuisse asiā. filij chā affri
cā τ filij iaphet europā. Isid. in li. Ethy. asserit cp orbis diuisus e in
tres partes b no equiter. Nā asia a meridie p orientem vscz ad septe
trionem puenit. Europa vo a septetrione vscz ad occidente ptingit.
Sed affrica ad occidentem p meridiez se extendit. Sola quocz Asia

Map of the world with illustrations of the fabulous human races in the left margin. From *Liber Cronicarum* (*The Nuremburg Chronicle*), by Hartmann Schedel, 1493. Courtesy of Dartmouth College Library, Hanover, N.H.

Sea monsters and mythical creatures thought to inhabit the northern seas and lands. Illustration from Sebastian Munster's *Cosmographiae Universalis*, 1550. Courtesy of Dartmouth College Library, Hanover, N.H.

Scenes of American life: the alligator hunt. From Theodore de Bry, *America*, 1599. Courtesy of Dana Special Collections, Dartmouth College, Hanover, N.H.

Lamia. Woodcut from Edward Topsell's *History of Four-Footed Beasts and Serpents*, 1608. Courtesy of Dana Special Collections, Dartmouth College, Hanover, N.H.

Manticora. Woodcut from Edward Topsell's *History of Four-Footed Beasts and Serpents*, 1608. Courtesy of Dana Special Collections, Dartmouth College, Hanover, N.H.

Illustration of a tree whose leaves turn into fish and birds; called the Credulity Tree. From C. Duret's *Histoire Admirable des Plantes et Herbes Esmerueillables et Miraculeuses en Nature*, 1605. Photo courtesy of Dumbarton Oaks, Trustees for Harvard University.

Illustration of the plant called the Scythian Lamb. From C. Duret's *Histoire des Plantes et Herbes Esmerueillables et Miraculeuses en Nature*, 1605. Photo courtesy of Dumbarton Oaks, Trustees for Harvard University.

A European view of Terrestrial Paradise. Woodcut from John Parkinson's *Paradisi in Sole Paradisus Terrestris*, 1629. Courtesy of Special Collections, Baker Library, Dartmouth College, Hanover, N.H.

Chapter Two

Hernán Cortés and
the Creation of the Model Conqueror

The Context of a Rebellion

Hernán Cortés set sail for the Indies from Palos de Moguer early in 1504. It was less than a year since Columbus, abandoned on the island of Jamaica, had written in his desperate *Lettera Rarissima* a last, somewhat inconsistent account of his perception of the New World, a perception that was to lead in less than twenty years to the destruction of his islands in the Indies.

The portrait of the New World presented in the Admiral's diaries and letters provided the foundation for a specific colonial plan that conceived of America as booty. In consequence, a complex structure was designed to implement the practice associated with booty—plunder—that came to constitute the first colonial model of economic organization in the Antilles. The main focus of this model was the acquisition of gold, which the demand for new currency had made extremely valuable. This demand derived from the scarcity of precious metals in Europe, a result in turn of Europe's trade deficit with India and the Orient.[1] In addition, the Spanish crown was incurring ever increasing debts connected with its numerous military campaigns.[2] All of this throws some light on why Columbus and his contemporaries were obsessed with gold, to the detriment of every other aspect of economic life in America. The *Lettera Rarissima* refers repeatedly to the higher value of gold, compared to that of any other merchandise:

From hence they will obtain gold. . . . The Genoese, Venetians, and all other nations that possess pearls, precious stones, and other articles of value, take them to the ends of the world to exchange them for gold. Gold is the most precious of all commodities; gold constitutes treasure, and he who possesses it has all he needs in this world, and also the means of expelling the souls of the dead from Paradise.[3]

Between the writing of this letter in 1503 and the conquest of Mexico in 1520, no fewer than fourteen thousand kilograms of gold were carried to Seville, without counting lost cargoes or contraband.[4] And as it became more evident that the new land was not Far East Asia but a new continent, lying like a barrier between Europe and the spice kingdoms, the material value of gold steadily increased. For a fifteenth- or sixteenth-century discoverer gold was a talisman representing the opportunity to acquire immediate wealth, break existing social barriers, and change overnight from an adventurer into a gentleman of means.

From the perspective of both the perception of reality and the organization of the colonial economy, this overvaluation and mythification of gold led to disastrous consequences, for it reduced and undermined the value of everything else in America. It was part of Columbus's initial perception of the New World as a source of commodities for the European market, and it became only more entrenched in his mind with time, as his song in praise of gold in the *Lettera Rarissima* clearly shows. After all, the existence of spices—the second item in importance on his list—became more and more doubtful as he found himself unable to confirm the signs of clove and pepper he had initially claimed were everywhere to be seen. The only pearl banks, located off the island of Margarita, did not appear to offer an inexhaustible supply regardless of a spectacular initial cargo carried back to Spain by Hojeda. And the precious stones augured by so many of Columbus's literary sources had not materialized. There was abundant brazilwood, fully confirming Columbus's early indications. But its trade did not promise the settlers any great wealth, for the crown had reserved for itself a monopoly over the product to export it to Flanders where, sold as dye, it could be used to pay for the importation of cloth.[5]

The only remaining source of wealth was agriculture, but this involved a twofold problem. First, there was the need to adapt European agricultural products to the new climate.[6] Despite the claims of the Admiral, who envisaged Hispaniola covered with vineyards and olive orchards like the islands in the Mediterranean, nature in the tropics was resistant to this kind of change, and the transplantation of trees, vineyards, plants, and grains in the New World was in the beginning not at all successful. Second, there was the attitude of the men who traveled to the Indies in the early days of the colony. These men had no interest in farming. In the writings of Columbus, Cortés, Bartolomé de Las Casas, and others, we find similar critiques of the behavior of the first colonists. They had not come to America to work, "to they themselves dig and plow" as Las Casas would say, but to get rich quickly and return to Spain. Columbus gives a bitter account of the designs of the settlers in a letter to the sovereigns written during his third voyage:

> because they came simply believing that the gold was there to be shoveled, and the spices already bound, and everything at the water's edge, ready to be stowed in the vessels—so blinded were they by greed. And they did not consider that, assuming there was gold or other metals, it would all be in the earth and that the spices would be growing on trees: that the gold would have to be dug for and the spices picked and dried.[7]

Twenty years later Cortés, by then governor of New Spain, remarked in a letter to the king on the character of the Spanish emigrants in even less flattering terms, "It is well known that most of the Spaniards who pass through here are low, strong, and given to many vices and sins."[8] Plunder was the most natural of activities in the minds of the early colonists, the most expeditious means of obtaining the booty they coveted and returning to Spain suddenly transformed into wealthy, respected *Indianos*. In fact, the difference between them and the Admiral came down to a matter of methods. America represented booty to each, but while Columbus applied his mercantile philosophy to making plans for its most efficient exploitation, the colonists, influenced by a long tradition of wars and conquests rewarded by plunder and rapine, proposed to benefit from whatever they found and to leave when supplies were exhausted.

The history of the Indies between 1492 and 1520 shows that plunder won out over Columbus's plan to utilize resources rationally. It created a deformed economy, incapable of providing the basic commodities it needed, with virtually all productive activity oriented toward the search for gold. As a result, natural and human resources were quickly exhausted. Gold production, which represented 1,434,664 ducats between 1511 and 1515,[9] began to decline immediately thereafter and started to run out by 1520. This was accompanied by a progressive decrease in the supply of native labor, which was essential to the production of any merchandise since, as Columbus accurately remarked, the settlers "were not workers."[10] So true was this that the value of an estate in the colony was measured by the number of natives available to work it.[11] The intolerable rate at which the natives were exploited by the colonists, the harsh treatment they received, disease, and the persistent lack of food caused an appalling decrease in the native population of the Caribbean. Between 1492 and 1514 the native population of Hispaniola fell from 500,000 to 32,000.[12] The concern caused to the crown and the colonists by this drop in demographics was apparent as of 1514, although the royal policy on the distribution of land and natives and the settlers' preoccupations were no doubt influenced more by the fact that the colony depended on the natives to run its estates than by any humanitarian considerations. Any decrease in the amount of labor in the colony implied of necessity that the settlers would become poorer and the royal income would be diminished.

The first expeditions to the Lesser Antilles, the Bahamas, and ultimately the mainland, together with the increasing shift of the center of the colony from Santo Domingo to Puerto Rico and eventually to Cuba, must be viewed in the context of the exhaustion of gold reserves and the drastic decrease in the labor supply. The colonial population began to spread to Puerto Rico and thence to Cuba as of 1508, but even as early as 1505 there were regular expeditions in search of labor to those islands that the king himself had called "useless." Bartolomé de Las Casas briefly describes the first "exploratory" expeditions that set out from the Greater Antilles:

> Around that time—although they were looking for the Yucaya people about whom we have spoken a great deal already in Book 2, describing how our Spaniards killed them—when the colonizers saw that the Indians on the island were vanishing, although they did not stop killing them, those who had collected a little money gained with the blood of the dead would get together, and they would equip one or two vessels or more to go in search of the innocent people living on the islands among the hills, hidden from the horror they had managed to flee.[13]

The settlers set out with "a quick eye for any signs of gold," says Las Casas, aptly giving the name of "assaults" to these expeditions in search of gold and slaves.

From 1509 on, several expeditions set out for the mainland from Santo Domingo, Cuba, and Jamaica. Although their purpose became progressively broader, they remained conditioned by the need to replenish the labor and booty that were clearly becoming in short supply in the colony.[14] Initially these expeditions seemed to offer little new in the way of discovery or exploration. Firmly rooted in Columbus's representation of American reality, they were designed rather to compensate for the worsening scarcity of resources available to the colony by spreading the pattern of plunder to as yet untapped territory. The 1509 expeditions under the command of Hojeda and Nicuesa, the 1515 voyage from Jamaica prompted by Francisco de Garay, and the 1518 expedition organized by Velázquez and led by Juan de Grijalva expressed the same basic approach and objectives. As conceived by the expeditionaries, the new lands were to be brought into the socioeconomic sphere of the colony exclusively by means of the capture and traffic of slaves and the plunder of booty, especially gold.[15] The purpose of these ventures to the mainland was quite different from the one eventually sustained by the Hernán Cortés expedition shortly thereafter. Nonetheless, they had an undeniable impact on the plans for this latter voyage.

The first of such expeditions took place between 1509 and 1510, under Diego de Nicuesa and Alonso de Hojeda. By means of intrigues supported by Bishop Fonseca, Nicuesa and Hojeda had obtained a concession from the king providing them with licenses and governorships and allowing them to settle in Veragua and Urabá (respectively, Colombia and Panama) and barter there. There is no report of the expedition written by any of its participants, but Las Casas provides an account in quite some detail. As he tells it, Nicuesa, the brains of the expedition, was motivated by the "scent of the news of riches, which the Admiral who first discovered these lands had furnished and he had heard."[16] The expedition was planned as an attempt "to barter" and "to settle" on the mainland along whose coasts the Admiral had sailed during his fourth voyage. But Las Casas carefully redefines the meaning of these two words in the context of the expedition. He explicitly equates "to settle" with "to bring war and spread disease"—the inevitable result of which would be the destruction of the new lands and the disappearance of their inhabitants;[17] "to barter" is to plunder material goods and capture slaves for trade with Europe and the colony. Las Casas refers to the "great evil done to the population of Cartagena by those who have gone there in the past with the pretext of bartering," and he remarks that with "the greed of the explorers gradually growing, which they disguised by the name of barter, they organized armadas with which they captured large numbers of Indians, whom they sold without license as slaves in Hispaniola and the other islands."[18]

Las Casas is frequently impassioned in his judgments of the behavior of the colonists. But in this case, as in so many others, the conduct of the two men in charge of the expedition—an account of which Las Casas apparently heard from one of the survivors—shows his assessments and definitions to be accurate. As soon as Hojeda stepped ashore on the mainland he appears to have "suddenly come upon a town named Calamar and quickly captured some Indians, sending them here to sell as slaves." This done, Hojeda and his crew, "blinded by their greed and sinful inclinations, spread through the woods in search of things to steal." Nicuesa's behavior during his first contact with the new land and its inhabitants seems to have been even worse, though he tried to justify himself by saying that he had acted in reprisal. When Nicuesa arrived to assist Hojeda, the natives "fled in their great fear from their houses, some with and others without arms, and not knowing where the Spaniards were, they kept running into them only to be disemboweled; fleeing from these they came upon others who tore them to bits. When they ran back into their houses, the Spaniards set fire to them and burned those inside alive."[19]

Having thus taken care of the native rebellion, Nicuesa and Hojeda parted and went to their respective territories, to "colonize." Las Casas remarks laconically on Hojeda's first foundation of a colony: not finding the gold indicated by the Indians, "he looked for a site, disembarked his people, and put a settlement he called Saint Sebastian on top of some hills . . . had the place never been settled, this would have been no offense to God, for an infinite number of sins would indeed have been prevented." This is how the "sinister village" was created, used by Hojeda as a base for implementing the mode of colonization practiced in the Antilles, which consisted, in Las Casas's words, of "harassing, robbing, and capturing" the natives.[20] Diego de Nicuesa followed the same pattern, except that he made no pretense at founding anything, merely grabbing whatever he could to remedy a situation that was becoming more critical with each passing day. "He sent off the young and the old, the sick and the healthy, into the water, the swamps, the hills, and the valleys to attack the Indians' villages and farmlands."[21] When several months later Anciso joined the survivors of the group left behind by Hojeda at Urabá, he prevented them from returning to Jamaica and persuaded them to continue "colonizing and settling." The argument he used was a reflection of the way he conceived his own venture, designed once again for the purpose of plunder. Las Casas provides the following summary: "Finally, using entreaties and arguments, and luring them with the prospect of going on land and capturing slaves to send or bring back to this island . . . he got them to return to Urabá."[22]

The second expedition to the mainland from the Antilles was led by Francisco Hernández de Córdoba, who set sail from Cuba on February 8, 1517. Bernal Díaz mentions that the expedition was financed by Hernández de Córdoba with each of his crew members contributing a share, although Diego de Velázquez provided material assistance and negotiated and issued licenses to settle and barter in the new lands. The pilot of the expedition was Antón de Alaminos, who accompanied Christopher Columbus on his fourth voyage and Juan Ponce de León when he discovered Florida. Las Casas, who was a friend of Hernández de Córdoba and knew him well, maintains that from the outset the purpose of the expedition was to capture Indians wherever they could be found. He also says that Alaminos insisted on sailing south of Cuba toward the west, "in great hopes of finding well settled land, richer than any so far discovered."[23] Accordingly, instead of setting out for places they knew had already been plundered, the expedition changed its direction toward new sources of human and material booty, which Alaminos claimed lay in Veragua. Bernal Díaz, who was not always the most scrupulous eyewitness in his portrayal of events, especially when a more favorable slant could be given to his role and that of other anonymous conquerors, admits that Velázquez's instructions for the expedition "stated that we were to set out prepared for war, and load the ships with Indians from the islands to sell them as slaves in order to pay for the vessel." He virtuously hastens to add, however, that he and the other soldiers, knowing that what Velázquez desired was not just, refused and told him that "neither God nor the King has ordered us to make free men slaves."[24] In any event, both sources mention that the capture of slaves was the main purpose of the expedition, followed by the inevitable search for gold. Las Casas speaks of the wealth of Veragua, described by the Admiral as being especially rich in gold mines.[25] Bernal Díaz refers to "rich lands, and people possessing gold, silver, pearls, and other riches," and he mentions a royal accountant on board whose responsibility it was to withhold for the crown one fifth of anything obtained.[26]

In any event, the activities of the protagonists of this new expedition would appear to confirm that, once again, its central purpose was the acquisition of booty. Hernández de Córdoba's communication with the natives whom he seized along the coast was designed exclusively to ascertain "whether the land contained that metal." He asked them on many occasions whether there was any gold on the island and promised to release the Indians held on board as prisoners if they would lead him to it.[27] Díaz makes it clear that the purpose of the expedition was plunder when he recalls in his *Historia* how the cleric González "loaded up with small chests and idols and gold and took all these things to the ships."[28]

Regardless of the fact that the purpose of the expedition was clearly restricted to plunder, there is something new in Díaz's account, the importance of which was not to be overlooked by Velázquez and even less so by Cortés. This new element consisted of several signs of a more highly developed culture than any found thus far in the New World. There were houses built very skillfully of "stone and mortar"; enigmatic sculptures; temples containing bas relief designs in stone and clay; clothing that showed the people who wore it to be "more endowed with reason than the Indians in Cuba";[29] and beehives, also described by Las Casas.[30] Ultimately, the success of the venture was to consist, as far as Velázquez was concerned, more in the discovery of these signs of an advanced Indian civilization than in the acquisition of material objects. Díaz found it hard to understand why so much importance was attributed to the "stone and mortar" houses, the "tiny gold fishes," the idols through which the Indians "sublimated their art."[31] Velázquez, however, evidently believed that these things were of great consequence as an indication of the great cultural and material wealth to be had on the mainland, a judgment reflected by the haste with which he began to prepare another expedition to exactly the same region visited by the first. This last preparatory expedition to the conquest of Mexico sailed from Cuba on May 1, 1518, under the command of Juan de Grijalva.

It is difficult to judge from existing documentation on this expedition whether Juan de Grijalva has come down in history as the most dimwitted or the most scrupulous of discoverers and conquerors in America. There is no question, however, that he followed his governor's orders more obediently and scrupulously than anyone else in the history of the conquest, a fact that earned him no small amount of criticism and insults from his own men. Bernal Díaz thought him brave and energetic, but Juan Díaz, the chaplain of the expedition, could not hide his irritation at Grijalva's lack of initiative and held him responsible for the mediocre results of the expedition. "Had we had a good captain," says Juan Díaz, "we would have obtained more than ten thousand castellanos; but because of him we could neither trade nor exchange our merchandise, nor settle on the land."[32] In any event, Grijalva's absolutely consistent, obedient, law abiding behavior provides an indication of the nature of Velázquez's instructions and sheds light on his intentions for the expedition. Bernal Díaz says, "It appears that the Governor's instructions to the expeditions were that they should obtain all the gold and silver they could by barter, and settle if they dared and if the land was suitable for settlement, but otherwise return to Cuba."[33] But Grijalva's systematic refusal to do anything more than explore and collect booty, as remarked by Juan Díaz, would appear to indicate that Velázquez had given him no orders to settle. Las Casas explains his attitude, claiming that rather than cowardice it reflected Grijalva's faithful observation of his instructions:

> Juan de Grijalva was by nature so disposed that his obedient and humble attitude and other good qualities would have made him not a bad friar; for this reason, not all the world together would have succeeded in changing his mind one iota from what he had been instructed to do, even if he knew he would be cut to pieces. I was acquainted with him and talked with him a

great deal, and I always knew him to be inclined toward virtue, obedience, and good habits, and very compliant regarding anything his superiors ordered him to do. Thus, in spite of all their enteaties and importunate arguments, they were unable to make him settle, which he claimed he had been forbidden to do by the man who had sent him; he maintained that his orders were limited to discovering and bartering, and that in carrying them out he would have fulfilled his obligation.[34]

According to this version, Velázquez's instructions contained an explicit prohibition against *settling and conquering*, which seems logical considering his ambitions and the fact that he was still lacking the required royal license. Indeed, he made haste to obtain such a license as soon as he learned the results of this last expedition.

The above three expeditions were part of a plan similar to the one that had shaped the social and economic organization of the Spanish colony in the Antilles. As a colonizing project, therefore, they offered nothing essentially new, but they were extremely important as geographical exploration. As such each of the three expeditions constituted an important stage in the process of correcting the imaginary referent that had informed Columbus's representation of America. The validity of the model created by Columbus based on both his fantastic and his geographical sources was questioned and increasingly undermined.[35] The notion that America was above all a source of booty persisted, but rather than indulging in descriptive confirmation, the explorers were now more inclined toward making inventories of what they found that were objective and faithful, albeit selective, in terms of the existing colony's requirements. Even before Columbus's fourth voyage, we can see how the process of systematic exploration of the mainland began to unfold. As a result of Alonso de Hojeda's 1499 expedition in search of the pearl banks reported by Columbus in his third voyage, the entire coast of Venezuela was explored and charted. That same year Vicente Yáñez explored the coast from Cape San Agustín to the estuary of the Orinoco—not the Amazon as has often been claimed.[36] One year later Alvarez Cabral followed the coast of Brazil as far south as the Amazon, while Rodrigo de Bastida and Juan de la Cosa explored the coat of Venezuela as far as Panama. Two years later Columbus sailed indefatigably along the coasts of Colombia and Panama in search of a strait leading to the Indian Sea and the Spice Islands. In 1509 Hojeda and Nicuesa set out to explore the same region, drawn by Columbus's claims that it was full of treasure. Francisco Hernández de Córdoba's 1517 expedition continued, surveying the coast and exploring the strip along the Yucatan, and Grijalva, who sighted land at Yucatan in May

1518, continued on northward as far as San Juan de Ulúa and present day Veracruz.

With the growing awareness of the configuration of the new continent, America began to be perceived as a new geographical entity quite different from the imaginary model Columbus had so persistently sought to confirm. The other discoverers active in the region between 1503 and 1518 learned to observe with an ever more objective eye the lands that gradually revealed themselves for what they in fact were: a new continent, different from Asia, unknown to them and unexplored before that time. As Columbus's fantastic model lost validity as a referent, certain ways of representing the monstrous and the marvelous became less prevalent. This did not mean, however, that the fantastic dimension associated with the new reality was no longer there. No one was searching any longer for the mythical gold mountains defended by giant ants described by Aeneas Sylvius; but from the time of Columbus to that of Cortés and in fact for many years afterward, there continued to be reports, repeated by guides and explorers, of all sorts of fantastic creatures and places. Remarking that "the men of that period were disposed to believe all kinds of extra, infra, or supernatural revelations, or rather, revelations that extended and transfigured the meaning and scope of the natural world . . . never before imagined, marvelous, or horrifying forms of life that had remained hidden from the old world," Salvador de Madariaga describes the prominent role that the marvelous played in the worldview of any medieval or Renaissance Spaniard.[37] Irving A. Leonard, on the other hand, points out that the Spaniard's inclination for myth and fantasy was considerable even for the period, and he explains why this should have been so historically:

> The relative isolation of Spanish life from that of the rest of Europe, the ever-present proximity of the unknown in the dark waters of the Atlantic, and the mingling of European and Arabic cultures, all tended to foster a sense of mystery and fantasy. This introspective preoccupation with the extraordinary was stimulated enormously . . . by the tales of returning sailors. . . . They brought rumors of mysterious islands with strange forms of life, hydras, gorgons, Amazons, mermaids. . . . The Spanish listeners, perhaps reacting to the stark realism of their immediate surroundings, escaped into flights of fantasy.[38]

This marked disposition toward the mythical, the fanciful, and the marvelous can be seen in, among other things, the incredible popularity that novels of chivalry achieved during the sixteenth century. Published in many editions, they took hold of the Iberian Peninsula to such a degree that laws were passed restricting or banning them. The blurry line of demarcation between reality and fiction affecting people's perception persisted throughout and beyond the age of exploration. In 1497 Columbus had spoken of mythical monsters and of Terrestrial Paradise. Moreover, in 1512 Ponce de León sailed about, lost in the Caribbean for more than six months, in search of the Fountain of Youth, until he came by chance upon a peninsula that he named Florida. And five years later, Juan Díaz mentioned having heard that at the tip of the Yucatan Peninsula there were Amazons and that an Indian chieftain had spoken of white men with enormous ears living on some nearby islands.[39] Velázquez referred to both the Amazons and the monstrous-looking men in his official instructions to Hernán Cortés on the occasion of the expedition to Mexico in 1519. In these instructions he wrote "they say there are people with large, wide ears and others with faces like dogs, and also where the Amazons are, which these Indians you are taking with you say are near there."[40] And in his *capitulaciones*, spelling out the terms of Cortés's license to lead the expedition, he specifically instructed him to investigate such claims.[41]

The fantastic and its two aspects—the marvelous and the monstrous—were no longer the key to identifying the new lands with Columbus's imaginary model and its referent.[42] But they persisted in the minds of the discoverers and continued to be reflected in their reports. Associated with the "ancient tales" that inspired Columbus and the "lying histories" of the novels of chivalry, they continued to provide an important incentive for exploration and remained a constant in the way the New World was perceived. The objective situation, however, was now quite different from the one that had allowed Columbus to adjust what he found in America to fit his literary models. For example, although Juan Díaz referred frequently to the Yucatan as an island, an essentially correct perception of the geography of the new continent gradually emerged. This involved a configuration decidedly in contrast to the one put forward by the Admiral, who had expected to find a number of archipelagos that he believed marked the path toward Cipangu and the east coast of Cathay.

The geographical objectives of the explorations that took place between 1503 and 1518 became increasingly clear. And however true it may be that what the colonizers had in mind was simply to expand the area of plunder, the journeys to the mainland represented a fundamental contribution to the reevaluation taking place. The last three, especially those led by Hernández de Córdoba and Grijalva, provided a considerable amount of concrete information on the new lands and their inhabitants, opening up possibilities that seemed far more auspicious than the initial plan to convert the natives, use them as labor, and pillage their territory. Velázquez reacted promptly to this early evidence of highly promising civilizations.

While sending off one expedition after another to gather information, he took measures to ensure that he would have a monopoly over the use of the new lands and their inhabitants. Meanwhile, Cortés, who was about to be appointed to command the next expedition to the mainland, conceived a project, based on the evidence of cultural and material wealth gathered during Hernández de Córdoba and Juan de Grijalva's first contacts with the Mayas and the subjects of the Aztec empire. This evidence involved not only the gold, silver, gems, and tortoise shell brought back by Grijalva to Cuba but also the level of civilization reflected by the symbols and motifs on the objects found, and their superior workmanship.

Because of the lack of documentation there is no way of knowing the real origins of Hernán Cortés's plan for the conquest of Mexico. Everything about his behavior, however, from the skill he used to get Velázquez to appoint him captain of the expedition to his first initiatives when he reached the mainland, would indicate that nothing he did was improvised. As they waited for a royal license to arrive, Velázquez had in mind that Cortés should use the time to gather the information needed to take over the new lands as efficiently and advantageously as possible; but Cortés, who intended to use Velázquez's support to start on a venture that would ultimately have nothing to do with the governor's objectives, set about contacting all the influential people he knew. Velázquez's objectives for this expedition were very similar to those implicit in the behavior of the scrupulously obedient Grijalva; that is, they involved no more than the design to obtain information on the land and its inhabitants, collect any valuable objects, and promptly bring this all back to Cuba.

Bernal Díaz says that although it was publicly announced that the purpose of the expedition was to settle the land, Diego Velázquez's "secret intention was not to settle but to trade."[43] The instructions Velázquez gave to Cortés before a notary on October 23, 1518, confirm Díaz's claim and provide considerable information on Velázquez's general plan and the function assigned to the expedition.[44] This function comprised four essential aspects. Cortés was appointed captain of the expeditionary fleet, with orders to *record* as much information as possible, *communicate* it promptly and in detail to Velázquez, scrupulously *supervise* the storage of the objects obtained in a chest made fast with "two or three locks," and *preach*, if the occasion arose, the fundamental tenets of the Catholic religion.[45]

It soon became apparent that Cortés's idea of the expedition was quite unlike Velázquez's notion of a simple survey and that he conceived his own role as being fundamentally different from that of a mere recipient and conveyor of information. Bernal Díaz says that Cortés "ordered a proclamation to be made to the sound of trumpets and drums, in the name of His Majesty and of Diego Velázquez as his Viceroy and of himself as his Captain-General, that anyone who wished to could accompany him to the newly discovered lands, to *conquer* and *settle*."[46] The inconsistency between the purpose of the expedition as published by Cortés and the terms of the governor's instructions may have been thought by Velázquez to be a mere ruse to attract people to join it; or perhaps Cortés's announcements did in fact reflect Velázquez's secret objective. This is relatively inconsequential, however, and it appears that Velázquez was not in the least disturbed by the notices until they were followed by more suspicious and alarming indications. Velázquez had planned the expedition along the lines of the earlier one led by Grijalva, meaning that only four vessels would be used. But shortly after Cortés was appointed, and clearly as a result of his diligent efforts, it became evident that the preparations for the expedition went far beyond any others made before that time. The amount represented by Cortés's ultimate share in financing the venture is much debated to this day. Claims have ranged from two thirds of the total cost, to seven ships, to half the capital in vessels and supplies, according to Montejo, Puertocarrero, and Gómara, respectively. By all accounts, however, his portion was very substantial, and he drew upon his own resources to equip the expedition to the point of going into debt.[47] In view of the spectacular preparations underway, and the comments and rumors all over the island suggesting a possible revolt by Cortés (who as Velázquez's jester Cervantes El Loco told the latter "knows how to look after himself, as everyone can tell you"), the governor—who according to Bernal Díaz had always feared that Cortés would "rise up against him"[48]— decided to face danger and suspicion directly, and withdrew Cortés's mandate. Warned of this, probably by one of his many friends at Velázquez's court, Cortés ordered the ships to set sail ahead of time without advising the governor. This was his first move in a complicated set of events in which he gradually removed himself from Velázquez's authority and created a situation whereby, although formally and on the surface obedient, he was in fact in a state of rebellion.[49]

The highly unusual nature of the fleet organized and outfitted by Cortés provides the first unequivocal evidence that his intentions differed from those of Velázquez. One need only compare its 12 vessels and 600 men with the 3 vessels and 110 men in Hernández de Córdoba's expedition, or 4 vessels under the command of Grijalva, to realize what was involved. This may, however, have been the only clear indication of Cortés's ambitious project before he left for the mainland on February 15, 1519. In his negotiations with Diego de Ordaz and Francisco Verdugo in Trinidad, as well as with Pedro Barba, Cortés repeatedly insisted that he was loyal to the governor who wished to dismiss him; and Bernal Díaz speaks of the warm, friendly letters he wrote to Velázquez, filled with claims of an obedience that his actions had clearly begun to contradict.

The Narrative Structures of a Fictional Justification

The first reference we find to the feverish addiction to letter-writing that was to be characteristic of Cortés for the rest of his life is made during the three months following his rebellious departure. It comes from Bernal Díaz, who summarizes the first letters and indicates their function. From Trinidad "Cortés sent a very friendly letter to the Governor, expressing his astonishment at His Honor's decision, and saying that his only desire was to serve God and His Majesty, and to obey Velázquez as the King's representative." Díaz describes Cortés's letters to the governor, written this time from Havana just before sailing for the mainland: "At the same time, Cortés wrote to Velázquez in those agreeable and complimentary terms that came so easily to him, saying that he was setting sail next day and would remain his humble servant."[50] If we are to be guided by Díaz, the political function of the letters was to ease Velázquez's mind while Cortés completed his arrangements: a function realized by Cortés's seductive rhetoric, by the gentle tones and good words that "came so easily to him." These first letters are important not only because of the early example they provide of the twofold function of Cortés's writing, that of justifying his actions while seducing his readers. They also reveal that his repeated avowal of obedience to Velázquez had absolutely no foundation in reality and as such offer an early harbinger of the thorough fictionalization that was to come in his later narrative discourse, under the guise of impeccable documentation.

In Cortés's *Cartas de Relación*,* the process of fictionalization is focused on two points: the representation of rebellion as service, and of the rebel as model conqueror. The former, around which the first three letters are largely organized, leads to recognition by the king of the validity and legitimacy of Cortés's plan for conquest. The latter, richer and more complex, constitutes a central organizing principle of Cortés's narrative from his first letter to his last.

The narrative adopts the form of a legal document, the aforesaid *Carta de Relación*, which in the sixteenth century represented something between

*The *Cartas de Relación* will be referred to here generally as Cortés's *Letters* or *Letters from Mexico*.—TRANS.

an epistle and a legal statement. It provided information on a multiplicity of objects, commented on human action and behavior, and described the thoughts and impressions of the author and those around him. But, as a legal document, it pledged the writer's word to the veracity of its contents. By its very concept it constituted a guarantee or certificate of the truth of its statements. Cortés almost always adds the adjective "true" to the noun "relation" as a sort of reiterated guarantee of credibility. Thus both the genre chosen and the explicit repetition of the adjective have a similar function: they create a presumably objective, documented framework for Cortés's text. And both the form chosen for the text, and the text because of its form, establish a reciprocal set of fictitious guarantees supporting the impartiality, veracity, and authority of the message.

In all his letters, the narrator's awareness of the commitment inherent to his narrative form is dramatized by his describing certain incidents in ways that enhance the authenticity of everything conveyed. The second letter, for example, suggests that to "provide an account" of certain volcanos is only possible if the narrator has explored them: "Because I have always wished to render your Highness very particular account of all the things of this land, I wished to know the explanation of this which seemed to me something of a miracle; so I sent ten of my companions, such as were qualified for such an undertaking, with some natives to guide them; and I urged them to attempt to climb the mountain and discover the secret of the smoke, whence it came, and how." In the same letter, he asks Moctezuma to allow him to inspect the gold mines himself so that he can "report on them to the King." Both of these examples imply that direct observation is a prerequisite for knowledge—not only geographical knowledge but everything reported by Cortés. His reluctance to remark on any geographical information whose "secret" has not been revealed to him personally includes everything that comes within the purview of his selection and the criteria underlying this selection, implying that his discussions refer only to things that have been factually proven.

The text's authority to speak, derived structurally from its form and stylistically reinforced by the repeated use of the adjective "true," is thus complemented by a feature often found in the chronicles of the period: the use of an eyewitness account as a method of establishing credibility. Bernal Díaz and Las Casas, among others, maintained that there were only two valid ways of reporting on the experience of the conquest: as an eyewitness who may or may not have taken part in a given event but who has nonetheless observed it firsthand; or as a compiler and reporter of information based on the experience of others, but not shared in or directly observed by the chronicler. Writers in the manner of Díaz believed the second approach to be unacceptable, and his polemic with Gómara revolved precisely around this issue. Díaz held that not only had Gómara used a different method to gather and present historical information, but his version was a "sloppy invention," his information was false, his dates and figures mistaken; he had exaggerated or undermined the true merit of things, produced a sloppy, worthless document; and "the gentlemen in the Royal Council of the Indies should have the errors in his books deleted."[51]

Las Casas agrees with Díaz that no credit should be given to Gómara's method or its results. He frequently accuses him of "untruthfulness" and "insolence," which he attributes to the absurd presumption of discussing things never witnessed. "Gómara," says Las Casas "who wrote the *Historia de Cortés*, who lived with him in Castile after he had become a Marquis, who never went to the Indies nor saw anything there . . . writes many favorable things about him that are in fact not true,"[52] and "the priest Gómara makes many very false statements in his *Historia*, having neither seen nor heard any of the things he describes."[53]

The rejection of Gómara's method implies that the only valid report is that of the eyewitness.[54] This is stressed stylistically by Las Casas, when he refers explicitly and repeatedly to his firsthand contact with the people whose story he is telling. He specifies where, when, and how often he saw them, defining the nature of his relationship with each of the important characters: his acquaintances—Cortés, for example, and Cortés's father, whom he "knew very well"; his personal friends, such as Grijalva; and his relatives. The same emphasis on indicating the author's closeness to the situation may be found in Bernal Díaz, except that Díaz carries a step further his implicit identification of what he observes with what is in fact true. After contrasting Gómara's historiographical method with his own eyewitness account, he compares their respective aesthetic values. For Díaz, what is *beautiful* is what is *true*. His is then a sort of aesthetics of truth, which he formulates explicitly by saying that "correct and elegant writing consists of having told the truth in everything I have written."[55] Gómara's aesthetics on the other hand exemplifies for Bernal a preference for beautiful rhetoric over documentary truth. Histories prefaced by "prologues and preambles filled with high-sounding arguments and rhetoric" are unacceptable as historiographical accounts from the perspective of chroniclers such as Díaz and Las Casas, for whom true knowledge comes only from direct experience. Their argument in defense of their own authority, adduced repeatedly by both chroniclers to refute the contentions of Gómara and others like him, is that they *knew* the characters, *witnessed* the action, or *took part* in the events.

Cortés's account of the conquest of Mexico is in conformity with the requirement that the reporter be a witness. At the same time, its author acknowledges using a specific method of selecting information, the explicit criterion involved being "the interest of the king." His role as an eyewitness enhances the validity of his message, a message whose accuracy appears to be guaranteed by his relationship to his material—he has participated in the events, his intentions are in good faith—and by the narrative form he has selected. His guarantee is fictitious, however, because as an examination of the letters will reveal, their apparently objective, formal, documentary structure constitutes a verbal strategy at the service of a political purpose, as the first step toward a complex fictionalization of the reality of his conquest. It was Cortés's intention to produce an extremely rational set of persuasive documents with an immediate political purpose. But by electing to narrate, within the documentary framework of a *relación*, a highly personal, mythified version of the conquest of Mexico, he goes beyond the bounds of discourse appertaining to a "true history," making them meaningless and converting the *relación* into a literary convention that becomes an integral part of the narrative structure of the fundamentally fictional discourse it introduces and shapes.

The intermingling of documentary and fictional forms in a single text was nothing new. Reflecting the blurred distinction between reality and fantasy described by Leonard,[56] it was to be found in a long line of chronicles and historiographical works dating back several centuries in which fable was combined with reality, fiction with history, the marvelous with the everyday. These included accounts both general and particular of the actual or blatantly fabulous experiences of extraordinary men, which provided no transition or word of warning to the reader as the narrative passed back and forth between the real and the imaginary.[57] The huge success of the "lying histories" of the novels of chivalry and the reforms introduced by the works of Erasmus, calling for literature containing anything considered immoral or false to be banned and replaced by "true histories" with an edifying and didactic purpose, combined to create a greater urgency to distinguish between reality and fantasy, between historiography and fiction.[58] But at the beginning of the sixteenth century, the connection between factual and imaginary accounts was often so close as to make the two kinds of narrative implicitly equivalent. The loss of distinction between what was real and what was imaginary had been introduced and facilitated in part by the development of the chronicles.

Leonard believes that the increasingly fictitious nature of these chronicles, which continued to be presented as authentic accounts of factual events, was one of the sources of the growing confusion between the real and the imaginary that reached a peak when the novels of chivalry became a collective passion:

> From bare recitals of fact, they became in time accounts ornamented with unrealistic details and the injection of increasing doses of invented elements without, however, losing any of their prestige as authentic records. . . . This work . . . was a revision of what passed for history in the old chronicles, incorporating details, incidents and characteristics of the now current romantic fiction but, since it dealt with a familiar historical episode, the ordinary reader did not question its veracity. Thus the complete acceptance of the parallel romance of chivalry itself was facilitated.[59]

In the context of a tradition in which the novels of chivalry could intermingle with the chronicles of the Middle Ages and the Renaissance and adopt their pseudohistoriographical forms without any problem of continuity, the processes by which Cortés fictionalized events in his *Letters* are remarkably subtle and austere. Nothing in Cortés's narrative suggests an intellectual trajectory comparable to that found in the writings of Fernández de Oviedo. Oviedo's interest in the novels of chivalry is documented by fact that he translated one of them in the early stages of his career.[60] But in the representation of the New World that Cortés developed throughout his writings the fantastic is consistently absent. Even after a close examination of the *Letters*, it is impossible to prove and difficult to support the importance attributed by Leonard to the influence of the novels of chivalry as an impelling force in the conquest of Mexico and the explorations that followed.[61] It is likely that Cortés shared the general taste for adventure reflected by the popularity of the novels of chivalry. But that this should be so does not necessarily mean that he adopted them as a literary model, or that the particular ways in which they expressed the period's thirst for adventure influenced his project or his actions. Leonard concludes on the basis of Cortés's fourth letter, that "his lieutenants, as well as he himself, were heading expeditions with instructions to locate the Amazons and other oddities, along with gold and silver mines"; and insists that "chief among the latter objectives were the Amazon women."[62] Cortés did indeed refer to the Amazons in his letter of October 15, 1524, but he was repeating a report by Cristobal de Olid, who had heard it from the chiefs of the province of Ciguatan. (The information on the location of the Amazons comes, according to the letter, from the chiefs of Ciguatan; the report on their existence and their wealth from de Olid.) Actually, Cortés *doubts* what he learns and feels constrained to *verify* it, which is much more consistent with his usually rational approach than with the belief in the fantastic attributed to him by Leonard.

The fictionalization process used by Cortés cannot really be traced, then, to the "lying histories" either as an imaginary model or as belonging to the same literary tradition. This process and the narrative discourse it produced are qualitatively different from those of both the novels of chivalry and a more recent referent, the discourse of Columbus. Indeed, if ever a fiction has been built on the clearest and most specific analysis of concrete reality, it is the one contained in the *Letters.*[63]

Cortés's first move in his fictitious representation of the conquest of Mexico is his transformation of *rebellion* into *service.* The point of departure is a transgression that initially appears to have no clear goal: it is a questionable disobedience that clearly threatens the established order. In his first three letters (that is, until the king implicitly accepts his rebellion by appointing him governor and captain-general of New Spain), Cortés shapes his transgression gradually, giving it the content it needs to appear as if it were service. First, he describes—and rejects—the order represented by Velázquez, whose motivation and behavior are projected to encompass the entire colonial model created and represented by himself and others of similar ilk. The human portraits in Cortés's letters are all given in terms of an implicit referential code, the code of vassalage. The portrait of Velázquez, rather than drawn directly by a judgment or character description, is almost always an indirect one, conveyed by reference to his behavior and the objectives this behavior reflects, and focused on the absence of the attributes typical of the ideal vassal.

Cortés's first letter has been lost. Any understanding of the events referred to in the first letter must therefore be gleaned from the summaries provided in both the second and third letters. A point stressed in the summaries is that Velázquez's interests are in opposition, not similar or subordinate, to those of the king. This is illustrated by Velázquez's decision to intercept a vessel dispatched by Cortés with his agents Puertocarrero and Montejo aboard, carrying instructions to hand over to the king all the gold and precious stones obtained thus far, rather than merely the obligatory one-fifth. The agents were also carrying Cortés's first letter and the *Letter from the Justiciary and Municipal Council.* Cortés expresses neither a judgment nor an opinion, stating simply that

> they had determined to seize the brigantine which was in the port with bread and salt pork aboard. They intended to kill the master of it, return to the island of Fernandina and inform Diego Velázquez of how I had sent a ship to Your Highness, and also of what she was carrying and what course she was to take so that the said Diego Velázquez might send ships to lie in wait

and take her. As soon as he knew this, he did so, for, as I have been informed, he sent a caravel after that same ship which, if she had not already passed, would have been taken.[64]

From the perspective of the code of vassalage, because the interest of Velázquez and his followers stands in the way of that of the crown, their attitude amounts to treason. And Cortés's harsh punishment underscores the seriousness of their crime: "On hearing the confessions of these miscreants, I punished them according to the law and as, in the circumstances, I judged would do Your Majesty greatest service."[65] Velázquez is a traitor, his men are delinquent, and Cortés has implemented justice in the service of the king. His actions seem impeccably consistent, and yet what he is presenting is a highly fictionalized account. This also applies, given the legal and political context of the period, to his foundation of Rica Villa de la Veracruz and his appointment, by his own *cabildo* or municipal council, as captain and chief justice. He presents the conclusion of a syllogism contrived to make his rebellion appear legal as if it were a valid premise. But outside this context and the general consistency of his letters, it is Cortés who is delinquent and a traitor, and the "justice" he claims to be administering is a seditious act against "delinquents and traitors" who are in fact the representatives of legal authority. This reversal of roles produces a fictionalized version of reality, whose nature is not in the least altered by the impeccable Aristotelian logic of the method used to achieve it.

The elements that articulate Cortés's fictionalized reconstructions—selection, reordering of events, subjective redefinition of concepts and meanings—are not fully developed in this first example but become increasingly clear in subsequent letters. In his second letter, for instance, Cortés uses one of the most important episodes of the conquest of Mexico, the loss of Tenochtitlan, for the purpose of conveying a full impression of Velázquez and the order he represents. The many versions that have survived of the development of events leading to the *noche triste** may be divided into two groups: those provided by the members of Cortés's army and those provided by the natives. A major difference between the two groups concerns the slaughter in the Temple during the celebration of the feast of Toxcatl and the death of Moctezuma. The native versions attribute the Aztec rebellion to the slaughter ordered, without any justification, by Pedro de Alvarado. The events are narrated in the *Ramírez Codex* as follows:

*On the *noche triste* (June 30, 1520) the Spaniards made their famous retreat from Tenochtitlan.—TRANS.

In the meantime, Pedro de Alvarado, who had remained in Mexico as [Cortés's] lieutenant, urged Moctezuma to have the lords his vassals hold a *mitote* as was their custom, all richly attired and unarmed, to display the gallantry and greatness of the kingdom; and the king did so . . . and when, elegant and proud, etc., they all appeared, Pedro de Alvarado, who had left some people guarding Moctezuma . . . used the others to attack the poor dancers; and they killed most of them and took the treasures they were wearing away from them: which so afflicted the city that it all but perished that very day.[66]

Alvarado's action is reported similarly, though more succinctly, in the *Aubin Codex*, where it says that "The singing had barely begun when the Christians appeared one by one; they passed among the people and then went to place themselves at the entrances in groups of four. They then dealt the leader of the dancers a blow. . . . Then there was general confusion, which led to complete ruination."[67] The version provided by Fray Bernardino de Sahagún's informants corroborates these two accounts, stressing in particular the cruelty with which Alvarado's soldiers murdered the best of the Aztec warriors, using to their advantage the requirement that the latter be unarmed during the ritual dances.

The Spaniards decide to kill the people. . . . With everything thus organized, they immediately enter the holy square to kill the people. . . . Next they surround the dancers and leap to where the kettledrums stood: they slashed at the man playing and severed both his arms. Then they cut off his head, and it fell at a distance. . . . Some they attacked from behind, and their entrails fell all over the ground. Others had their heads torn asunder. . . . All the entrails fell on the ground. And there were some who tried to run: they dragged their intestines with them and their feet seemed to get tangled in them. . . . The warriors' blood flowed like water: it . . . stagnated like water, and the smell of blood and of the entrails that seemed to be dragging rose in the air . . . what angered the Mexicans so much was that their warriors were killed without even realizing they were under attack, and that their captains were killed treacherously.[68]

The native versions present more or less the same interpretation of the slaughter—the Aztec warriors were shut in on purpose while unarmed, so that they could be liquidated. They also agree in claiming that this slaughter was the direct cause of the rebellion of the people of Tenochtitlan against Alvarado.

On Cortés's side, it is interesting to compare his own version of the events with the account provided by some of his men. Bernal Díaz was away with Cortés when the massacre took place, but he includes in his report what he learned from the envoys of Moctezuma and from Alvarado and his companions, upon returning to Tenochtitlan. His account is essentially consistent with the three native versions, but there are differences of interpretation:

> Four important chiefs arrived whom the great Montezuma had sent to Cortés to complain about Pedro de Alvarado. With tears streaming from their eyes, they said that Alvarado had come out of his quarters with all the soldiers whom Cortés had left him, and for no reason at all had fallen on their *Caciques* and dignitaries, who were dancing and celebrating a festival in honor of their idols Huichilobos and Tezcatlipoca, for which they had Alvarado's permission. Many Mexicans had been killed and wounded.[69]

Díaz then complements his account of a native version with a transcription of Alvarado's own account to Cortés. According to Alvarado, the Aztecs had conspired against him. Encouraged by the promises made by Narváez to Moctezuma, as well as by the decrease in numbers among the Spaniards after the departure of Cortés, the Aztecs were planning to attack the fort and kill everyone in it immediately following their celebrations in honor of the god Toxcatl. From this perspective, the slaughter was no more than a simple measure taken in anticipation of the attack expected from the Aztecs. Both versions recounted by Díaz agree that a slaughter did indeed take place in the temple, and that it was the direct cause of the Aztec rebellion and seizure of the fort. They disagree, however, in their interpretation of the nature of the slaughter: for the Indians it was a treacherous, gratuitous act of cruel aggression, while for the Spaniards it was a defensive measure against an imminent Aztec attack.

There is also disagreement between the Spanish and Indian assessments of another fundamental event leading to the *noche triste*: the death of Moctezuma. According to Hernando Alva Ixtlilxochitl, "they say that one of the Indians threw a stone at him, which killed him; but the vassals say the Spaniards killed him, wounding him with a sword in the lower part of his body."[70] The *Ramírez Codex* is even more explicit:

> Finally, finding himself among more than 900 Spaniards and his friends, the Marquis made a decision which he painted differently, but God knows what really happened, and this was that at the dawn watch the hapless Moctezuma was found dead. The day before, during a great attack, he had been placed on a low, protruding rooftop to talk to them, and they began to throw [stones] that they say hit him; but even if they did, they could not have injured him because he had been dead for more than five hours, and there were those who said that because no wound could be seen on him, a sword had been thrust into the lower part of his body.[71]

Bernal Díaz, on the other hand, attributes Moctezuma's death to stoning by his subjects, claiming that Cortés had had him taken to the rooftop to pacify the Mexicans:

In view of this situation, Cortés decided that the great Montezuma should speak to them from the roof and tell them that the attacks must cease, since we wished to leave the city. . . . Montezuma was hit by three stones, one on the head, one on the arm, and one on the leg; and though they begged him to have his wounds dressed and eat some food and spoke very kindly to him, he refused. Then quite unexpectedly, we were told that he was dead.[72]

Díaz adds that Cortés and his men sincerely mourned Moctezuma, which is easy to understand since with his imperial prisoner dead, Cortés had lost what he believed to be an essential pawn in his attempt to recover control over the situation at Tenochtitlan.[73]

It is interesting to compare Cortés's own version of the events with these other accounts. In spite of the above variations, all versions offer a similar account of the sequence of events leading to the flight of the Spaniards on the *noche triste*. Cortés's profoundly different version in his second letter, corroborated again in the summary at the beginning of the third, is therefore all the more extraordinary. He excludes anything that cannot be suited to his objective—an essential aspect of which continues to be the portrayal of his rebellion as service—and carefully reworks the material selected for inclusion. He avoids making any account of two absolutely fundamental incidents: the slaughter in the temple perpetrated by Alvarado and his men, and the freeing of Moctezuma's brother, Cuhitlaua.

The crucial importance of the slaughter is made clear in *all* the Indian and Spanish versions, which are unanimous in presenting it as the incident that unleashed the rebellion. The freeing of Cuhitlaua was equally decisive, for it involved the removal of the subjected Moctezuma, and augured the organization of a resistance movement and an attack by the Aztecs under the command of a new military and religious leader. Instead of providing a factual report on the slaughter initiated by Alvarado or on his own serious mistake, which led to the loss of Tenochtitlan and all the Aztec treasure, Cortés creates a fiction, omitting these central incidents and blaming the rebellion on the fact that he was obliged to leave the city. All that had occurred was that "the Indians had attacked the fortress and set fire to it in many places and tried to mine it, and . . . the Spaniards had been greatly pressed and in great danger, and might yet be killed if Mutezuma did not order a cease fire, for although they were not at present being attacked, they were still surrounded and not permitted to venture outside the fortress at all."[74] Cortés returns to this version in his third letter, explicitly emphasizing that there was no reason for the natives to revolt: "for no good reason, all the natives of Culua, that is, those from the great city of Temixtitan, and those from all the other provinces which are subject thereto, had not only rebelled against Your Majesty, but moreover had killed many men who were our friends and kinsmen."[75]

This omission of central events, which constitutes the first step in Cortés's narrative construction of a fictionalized account of the loss of Tenochtitlan, is complemented by his careful reelaboration of the material describing the events he chooses to narrate. A good illustration of this is provided by the differences in the various accounts of Cortés's arrival at Alvarado's besieged fortress. Bernal Díaz's version is factual, focusing on Cortés's investigation into the causes of the rebellion and on Alvarado's arguments and excuses. Díaz quotes Cortés verbatim as having told Alvarado that what he did was "a bad thing and a great mistake," and he carefully transcribes Alvarado's explanations.[76] Cortés, on the other hand, creates his version after the fact and after deciding not to report the incident of the slaughter. Building his fiction around everyone's happiness at being together again, he turns the disagreeable scene described by Díaz, full of accusations and protestations, into an idyllic instance of harmony, solidarity, and camaraderie.[77]

The same procedure applies to the account of the death of Moctezuma. According to Cortés:

> Mutezuma, who together with one of his sons and many other chiefs who had been captured previously was still a prisoner, asked to be taken out onto the roof of the fortress where he might speak to the captains of his people and tell them to end the fighting. I had him taken out, and when he reached a breastwork which ran out beyond the fortress, and was about to speak to them, he received a blow on his head from a stone; and the injury was so serious that he died three days later.[78]

The change here consists of the addition of the apparently innocent words "asked to be taken," which by attributing the peace initiative to Moctezuma make him the cause of the sequence of events leading to his death by stoning. Cortés thus transfers his own responsibility for Moctezuma's death to Moctezuma himself and his subjects and once again converts what actually transpired into a fiction. A death caused largely by Cortés's misunderstanding of the true significance of Cuhitlaua's appointment and by his order to Moctezuma to address his subjects is turned into a suicide for which only Moctezuma is responsible and an act of aggression for which only the Aztecs are to blame.[79]

But why are there so many omissions, reelaborations, and distortions in Cortés's account of the loss of Tenochtitlan? Díaz's version, the *Ramírez Codex*, and other documents show that Cortés was aware of the facts and understood their implications, and hence his omissions and reelaborations must have been deliberate and calculated to fit a general design to present things differently. Certainly one of Cortés's purposes was to put himself and his men in a favorable light, downplaying the problematic aspects of their role in the conquest and loss of Tenochtitlan. But a close examination of his second letter reveals that the cornerstone of the transformation of his rebellion into service was his characterization of Velázquez and his followers as traitors. His characterization includes a careful presentation of their actions and their consequences that would show them capable of sacrificing the king's interest to their own goals. By presenting Velázquez as the one person responsible for the Aztec rebellion and, consequently, the loss of Tenochtitlan and all its treasures, Cortés's rebellion would be implicitly perceived as service on the part of a faithful vassal forced by circumstances to rise up against a traitor, and not as a transgression of the royal order and an act of disobedience against the governor. In his narrative Cortés often violates chronology and includes impressions, judgments, and reflections that could only have occurred to him after the fact. Again, this is no slip of memory, but a deliberate strategy. Its effect is twofold. On the one hand, it allows him to present himself as the clairvoyant leader who foresees to the last detail the implications and disastrous consequences of the actions of Velázquez and Narváez. On the other hand, it gradually prepares the reader for the final and inescapable characterization of Velázquez the traitor as *the* cause of the "groundless" rebellion of the Aztecs.

In his second letter, Cortés narrates Narváez's arrival in Mexico in a presentation that recalls, in its main lines of characterization, that of his first letter, the one lost and summarized at the beginning of the second. Narváez's expedition is portrayed as having been prompted by the conflict between the interests of Velázquez and those of the king: "They had sent that fleet and their men against me," says Cortés, "because I had sent the report concerning this land to Your Majesty and not to the aforementioned Diego Velázquez . . . and the said Diego Velázquez was preparing a fleet, . . . knowing full well the harm and disservice to your Majesty that this might cause."[80] This is his first direct accusation of treason against Velázquez under the code of vassalage, but it is not the last. Ignoring the loyal recommendations of the ever loyal Cortés, Velázquez repeats the same crime by inciting the natives to rebel against the Spaniards, sending "messengers to Mutezuma to tell him he would be freed and that . . . Narváez had come to seize me and all my company and would afterwards leave the land. He said he did not want gold but that once he had captured me and all those with me he would leave the people of this land in complete freedom."[81] The "disservice" involved here is so obvious that Cortés does not bother to highlight its importance. The third act is even more serious. Cortés says in his second letter that Narváez "in the name of Diego Velázquez . . . intended to proceed against us and take us by force. To this end he was in league with the natives, especially with Mutezuma by way of his Messengers."[82] This now is high treason, with Velázquez and his men siding with the Aztecs against the king and his loyal representatives.

Besides characterizing Velázquez and his men indirectly by describing their actions, Cortés continues to make harsh, explicit statements about them, calling them "foreigners," then the authors of a "disservice," and finally "traitors and perfidious vassals who had rebelled against their sovereign and sought to usurp his realms and dominions."[83] Just as he is about to depart from Tenochtitlan, Cortés presciently remarks that he feels that he should not really dare to leave the city because of the attitudes he has observed, "for fear that once I had done so the inhabitants would rebel and I would lose all the gold, the jewels, and even the city itself; for once that was lost the whole country would be lost also"; but that in view of the great trouble brewing and having seen "the great harm that was being stirred up, and how the country was in revolt because of Narváez," he feels obliged to confront Narváez in defense of the interests of the king. Narváez is thus made to appear responsible for Cortés's absence and its consequences.

This entire version, so neatly put together after the fact, illustrates how Cortés converted everything connected with the loss of Tenochtitlan into a fiction in support of his characterization of Velázquez and his men, with the design in turn of making his rebellion against Velázquez appear justified. The systematic omission of anything that might have divided the responsibility between himself and Velázquez responds to the calculated need to present the latter as a traitor and to blame the most serious disaster of the conquest of Mexico directly on Velázquez's thirst for power and his repeated betrayal of royal concerns. Presenting the legitimacy of his own behavior as a matter to be taken for granted, Cortés omits certain episodes, reworks others, and reverses the roles of the two central figures.

On the surface, Cortés's discourse appears to be shaped by impeccable logic. His choice of the narrative form of the *relación* fictitiously guarantees the truth of a narrative that gradually substitutes a highly subjective, fictionalized representation for the accurate account of the events it promises. But within this representation the inner logic of the discourse fictitiously demonstrates that, despite existing laws and misleading appearances, Cortés's rebellion is fully justified. In the context of Cortés's narrative, his rebellion loses its disruptive potential and becomes an exemplary service to the king.

Thus the first stage in transforming rebellion into service is aimed at disqualifying Velázquez as a legitimate representative of the king. In the second phase, the focus is on making Cortés's rebellious venture appear to be the reverse of everything represented by Velázquez and his plans for colonial expansion. Once again, the technique consists of an apparently objective description, concealing the fact that certain key elements have been carefully selected and refashioned. The narrator rarely assesses anything he has done directly, allowing the exemplary quality of his actions to become apparent "naturally" by virtue of their results and their implicit contrast with the designs and actions associated with Velázquez.

The fact that Cortés's first letter is missing is particularly unfortunate, since it deprives us of the first direct presentation he makes of his rebellion as a move in opposition to the intentions of Velázquez. But in both the *Letter from the Justiciary and Municipal Council* and the accounts by Bernal Díaz and Andrés Tapia, the opposition centers on the fact that Cortés proposed to *settle* whereas Velázquez proposed to *barter* or *trade*. Díaz goes so far as to assert that Velázquez's instructions stated explicitly that "as soon as you have gained all you can by trading you are to return."[84] The *Letter from the Justiciary and Municipal Council* stresses Cortés's plan to explore. Again, this sets him apart from Grijalva or any of the other former expeditionaries who failed to carry out any significant exploration of the new lands.[85]

With slight variations, all the direct accounts of the events are focused on the discrepancy in objectives (to barter versus to settle), reflecting two qualitatively different plans. It is very likely that, when the time came for Cortés to convince his men to accept his ideas, he found it more politically expedient to limit the difference to these two points and the potential for material gain represented by each approach. Barter offered only limited benefits, since most of what might be acquired was to be surrendered to the governor. But settlement opened up endless possibilities, adding to the spoils to be won in battle the lands and Indians that would be granted as a reward. Soldiers returned from a barter operation tired, often wounded, and rarely compensated for their service. The gains were for the governor and for his captain, who was given gold and *encomiendas* for his efforts. According to Bernal Díaz, all of this was referred to in the discussions that took place among Cortés's followers just before his election as captain-general and chief justice and before the foundating of Rica Villa de la Vera Cruz:

Sir, do you think it was right of Hernando Cortés to have brought us here by deceit? He proclaimed in Cuba that he was coming to settle, and now we discover that he has no authority to do anything but barter, and these men wish us to return to Santiago de Cuba with all the gold that has been collected. That will be the ruin of us all, for Diego Velázquez will take all, as he did before. You, sir, have already been to this country three times, counting the present expedition, spending your wealth and contracting debts, and have been in peril for your life many times from the wounds you have received. Many of us gentlemen, who feel that we are your friends, wish to convince you that this state of things must end.[86]

For these men, a change in the plans could imply something qualitatively different from a simple increase in booty: it represented the chance for an ordinary solider to become an *encomendero*.

The vague notion conveyed by the words "to settle" becomes more precise and defined in the *Letters* as Cortés reveals that his plan for conquering the new lands and incorporating them into the empire involves something quite different from the form of socioeconomic organization that had shaped the colony. Everything in his first three letters, however, appears to be governed by his need to ensure that Velázquez's project is perceived as involving treason rather than trade, and that his own is understood to be focused on service rather than conquest. The greed and irresponsibility of the former are highlighted by the disinterest, generosity, and foresight of the latter. Velázquez has reduced his interest in the new lands to becoming rich at their expense without concerning himself about whether they are destroyed, or whether his approach will harm the interests of the king, which, traitor that he is, he always subordinates to his own. Cortés's behavior, on the other hand, is always absolutely unselfish, his generosity is always exemplary, and he is motivated solely by the desire to be allowed to serve his king and lord, and to bring him further greatness. Cortés's presentation of everything he chooses to say is subordinated to the purpose of depicting his enterprise as loyal service. Thus he tells us that what moved him to stop at Mexico, disobeying Velázquez's orders, was the desire to make Moctezuma "subject to your Majesty's Royal Crown"; that his only reason for punishing Velázquez's men and destroying the ships was to prevent any interference with "all that in the name of God and Your Highness has been accomplished in this land";[87] and that what sent him off to confront Narváez was his desire to protect the royal interest.[88]

Cortés presents his design not only as service but as service seeking no other reward than to serve. In his exhortations to his soldiers he maintains over and over again that his overriding purpose is to *serve*; shortly before setting out against Narváez, who, we must not forget, represented Veláz-quez, the king, and all legally constituted authority, he says:

> Once I had seen that there was no way by which I could avoid the great harm that would ensue and, furthermore, that the natives of the land were becoming more rebellious each day, I entrusted myself to God, and, setting aside all fear of what might ensue, and considering that to die in the service of my king and in defense of his lands against usurpation would win for us all great glory, I ordered Gonzalo de Sandoval, alguacil mayor, to seize Narváez.[89]

The fiction is complete if we consider that the usurper was Cortés and the loyal servant Narváez. But the point of this paragraph is to show that the dangerous and potentially fatal path of glory chosen by Cortés is equated with loyal service to the king, in clear opposition to the attitude of men like Velázquez, who was endangering the royal interest by making it subordinate to the primary goal of increasing his own profits and power. Thus, to yield to Velázquez's pressure would constitute treason rather than obedience, whereas to disobey him amounts to yet another act of service. Cortés himself states very clearly that: "I would not be persuaded by bribes to do as they asked, for I, and those who were with me, would rather die in defense of the land which we had won and now held in subjection for Your Majesty than be disloyal or traitors to our king."[90]

His conclusion is inescapable, given the internal logic of his discourse: obedience to the governor is tantamount to complicity with a traitor, and insubordination represents the very best kind of service to the king. The first goal that articulates Cortés's fictionalized account of his conquest has been reached: *Rebellion* is metamorphosed into *service*. There is one last fictional element, however, that will be used to even further reinforce this critically necessary transformation: providentialism. Invocations to God, the Virgin, and all the saints of the heavenly court—especially St. Yago and St. Peter—were a natural part of the language, at a time in history when the development of events was believed by most to be part of a divine master plan. Such invocations, which appear frequently in the discourse of Bernal Díaz and Cortés, were often rather automatic and meaningless. But Cortés goes beyond the standard God-referent clichés of the day, presenting his actions as the work of Providence. These invocations are very specific, and they present God as Cortés's ally vis-à-vis both the Aztecs and the followers of Velázquez, legitimizing his insubordination by the evidence of divine support and protection. The first incidence of this occurs during the clash with the men sent by Garay, shortly after the foundation of Rica Villa de la Vera Cruz, when God prevents the gun threatening one of Cortés's captains from firing: "he tried to fire his harquebus," says Cortés, "which would have killed the captain I had put in charge of Vera Cruz had not Our Lord prevented the fuse from igniting."[91] From this time on, Cortés refers repeatedly to this support during each of his confrontations with the representatives of Velázquez. For example, upon defeating Narváez he says that "they were very glad that God has so provided . . . that if God had not mysteriously assisted us."[92] He offers the same kind of providentialist explanation for his most resounding victories over the natives. In Tlaxcala he says that "it truly seemed that God was fighting for us, because from such a multitude, such fierce and able warriors and with so many kinds of weapons to harm us, we escaped so lightly" adding a reference to "the victory which God had been pleased to give us."[93] In the battles before the *noche triste*, Cortés remarks that he and his men received "the help of God and his Blessed Mother." In Otumba he says that "it seemed that the Holy Spirit had inspired me in this," to explain his own foresight, and the battle is decided in favor of the Spaniards because "Our Lord was pleased to show His power and mercy."[94] And finally, as they prepare to attack Tenochtitlan, the arrival of a reinforcement of men and weapons is described by Cortés as a miracle sent by God: a miracle crucial to victory in battle that "it had pleased God to grant to the Spaniards."[95]

With exemplary modesty, Cortés attributes to God, the Virgin, and all the saints the merit for some of his most spectacular military triumphs. The result of such humility again transforms what actually transpired into a fiction in which the events reflect divine will rather than the military genius of Cortés and the valor of his men. The presentation of God as Cortés's most faithful and constant ally, and of his rebellious venture as repeatedly favored and defended by Providence, is a crucial move. It constitutes the best possible means of establishing legitimacy in the context of an ideology informed by both medieval and Renaissance elements, for which the concept of the divine origins of the monarchy implies the closest of alliances between God and the king. Cortés has not yet obtained the king's support, but by giving this providentialist cast to his action, any denial of such support would have to be in flagrant opposition to the will of God. His rebellion, already metamorphosed into service in Cortés's highly fictionalized accounts of himself, Velázquez, and their respective plans, is now finally legitimized by being presented as an expression not of an individual or collective will but of the will of God.

The Creation of a Model

In all the surviving portraits, from official paintings such as the one on display in the Hospital de Jesús in Mexico City to the large number of stylized drawings in the native codexes, Cortés's main features remain essentially the same. His stance is determined, his expression half dreamy, half ironic; his legs are well built, his hands both strong and dainty. He is a small man, with a rather large head; his expression is alert, his appearance somewhat fragile. The conventional details of the portraits do not provide much information beyond these impressions, and we must look to the texts of his contemporaries for a fuller description.

Las Casas, who presented Columbus in the best possible light by continually excusing and justifying his actions and perceptions, adopts a much more critical attitude toward Cortés. Among all the contemporary characterizations, his is the most negative. Cortés appears in the *Historia de las Indias* as a complete opportunist who did nothing but use everything and everybody for his own purposes. His only merit is that of "knowing Latin because he studied law in Salamanca and obtained a degree there." Otherwise he was fond of "talking and telling jokes," from which Las Casas hastens to conclude that he did not have the discretion necessary to be a good secretary. He was "crafty," "pedantic," a "haggler," niggardly, false, ungrateful, envious, and of "extremely humble origins."[96] Tapia's portrait, on the other hand, has little in common with the version by Las Casas. His comments and his description of Cortés's actions and exhortations to his men present him as being a most exceptional and "well liked" man. He is intelligent, brave, fair, a good politician, possessed of great military genius, and very popular with his men.[97]

Bernal Díaz's characterization is the richest and most detailed. He proposes to describe for the reader "Cortés's nature and dimensions" and expresses profound admiration for all the many qualities he attributes to him. He begins with a physical description:

> He was of good stature and build, strong of body and limb, and well proportioned; his complexion was greyish in hue and his expression not very animated, and had his face been longer it would have been more handsome; his eyes were both kind and grave. His beard was rather dark and somewhat sparse, and his hair, as it was worn at the time, likewise. He was slender, with a high chest, straight back, and flat stomach. He was somewhat bow-legged but well set upon his limbs. He was a good horseman and skillful in the use of all kinds of weapons, on foot and on horseback, and he fought very well with them. Above all, he was courageous and spirited, and that is what matters.

This physical description is followed by a considerable amount of firsthand information on his personality. According to Díaz, Cortés got into "mischief with the ladies," in consequence of which "he sometimes fought against men valiant and dexterous in the use of their swords, and he always won." He was austere and little inclined to ostentation, "but showed in every way that he was a great gentleman." He was cultured and fond of literature, "knew Latin . . . was a bachelor of law, and something of a poet." He was "the first" to appear when work had to be done, and in battle "I always saw him enter the fray with the rest of us." He was a good warrior, very courageous, wise, highly daring, "very reasonable," although "extremely stubborn." Díaz concludes his portrait with a reference to Cortés's fondness for gambling. "I have not mentioned many other of our Marquis's feats of skill and courage . . . and I will say that he was very fond of cards and dice."[98]

However, when we compare Díaz's long, detailed description of Cortés's personality with the extraordinary complexity of the portrait carefully woven by Cortés in his *Letters*, Díaz's characterization shows no more insight than the other portraits mentioned above. In the *Letters* Cortés's self-portrait as a hero and model is no secondary aspect of the discourse. His transformation from a rebel into a model is one of the immediate purposes of the *Letters*, and the pivot of the fictionalization process. Through a gradual process of self-mythification, Cortés is transformed into a model that functions as the central element linking the transformation of his rebellion into service—the first goal of Cortés's fictional representation of the conquest—with the formulation of his ultimate goal: the creation of the political entity of New Spain under his expert leadership. The specific features of Cortés's self-portrait correspond to the complex functions that he must perform, from easing the mind of the king by repeatedly asserting his obeisance to the latter's authority, to guaranteeing the success and validity of his venture, implicitly representing it to be a projection of his own exemplary qualities. Cortés's fictional self-characterization in the *Letters* develops in two well-defined stages. The first involves the gradual transformation of Cortés into a mythical hero, and it unfolds during the period of the first four letters, reaching its highest point during the fall of Tenochtitlan. The second, which lasts through the disastrous expedition to Honduras described in the fifth letter, shows a gradual humanization and problematization of the mythical figure created in the earlier letters. The fact that the fictional dimension of the character appears most marked in the first three letters—corresponding to the period before the king recognizes Cortés's merit and the legitimacy of his conquest of Mexico—serves to emphasize that the fictionalization is deliberate and oriented toward certain highly political, rather than literary, objectives.

Ideologically, the attributes of the fictionalized Cortés appear to be rooted in the interface between the medieval and Renaissance worldviews that were characteristic of Spain during this time. The medieval dimension of Cortés's characterization draws upon the feudal code of representation, presenting a model who is both a loyal vassal and a perfect Christian. The Renaissance dimension is manifest in the qualities Cortés selects to represent himself as an outstanding leader, who ensures that his plans are put into effect on the exact terms he has designed for the purpose, and in his implicit formulation of a political philosophy founded on the use of reason as a privileged instrument of knowledge and on the conviction that the ends justify the means.[99] The point of departure of Cortés's fictionalized self-representation is the figure of a rebel who has taken defensive action to protect himself against legal punishment. But starting with the brief description of the destruction of the ships (at the beginning of the second letter), he gradually becomes a hero. For the narrative presents this rebel, acting out of a need to protect himself, as a prudent leader who knows what must be done to ensure the success of an enterprise construed as a "great service" to the king. This is the first stage in a metamorphosis that continues throughout the succeeding four letters as Cortés selects and refashions his material, adjusting it to present himself as the sum of the virtues required for the successful realization of his plan and eliminating anything not functionally suited to his purpose.

The technique used to portray the character in the *Letters* is consistent with literary models to be found in epic poetry. A simple comparison of the character in the *Letters* with the Cid will show that a similar narrative strategy has produced them both. Both characterizations draw on all the qualities needed to carry their action to a successful conclusion, although the specific goals are quite different. It had been the Cid's mission to put an end to the fragmentation of feudal power in medieval Spanish society and make way for the establishment of a centralized monarchy. The mission of Cortés was to conquer a new kingdom and achieve an essentially reformist personal political objective, within the structure of the Christian empire and under a monarch with absolute sovereignty.

The Cid's enterprise had been rooted in the ideology of the Spanish *Reconquista* of the Iberian Peninsula, which expresses the worldview of medieval Spain. Cortés's enterprise, as defined by the character in his *Letters*, reflects the very essence of the political philosophy of the Renaissance as embodied in *The Prince* by Machiavelli. Cortés could not have read Machiavelli's *The Prince* before writing his *Letters*, for although Machiavelli composed his work in prison around 1513, the first edition was not published until after his death, in 1532. Nonetheless, the Cortés of the *Letters* is fashioned in terms of the very same Renaissance philosophical principles of political realism that in *The Prince* are carried to their ultimate consequences.

Arnold Hauser observes with good reason that Machiavelli did not invent Machiavellianism and that years before he wrote his book Italy was already governed by princes who had virtually been born Machiavellian. Machiavelli's achievement was that he formulated consistently and systematically a philosophy based on the notion that Christianity and the principles of politics should be kept separate, a notion that became the foundation of the political realism of the Renaissance.[100]

It should therefore come as no surprise that many of Cortés's actions embodied the political concepts developed by Machiavelli. Henry R. Wagner maintains that even if Cortés did not imitate Cesare Borgia he unconsciously followed his path, and he explains this by the fact that both men were Spanish.[101] The similarity between them, however, or between either of the two and any other great Renaissance politician is a result of their having shared some of the central principles of political realism rather than a consequence of their common nationality. Yet Cortés's political realism, implicit in everything he did and wrote, cannot be attributed as proposed by Wagner to the working of his subconscious. His ability to formulate rationally the central components of a philosophy that was exactly suited to the demands of his age distinguishes him from the large number of princes alluded to by Hauser and makes him a predecessor to the character created by Machiavelli. The capacity of Machiavelli's prince for analyzing concrete reality (on which the rational political philosophy of the Renaissance was based) is identical to that underlying the characterization of Cortés.

There is no clear connection, however, between the hero of the *Letters* and the fabulous characters of the novels of chivalry—whose actions, according to Leonard, all the conquistadors wished to emulate. It is likely that, in more or less conscious ways, many conquistadors followed the chivalric model, but in this regard Cortés was a notable exception. Leonard is surprised at not finding more references in the *Letters* to chivalric characters or fantastic phenomena, such as those that do occur occasionally in, for example, Bernal Díaz's *Conquest of New Spain*. But Cortés's *Letters* and other personal correspondence make it clear that the importance of such models was, in his case, negligible. He appears not as an *imitator* but as a *creator* of models, and the origins of what he creates are to be found in a rational analysis of objective reality, rather than in preexisting literary models or the realm of the fantastic. Columbus fictionalized his representation of American reality to identify it with a preexisting imaginary model. Cortés, on the other hand, used his rational analysis of reality and of the objective situation around him as the basis for making the hero of his *Letters* the very embodiment of the political philosophy of his day. The fictionalization in Columbus's discourse was based on a process of reducing American reality and undermining its value. The fictionalization of the narrative discourse of the *Letters* reflects, on the contrary, a rational analysis and profound understanding of the historical and political circumstances of their author's time.

The first element in Cortés's fictional characterization as a model is the presentation of himself as a warrior and military leader. This role corresponds to one of Cortés's main functions during the occupation and conquest of Moctezuma's empire and reflects one of the most important attributes of Machiavelli's Renaissance prince. "A ruler, then," says Machiavelli, "should have no other objective and no other concern, nor occupy himself with anything else except war and its methods and practices, for this pertains only to those who rule. . . . A ruler who lacks such expertise lacks the elements of generalship. For it enables one to track down the enemy, to encamp one's army properly, to lead an army toward the enemy, to prepare for battle, to besiege fortresses or fortified towns, in ways that conduce to victory."[102] Starting with his decision to destroy the ships, Cortés projects his foresight as an eminently clear indication of his military genius. He first presents himself as a model by attributing to himself, every time he is successful, the capacity for having accurately anticipated the moves of the enemy. Simultaneously, he transforms or simply does not refer to any incident in which his lack of foresight has produced negative consequences. One of the clearest examples of this involves the incident in which he overturns the idols in the Great Temple at Tenochtitlan.

Cortés presents his decision as being appropriate to the circumstances of the Spaniards, and its immediate results as, of course, positive:

> The most important of these idols, and the ones in whom they have most faith, I had taken from their places and thrown down the steps . . . Mutezuma and many of the chieftains of the city were with me until the idols were removed, the chapel cleaned and the images set up, and all wore happy faces. I forbade them to sacrifice living creatures to idols as they were accustomed. . . . And from then on they ceased to do it, and in all the time I stayed in that city I did not see a living creature killed or sacrificed.[103]

But Bernal Díaz's account, which is much more consistent with the development of the events that led to the *noche triste*, shatters this idyllic presentation of the episode and its consequences. According to Díaz, Cortés's provocation was based on a miscalculation regarding the strength of the position of the Spaniards in Tenochtitlan. This position had already been considerably weakened with the arrival of Narváez and his men at Veracruz, and the consequences of Cortés's bad judgment were negative from the beginning. His action provoked immediate indignation among the Aztecs, who responded by sending a clear ultimatum to Cortés and his followers:

> No sooner had we set up the image of Our Lady on the altar and said mass, than Huichilobos and Tezcatlipoca seem to have spoken to their *papas*, telling them that they intended to leave their country, since they were so ill treated by the *Teules** . . . and the *papas* . . . must convey it to Montezuma and all his captains, so that they might at once attack us and kill us. . . . Montezuma sent Orteguilla to our Captain with the message that he wished to speak to him . . . the great Montezuma addressed them in these words: "My lord Malinche and captains, I am indeed distressed at the answer which our *Teules* have given to our *papas*, to me and to all my captains. They have commanded us to make war on you and kill you and drive you back to the sea. I have reflected on this command, and think it would be best that you should leave this city before you are attacked, and leave no one behind. This, my lord Malinche, you must certainly do, for it is in your own interest. Otherwise you will be killed. Remember that your lives are at stake."[104]

The fictional transformation of this episode is fundamental. It allows Cortés to appear as a man of great foresight well able to gauge his strength, evaluate his circumstances, and predict the consequences of his action. His move is fictitiously presented as having consolidated order, eliminated the practice of sacrifice, and enhanced the authority of the Spaniards. His decision to leave the defense of Tenochtitlan in the hands of no more than one hundred men is made to seem heroic, not imprudent, on the grounds that the city was peaceful and secure; there were no signs of upheaval among the natives, who appeared contented and respectful of Spanish authority; and Alvarado's troops could easily defend the stronghold if the need arose. But according to Díaz's account of Cortés's decision and the events that followed, the historical facts were very different. The residents of the city had given a perfectly clear indication of their intention to rebel, in the form of an ultimatum inspired by their gods. In this light, Cortés's heroism was in fact a desperate move, his foresight questionable

---

*Name given to the conquistadors by the Aztecs when the two groups first encountered each other. The word comes from the Aztec *teotl* or *teutl*, meaning "god." The Aztecs believed that the Spaniards were gods, or the children of the sun.—TRANS.

indeed, and the catastrophic violence inflicted by Alvarado in the temple recovers its original meaning, perhaps, as an expression of anguish and terror in the face of a situation that was becoming more impossible to withstand every day. The result of Cortés's provocation in the temple was to unleash rebellion, not to consolidate the obedience of the Aztecs. Díaz implies that the period between the overturning of the idols and Cortés's departure for the coast was uneasy and uncertain rather than peaceful: "Meanwhile we in Mexico went about in a great depression, fearing that any moment we might be attacked. Our Tlascalan auxiliaries and Doña Marina told Cortés that this was imminent, and the page Orteguilla was always in tears. We all kept on the alert . . . since we never took off our armour, gorgets, or leggings by night or day," says Díaz, eloquently summarizing the actual circumstances of the Spaniards in Tenochtitlan following the incident in the Great Temple.[105]

Casting himself as a model of prescience, Cortés converts his thoughtless impulse into an instance of extraordinary foresight. The consequences of his action—the events leading to the *noche triste* and the loss of Tenochtitlan—are placed in a favorable light, with no hint of the problematical potential of the deed that caused them. Through the selection and reordering of events that shape the narrative, Cortés emerges as a leader gifted with unfailing clairvoyance. This quality allows him to imagine or anticipate, at the outset of each battle, everything that promises victory to the Spaniards. His army is invulnerable to ambush because he is always "on guard"; the surprise attacks of the Tlaxcaltecas founder against his better organized defense; he knows that the natives are unlikely to attack at night, their witch doctors having advised them not to; at Otumba a prediction inspired by the Holy Spirit, with whom Cortés seems disposed on this occasion to share his glory, saves the Spaniards from total destruction; during the reconquest of Tenochtitlan described in the third letter, his foresight is responsible for the most unusual military triumphs and for the successful outcome of his campaign.

Second in importance to Cortés's portrait as a military model is his courage. His unusual valor was real enough, as testified to by his soldiers and other contemporaries. But in the discourse of the *Letters* this quality takes on a mythical dimension. His courage is implicit in such actions as using Velázquez's own ships to rise up against him, or entering unknown territory with only a handful of men. But at key moments in the development of the conquest, it is given a cast both decisive and superhuman. Where his courage is concerned, the fictional component involves the presentation of Cortés's undeniable personal valor as the *sole* factor leading to the success of an enterprise, to the exclusion of all others. The impression this conveys is decisively heightened by the frequent—and on occasion systematic—use of the first person singular rather than the much more fitting first person plural to describe certain episodes. In the wars against the Tlascalans, for example, the use of the first person singular transforms the import of the action, attributing the success of the campaign exclusively to Cortés's superhuman courage: "I had done them much harm without receiving any . . . I burnt five or six small places . . . I burnt more than ten villages . . . the inhabitants fought with us . . . I attacked two towns, where I killed many people." And in the battles preceding the *noche triste* it is again Cortés's courage that saves the situation over and over again: "I rode as fast as I was able down the whole length of the street with some horsemen following me, and without stopping I broke through those Indians, recovered the bridges and pursued the fugitives to the mainland."[106] His men simply "follow him," his herculean courage bearing the entire burden of the battle. Cortés's courage is thus fictionalized constantly throughout the accounts of the retreat on the *noche triste*, the events surrounding the battle of Otumba, and the high points of the reconquest of Tenochtitlan.

The use of the first person singular creates a fictitious division between Cortés and the rest of the men. Cortés gives the appearance of being isolated, always successfully solving things thanks to one of his particular qualities. This quality may be diplomacy, astuteness, the art of persuasion, justified violence, or, as in the cases just described, courage. Where the latter is concerned, the first person singular not only projects the attribute beyond human limits, it creates an illusion of invulnerability, casting upon the character the aura of myth.

Cortés's third model quality relating to what Machiavelli called the art of war is his talent as an outstanding strategist and tactician. His characterization as strategist begins with his subjective presentation of the Mexican territory. The rivers, valleys, mountains, and plains of Mexico, the towns, streets, and plazas of the complex Aztec empire are all converted into a gigantic military objective. This reduction of reality to its strategically relevant aspects occurs frequently in the second letter and becomes in the third almost the only form of representation used. The earlier code, focused on the figure of the discoverer and on relating the dominions of Moctezuma to the objectives of other expeditions (Seville and Granada during the *Reconquista*, Africa and Asia during an earlier stage of the Renaissance), is replaced almost entirely in the third letter by a military code of representation. Beauty, initially identified with wealth, culture, and refinement, is now associated with military victory: *fighting* is beautiful, and cities described in the second letter in the language of aesthetics and culture have now become nothing but military goals.

This transformation of Mexico the fabulous, as perceived in the first letters, into a Mexico consisting of the sum of all the tactical objectives of the reconquest of Tenochtitlan highlights Cortés's talent as a great strategist. His skill in preparing for the reconquest by founding Tepeaca and thereby securing a means of retreat toward the sea, building ships, and blocking passage along the bridges during the advance toward the center of Tenochtitlan, all provide a good illustration of his unusual abilities. But just as with his courage, the fictional dimension of the portrait involves not the characteristic or quality itself but the way it is attributed to him in the discourse. Cortés is not only a good strategist and tactician; he is the model and prototype of them all, and within the context of the *Letters*, the only one around. Díaz expresses indignation over the fact that in his *Historia*, Gómara attributes certain qualities exclusively to Cortés. But the same perception, according to which the hero single-handedly plans infallible strategies virtually all the time, shapes the narrative of the *Letters*. Success is always presented as the sole result of an initiative conceived exclusively by Cortés, and anything not of his conception inevitably leads to failure—illustrated by the few failures that do not go unreported in the *Letters*, all of which are explained in terms of somebody else's disobedience.[107] Where the fiction of the *Letters* is concerned, there can be no error, surprise, or failure possible for a mythical hero endowed with extraordinary talents that are shared with no one and that constitute the very guarantee of victory.

The final element in Cortés's fictional portrayal of himself in the *Letters* as a model of military leadership involves his use of violence. The rationale that justifies violence and terror as tactical measures is the numerical disproportion between the native and Spanish armies. Within this context, the use of terror becomes one of the most important weapons of the conquest. By subordinating his description of terror to his self-characterization as an exemplary tactician and by giving violence the appearance of a necessary measure, Cortés provides a fictitious justification for some of the most controversial episodes of the conquest.

The massacre of Cholula is one of the most revealing examples. There is considerable disagreement over the episode among biographers and historians. All eye-witnesses on the side of the Spaniards maintain that the behavior of the Cholultecas was treacherous, whereas the native versions recorded by Sahagún disagree. The latter, however, are explicit about the

Cholultecas' determination never to surrender, convinced that their gods would free them from Spanish domination.[108] Whatever the true reason, the repression ordered by Cortés at Cholula was so bloody that it is hard to justify it even on the hypothesis of genuine signs of treachery. Furthermore, rather than a battle, what actually took place was the calculated massacre of thousands of defenseless natives and the subsequent destruction of a large part of the city. Andrés Tapia describes the events:

> And then he ordered most of those men killed, leaving some of them in prison, and he ordered a signal given for the Spaniards to attack the ones in the courtyards and kill them all, and this was done; and they defended themselves as best they could and tried to hit back; but since they were closed into the courtyards, with the entrances blocked, most of them died. After this, we Spaniards and the Indians who were with us formed squadrons and went into many parts of the city, killing warriors and setting fire to houses. . . . Thus it was that everything possible was done to destroy that city . . . and it took two days to destroy the city.[109]

Bernal Díaz, on the other hand, devotes less attention to the slaughter and the destruction of the city than to the treachery of the Cholultecas, whom he virtually accuses of having pots of chile sauce prepared in which to cook the Spaniards.[110]

Cortés's version is short and pragmatic. In his second letter, he briefly lists early signs of treachery later confirmed by information that Marina received from a Cholulteca woman and states that he decided to take action before being kept from doing so by the events. He downplays as much as possible the violence inflicted and refers to the torture and execution of the top leaders, mentioned by Tapia and Bernal Díaz, simply by saying that the victims were left bound up in a room. The slaughter of thousands of unarmed natives within an enclosed courtyard is reduced to one sentence, which does not express, even syntactically, the direct relationship between the actions of the Spaniards and the death of the natives: "and we fought so hard that in two hours more than three thousand men died." In regard to the destruction of the city, he says only that he "ordered some towers and fortified houses from which they were attacking us to be set on fire," and he records the repression as lasting "five hours" instead of two days.[111]

The result of these changes is a considerably fictionalized version of the events. Violence appears as necessary action, planned as such by Cortés who is presented as the prototype of a man capable of controlling a difficult situation by appropriate means. His report reveals nothing controversial: a highly questionable decision is represented as having been necessary and even unavoidable, and the true scope of its effects are minimized. The function of the fictionalization is twofold. It implies that such violence is justified, and it portrays Cortés as a military leader who may be relied on to act in the best way possible, in any situation whatsoever.[112]

The second feature that complements Cortés's self-portrait as a fictional military hero in the *Letters* is his role as a *politician*. This role is founded on his ability to use negotiations as a means of making very considerable advances in the conquest, while at the same time strengthening his military position through the establishment of alliances. Violence and aggressiveness are never presented as the best approach to conquest, but only as the last resort after all other possible forms of negotiation and persuasion have failed. Whereas Cortés the warrior had destroyed and killed mercilessly whenever it seemed necessary, Cortés the politician seduces everyone, Mexican or Spaniard. Throughout the *Letter from the Justiciary and Municipal Council*, he presents himself as being so effective in this regard that both the unity and military competence of the Spaniards and the overwhelming increase in the number of natives disposed to join them appear to be more the result of his negotiating talent than of any of the disciplinary or repressive measures that he in fact never hesitated to apply. By his account, the attempted rebellion by Velázquez's followers was put in check by the irresistible persuasiveness of his extraordinary speeches, in which he reminded them of the purpose of their glorious mission and skillfully manipulated an array of political, religious, social, and material incentives. Any reference to the disciplinary measures used to implement the designs of his beautiful oratory—which ranged from imprisonment to hanging—is limited to an occasional vague remark about some undefined punishment. "I punished them according to the law and as, in the circumstances, I judged would do Your Majesty greatest service," says Cortés, in a brief comment on the disciplinary action taken against Escudero and Carmeño, whom he ordered hanged, and against Umbría, who was whiplashed and had his feet cut off for trying to rebel.[113] Cortés's authority and control are presented as if his ability to apply them derived entirely from his power of persuasion, a power that appears to derive from Cortés's own nature. He appears as a superior being in possession of the truth, capable of securing obedience, respect, and subjection by merely conveying this truth to those around him and keeping them reminded of it.

The version of the conquest contained in the *Letters* explicitly presents the use of force as a secondary instrument, applied only after peaceful methods have failed. The measures taken to impose control, authority, and vassalage always follow the same sequence: solicitation, persuasion, negotiation, repeated pardons, and attack. But the latter is resorted to only when Cortés is unable to achieve his objectives politically by using his extraordinary faculties of diplomacy and persuasion. The approach implicit in his actions and speeches comes down to two basic principles, which Machiavelli describes as reflecting the political philosophy of the Renaissance. The first, "divide and conquer," is exemplified by Cortés's political alliances throughout the conquest. "What usually happens," says Machiavelli, "is that, as soon as a strong invader attacks a country, all the less powerful men rally to him, because they are enviously hostile to the ruler who has held sway over them . . . and using his own forces, and with their consent, he can easily put down those who are powerful, thus gaining complete control of the country."[114] As soon as Cortés senses the discontent among Moctezuma's subjects and their desire for freedom from Aztec control, he puts this idea into practice. Soon after forming an alliance with the Tlaxcaltecas, he explicitly clarifies the applicability of this basic policy to the entire venture of the conquest: "When I saw the discord and animosity between these two peoples I was not a little pleased, for it seemed to further my purpose considerably; consequently I might have the opportunity of subduing them more quickly, for, as the saying goes, 'divided they fall.' . . . So I maneuvered one against the other and thanked each side for their warnings and told each that I held his friendship to be worth more than the other's."[115] The second principle involves knowing how to alternate effectively between harshness and kindness in dealing with both the Spaniards and the natives; how to apply "a shovelful of limestone and another of sand" in the words of a Spanish saying, or, using Machiavelli's more sophisticated expression, how to find a balance between cruelty and mercifulness.[116] In the *Letters* a reference to Moctezuma's imprisonment, for instance, is followed by Cortés's "kind words" and protests of respect and obedience. The even more problematical measure of "putting him in irons" is followed by a description of Cortés's great show of magnanimity and "good treatment," consistent with the policy that has characterized his relationship with the natives and his own men all along.

Cortés's representation of reality, in which the success of his diplomatic campaign to impose his authority is ascribed entirely to his political talent, is complemented by the avoidance of any reference to political mistakes and their consequences. The best example of this is the episode in which Moctezuma's brother Cuhitlaua is set free. Henry Wagner summarizes the importance of this by saying that of Cortés's many mistakes during the week following his return to Tenochtitlan after defeating Narváez, it may well have been the liberation of Cuhitlaua that marked the beginning of disaster.[117] Madariaga mentions the accounts by Cervantes de Salazar and Torquemada to show that freeing Cuhitlaua was a very poor move, in terms of the negotiations Cortés was conducting with Moctezuma and his people to try to recover control over the city.[118] Bernal Díaz and the native informants present Moctezuma's transfer of power to Cuhitlaua as an accomplished fact, without going into what led up to it. It does not seem unreasonable to conclude, however, that it was Cortés who freed him, for reasons that cannot be clearly ascertained from existing documents. Cuhitlaua had been a prisoner in the palace before Cortés left Tenochtitlan. One week after his return, Cuhitlaua was free and had been elected by the Aztecs as the political and religious leader of the rebellion. The only person with sufficient authority to free any of the royal prisoners was Cortés, and regardless of whether the decision was made individually or collectively, the responsibility for the mistake fell to Cortés as the Spanish leader. To have avoided any reference to the freeing of Cuhitlaua and the manner of his appointment as leader of the Aztec is consistent with Cortés's narrative strategy, in which any action that might undermine the characterization of the hero as the perfect representative of every relevant virtue is simply left out.

In the chapter "Those who became rulers through wicked means," Machiavelli says: "Hence, it should be noted that a conqueror, after seizing power, must decide about all the injuries he needs to commit, and do all of them at once, so as not to have to inflict punishments every day. Thus he will be able, by his restraint, to reassure men and win them over by benefiting them."[119] By the end of his campaign, Cortés's conduct would appear to have been exactly consistent with this philosophy. In the narrative discourse of the *Letters*, the fall of Tenochtitlan marks, without any real transition, the end of the presentation of the hero in terms of the virtues required for war and aggression and sets the stage for his characterization in terms of his third main function, his role as *governor*. Harshness gives way to magnanimity, aggressiveness turns into compassion, and punishment is replaced by pardon. Instead of an analysis of military affairs, a warrior's perception of his enemy, there is a new humanity, expressed in the form of repeated displays of compassion and clemency. The Aztecs, portrayed as "dogs" or "traitors" throughout the third letter, are now "sad": "So great was their suffering that it was beyond our understanding how they would endure it." Gone is the implacable warrior of the campaign to recover Tenochtitlan, replaced by a Cortés who, as he organizes his new government, presents himself as the lenient defender of the very Indians he previously attacked so mercilessly. When Cuauhtémoc hands him his dagger asking him to kill him Cortés pardons and encourages him, telling him he has "nothing to fear," and he advises the reader that a conqueror's first obligation is to protect the unfortunate people he has conquered.[120]

The portrayal of Cortés as a model governor focuses on two aspects. First, he is a compendium, in the style of Machiavelli's prince, of all the ideal attributes of the governor of a newly founded state. Second, this new state, shaped entirely by the measures the ideal governor chooses, is a thoroughly unproblematical model of order, justice, and peace. In the context of this Utopian arrangement, anything problematical or controversial that arises is blamed on those wishing to undermine Cortés's authority. This narrative strategy allows Cortés to enhance his image as the prototype of a perfect Renaissance governor while stressing the threat posed to the king's interests by his adversaries—especially Velázquez and Bishop Fonseca.

According to the *Letters*, Tenochtitlan had no sooner been conquered and the peace consolidated through the issuance of pardons than Cortés undertook an amazing number of activities. He redistributed land and rebuilt the city, settled new sections and founded new towns, discovered mines and erected arms and munitions factories, organized a communication network to connect all points in the new state to the capital, reestablished trade, improved the imperial economy, and converted the natives to Christianity. He planned expeditions to explore and conquer new territory and spread his dominions beyond the limits of the former empire, so as to be able to control the ports and coastlines and link the new kingdom with the highly prized spice islands to the east. Speaking of the reconstruction of Tenochtitlan, he says: "They have worked so rapidly that many of the settlers' houses are already finished and others well underway. And because there is an abundance of stone . . . they are such fine and large houses that Your Sacred Majesty may be certain that in five years this city will be the most noble and populous in the known world, and it will have the finest buildings."[121] This plan to create the most noble city in the world is consistent with his design to represent his activities as governor as being oriented toward the creation of a Utopian state, largely defined in terms of its contrast with the model of the colonies in the Antilles. Cortés refers to this contrast in his fourth letter in a remark on how his decisions and orders were received by the settlers:

> Some of the Spaniards who reside in these parts are not entirely satisfied with some of them, especially those which oblige them to settle on the land, for most of them expect to do with these lands as was done in the Islands when they were colonized, that is, to harvest, destroy, and then abandon them. And because it seems to me that it would be unpardonable for those of us who

have had experience in the past not to do better for the present and the future by taking measures against those things which are well known to have caused the ruin of the Islands, especially, as I have written to Your Majesty many times, because this land is of such magnificence and nobility, that God, Our Lord, may be so well served, and Your Majesty's Royal revenues much increased.[122]

Cortés's plans for the state now call for a general *development* of the colonial resources to replace the former model of plunder. Centers are to be created and organized for the development of agriculture, handicrafts, and trade. The earlier obsession with gold as the sole symbol of wealth, so present in Columbus's discourse and reflected by the economic model adopted in the Antilles, is to be set aside: exploration will henceforth be oriented toward the mining of copper, tin, and iron for weapons and tools, so that New Spain may become independent from her current suppliers. With Cortés in command, rapine and corruption will be replaced by production and a government organized for the benefit of all. The unfortunate destruction of the colonies in the Antilles is to be followed by a Utopian project for creation and development, within the framework of an authoritarian and paternalistic, but just, regime. The disappearance of the population in the Antilles is presented as being one of the governor's main preoccupations; he takes measures, enacts laws, and punishes those guilty of offenses against the natives, evidently wishing to guard the Mexican population from the fate suffered by those subjected to the *encomienda* system in the earlier colonies. In May 1524 he signed a series of government ordinances designed to protect the natives by regulating their working hours, the frequency with which they could be moved about, their daily diet, and religious instruction. The ordinances also explicitly prohibited the use of natives in the exploitation of the mines. In his letter to the king dated October 15, 1524, Cortés justifies his disobedience of royal instructions ordering him to put an end to the controlled distribution of natives and to allow them free contractual and commercial relations with the Spaniards. He argues that his system of distribution is part of a broader plan to protect natives from the abuse of settlers whom he describes as "low, fierce, and given to a variety of sins and vices." He goes on to propose his plan for establishing a prosperous, well organized, just state, which would truly concern itself with converting the natives to Christianity, and which would allow slavery only in punishment for rebellion.[123]

Cortés describes himself in terms thoroughly consistent with the demands of a Utopian Renaissance state as he conceives it, and thus as the best man to govern it. To highlight the perfect match between the man and the enterprise, the *Letters* refer repeatedly to the dependency of the latter upon the former. The person and presence of Cortés are made to appear irreplaceable. Within the fictionalizing construct of the *Letters*, they become the central support without which the entire state would founder.[124] The only difficulties acknowledged in his Utopian version of reality immediately following the conquest are associated either with interference on the part of his Spanish opponents or with the behavior of natives not yet incorporated into the new state. It is outsiders alone who can threaten—through ignorance, as in the case of the natives, or ambition, as in the case of the envoys of Velázquez and Fonseca—the welfare of the harmonious state he has organized and put before his king.[125]

Cortés's self-characterization as governor of the new state completes his image as a Renaissance hero. A better conqueror, negotiator, organizer, and leader than anyone else, he embodies all the virtues prescribed by Machiavelli for a Renaissance leader. Consequently, no one could be better able to make of Mexico a perfect Renaissance state. But this very fact is inherently problematical: in a context in which power is highly centralized in the figure of an absolute monarch, the qualities that make Cortés appear heroic and fit to be a perfect governor also make him potentially danger-ous. The Cortés who comes across in the *Letters* embodies the political philosophy of Machiavelli's *Prince*. But Cortés was a vassal, not a prince, an adventurous *hidalgo** who as a result of certain qualities and merits not in keeping with his station had risen at a heady, even alarming, rate. But the political structure within which Cortés operated revolved around an absolute monarchy and tolerated no dispersion of power. The same qualities that would have made him a model in his time, had he been a prince, made him a most threatening subject.

The last central element in the fictionalization of Cortés's characterization in the *Letters* reveals the extent to which he was aware of this potential threat. The first stage of the fictional characterization transforms the rebel into a Renaissance hero. The second turns this hero into a model by reinscribing Cortés's figure within a structure of vassalage. Ironically, this narrative strategy validates Cortés's personality and action by linking them to medieval ideological parameters quite different from the ideals of the Renaissance, which Cortés so perfectly embodied.[126] But it allows Cortés to appear in fictitious harmony with the hierarchical structure of power headed by God and the king. In his statement to the king on May 15, 1522, Cortés alludes to the hierarchical nature of the existing power

*From "*hijo de algo*." In Spain, a gentleman by birth belonging to the lower nobility.—TRANS.

structure in the following terms: "for works will be seen in these things wrought not by our hands but by God, through whose favor so many services have been rendered Your Majesty here, which I will not mention because I do not wish to lengthen my account, and because, in part, I have been their minister."[127] From the top of the pyramid God has granted favors to the king, who sits directly under Him, through the good offices of Cortés, who represents himself to be the minister of God and the vassal of the king. Cortés used this pyramid of relationships fictitiously over and over again to make himself appear subordinate to the laws of the king and the will of God. Objective reality, however, was quite different, for he was in fact a disobedient rebel in the process of acquiring enormous personal power. The interests and objectives that had motivated him to embark on the conquest—including the desire for power, glory, and wealth—are presented in his *Letters* as nothing other than the wish to serve the king, even to the point of sacrificing his own life should this be necessary. Thus in his second letter Cortés offers as the only reason for his decision to go inland and conquer the Aztec empire his desire to bring Moctezuma "to your Majesty either as a prisoner or a subject, or dead," and in the fourth letter he remarks that "the least of these expeditions which have been dispatched has cost me more than five thousand *pesos de oro* of my own, and those led by Pedro de Alvarado and Cristóbal de Olid have cost more than fifty thousand. . . . But as it is all in the service of Your Caesarean Majesty, even were it to cost me my life in addition, I should count it a greater favor."[128] Within the fictional narrative structures of the *Letters*, glory, profit, and power belong to the king. Cortés claims in fictitious humility to be satisfied with being a "minister" or "cause," and in any event never more than a vassal whose sole desire is to serve the royal interest.[129] The development of the conquest is described in similar terms. Its objective is to make the natives vassals. Cortés is merely an intermediary, with no interest of his own, intent on granting to the natives, in due order and in representation of his king, the grace of vassalage.[130]

Cortés's calculated use of repeated references to the hand of Providence to legitimize his will, knowledge, action, and final goals, completes a narrative strategy designed to present his power firmly integrated within the political framework presided over by the monarchy. Inspired by God's will, Cortés's most dramatic choices—from destroying the vessels to embarking on the expedition to the Hibueras—become acts of *obedience*. Cortés has been chosen by God and his action embodies God's will. Rather than making his own choice, the fictional hero of the *Letters* appears to execute not his own plans but those of the divine will. Knowledge is consistently presented as divine inspiration, action as part of a holy war, while the enterprise itself becomes a sacred mission.[131] By systematically presenting God as his ally and the author of his victories, by repeatedly invoking Providence, the Holy Spirit, and the Holy Trinity, Cortés fictitiously dissociates his power from its true source—his personal characteristics and actions—disguising and neutralizing it by attributing its effects to divine will.

Cortés's use of the fiction of vassalage in his discourse was crucial, for in point of fact, the feudal model to which he wished to adapt his self-characterization as a Renaissance hero was becoming increasingly challenged by his very actions and by the specific circumstances of his conquest. Having disobeyed Velázquez, he was already guilty of insubordination. He had destroyed vessels that did not belong to him. He had created a state, concentrating its power in his own hands as governor and relegating the role of the monarch to that of a supervisor. Throughout the process of conquest he had generally conducted himself in an independent manner more fitting for a king than his servant. He was fully aware that the king had the power to destroy him[132] and that his only chance of retaining the very considerable power he was acquiring through his conquests and achievements was to present these as action at the service of God and the king and to characterize himself as a humble vassal. This is precisely the function of his recourse to vassalage as a social form founded on an ideology that included a belief in the divine origins of the monarchy and a messianic conception of history and human conduct. Hence his self-characterization as a Renaissance hero in terms of a pyramidal order presided over by God, and the presentation of his actions as choices whose inspiration and success are attributable to the divine and whose material results will accrue to the crown.

Rather than offering a brief, faithful account of the facts, the *Letters* are designed to create a series of fictional models suited to Cortés's plans for the acquisition of fame, power, and glory. Unlike Columbus's deliberate fictions, however, Cortés's discourse is founded on a lucid analysis of concrete reality. Columbus's mode of perception was at the core of an inaccurate representation of America that fictionalized the new realities. This fictionalization characterized the New World as a combination of myth and booty following the terms of the archetype created by Columbus from his literary sources. In the *Letters*, on the other hand, the perception of reality is in essence analytical and objective. Rigorous in his perception, Cortés notes down, analyzes, and classifies with great accuracy all the predominant features of the mainland he is exploring and conquering. Nothing in the narrative discourse of his *Letters* suggests that his representation of what he experienced was ever determined by the myths or fantasies of preexisting literary models. Bernal Díaz and Andrés de Tapia fall within Columbus's tradition. Like him, they often organize their conceptualization of the unknown around things marvelous or monstrous. In his first description of Tenochtitlan, for example, Díaz identifies the city with the models in the books of chivalry, transforming it into a marvelous site somewhere between reality and dream:

> And when we saw all those cities and villages built in the water, and other great towns on dry land, and that straight and level causeway leading to Mexico, we were astounded. These great towns and *cues* and buildings rising from the water all made of stone, seemed like an enchanted vision from the tale of Amadís. Indeed, some of our soldiers asked whether it was not all a dream. It is not surprising, then, that I should write in this vein. It was all so wonderful that I do not know how to describe this first glimpse of things never heard of, seen, or dreamed of before.[133]

And his descriptions of sacrifices, cannibalism, and sodomy, together with Tapia's account of the interior of the Great Temple at Tenochtitlan, tie with insistent truculence the bloodstained outward signs of a cruel religion to a literary tradition for which any unfamiliar or unexplored territory was simply monstrous.

Compared with these descriptions, Cortés's perception of Mexico and the Aztec empire is unusually clear and analytical. His description of Tenochtitlan, for example, is a model of rational classification. Everything is presented in sequence, in terms of its social and economic function and the degree of culture and civilization it reveals. The things he describes are marvelous not because of their association with established ideological or literary models, but in their own right and because of their impact when taken all together. Europe as a point of economic or geographic reference, used so insistently by Columbus, is drawn on occasionally in the first four letters in relation to Mexico and the Aztec empire, to make it easier to communicate the multiple dimensions of an entirely new reality. But by the fifth letter Cortés states explicitly that this new reality simply cannot be described and any attempt to do so "from over here" would never be understood "over there": "and they are things that Your Highness should know about; if only to persist in my custom of faithfully informing Your Majesty of all my deeds, I shall therefore relate these events briefly, as best I am able, for were I to attempt to describe them exactly as they happened *I am certain that I would prove unequal to the task and that my narrative would not be understood.*" He remarks again on the difficulty of communication toward the end of his letter, claiming that the only way to understand a reality so new and qualitatively different is by experiencing it directly, and illustrating his point with comments on the natural environment encountered during the expedition to the Hibueras: "we began to climb a pass which is the most remarkable sight in the world to see, and the most perilous to cross, for *even though I attempt to describe* for Your Majesty the cragginess and extreme harshness of these mountains, *not even one who is more skilled at writing than I could adequately express it, nor could one who heard of it understand it fully*, unless he had himself experienced the crossing of it."[134] Both quotes imply a rejection of Columbus's approach and of his representational strategies. In the *Letters*, the direct experience and careful observation of the new realities become the only valid forms of understanding and knowledge. Imaginary models and European referents give way to a growing awareness of the inadequacy of Old World languages to convey New World realities.

In the *Letters*, the fictionalization of events and characters is governed entirely by Cortés's need to legitimize his venture and consolidate his power. Its structure is calculated and impeccably rational. The narrative takes a form usually associated with an official document, suggesting a direct equivalence between the content narrated and the truth. At the same time, the philosophy implicit between the lines appeals to a Renaissance ideology that would hold from Machiavelli to St. Ignatius of Loyola that the end justifies the means and that the legitimacy of an action is determined by its success. Within this framework, the fiction Cortés creates—selecting, reorganizing, and reelaborating the material examined above—masterfully replaces the *true account* promised by his statements and implicit in the form of the *relación*, by three fictional models: conquest, hero, and state.

A model hero, such as the one Cortés creates in his *Letters*, can have no weakness. Doubt, suffering, and emotion, or any other element that could make the fictional character vulnerable, must be eliminated. That explains the conspicuous absence of Cortés's *body* from the *Letters*. We will not find it in the first three letters where, at most, we see a quick reference to his arm—wounded during the *noche triste*—or to his forehead—stoned during the retreat. We must turn instead to Andrés de Tapia's account, which speaks of the frequent laxatives to which Cortés resorted, one of which may easily have caused the failure of the attack on Tlaxcala; or read Bernal Díaz, who mentions the chamomile tea Cortés had brought from Cuba to relieve his frequent physical afflictions. The model conqueror created in the first four letters never doubts, fears, hesitates, or suffers. It is only in the fifth that he becomes progressively humanized and problematical. But that is only because the change in circumstances has removed the need for him to present himself as an invulnerable superman.

Columbus's fictionalization of America had been based on two very simple processes: one, a transformation of the new reality by identifying its attributes with those of a preconceived imaginary model; the other, a reduction of these attributes to whatever could be turned into merchandise for the markets of late fifteenth-century Europe.[135] Cortés's narrative discourse, on the other hand, involves simultaneously medieval ideological models and Renaissance philosophical principles in its creation of a fictional representation of the conquest, the conqueror, and the state; a representation that was to provide a model for the subsequent development of the conquest of the New World. His fictional representation does not focus on the transformation of America according to literary models but, rather, on a mythical presentation of the hero, an idealized account of his conquest, and a Utopian characterization of his state. Columbus's fiction-alization of America was founded on an irrational act of will. Cortés's transformation of reality involves a highly sophisticated manipulation of logical structures, presenting conclusions as premises twisting and con-founding apparent syllogisms and turning language and logic into the perfect weapon for the acquisition of power, fame, and glory. Cortés's fiction is shaped by reason, and the final result of his narrative is the creation of a series of models that reveal, through all the many aspects that make them a fiction, their creator's impeccable rationality and his profound understanding of the historical reality he proposed to pacify, seduce, and control.

Part Two

Demythification and Questioning

Chapter Three

From Failure to Demythification

A Collective Penchant for Myth

Cortés's rigorous rationalism and his keen understanding of his contemporary historical context were by no means the rule. In fact he was quite an exception in the process of discovery and conquest of America. Most of the expeditions that crossed the continent expanding the boundaries of the explored territories during the sixteenth century had wholly fantastic projects and sought fabulous objectives. The expansion of the Spanish empire and the exploration of the American continent took place under the seductive sign of myth.

The Spanish conquest has been traditionally associated with three main incentives: "Gold, Glory, and Gospel."[1] These reflected a military philosophy inherited from the long period of the *Reconquista*, together with a desire for worldly glory and renown so characteristic of the Renaissance. But there was an at least equally important fourth factor: the fascination exercised by the marvelous, a fascination that took the form of endless versions and reelaborations of a small repertory of myths.

Irving A. Leonard has studied certain fundamental aspects of the sixteenth-century Spaniard's credulity regarding a wide variety of fantastic tales, and he maintains that the novels of chivalry (or "lying histories" as they were called by the moralists) had an unquestionable influence on the conquest and its protagonists.

> Like the motion pictures of a later day, these romantic novels exerted a
> profound influence on contemporary conduct, morality and thought patterns,
> and they furthered the acceptance of artificial standards of value and false
> attitudes toward reality. . . . They brought a touch of color to the drab lives
> of their readers. The latter, despite the denunciations of moralists against
> these "lying histories," continued to find in them authentic portrayals of life
> from which they derived not only patterns of behavior as well as ideas of a
> larger reality but incitement to greater endeavors.[2]

But the enormous popularity of these novels in both Spain and America,
where they were probably read by a large number of conquistadors, would
appear to be a symptom rather than a cause of the Spanish inclination for
myth. The novels of chivalry did indeed shape the imagination of the
Spaniards, often leading them to identify the unknown with the fantastic
tales presented more or less convincingly in their pages. And Bernal Díaz
was certainly not the only informant who drew on this material to describe
what was most unusual about America.[3] The national passion for the
novels, however, may have been no more than one of many indications of
an enormously complex process involving the gradual loss of touch with
a reality that appeared more problematic and less marvelous with each
passing day. This is the process that reached its climax in the seventeenth
century—with the tragic contrast between worn out, old myths and
relentless reality that Cervantes dramatizes in *Don Quixote*—in a Spain
that, Pierre Vilar has said, preferred to dream than face the growing
burden of its problems.[4]

The complex origins of this growing disconnection from reality, this
"irrealismo español" in the words of Vilar, go beyond the scope of this
work.[5] Opinions vary from one extreme represented by Vilar, who believes
that any serious understanding of the question requires a thorough analysis
of the social foundations of the period, to another represented by Leonard,
whose explanations can just as often be as suggestive as they are unsatis-
factory. Says Leonard: "The relative isolation of Spanish life from that of
the rest of Europe, the ever-present proximity of the unknown in the dark
waters of the Atlantic, and the mingling of European and Arabic cultures,
all tended to foster a sense of mystery or fantasy. . . . The Spanish listeners,
perhaps reacting to the stark realism of their immediate surroundings,
escaped into flights of fantasy and, as their imaginations became incan-
descent, they flamed into a passion for adventure, for discovery."[6]

Whatever its origins might be, the inclination of sixteenth-century Spaniards to believe in chimeras, myths, and fabulous tales is shown by the
historical record to have been very strong. In the New World, the unusual
strength of this inclination was evidenced not only by the constant for-

mulation of fabulous goals and mythical objectives but also by their persistent popularity in the face of negative experiences and failures that might have been expected to put a check on the explorers' indulgence in imaginary elaborations.

The mythical objectives of the expeditions were not individual creations; they were all more or less related to vague legends and stories belonging to Western, Asian, or even Native American traditions that the Spaniards gathered from their often mistaken understanding of the information they received from the natives. In some cases the Spaniards identified the scant contradictory reports they received from the natives with their own fables and mythical goals, although the grounds for such identifications were often unclear. In others, a Native American myth was found to be similar to a European legend. In still other instances, the belief in a mythical objective was the result of false information that contained outright lies and inventions, such as the fabrications by Fray Marcos de Nizza and some of the Indian guides and captives.

Among the many fantastic expectations of the conquistadors, two myths in particular had a very marked impact on the exploration of the northern part of the continent: the Fountain of Youth and the Seven Enchanted Cities. Marvelous elixirs that restored one's youth were part of the traditional lore in both Europe and Asia. The Chinese spent many long years in search of such an elixir, and there are references in the West, from the Classical period through the Middle Ages, to many potions and rituals that could magically restore one's youth.[7] Sir John Mandeville's reports on his alleged journeys include a full description of a fountain of youth located near the city of Polumbum, which he called the *Fons Iuventutis*.[8] In America, meanwhile, the Indians from the Orinoco to Florida possessed a similar tradition of youth-restoring rivers located at several different sites. The marvelous properties of these rivers came from the fabulous trees that bathed their roots in their waters.[9]

The myth that inspired men like Ponce de León was a combination of the European and American versions. The first author to have put the two together was Pietro Martire d'Anghiera in his *Decades of the New World or West India*, and the combined version appears again in the chronicles of Gonzalo Fernández de Oviedo, Francisco Lopez de Gómara, and Antonio de Herrera. The attitude of the Spaniards regarding the existence of the magic fountain varied. Its discovery was the central goal of Hernando de Soto's first expedition to Florida. In 1515 Juan Ponce de León, who believed in its existence, organized an expedition to Bimini, where he thought he would find it, having based its location on accounts by natives in the Antilles. Unsuccessful in Bimini he continued on his journey and reached the tip of Florida, where he returned with a larger expedition in 1539 hoping to find the fountain there. Gonzalo Fernández de Oviedo, on the other hand, is consistently skeptical in his references to the prodigious fountain, attributing the information on it to the natives. Harshly critical of Ponce de León, he says: "he went in search of that fabulous fountain of Bimini, which the Indians said made old men young. And I have seen this . . . weakening the brain instead of improving the strength, turning men into youths in their actions and understanding. And among these was Juan Ponce as long as he persisted in his vain belief in the nonsense he heard from the Indians, on which he spent so much to equip men and vessels."[10] And he refers again, further on, to "that fountain of Bimini that the Indians had said would give new youth, freshness, and vigor to anyone who drank its waters or bathed in it, and it was all in vain as might be expected of anything so fabulous and untruthful, and he realized that he had been tricked and misinformed."[11] Most of the people in the area were, however, far from being as convinced as Oviedo was that the current rumors about fabulous objectives were untrue. Lucas Vázquez de Ayllón's expedition to the Carolinas—organized eight years after Ponce de León's first expedition to Bimini—is a case in point. According to Pietro Martire d'Anghiera, reports of a wonderful fountain that could restore the youth of anyone who drank its waters provided one of the main incentives of this expedition. A native servant by the name of Andrés had stated, in the presence of Lucas Vázquez de Ayllón and the president of the High Court of Hispaniola, that his elderly father's health had been restored immediately after drinking some of the water.[12] Neither Ponce de León nor Vázquez de Ayllón ever discovered the marvelous fountain; nor did the Caribbean natives discover any of their magical rivers, even though they had been searching the Florida coastline since well before the arrival of the Spaniards, to the point where according to Herrera "there was not a river or stream in Florida, from Lagunas to Pantanos, where they had not bathed."[13] But this did not soon dispel the myth, and many years would pass before rumors about magical waters that restored youth eventually disappeared.

The myth of the fountain of youth encouraged expeditions to the Florida peninsula and the eastern portion of the North American continent. Other explorations to the north, from the Mexican frontier to the great central plain, often set out in search of another goal that was no less chimerical: the seven enchanted cities, later known as the Seven Cities of Cibola. The earliest Western version of this myth has been traced to a medieval

Portuguese legend. Ferdinand Columbus refers to it in the biography of his father, and Herrera includes it in his *Historia general*. According to the legend, when the Moors entered Spain after Roderick lost the kingdom, seven Portuguese bishops fled from the invaders. They sailed with their people to a great island where each founded a city. To keep anyone from thinking of returning to the peninsula, they set fire to their ships. The legend claims that all this occurred around the year 714.[14] The mysterious island in question is identified as Antilla on Martin Behaim's map of 1492, which contains a notation placing the flight of the bishops in 734: "In the year of Our Lord 734, when all Spain was under the dominion of pagans from Africa, the island Antilla named Septe Ritade was settled by an Archbishop from Porto in Portugal, six other bishops, and a number of Christians, men and women, who had fled from Spain taking with them their cattle and their property." In 1508 Johann Ruysch's map of the world placed the mythical Antilla in the middle of the Atlantic halfway between Hispaniola and the Azores, and Antilla appeared later on Schöner's map published in 1523.[15]

Several expeditions were undertaken in the fifteenth century by the Portuguese, with the intention of discovering and exploring the mythical island and its seven cities. According to Ferdinand Columbus, at the time of Henry the Navigator Portuguese vessels actually landed on the island, but crew members were afraid to accept an invitation by the residents to be taken to see their chief, and they hurried back to Portugal.[16] The most famous of such projects was that of Fernan Dulmo, a Flemish explorer to whom the Portuguese crown granted a license in 1485 to explore "a large island or islands, or the mainland beyond our coastline, believed to be the island of the Seven Cities."[17] Nothing further is known about Dulmo, or about whether or not he in fact ever departed in search of his mythical objective.

In the New World, the medieval legend of the seven bishops appears to have combined with another myth existing among the Indians of Mexico: the religious myth of Chicomoztot, which described the origin of the seven tribes of the Nahuas. Enrique de Gandía remarks on the likely fusion of these two versions as follows: "The account of these seven mysterious caves may have been confused with the seven cities, or evoked the legend of the seven medieval cities."[18] In any event, the Nahua myth of the seven caves may explain the numerous native versions that appear to refer to seven important sites or villages north of the Mexican frontier, in the place of origin of the tribes that moved toward the central valley of Mexico long before the arrival of the Spaniards. And the fact that many of the Spaniards were familiar with the ancient Portuguese legend may explain why the Indian myth was so rapidly assimilated.

Because so very little was known about the nature of the American continent throughout the first half of the sixteenth century, it was natural for adventurers and dreamers to imagine in its unexplored territories all the myths they knew from both Western and Native American sources. And their fantasies were nourished further by another no less important source: the fantastic tales passed along by both natives and Spaniards throughout the period of exploration and conquest. One of the most remarkable of these was Fray Marcos de Nizza's largely fictional account of an actual expedition in search of the Seven Cities. In 1536 shortly after Alvar Núñez Cabeza de Vaca, Dorantes, and Esteban returned to Mexico following their long journey by foot from Florida to the capital of New Spain, Viceroy Antonio de Mendoza conceived the idea of organizing an expedition to the interior of North America, in search of certain marvelous cities he had recently heard about. The person responsible for these reports was not Alvar Núñez, whose *Naufragios* never mention anything suggesting the seven enchanted cities or any other mythical goal. It was, rather, a native from the American southwest (a *Tejo*) held captive and owned by Governor Núñez de Guzmán.[19] He claimed to be the son of a trader who had often visited several fabulous cities on the other side of the desert. He also claimed that his father had exchanged feathers for large amounts of gold and silver, which were very plentiful there. Crossing the desert to the north of Mexico, one would come after forty days to the seven mythical cities, which the captive insisted were all larger and richer than the city of Mexico itself.

During the winter of 1537 Antonio de Mendoza tried repeatedly to persuade Alvar Núñez to lead an expedition to the region in question, but Núñez declined and returned to Spain, where he intended to request his appointment as Adelantado of Florida. This did not deter Mendoza, however, and in March 1539 a small expedition left Mexico under Fray Marcos de Nizza; Esteban, the black *alamanzor** who in 1526 had survived the Narváez disaster with Núñez and Dorantes, went along as a special guide.

Except for Fray Marcos de Nizza's fantastic account, everything would appear to indicate that the expedition was a complete failure and never achieved its goal of finding the seven wonderful cities. Esteban lost his life at the hands of the natives, and it seems likely that upon learning of his death, Fray Marcos decided to turn back with no more than a quick glance

---

*Esteban is referred to in English texts as a "Moor" or a "Black Moor."—TRANS.

at the first Zuni settlements he saw from the distance. Admitting his agitation at the news of Esteban's death, he writes that "learning the terrible news I feared I would be lost, and my fear was not so much for my own life as it was that I would never be able to report on the great land discovered."[20] In the same report, however, he says that in spite of the circumstances, he decided to go ahead with the exploration: "I told them that whatever happened, I would see the City of Cibola . . . and I continued on my way until I saw it, on a plain nestled against the curve of a hill."[21]

There is no way of knowing how far Fray Marcos de Nizza got during his explorations, but what subsequent expeditions proved beyond question was that his report concerning the nature of the vast lands he claimed to have covered was one of the more fictitious accounts written during the discovery. Viceroy Mendoza had given him very clear instructions to explore and gather information: "You will very carefully observe the people, whether there are many or few, whether they live together or scattered about; the quality and fertility of the land, the temperature, trees, plants, and domestic and wild animals, whether the terrain is rough or smooth, whether the rivers are large or small and what stones and metals they contain; and you will bring back or send any samples you can obtain, for the information of His Majesty."[22] But either Fray Marcos gave a highly personal interpretation to the word "information," allowing him to present the most fantastic conjecture as actual fact; or he was even more predisposed to fantasy and credulity than his myth-loving contemporaries; or perhaps he fictionalized what he saw because he really hoped that Viceroy Mendoza's expectations would eventually be fulfilled and believed that the marvelous things promised by Nuño de Guzmán's *Tejo* would soon appear in the vicinity. The fact is that his account provided the first complete American formulation of the myth of the Seven Cities derived from the Portuguese legend, updated and improved with information from native guides and settlers whom Fray Marcos claimed to have questioned repeatedly.

There are four versions of the myth in Fray Marcos's account. The first he attributes to Native Americans living near Petatlan, just north of the Mexican border, who in answer to his question whether there were "many settlements there . . . and people who were more rational and sophisticated" answered that at a distance of four or five days' journey inland, there were "many large settlements where people wore cotton. And when I showed them certain pieces of metal . . . they took from among them a piece of gold and told me that the people in the valley had pots made of the same substance, as well as certain round things they wore in their ears and

noses, and some small spatulas they used to wipe off their perspiration."[23]
The second account he claims to have heard from a native who had been
walking up ahead with Esteban and returned to give him a report.

> He maintains that there are seven very large cities in this first province, all of
> them under a single chief, with large flat-roofed houses made of stone and
> limestone. The houses stand one, two, and three stories high, except for the
> chief's which has four stories. The façade of the more important houses is
> finely worked with turquoise, which he says is very abundant. The people
> are very well dressed. He described many other features of these seven cities,
> and some even more remarkable provinces further ahead. I asked him several
> questions about how he knew all this, and he answered me at length very
> reasonably.[24]

The third version is claimed to come from the Native Americans who
lived on the land near the mythical location. It involves a more detailed
repetition of the first two accounts, with the addition of the names Marata,
Acus Totonteac, and Cibola, and an elaboration on the level of civilization
of the people, who "wear strings of turquoises . . . and some wear very
good blankets and others carefully worked cowhides . . . and the women
are dressed in like fashion, covered down to their feet." Detailing the
fabulous wealth in these cities, Fray Marcos says that "everyone wears
fine, good turquoises hanging from their ears and noses, and these same
stones are used to decorate the main doorways of Cibola."[25]

The fourth version is attributed by Fray Marcos to a "rather old" but
"very reasonable" native and resident of Cibola itself. His authority
confirms the accuracy of the previous accounts:

> Cibola is a great city, with a large number of people, streets, and parks. . . .
> In some sections there are very large houses ten stories high, where the most
> prominent people in the city meet on certain days of the year; just as the
> other versions claim, the houses are made of stone and limestone, and the
> façades of the main houses are laid over with turquoises. He told me that the
> other seven cities are like this one and that the greatest is Ahacus. He also
> told me that toward the southeast lies the kingdom called Totonteac, which
> he says is the greatest in the world, with the largest amount of people and
> treasure; that the people there wear cloth like the piece I have brought and
> other kinds even more delicate, taken from animals that were shown to me;
> and that the people are very courteous.[26]

Thus far Fray Marcos may be excused, on the grounds that he was
merely transcribing information provided by the natives. The fabulous
character of their tales later proved to have little connection with reality.
However, there are several points of Marcos's account that show that he
himself actively created fabulous tales rather than simply passing along

the inventions of others. For example, he insisted on certifying and giving credit to the information provided by the natives. Far from keeping any critical distance, he hastens to stress that he and Esteban have taken the accounts to be true, for good reason: "and Esteban sent word to me that ever since he left he had never once caught the Indians lying, and that so far everything had turned out as they said it would and he expected this to continue. And I believe this to be true, for as of the day when I first heard of Cibola, whatever the Indians told me about I have since seen."[27] Second, he gives a false description of Cibola, the first of the seven cities and, according to the natives, the smallest. "It is very beautiful, the most beautiful I have seen in these parts; judging from where I looked upon them from the hilltop, the houses are just as the Indians described them, made of stone, flat-roofed and several stories high. The population is larger than that of the city of Mexico."[28] His transformation of a small Zuni village of adobe houses into a city larger than the city of Mexico is a clear illustration of Fray Marcos's story-telling abilities. And this time the responsibility cannot be attributed to the natives, for he explicitly declares having seen these things with his own eyes, from a hilltop. Moreover, this is not the only example of the way he described places he perhaps did in fact find, but which he idealized in his fancy to the point that later explorers seriously doubted whether he had been there at all. On one occasion, for example, he said that he had "always been well supplied with deer, hares, and partridges of the same color and taste as those in Spain although somewhat smaller in size,"[29] referring to the arid Southwest where subsequent explorers were constantly plagued by hunger.

However, perhaps his most spectacular creation was his transformation of the American buffalo into a fantastic combination of a rhinoceros, cow, and billy goat. The buffalo was "an animal with a single horn in his forehead curved toward his chest, from which grows a straight spike that makes him so strong that he breaks everything he runs into. His skin is the color of a billy goat's, and his hair is as long as my finger."[30]

Fray Marcos's account of fabulous regions said to hold incredible treasures somewhere in the hinterland of North America was the first written version of the myth in the New World, but not the last. Chroniclers from Lucas Vázquez de Ayllón to Vázquez de Coronado referred over and over again to a region of fabulous riches that lay somewhere in the unexplored interior of North America. Behind the differing versions of its true nature and location, we often find the same source: a native captive, fueling the dreams that could only lead to expeditions doomed to failure. The captive's tale usually confirmed the existence of mythical kingdoms about which there were rumors all over the colony. The first of these "weavers of fables" to be recorded was the Yucayo called Andrés Barbudo ("because he alone among his beardless fellow countrymen had a beard," says Pietro Martire d'Anghiera), who convinced Ayllón, the dean of Hispaniola, and Figueroa, the president of the Senate, that the fountain of youth was somewhere in Florida. Andrés called upon "many people brought from his nation, Yucaya" as witnesses to the magical rejuvenation of his own father, "who maintain that they saw the man in a virtually decrepit state and later made young again, and full of strength and energy."[31]

Lucas Vázquez de Ayllón, on the other hand, had a native servant named Francisco who elaborated on Barbudo's tale. Gonzalo Fernández de Oviedo refers to his encounter with Francisco at Ayllón's house in 1523: "I was wearing a large round pearl, a perfect specimen weighing 26 carats, which I wanted him to see because he said that the Indian had told him that those in his country were large and excellent. Ayllón told me that it was very small compared to the ones promised him by his servant, and I was all the more sure that the latter was deceiving us; that his desire to return to his homeland had led him to tell the Licenciado about things he knew he liked, and to put together very cleverly information that should not have been believed."[32] Ayllón's expedition to the Carolinas in July 1523 indicated that he did not share the skepticism later displayed by Oviedo in his *Historia*, once the failure of the expedition and Francisco's flight into the woods of his native Chicora immediately upon landing had already proved Oviedo to be right.

A few years later, Nuño de Guzmán's *Tejo* captive added other inventions to the myths of Andrés el Barbudo and Francisco de Chicora. Pedro de Castañeda introduces his *Relación de la jornada de Cibola* with a brief summary of his stories.

> This Indian said that he was the son of a trader, now dead, and that when he was little his father had traded in feathers in the hinterland, returning with large amounts of the gold and silver that abounded there, and claiming to have seen very large towns comparable to Mexico and its surroundings. . . . [He said] that he had seen seven very large towns, with streets paved in silver. It took forty days to get there, walking northward along a path between two seas over uninhabited territory, where the only grass growing was no more than one *xeme** high.[33]

Encouraged by such promising news, Nuño de Guzmán hastened to organize an expedition to the mythical seven cities, which reached no

---

*Measure based on the span between the tip of the thumb and the index finger.—TRANS.

further than the region around Culiacan. But when Fray Marcos de Nizza's fantastic *Relación* confirmed this first report of the myth in America, Viceroy Mendoza decided to look for the cities himself. While he was finishing his preparations for the Coronado expedition, he sent out a small group under Captain Melchor Díaz to verify some of Fray Marcos's sensational information. The result was predictable: Melchor Díaz returned with the news that the weather had kept him from going very far, but that nothing of what he had seen confirmed Fray Marcos's optimistic reports. The Native Americans themselves, mentioned by the friar as having provided a detailed account of the seven cities of Cibola, assured Melchor Díaz that all that was there were four small villages of adobe houses and three others that were somewhat larger but similar in type. They said that the residents did indeed own turquoises, but far fewer than Fray Marcos had indicated, and they denied knowledge of any metal in the region, mentioning specifically that they knew of no evidence of gold or silver. The fact that this information, provided confidentially to Don Antonio Mendoza, was not sufficient to discourage him from launching Vázquez de Coronado's expedition simply proves again that anything that might be absorbed or interpreted as a confirmation of previous myths had a strong hold on the imagination of the conquistadors—even on a man usually as calm and prudent as the viceroy. Presented in the form of legends, children's stories, ballads, chronicles, or novels of chivalry, these myths constituted an aspect of the imaginary shared by them all as members of a common Western culture.

As Coronado's expedition advanced, the truth of Melchor Díaz's report and the fantastic character of Fray Marcos's *Relación* became increasingly clear, and the men would probably have soon turned back had the discredited myth of the seven cities of Cibola not been revived by the inspired fables of another native captive, called by the Spaniards "the Turk."[34] The Turk was a gift from the native chief Bigotes to Alvarado, who was leading the vanguard of Coronado's expedition to Cibola. No sooner had the Turk found himself among the Spaniards—whose morale was at one of the lowest points of the entire expedition—than he began to recount some fantastic tales about the land he had come from and to where he offered to guide them:

> he said that in his country there was a river two leagues wide running over low land, with fish as large as horses, and a great many very large canoes carrying more than twenty oarsmen on either side. The canoes had sails, and their masters sat in the stern under a canopy, and there was a great golden eagle on the bow. He said that the lord of all that land took his afternoon nap under a great tree hung with golden bells that wafted in the breeze. The

tableware was made of silver and the dishes, pitchers, and bowls were all made of gold. He called gold *acochis*, and they believed him because they showed him tin ornaments and he smelled them and said they were not gold, and that he was very familiar with both gold and silver.[35]

Although he was questioned cleverly and repeatedly, the Turk kept to his story and won the confidence of not only Alvarado but Coronado and most of the members of the expedition, some of whom went so far as to attribute supernatural powers to him and claim that he was trafficking with the devil.[36] The expedition did not return to Mexico, wandering instead for two miserable years through the vast central plains of North America in search of the Turk's mythical Quivira. But far from finding a marvelous city, all they saw were "cows and the sky."[37]

The last of the Native American captives and guides whose fables provided much of the incentive for exploring the northern continent was the youth Pedro, who in 1540 led the expedition of Hernando de Soto to disaster. Pedro was captured with several other natives by Juan Gaytán during the battle of Napetuce in Appalachia, and he claimed that he was from a large city far to the east, called Yupaha. Governed by a woman, Yupaha was large and populous, and had abundant gold. When questioned by the Spaniards, Pedro described how the gold was extracted from the mines, melted down, and refined, "based on what he had seen or been shown by the devil. Thus all those who knew anything about such things said that it was impossible to explain them in so much detail without having seem them, and from then on everyone believed what the Indian told them."[38] This is when Hernando de Soto's troubles began, and it could well be said of Pedro (who asked to be called by that name after he was baptized) that "he was the cause of all the bad things that came to pass"[39]— just as Castañeda had said of the Turk.

Pedro does not appear to have had as fertile an imagination as either the Turk or Andrés el Barbudo, but he did have the habit of claiming that "he had seen what he in fact knew only from hearsay and of exaggerating the things he did know of directly."[40] Following his indications, De Soto and his men wandered around lost for several weeks without food or water, before coming upon the dominions of the great matriarch Cutifachiqui. If we are to believe the Gentleman of Elvas, they discovered some five hundred pounds of pearls in the coffers there. They decided not to stay, however, and left in search of fabulous treasures that according to Pedro were located in the region of Coca, but which never materialized.

Indian legends, ancient myths from Asia, Greece, and Rome, stories from the Middle Ages, descriptions bearing little relation to the lands their authors claimed to be describing, reports by both the Spaniards and the Native Americans that were more fantastic than any of the false tales that provoked the fury of the moralists or the censure of the Inquisition: all of this material contributed to shaping the view discoverers and conquistadors had of the world and of the meaning of their conquest. But with the conquest of Peru, there were two concrete, verifiable wonders to add to the existing, ever broadening repertory of fable and myth: the Aztec and Inca empires. The accounts of these conquests, which their chroniclers presented with a combination of real evidence of booty obtained and a fictionalization that attributed to them almost magical qualities, further increased the stock of models that promised success to the many ambitious dreamers set on becoming powerful.

The accounts attributed to the natives by the Spaniards contain frequent allusions to splendid mythical places. The referent for these was, alternatively, New Spain, Peru, or the treasures of Cuzco or Tenochtitlan. The latter two provided the main inspiration for describing the fabulous invented cities promised by both Native Americans and Spaniards. When Fray Marcos speaks of the inhabitants of the land in the region of Cibola he says: "People speak of Cibola here as much as they do in New Spain of Mexico or in Peru of Cuzco."[41] Upon making out the village of Cibola on the horizon—which he probably never saw before going there with Coronado's expedition—he calls it "larger than the city of Mexico." The model is no longer Seville, Cordoba, or Granada to which Columbus so frequently compared the lands and settlements of the New World, but Mexico. Elvas for his part stresses the importance of Peru as a model for the members of De Soto's expedition. Discussing De Soto's unexpected decision to be guided by Pedro's false promises and to continue searching for Coca instead of remaining with the *cacica** Cutifachiqui, in whose dominions he had found food, water, hospitality, and five hundred pounds of pearls, Elvas explains:

> Everyone else thought that the spot would make a good place to settle, for all the vessels from New Spain, Peru, Santa María, and the mainland would stop there en route to Spain, and the land was good and promised to be fruitful. But the governor was set on finding treasure similar to that of lord Atahualpa of Peru, and he would not be satisfied with either the good land or the pearls, even though some of the latter were worth their weight in gold.[42]

Hernando de Soto paid for his mistake and his obstinacy with his life. His experience, like that of so many others, proved that it was Mexico

*Woman chieftain.—TRANS.

and Peru that were the exceptions, not the terrible swamps, deserts, jungles, and ambushes where so many expeditions, intent on matching the legends of two cultures and many centuries with American reality, would find nothing but failure.

The Narrative Discourse of Failure

The initial narrative discourse on the conquest of America was shaped by success. This success was problematical for Columbus, but he managed to avoid disappointment by refraining from drawing realistic comparisons between his findings and his expectations. His representation of America was almost as far from the truth as Fray Marcos de Nizza's report on the seven wondrous cities was; and much as with the latter, the fiction he created protected him from having to view his enterprise as a failure.

The representation of the conquest and the model of the conquistador created by Hernán Cortés, by contrast, was based on a careful selection, reorganization, and reelaboration of historical material designed to provide a fictional context within which everything their author did led to legitimate and undisputable success. Thus even his mistakes and disobedience were transformed and presented as necessary to the masterfully conceived plan for the successful conquest of the Aztec empire.

Along with this mythification of reality, action, and personalities, however, there evolved another quite different discourse. This discourse would be grounded in failure and it would proclaim the value of misfortune and the merit of suffering. It is to this discourse of failure that we must look to find the first critical appraisals of American reality.

It would be inaccurate to suggest that the mythifying discourse of Columbus and Cortés and the discourse of failure developed in a chronological sequence. The second does not follow the first but, rather, evolves gradually even within the narrative of the first group of authors. Disappointment is expressed repeatedly in Columbus's *Letter from Jamaica*, where we already find some of the central elements that will shape the discourse of failure. The first element is his view of nature as the sum of violent, uncontrollable, hostile, destructive forces. The coastline appears exceedingly rugged and uninviting; the water is full of worms that bore holes in the bottom of the ships; the waves break the lines and carry off the anchors; the sea is a never ending scene of devastating, apocalyptic storms:

> never was the sea so high, so terrific, and so covered with foam; not only did
> the wind oppose our proceeding onward, but also rendered it highly danger-
> ous to run in for any headland, and kept me in that sea that seemed to me a

sea of blood, seething like a cauldron on a mighty fire. Never did the sky look more fearful; during one day and night it burned like a furnace, and every instant I looked to see if my masts and sails were not destroyed; for the lightning flashed with such alarming fury that we all thought the ships must have been consumed. All this time the waters from heaven never ceased descending, not to say that it rained, for it was like a repetition of the deluge.[43]

For the first time, nature is represented as powerful, stubborn, impossible to disguise in myth. Altogether different from anything encountered before, its violence nullifies Columbus's European models and provides the source of a constant theme of the discourse of failure—one that persists in present-day Spanish American literature: the impotence of people and their defeat at the hands of nature.

Suffering is the second major theme that ties Columbus's *Letter from Jamaica* to the discourse of failure. Here suffering is both physical and mental. Anguished, alone, exhausted, ill, hopeless of being able to avoid disaster, he complains, weeps, and despairs over circumstances resulting only from "the honest devotedness I have always shown to your Majesties' service." This sets the stage for a third central element of the discourse of failure: the insistence on the value of suffering, the presentation of failure as a different kind of service as deserving of recognition and reward as success. "I was twenty-eight years old when I came into your Highnesses' service," says Columbus, "and now I have not a hair upon me that is not grey; my body is infirm."[44] Neither suffering itself nor the hostility of nature, however, are the central themes of the *Letter from Jamaica*. For regardless of the desolation conveyed, the success of the discovery is never at issue; what gives the letter its tragic character is not doubt or failure, but the narrator's sense of having been ungratefully abandoned by the crown, his achievements unjustly ignored.

Cortés's fifth letter can be seen chronologically as the first text of the narrative mode that I have called the discourse of failure. This letter differs qualitatively from the author's preceding ones and offers quite a bit more than the few initial indications of such a discourse that we find in the *Letter from Jamaica*. A complex text, the fifth letter marks the transition from myth to failure. While still retaining certain aspects of the former mythifying discourse, it begins to articulate the central narrative patterns of the discourse of failure. Cortés is still a central figure, a perfect model equal to his epic assignments while at the same time able to adjust masterfully to his new circumstances. The unfailing military conquistador becomes a discoverer and a peacemaker. He observes the terrain; looks for natural communication routes; examines the natives' crops, agricultural methods, and forms of organization; evaluates the potential for development everywhere he goes. The conqueror of the Aztec empire is now an engineer, operating in an environment where the enemy is more likely to be the marsh and the jungle than any scattered groups of natives. Giving directions for the construction of an extraordinary bridge, he says after its completion that "it is made of more than a thousand timbers, of which the smallest is almost as thick as a man's body, from nine to ten fathoms in length, not to mention an immense quantity of light timber."[45] Indefatigable as ever, he organizes exploratory and survey missions and searches for access routes, food, and water with the same flawless efficiency that he devoted earlier to his strategy for the siege and reconquest of Tenochtitlan. It is true that his physical and biological needs, never mentioned in his earlier dispatches, are now the source of considerable suffering. But his clairvoyance, his almost magical control over the situation, the divine agency that seems to have singled him out for protection and prepared him alone to conquer Mexico and organize a new state, continue to cast him as a hero without equal amidst the jungles and marshes of Central America.

Cortés is as capable as ever of handling any situation, even one as chaotic as the one described in the fifth letter. But the organization of this letter points to the beginnings of the discourse of failure. The narrative no longer reflects the author's need to present himself as a flawless hero and although he does not go so far as to speak concretely of "failure," he questions his own journey and its validity in decidedly critical terms: "I cannot describe to Your Majesty the great joy which I and all my company felt on hearing this news in Tanyha and knowing that we were now so close to the end of our so uncertain a journey."[46] After having presented his actions as the reflection of an impeccable plan and the divine order of things in his first three letters, Cortés now describes an "uncertain journey" whose imprecise objectives change constantly, and whose execution consists more of wandering about at the mercy of the accidents of the terrain than implementing a rigorously conceived plan.

Since in the fifth letter the presentation of reality need not support an ideal characterization of the conquistador or the conquest, it can be more objective. This presentation involves a new sequence of elements that, besides organizing a good portion of the narrative in this last letter, turn out to be central structural factors in the subsequent development of the discourse of failure.

The presence of a mythical goal constitutes the first of these elements. For Ponce de León this was to be the Fountain of Youth; for Vázquez de Coronado, Fray Marcos de Nizza's Seven Cities of Cibola; for Hernando de Soto, another Peru filled with treasures. Cortés's mythical objective is related by analogy to the recently conquered Aztec empire. What appears to have moved him to undertake his expedition to Honduras, putting aside his privileges and obligations as governor of New Spain, was an abstract, nonexistent "new Mexico"; and the design to suppress Olid's rebellion seems to have been little more than a pretext for not revealing his true motives.[47] Cortés himself remarks on the latter explicitly toward the end of the fifth letter:

> and I am certain that your Majesty will benefit greatly from it and that it will be another Culúa. For I have received news of very large and wealthy provinces with powerful lords richly attended . . . and having made inquiries about it throughout my journey, have discovered at last that it is eight or ten days' march from that town of Trujillo; . . . and such wonderful news has been received of it that I marvel at what is said, for even if two thirds of it prove false it must exceed Mexico in riches and equal it in the great size of its towns, the multitude of people and the government thereof.[48]

Contrary to the Mexican experience, the project was doomed to failure because it sought something that simply did not exist. But Cortés did not realize this until other factors forced him to abandon his search.[49] As he saw it, what kept him from another spectacular triumph was not the fabulous character of his pursuit but a formidable new obstacle: nature. In his fifth letter nature gets center stage, playing consistently, for the first time, the prominent role it was to occupy in all subsequent texts of the narrative discourse of failure. Introduced as a specific subject in Columbus's *Letter from Jamaica*, nature as described by Cortés becomes a force unimaginable in a European context, which transforms human action and converts the search for power, glory, and fame into a struggle for survival.

Like Columbus before him, once American reality asserts itself in his discourse, Cortés no longer refers to Europe as the standard. From the very beginning of the fifth letter he announces that he will try to explain the events of the journey as well as he can, "for were I to attempt to describe them exactly as they happened I am certain that I would prove unequal to the task and that my narrative would not be understood." His perception is accompanied by an awareness of the impossibility of conveying so fundamentally different a reality to the king, in the absence of a shared point of reference: "for even though I attempt to describe for Your Majesty the cragginess and extreme harshness of these mountains, not even one who is more skilled at writing than I could adequately express it, nor could one who heard of it understand it fully, unless he himself had seen it with his own eyes and had himself experienced the crossing of it."[50] His letter implies that *difference* is the crux of the problem, and that any other European in his situation would also find it impossible to convey what he had seen and felt.

In the desolate and hostile territory that Cortés explored relentlessly for many months, following roads that had been erased by weeds and water, the few existing settlements were deserted. His progress "along a very narrow track . . . between the highest and steepest mountains" was constantly blocked by "great marshes and the roots of the trees," and whenever he tried to take another path, he would find himself in a more dreadful marsh, such as the "great marsh which lasted for two cross-bowshots, the most frightful thing the men had ever seen." Leaving the marshlands behind to start laboriously up the mountains, he finds himself in different but no less hostile territory. "This forest was so dense that we could only see a pace in front of us or, looking up, the clear sky above us; and so thick and high were the trees that even those who climbed them could not see even a stone throw's distance." A scarcity of water is immediately followed by "a torrent of rain amid the most unbelievable plague of mosquitoes. Indeed, so rough was the road and so dark and stormy the night that two or three times, when I attempted to find the town, I failed even to find the road." At times the violence of nature is conveyed by its effects, as in the description of a mountain pass whose awesome nature Cortés admits to being unable to express:

> Let it suffice for Your Majesty to know that we spent twelve days covering the eight leagues of the pass, that is until the end of our train was over, and that we lost sixty-eight of our horses, which either fell over the cliff or were hamstrung; and the remainder were in such a sorry state that we did not expect any of them to be any use again. Thus sixty-eight horses died from their injuries or exhaustion in that pass, and those who escaped were not fully recovered for more than three months.

In this environment, where even a compass is useless, the Spaniards wander about lost for weeks at a time: "We had almost abandoned hope because we had no guide and our compass was useless, for we were surrounded by the most rugged, dense mountains ever seen and unable to find a way out anywhere."[51]

In the context of this inhuman, destructive environment action is transformed, and nature, at first no more than an obstacle to be overcome in the course of reaching an objective, gradually becomes the central focus of the text, shifting the reader's attention away from everything else. The ceaseless struggle against it, as it assaults the members of the expedition in a thousand ways and increasingly threatens their survival, comes to be the organizing purpose of their daily activities. Cortés the "engineer" designs roads and bridges to save his army from the horrors of the marshlands; his men hew timber, open trails, search for food, dig wells, build rafts. The enemy is no longer the native but the environment. Action, once designed to obtain booty and subjugate the natives, and thus represented in the discourse of mythification, now consists of strenuous efforts to control the forces of nature that assault the expedition from every quarter. Cortés rarely admits to the difficulty of his labors in his earlier letters; in the fifth, however, he refers over and over again to how "great," "numerous," and "major" are the efforts endured by him and his companions.

The glory and fame that could be won by faithful vassals of the king in the conquest of new lands motivated the action in the earlier texts of Cortés and Columbus. But in the discourse of failure, what impels the action is *necessity*. Taking several forms, including hunger, cold, sickness, and thirst, necessity transforms the epic action of the discourse of mythification into the desperate wanderings of the shipwrecked. Hunger, later to become a main theme of the best examples of the narrative of failure, appears for the first time in the fifth letter: "for ten days we had eaten nothing but palm nuts and palmettos, and even of these we had only a few, for we no longer had the strength to cut them," says Cortés. The prospect of obtaining a few loads of corn or cocoa, or a few chickens, is enough to make him postpone more glorious plans and shift the direction of the entire expedition. Hunger is accompanied at times by cold or thirst:

> All the time we were crossing the pass it rained without cease, all day and all night long, but those mountains were such that they did not retain water, and consequently we suffered greatly from thirst, most of our horses dying because of it. And were it not for the water we collected in pots and other vessels while encamped in the huts and shacks we built to shelter us, as it rained enough to provide water for us and the horses, no man or horse would have escaped from those mountains.[52]

Although the problems of shelter and water never surpass in importance the actual experience of hunger as a theme, these sometimes prosaic sometimes desperate efforts replace the glorious epic goals of the earlier model of action.

The realistic presentation of America; the gradual displacement of fabulous mythical objectives; the shift from epic exploits toward common daily tasks; the replacement of riches, glory, and power by necessity as a fundamental incentive for action make the fifth letter the first clear example of the discourse of failure. But Cortés continues to cast himself as a model somehow unaltered by the new situation, and this continuity in his characterization still ties the fifth letter to the narrative discourse of the first four. Moreover, within this last letter, the development of the action and the transformation of its objectives are presented not as failure but as a transitional stage planned and calculated by Cortés in his newly acquired role. His inability to reach successfully his mythical objective[53] is presented not as an error of purpose but as recognition of the need to suspend his search for reasons of extreme political urgency. The result of these ambivalences is a hybrid text, halfway between mythification and failure.

Spain's exploration of North America between 1526 and 1542 included three major expeditions, led by Pánfilo de Narváez in 1526, Hernando de Soto in 1539, and Vázquez de Coronado in 1540. The three expeditions explored different regions, but they had at least two points in common. First, their goals were all fabulous, inspired by myths such as that of the Seven Enchanted Cities or the Fountain of Youth, or real models such as the Inca and Aztec empires. Second, they all ended in devastating failure. Pánfilo de Narváez started out with five vessels, four hundred men, and eighty horses, and only three men survived. Wounded and defeated, Coronado returns with his men after two long years of crossing half the North American continent under conditions that decimated his army and exhausted his will to continue. Summarizing his failed project, Coronado writes to the emperor in 1541 that

> since my arrival in the province of Cibola whither I was sent on your Majesty's behalf by the Viceroy of New Spain, having found none of the things mentioned by Fray Marcos, I have explored an area for more than two hundred leagues around, and the most I have discovered so far is the Figuez river, with the villages nearby where I am at present. This would not be a good place to settle, however. It is four hundred leagues from the Northern Sea and more than two hundred from the Southern Sea, meaning that the distance is too great for any commerce. The land is very cold, as I've already described it to be, and it would appear to be impossible to spend a winter here: there is neither timber nor clothing to keep the men warm, but only the skins used by the natives and a very small number of cotton blankets.[54]

And, finally, Hernando de Soto died of an unknown disease near the mouth of the Mississippi River. His body was buried secretly, since the Spaniards feared that if the natives learned of his death they would kill the remaining members of the expedition. The three hundred survivors were forced to build rafts and sail across the highly dangerous waters of the Gulf of Mexico. They landed at Panuco in a state far more miserable than when, a year earlier, they had left in search of a mythical fountain and a second Peru.

In the writing of history, failure is often followed by silence, and many explorers—from Hojeda and Nicuesa to Lucas Vázquez de Ayllón and their men—kept silent about their expeditions. But the survivors of the expeditions of Narváez, De Soto, and Coronado chose to speak out and refused to let their tragic misfortunes be forgotten. Pedro de Castañeda, for example, declares his intention of giving a precise, eyewitness account of the events of Coronado's expedition, breaking with a tradition that relegated failure to oblivion: "Because they had not won the land nobody wanted to write about it, so that nothing would be known about what God for His own reasons had disposed that they should not have. . . . But I propose to provide a true account, rather than gain merit as a good writer or rhetorician."[55] In the preface to his narrative the author clearly states a second goal for his testimonial account: to settle any discrepancies in the versions of chroniclers and witnesses, and to anticipate any subsequent fictionalizing of the events by the expedition members "who love to describe what they saw and even what they fancy they lost."[56]

Castañeda was not alone in preserving the memory of these events. Other accounts of Coronado's failed expedition that have been preserved include a less interesting version by Juan de Jaramillo; a *Relación del Suceso* by an anonymous author; and a *Relación Postrera de Cibola* written most probably by one of the expedition's friars.[57] As for De Soto's journey, it would be rescued from oblivion by a detailed account by one participant, the Gentleman of Elvas, and by a much briefer one by another, Luis Hernández de Biedma. Gonzalo Fernández de Oviedo, on the other hand, includes a shorter version of Rodrigo de Ranjel's account of the expedition in his *Historia general de las Indias*. Alvar Núñez Cabeza de Vaca, one of the three survivors of Narváez's expedition to Florida, would also choose to preserve the memory of another failed journey that would otherwise have been forgotten when he wrote his *Naufragios*. The *Naufragios* offers a detailed and fascinating account of Cabeza de Vaca's misfortunes as he traveled over a ten-year period from Florida to New Spain. A rich and complex work, the *Naufragios* is the most important text in the long sequence of accounts making up what I have called the narrative discourse of failure.

An examination of each of these texts reveals certain predominant aspects that set them apart from the narrative forms and central topics of the discourse of mythification, defining them as the different voices of the new and different discourse to which they belong. The first aspect involves their characterization of the natural environment. The discourse of mythification contains very little in the way of a thoughtful, aesthetic appreciation of nature in America. When there is any at all, it is generally related to an economic goal (Columbus) or a political one (Cortés). Columbus identified the landscape with his imaginary models or commercial designs. Cortés viewed it in his first three letters as either the sum of all the potential dangers and threatening signs that needed to be interpreted correctly if his enterprise was to succeed (second letter) or a succession of military objectives whose importance depended on their role in his strategy for conquering the empire. In the narrative discourse of failure, the *landscape* disappears altogether as an aesthetic concept or category of perception to be replaced by the *environment*. This includes the geography, climate, flora, and fauna of America, whose qualities, although varying from text to text, are always shown to be negative. The narrator of failure neither fantasizes after the fact nor mythifies what he discovers. He always perceives the environment as his worst enemy, relentlessly hostile and threatening. This hostility is apparent in the enormous excesses of nature itself, and in the feeling of alienation that results from trying to control it without understanding what it can do. Not only for Cortés but for many of the explorers, nature in America is destructive beyond measure; everything is "more" and "greater" than anything anyone has ever seen before, and thus impossible to convey or describe. Elvas makes frequent if laconic allusions to the enormous swamps and marshes of Florida and the southern coast which the horses could not penetrate and among whose branches the natives darted in and out and appeared and disappeared so quickly that there was neither a crossbow nor a harquebus that could catch them.[58] Coronado is amazed by the size of certain plains he compares to the sea: "I came upon some plains that were so large that I could find no end to them anywhere . . . and after walking for another five days in the direction I was given, I came upon plains so empty of any sign that we seemed to be in the middle of the sea."[59]

The narrator of the *Relación Postrera de Cíbola* elaborates on the mystery and terror of the central plains: "The plains go on and on, how far one cannot tell. . . . The land is so flat that a man can get lost by going half a league off course, as in the case of a horse that never appeared again, and two others that likewise disappeared, with their saddles and bridles, leaving not a trace."[60] The narrators of both Coronado's and Hernando de Soto's expeditions refer repeatedly to an endless number of rivers whose torrential floods have carried away men and horses; branches of the sea that cut deep into the land rendering it impassable; swarms of insects that not only make it impossible to sleep but transmit deadly diseases; an intolerable winter climate in the great plains and along the southern coast.

Moreover, American nature is inscrutable and unchangeable. In the narrative discourse of failure, the difficulties encountered by these vulnerable men almost entirely ignorant of the character of the New World, as they attempted to find what they needed to sustain themselves, are perceived systematically as aggression. Most of the hardships suffered by De Soto's and Coronado's companions illustrate this very well. The hunger they endured, referred to obsessively in all these texts; the cold, thirst, and diseases that afflicted them were very often the result of ignorance. Land will always seem sterile and unable to support life to those unable to identify the food-producing plants used by the native inhabitants. Water will always be scarce, when one does not know how to look for a spring. Elvas appears to have assessed the inadequacies of the Spaniards most clearly. After referring to the desperate situation of men who had fallen ill for lack of meat and salt he says: "The Indians do not want for meat; they catch large numbers of deer, chickens, rabbits, and other game, for which they have a great skill not possessed by the Spaniards; but even had the Spaniards had this skill they would have been unable to use it, for they walked most of the time and dared not leave the pathways."[61]

In an environment perceived as relentlessly aggressive, action can no longer be described in the epic terms of the discourse of mythification, and this shift from heroic deeds to struggle for survival constitutes the second structuring element of the narrative discourse of failure. In the narrative discourse of mythification, the representation of action showed three distinct stages: exploration, occupation, and domination. The correspondence—established, it must be recalled, after the fact—between the action and its results was perfect, as each stage was crowned by success. Columbus, for example, explored the Caribbean region convincing himself that what he had before his eyes was Japan, China, or, finally, the land of King Solomon's mines, Quersoneso Aureo, while in his journal and letters he recorded one spectacular achievement after another. And in Cortés's first three letters, the very directness and simplicity of his path from Veracruz to the center of the Aztec empire is like a metaphor of the conquest of Mexico to which it led him, guided by his genius and the will of God.

The second stage, occupation, consisted of several brilliant diplomatic episodes, involving repeated readings of the *requerimiento** and a succes-

---

* "The *requerimiento* or requirement was to be read, with or without interpreters, to the Indians before any attack might legally be made on them. . . . The middle section, which gives the document its name, requires the Indians to recognize the sovereignty of the Catholic Church, and in its place the secular authority of the Spanish Crown. The other demand is

sion of speeches and lectures by both the conquering and defeated parties. When occupation was no longer possible by diplomatic means, violence was resorted to—but this violence always appeared to be justified by the claim that the initial approach had been peaceful. The third stage, domination, was openly violent, its purpose being to bring everything explored and occupied under control. Its legitimacy was presented as undeniable by virtue of its association with a holy war.

The narrative discourse of failure implicitly cancels the epic model contained in the earlier accounts. In this new context the former mythical objectives begin to seem more and more implausible; adventurous initiative loses all direction, and *exploration* gives way to *wandering*. Paths become blurred and disappear, and at times the expeditionaries find themselves walking around in circles in the same general area without realizing it.

> We left from here and came to the Province of Xacatun in the midst of a dense forest, where there was no food. From there the Indians led us eastward toward some other hamlets where there was very little food, telling us that there were some Christians there like ourselves. It appeared later that this was not true, that we were the only Christians they could have heard about; but since we had gone about so many times in circles, they must have learned of our passing through on one of these occasions.[62]

Occupation of the land is never referred to in the narrative discourse of failure. That is, in the words of Pedro de Castañeda, "the land does not remain." The conquistador and his men are led on by the need to satisfy their most immediate necessities, leaving no more trace than Coronado's men, becoming lost forever in the tall grass of the prairies. Nor is there any mention of *conquest*. In the context of hideously hostile surroundings, the action of the discourse of failure becomes a struggle for survival. Military action, once idealized and mythified, now takes on an element of parody. There is a far distance indeed between Cortés's account of his military campaigns and the following reference by Castañeda to a native provocation: "And the following night, some two leagues from the town, some Indians began to cry out from their vantage point in such a way that although everyone was prepared, some of the men became so upset they saddled their horses backwards."[63] The well organized, aggressive action presented in the narrative discourse of Cortés's *Letters* gives way to a chaotic defensiveness, its painful and futile character replacing the precise heroic thrust of Cortés's representation of conquest. Energy, courage, and

---

that they permit the faith to be preached to them. This is then followed by a description of what will befall them if they fail to comply with these requests. The Spaniards will enter their lands by force and will make slaves of their wives and children." Cortés, *Letters from Mexico*, p. 454n.—TRANS.

honor have been replaced in the discourse of failure by fatigue and suffering, and all the men's efforts are absorbed by the struggle against destruction and death.

This transformation of the epic model has to do with a third aspect of the discourse of failure. Wealth, glory, power, and the myths surrounding them fade as incentives, and what now governs the way the expeditions are conducted is the reality of hunger, thirst, cold, and the threat posed by the natives. The objectives and values of the explorers change accordingly, and this redefinition of goals constitutes the fourth major element that defines the discourse of failure. The discourse of mythification as it appears in the texts of Columbus, Cortés, Díaz, Tapia, Cúneo, and others tended to present the search for gold, silver, and precious stones as the major objective. The products of the earth were only interesting to the degree that they could be identified with spices or with the proximity of fabulous dominions. Clothes and artifacts were appreciated only as a sign of the level of civilization of the natives, an indication of the quality of the booty in store. The only really acceptable booty was gold, silver, pearls, or precious stones; and the repeated questioning of the natives, at times involving torture and death, was designed exclusively to discover whether such prizes existed. The Spaniards' disdain of anything else shocked the Aztecs. Sahagún's informants called them "pigs who were anxious for nothing but gold," and the Florentine Codex contains an extremely eloquent description of their savage behavior when they succeeded in seizing the fabulous treasures of Moctezuma:

> And when they had all come to the house where the treasure was, called Teucalco, they removed all the artifacts made with feathers: clasps made of quetzal plumes, fine shields, golden disks, the necklaces worn by the idols, golden nose rings, bracelets, diadems, and armor pieces. The gold was detached immediately from the shields and insignias. Then they made the gold into a great ball, and they lit fire to the rest, no matter how valuable, and burned it all. . . . And the Spaniards melted all the gold down into bars.[64]

But such expectations diminished and eventually vanished as more and more expeditions failed. The goals of the Spaniards changed, for they were obliged to focus on far more basic objectives: how to protect themselves from the cold; how to find a remedy for their thirst and hunger. Booty became far more humble and basic: food, blankets, water, firewood. Often the direction of an expedition changed, when it was learned that there was an excellent supply of corn or chickens to be had in a distant village. The detailed lists prepared by the Gentleman of Elvas of the booty taken during his raids on certain native settlements are different indeed from Columbus or Cortés's inventories of treasures. The provisions captured during the "heroic" conquest of Cibola, following a rock-throwing battle with the natives, represent in the practical words of Pedro de Castañeda "what was most needed." The gifts offered to Coronado by the natives generally consist of no more than hides, helmets, and shields, but they are received "with great pleasure" and an attitude sharply in contrast with the arrogance described by the Aztec chronicles.[65] Elvas records the generosity of a Native American lord who sent "two thousand Indians bearing gifts including a large number of rabbits and partridges, cornbread, two chickens, and several dogs, all of which were as welcome as fat sheep to the Christians who were [sorely] lacking in meat and salt." He details the gifts from Chief Cutifachiqui, who offered the Spaniards blankets, hides, and several chickens; refers to the natives in one village who gave De Soto "seven hundred wild chickens" and to an occasion when the natives "offered [the Spaniards] any chickens they had or could get hold of"; and mentions a chief who "did the governor the great service of bringing him two deer hides."[66]

The demythifying descriptions of nature focus on the differences between Europe and America. Heroic action shifts to a struggle for survival. The incentive to acquire wealth and glory is replaced by the need to receive sustenance, thereby changing the very definition of booty and eventually the developmental rationale of all expeditionary undertakings. All these elements characterize the narrative of the discourse of failure. But there is one last fundamental element shared by these texts: the presentation of the narrative itself as *service*. Throughout the conquest, action is associated with glory, fame, and power, but these depend entirely on success. A conquistador who fails returns with nothing of value to offer and can expect very little in the way of glory or favor. It is in this context that the narrators of the discourse of failure begin to present their misfortunes as a form of service, as valuable and deserving of favor as any other more successful venture. Thus conceived, the purpose of describing their misadventures is not just to inform the king truthfully and in detail about everything that occurs but rather to claim recognition for hardships and sacrifices that express the utmost loyalty and consequently deserve the highest reward. Pedro de Castañeda states in the preface to his account that he is moved to write it "as a small service to Your Grace, which I urge you to receive as coming from a true servant and soldier."[67] Likewise Núñez, in his preface to the *Naufragios*, emphasizes the value of a man's *intentions* compared to *success*, which he attributes to fortune more than will:

Everyone has the will and desire to serve. However, aside from any advantages that may fall to a man, things can turn out very differently through no fault of his own but as a result of the whim of fortune or the will and judgment of God. Thus one man's service may turn out to be more worthy than he ever anticipated, while another's experience may be so contrary that his only proof of his purpose is his diligence, and even this can be so discreet as to go unnoticed.

He explicitly refers to his narrative of his misfortunes as a service to the king, begging that it "be received in the name of service, for it is all a man left naked could bring back with him."[68]

With no booty to add to the coffers of the crown, the account of the author's adversity must be turned into service, its value stressed and presented in support of his claim to the position and compensation he seeks: "I trusted that my *deeds* and services would be as clear and evident as those of my ancestors, and that I would not need to *speak* in order to be counted among those who so carefully and faithfully direct and manage the duties entrusted to them by Your Majesty, and are so favored by them. But . . . in the end I was left with no service to offer save for the *narrative* which I bring to your Majesty."[69] Núñez's service has not won him the rewards he had hoped for. His efforts have not been crowned by success. But against the backdrop of the implied opposition between words and deeds that Núñez is openly challenging, a new reality emerges. For the first time since the beginning of the conquest, *words* are endowed with an importance that makes them as valuable as the material booty won by more successful narrators.

Demythification and Criticism in the *Naufragios*

The point of departure of the narrative in the *Naufragios* is the same as in the other texts that constitute the narrative discourse of failure: the model formulated in the texts of the discourse of mythification. It can be divided into three main components. First, the mythical objective, the fabulous booty described in Columbus's fantastic hypotheses and verifications in his *Journal* and *Letters*. The actual existence of this mythical America promised by Columbus and dreamed of by so many others seemed to be confirmed by Cortés's conquest of Mexico and Pizarro's conquest of Peru.[70] The second component concerns the characterization of action as an epic military venture that shapes a legitimate and heroic project of domination, evangelization, and expropriation. The most thorough formulation of this model of action is to be found in Cortés's letters, government ordinances, and personal correspondence.[71] The third and last component is the model characterization of the conquistador as a mythical hero. This image is a creation of Cortés, who provided a description of all the moral, political, and physical qualities required for the successful conquest of America.[72] The narrative discourse of failure, however, moves gradually away from these models. The narratives of failure consistently undermine an imperialistic discourse in which action is identified with conquest, man with the conquistador, and America with booty, as their texts develop a critical demythification of the conquest that gradually puts an end to the initial models.

The *Naufragios* constitutes a perfect example of the discourse of demythification. In this work, America is presented in terms that link it directly with Cortés's fifth letter and implicitly cancel the model developed by Columbus. Against the latter's fabulous portrait of America inspired by Tarshish and Ophir, Cipangu and Cathay, as well as the Terrestrial Paradise, Núñez's text offers a rational, straightforward account of his recollection of the lands through which he wandered over a period of nine years. Núñez's America is no myth. It is a vast, wild, hostile territory, almost uninhabitable for the natives, entirely so for the Europeans.

In the description of American nature, there is only one European item mentioned as a point of reference: the hearts of palm eaten occasionally by the natives and Spaniards are similar to those in Castile and Andalusia. Here, as in other texts of the narrative discourse of failure, what characterizes the presentation of nature is its absolute lack of moderation, suggestive of primeval chaos, causing wonder and fear in the observer. "These [native guides] led us into a country difficult to traverse and strange to look at for it had very great forests, the trees being wonderfully tall and so many of them fallen they obstructed our way so that we had to make long detours and with great trouble. Of the trees standing many were rent from top to bottom by thunderbolts, which strike very often in that country, where storms and tempests are always frequent."[73] The swamps are too enormous to cross; the torrential force and fearful currents of the rivers pull men and horses alike into the water and drown them.[74] The huge oyster beds that Núñez and his men have to cross as they search for the sea Narváez had ordered them to look for are a good example of the constant harassment to which American nature subjects the discoverers. "For about one and a half leagues we walked, with water up to the knee, and stepping on shells [from which we received many cuts on our feet]. All this gave us much trouble."[75] Núñez's choice of words itself reflects his perception of nature as an aggressor: the Europeans are victims who "receive" the aggression (cuts from oyster shells) without being able to defend themselves or avoid the "trouble" inflicted. He carefully notes down everything he learns regarding the possible existence of gold, silver, and precious stones. But he stresses that he has seen only samples, signs, never any tangible evidence. And although these indications were to be referred to later by Hernando de Soto and Coronado in support of their own mythical objectives, they essentially serve no such purpose in Núñez's text, where in the final balance, America is presented in demythified terms that unequivocally contradict the mythical representations initiated by Columbus.

The shift from heroic action to a desperate struggle for survival is developed more thoroughly in the *Naufragios* than in any other text. This shift is already apparent in chapter 3, where in the account of the arrival of the expedition members in Florida we see them going through the usual formalities of assessing their position and reviewing the troops. Narváez solemnly takes possession of a handful of abandoned houses, and he is acknowledged as governor in a sort of phantom ceremony without a single native present. Provisions are brought to him by an army of starving, exhausted men, with a few horses too tired and thin to be of much use. The scene is desolate and pathetic, especially given the inevitable contrast with Cortés's conquest of Mexico and all its brilliant speeches and displays, which Narváez was trying to emulate.

Núñez's description of the invading army in the next chapter makes Narváez's expedition appear even more caricaturesque, compared to the model it tries to duplicate. "The pilots," says Núñez, "were at a loss . . . undecided as to what course to pursue. Moreover the horses would not be with us in case we needed them, and, furthermore, we had no interpreter . . . finally, we had not the supplies required."[76] In contrast to the leadership and strength of the invading army described by Cortés, Narváez's expedition is presented from the beginning as being weak, vulnerable, and disoriented. Narváez is a caricature of the hero. He has none of the qualities that make the Cortés of the *Letters* a model, and his arrogance and irresponsibility, his lack of foresight and military talent make him in the eyes of the prudent Núñez the cause of all the expedition's misfortunes. His army too is made to appear caricaturesque, with attributes far different from those of the model army of Cortés. Now it is the natives who show initiative and strength, who are threatening and aggressive. When the natives become too dangerous the Spaniards strike back only in self-defense.

Added to this substitution of weakness and vulnerability for those attributes of strength ever to be found in the discourse of mythification, there is an important change in the context in which certain key terms present in Cortés's narrative now appear. Most revealing is the verb "to take," which Cortés uses constantly to describe the successful achievement of a military objective. Cities, ports, rooftops, temples, are all "taken" by Cortés and his men, after a heroic battle. Núñez uses the word as well, but he applies it to an anti-heroic context. When the men come upon an island after sailing aimlessly for seven days he says: "we found plenty of ruffs and their eggs, dried, and that was a very great relief in our needy condition. Having taken them, we went further, and two leagues beyond found a strait."[77] The structure of the last sentence is identical to that of a great many formulaic summaries used by Cortés in his letters to describe the victorious progress of his troops during the conquest of Mexico. Here, however, the main item of interest is no longer an important military objective, but dried fish and eggs. The grotesque effect of the syntactic contiguity established between the military formula "to take" and so humble an objective conveys intensely and economically the disintegration of the epic model of action developed by Cortés.

Thus, there are already indications at the beginning of the *Naufragios* that the epic model of action is falling apart; but the actual process starts with a specific incident, and it is virtually completed in chapters 8 through 10. The incident is recounted in chapter 5 as follows:

> One horseman, whose name was Juan Velázquez, a native of Cuellar, not willing to wait, rode into the stream, and the strong current swept him from the horse and he took hold of the reins, and was drowned with the animal. The Indians of that chief (whose name was Dulchanchellin) discovered the horse and told us that we would find him lower down the stream. So they went after the man, and his death caused us much grief, since until then we had not lost anybody. The horse made a supper for many on that night.[78]

In Cortés's *Letters*, the figure of the horse is always the quintessential symbol of the military superiority of the Spaniards, making the *teules* superhuman in the eyes of the Native Americans. Cortés, Bernal Díaz, and Tapia refer to the terror their horses provoked among the natives, who believed them to have magical qualities; and they remark frequently on how important the role of the horses was in the conquest of Mexico. In contrast, there is nothing magical or glorious about the horse in the incident described by Núñez. Nor have the horses in this expedition given the natives reason to fear: unlike the Aztecs, these natives see them only in the rivers and swamps of Florida where, as Elvas was to observe years later, they become an obstacle more than a sign of superiority.

In this episode, the utility of the horse is identified for the first time with its potential as food for the Spaniards, indicating that the goal of *conquest* is in the process of being replaced by that of *survival*. The "magical deer" described to Moctezuma by his astounded envoys is reduced here to the humble function of providing a supper for the starved followers of Narváez. This marks symbolically the beginning of the end for the model set by Cortés, which completely disintegrates in chapter 8 of the *Naufragios*, where war is replaced by industry, and all the instruments of conquest, all the attributes of the conquistador are transformed into objects that can be used for flight or survival.

When the men realize that the land discovered is so bad that if they stay there death is their "sole prospect," their first impulse is to flee. But having agreed that their objective must be changed from conquest to *return*, they realize that great difficulties still stand in the way: "It seemed impossible, as none of us knew how to construct ships. We had no tools, no iron, no smithery, no oakum, no pitch, no tackling; finally, nothing of what was indispensable. Neither was there anybody to instruct us in shipbuilding, and, above all, there was nothing to eat, while the work was going on."[79]

The solution to all these impossible tasks involves a series of steps that symbolize the destruction of the model of conquest, and the transformation of the conquistador into an artisan. First, the instruments of war are melted down to make tools. Harnesses, so closely associated with the mythical attributes of the conquistador, and weapons, which have symbolized his power to prevail and control, become the implements of manual labor, more suited to a plebeian artisan than a noble warrior: "and [we] agreed to make of our stirrups, spurs, cross-bows and other iron implements the nails, saws, and hatchets and other tools we so greatly needed for our purpose." Second, the function of the horses is radically transformed as every part of the animal is used: "of the tails and manes of the horses we made ropes and tackles. . . . We flayed the legs of the horses and tanned the skin to make leather pouches for carrying water."[80] With their horses and weapons gone, the pursuits of the conquistadors are no longer glorious but industrious as they devote themselves to the manual labor of collecting palmettos and resin for oakum and pitch, making sails from their clothes, and tanning horsehide.

The last stage in the demise of mythical models involves the increasing fragmentation of the invading army. The very notion of an army kept together by a common mission vanishes; personal interest and security become the top priority. In chapter 10 of the *Naufragios*, Narváez and his men have been sailing near the coast shortly after having escaped from a native attack:

When it dawned the barges had been driven apart from each other . . . at the hour of vespers, I descried two barges, and as I approached saw that the first one was that of the governor, who asked me what I thought we should do. I told him that we ought to rejoin the other barge, which was ahead of us, and in no manner foresake her, and the three together should continue our way whither God might take us. He replied it was impossible, since the barge was drifting far away into the sea, whereas he wanted to land. . . . Seeing his determination, I took to my own oar and the other oarsmen in my craft did the same. . . . But as the Governor had with him the healthiest and strongest men, in no way could we follow or keep up with him. Seeing this, I asked him to give me a rope from his barge to be able to follow, but he answered that it was no small effort on their part alone to reach the shore on that night. I told him that . . . he should tell me what he commanded me to do. He answered that this was no time for orders; that each one should do the best he could to save himself.[81]

As the vessels begin to separate, Alvar Núñez embodies the impulse to hold on to the notion of an army in solidarity, Narváez its final relinquishment. By repeatedly requesting Narváez not to abandon the third vessel, to link his chances to his own and those of his crew, Núñez was appealing to one of the central aspects of the model created by the discourse of mythification: the Spaniards' unwavering solidarity.[82] But in reply to Núñez's urging that he heed the collective security of the army, Narváez insists that his overriding priority is his own interest, and when he finally tells Núñez that each should do his best to save himself, communication is broken off for good between the two men.

In Cortés's model, the action of a conquistador corresponded exactly with the will of his leader, and the action of the latter expressed the interests of the crown. In the above episode this chain of relationships is severed at the level of its central link, that of the leader. By putting his interests above those of his men and the crown, the leader Narváez destroys the model. Within the ideological context that implicitly frames the action, he becomes a traitor to his king and a man without honor.

Just as in the other texts of the narrative discourse of failure, the shift from an epic model of conquest to a struggle for survival brings about a replacement of fabulous objectives by others far more modest, whose value will be defined solely in relation to the desperate fight against cold, hunger, and thirst. In the *Naufragios*, all that remains of the fabulous objectives that prompted the expedition is the promising gold bell found at their first landing. But the bell's promise never materializes, and Narváez's hopes to discover "a second Mexico" are reduced to this small artifact. When Núñez speaks much later of his travels through the southwest of the United States, of turquoise and coral and significant signs of gold and silver in the northern regions of New Spain, these are no longer important objectives, for he has come to identify the virtues of the land with fertility, water, and the potential for excellent harvests. During the ten years following the discovery of the bell, the sole purpose of Núñez and the other survivors would be to defend themselves against the threat of death, by securing sufficient roots, shellfish, meat, or prickly pears to live on from day to day. Hunger endured by Núñez, Dorantes, Castillo, and Esteban over a period of more than eight years spent with the natives redefines the short term goals described in the *Naufragios*, which come to be associated with whatever means are required to survive under primitive conditions in a hostile environment:

> Now and then they kill deer and at times kill a fish, but this is so little and their hunger so great that they eat spiders and ant eggs, worms, lizards and salamanders and serpents, also vipers the bite of which is deadly. They swallow earth and wood, and all they can get, the dung of deer and more things I do not mention; and I verily believe, from what I saw, that if there were any stones in the country they would eat them also.[83]

The incentive to obtain such basic things as these is obviously unlikely to involve any of the concern for fame and glory displayed in the discourse of mythification. Here, as with other texts belonging to the narrative discourse of failure, *need* shifts and redefines objectives, plans, and courses of action. "So great is the power of need," says Núñez shortly before his last shipwreck, "that it brought us to venture out into such a troublesome sea in this manner, and without any one among us having the least knowledge of the art of navigation." And he adds, when he and his companions are obliged for the first time to treat the sick, "At last we found ourselves in such [need] as to have to do it, without risking any punishment."[84] The incentives of wealth, glory, and power have disappeared entirely from his account, for need has cancelled them out, organizing the action and confining it to the sole purpose of survival.

The same five main components present in the other texts belonging to the discourse of failure are thus also to be found in the *Naufragios*. Reflecting a basic change in perception and discourse, these are the first texts to demythify America, the conquest, and the conquistador. They challenge the models of land, action, and conquistador created by Columbus and Cortés and no longer present America as the repository of fantasy or fabulous booty. In the texts of the discourse of failure, America is no longer a myth. Its characterization reveals all the complexity of a new, hard-to-mythify reality.

The breakdown of the epic enterprise that takes place in these texts, on the other hand, challenges radically Cortés's concept of action. His total identification of action with conquest and his consistent subordination of individual action to a common historical goal become very problematical here. The focus is now on personal need and survival, and this flaws the earlier image of the conquistador as a selfless representative of the royal interest. Cortés's mythical hero had been an ideal construct, embodying all the virtues needed for the successful outcome of his epic goals. His character has been completely consistent with the objective requirements for the flawless development of the historical project he proposed to his king. But in the narrative discourse of failure, Cortés's fictional hero becomes human, makes mistakes, suffers, doubts, and fails. The abstraction of myth gives way to ambivalence and contradiction, and the conquistador, no longer a mythical, powerful hero, appears in all his frail humanity.

The demythification of land, action, and conqueror outlined above shapes the narrative discourse of failure. In the texts of this narrative discourse, the narrative typically begins with an acknowledgment of failure. This is followed by a systematic highlighting of the differences between the models created by the discourse of mythification and the reality revealed by actual experience. Earlier models become meaningless and are replaced in most cases by disorientation and disenchantment. It is in this context that the unusual character of the *Naufragios* first becomes apparent, for what its narrative reveals goes well beyond the record of a sequence of misfortunes and disappointments. The narrative of misfortunes here simply sets the stage for the gradual process of self-definition of a new critical consciousness. It is this consciousness that will, in the text, organize and present a qualitatively different perception of American reality, its discovery and conquest.

The narrative of the *Naufragios* is structured around two distinct central processes. The first, already discussed, relates to the demythification of the earlier models through the three main transformations that also shape the other texts of the discourse of failure. The second revolves around the progressive development of a critical consciousness. The new perception articulated by this critical consciousness will offer a very different representation of American reality and of the possible terms of the relationship between the Spaniards and that reality.

The point of departure of this second process is in chapter 11. Here we find Núñez and a small group of shipwrecked conquistadors on the island of Ill Fate. Their vulnerability is expressed in the text by the fact that what organizes—and distorts—their perception of reality is *fear*. The natives who have come to see the shipwrecked men are made to seem monstrous, illustrating by contrast the weakness of the latter: "our fright was such that, whether tall or little, it made them appear giants to us."[85] On the following days the men eat what the natives give them, and once they have stored up a minimum amount of provisions they decide to make one final attempt to reach the lost brigs, or the shore of the nearest colony. Their boat has sunk into the sand, but they uncover it and, taking off their clothes, try putting it out to sea: "Then we embarked. Two crossbow shots from shore, a wave swept over us, we all got wet, and being naked and the cold very great, the oars dropped out of our hands. The next wave overturned the barge. . . . The shore being very rough, the sea took the others and thrust them, half dead, on the beach of the same island again, less the three that had perished underneath the barge. The rest of us, *as naked as we had been born, had lost everything*."[86] This is Núñez's last shipwreck, and the words quoted here reflect both the last stage in the rejection of the former model of mythified conquest, and the beginning of the narrator's critical consciousness.

The complete demythification of the idealized model of military conquest had already been expressed metaphorically in the episode where Alvar Núñez and his men used their weapons for tools, their horses for provisions, and their clothes for sails. But their nakedness now signifies their absolute dispossession of the cultural and ideological context that had given the image of the conquistador and his enterprise its identity.

At the same time, however, something else begins to develop in the text, unrelated to this "lost" context, for nakedness has a twofold significance. Associated on the one hand with failure and death, it is an expression of the loss of contact with the original culture. Ever since the journals of Columbus, the clothing of the Spaniards had been considered a mark of their civilization, and the nakedness of the Native Americans, in contrast, a proof of their status as savages. The Spaniards' loss of their clothing might therefore be taken to represent their loss of civilization, that is, their death in terms of the Eurocentrism prevalent in that day. Núñez draws this equivalence between cultural dispossession and symbolic death when he says "and we looked like death itself." But, on the other hand, nakedness and death in relation to the European ideological and cultural context are in this episode associated with rebirth: "as naked as we had been born." It is this textual contiguity between death and birth, reinforced by the explicit connection between becoming naked and being born, that marks the beginning of a new consciousness. The development of this new consciousness, which gradually eliminates the earlier ideological models, organizes the critical perception of reality in the *Naufragios*.

To start with, this new perception involves a rejection of the Manichaean dichotomy often associated with epic forms of representation: infidels versus Christians in medieval epic poetry; savages versus civilized men in the discourse of Columbus; natives versus Spaniards in the *Letters* of Cortés. Chapter 12 marks the rejection of such divisions and their replacement by a form of solidarity that removes the opposition between Spaniards and natives. When the natives see that the Spaniards have been left naked and vulnerable after their last shipwreck ("with many tears. . . . Every one of us pitied not only himself, but all the others whom he saw in the same condition"), their initial reaction is such that it highlights the extent of the change in their respective roles: "when they saw us," says Núñez, "in such a different attire from before and so strange looking, they were so frightened as to turn back." But what seems remarkable to Núñez is that these men called savages, barbarians, and enemies throughout the epic versions of the conquest, far from taking advantage of the weakness of the invaders to destroy them, treat them like brothers and weep with them over their misfortune. "Upon seeing the disaster we had suffered, our misery and distress, the Indians sat down with us and all began to weep out of compassion for our misfortune, and for more than half an hour they wept so loud and so sincerely that it could be heard far away."[87]

Starting with this instance of shared weeping, the characterization of the natives and the Spaniards develops along lines that appear at times to reverse the roles assigned to each in earlier accounts. For here the Spaniards completely lose control and are reduced to "weeping," "asking," "begging," and "fearing." It is the natives who control the situation entirely; the initiative is theirs, and they "take" the Spaniards, carrying them so that their feet do not so much as touch the ground, warm them by the fires they light along the road, give them fish to eat, and shelter them in their huts. The reversal of roles observed here for the first time comes to a high point during an incident that challenges a central ideological assumption of the discourse of mythification. The incident concerns cannibalism. From Columbus to Cortés, including Tapia and Bernal Díaz, cannibalism provides the conquistadors with one of the most important means of justifying their actions. Columbus cites the widespread cannibalism he claims to have found in the Antilles in defense of his proposal to the queen for the organization of a lucrative trade in slaves supported by Her Majesty. Bernal Díaz grotesquely exaggerates the ritual cannibalism practiced by the natives of the Mexican plateau, adducing what he claims makes them inhuman savages as the justification for doing battle against them, enslaving them, and putting them to mass extermination.

For the average conquistador cannibalism was a perversion comparable to sodomy—another of Díaz's obsessions—which deserved the severest punishment and cast doubt on the very humanity of its practitioners. Indeed, such an aberration placed an individual in an ambiguous category, half human and half bestial, providing an excuse for the most terrible forms of violence, atrocity, and repression.

Núñez refers to two cases of cannibalism in his *Naufragios*. But the important thing here, more important than the act itself, is that in both cases the practitioners were Spaniards, not Native Americans. The first episode involves five Christians who had taken refuge on the shore near the settlement belonging to the natives who rescued Núñez. When the winter weather became very cold "five Christians, quartered on the coast, were driven to such an extremity that they ate each other up until but one remained, who being left alone, there was nobody to eat him." The second episode concerns Esquivel and his companions who in the month of November "from cold and hunger began to die. . . . Thus they perished one after another, the survivors slicing the dead for meat. The last one to die was Sotomayor, and Esquivel cut him up and fed on his body."[88]

With the description of the natives' reaction to this behavior, the reversal of roles implicit in the attribution of cannibalism to the Spaniards is complete. "At this the Indians were so startled, and there was such an uproar among them, that I verily believe if they had seen this at the beginning they would have killed them, and we would all have been in great danger."[89] What this reversal suggests is devastating to the model produced by the discourse of mythification. The presentation of the Spaniards as subhuman savages and of the natives as humane and civilized amounts in fact to the complete rejection of the earlier representations.

The demythification of the figure of the conquistador and the refutation of the epic model (in which humanity had been divided into two antagonistic camps, with the Spaniard representing reason, civilization, justice, the will of God, and the native embodying brutality, paganism, absence of reason) provide the foundation for a shift from a mythical to a more accurate perception of peoples. The mythical figures of the hero and the brute are profoundly transformed in the *Naufragios*. In this text, solidarity with the other in suffering and the reversal of roles just described mark the beginning of the humanization of the conquistador. First represented metaphorically in chapter 12 by the nakedness of the protagonists, this humanization materializes throughout a long sequence of metamorphoses of the figure of the mythical warrior. These metamorphoses express new forms of relationship that develop between the Spaniards and the natives, in contrast to the earlier alienating opposition between conqueror and conquered. But they also trace the development of a new ability to adapt to the environment, a development that necessarily involves the replacement of earlier mythically informed perceptions by a more objective and critical approach to reality. Throughout all this, the shipwrecked conquistador's sense of his own identity in relation to a context he must of necessity learn to understand will gradually be redefined.

Initially, physical nakedness is tantamount to cultural nudity. Cut off from his Western surroundings, Núñez is as ignorant as a newborn infant of the situation in which he must now commence to live. His first metamorphosis, which places him entirely at the mercy of the natives, his status halfway between that of a domestic animal and a slave provide a clear expression of his ignorance, vulnerability, and complete dependency. He is used for the most primitive tasks, the only ones he appears so far able to perform.

> Among the many other troubles I had to pull the eatable roots out of the water and from among the canes where they were buried in the ground, and from this my fingers had become so tender that the mere touch of a straw caused them to bleed. The reeds would cut me in many places, because many were broken and I had to go in among them with the clothing I had on, of which I have told. This is why I went to work and joined the other Indians. Among these I improved my condition a little by [making myself a trader], doing the best in it I could.[90]

In his second metamorphosis, then, he becomes a trader. The precise wording of his redefinition of himself—"I made myself"—is not fortuitous but deliberate, and it reflects a qualitatively different stage in his understanding of the new environment. He learns about the merchandise considered desirable by the natives: he knows what it is used for and how to obtain it; he establishes trade routes to exchange the products of the various tribes living in the territory he covers. He uses his role and his journeys to become more familiar with the customs of the natives and to establish a personal relationship with them, which turns out to be very useful once he begins his long trek back to New Spain.

In his third metamorphosis, Núñez becomes a physician and as such introduces a new application for religion. Used by previous conquistadors to justify violence and exploitation, religion in the *Naufragios* is turned into an instrument of healing and persuasion. The success of the miraculous healings performed by Núñez and the other survivors leads to the final metamorphosis in the development of this conquistador: the former shipwreck victim-slave-merchant-physician is now a child of the sun. While staying with the Aravare Indians he remarks: "During that time they came to us from many places and said that verily we were the children of the sun," and later, "[they] told them that we were children of the sun."[91] Ironically, the cycle of transformations ends where the discourse of myth-ification began, and develops in the opposite direction. Those who had been called gods by the envoys of Moctezuma are "swine" by the end of the conquest of Mexico. The miserable victims of the shipwreck at the beginning of the *Naufragios*—whom the natives had treated as little better than domestic animals, slapping and whipping them and plucking their beards for their diversion—end up as gods. In the first case, prestige and authority are lost and then compensated for by an escalation of violence; in the second, authority is recovered. But unlike the pattern portrayed by the discourse of mythification, authority in this latter circumstance is neither achieved nor preserved through violence; rather, it results from knowledge and a better understanding of a new situation. The opposition between violence and knowledge, expressed by such absolutely different processes, is what lies at the foundation of two radically diverse modes of encounter between the natives and the Spaniards. Cortés had used his "divine" authority to attack the Aztecs, to bring them under his control, and to deprive them of their property and freedom. Núñez and the other survivors of the expedition attempted to use their new position of authority to create for all a peaceful and more just relationship.

The radical contrast between the two attitudes is highlighted in the *Naufragios* by the Alcaraz episode. Here the violence and plunder associated with the conquest are carried to the extreme, and their presentation is stripped of any of the mitigating rhetoric or extenuating circumstances that might have embellished the picture in the case of a more complex character like Cortés. The Christians—Alcaraz and his men—are abusive, mendacious, cruel, and engage in every conceivable form of violence and inhumanity. The natives consider them bloodthirsty savages and flee from them as they would from the plague. In contrast, the impact of the humanitarian, peace-loving attitude of the shipwreck victims, whose re-lations with the natives are based on understanding, generosity, and justice, is particularly forceful. This attitude is dramatically different from the chaotic violence, aggression, and pillage inherent in the imperial ideology that shaped the conquest. But as Núñez becomes aware of this, he begins to realize the extent to which this awareness marginalizes him in relation to the prevailing ideology. The longed-for "return to civilization" becomes a painful recognition of his own critical rejection of the very "civilized" values that at one time had seemed to him unquestionable.

Alvar Núñez's new perception of his own identity, expressed in the

Naufragios by the metamorphoses he experiences as a conquistador-narrator during his long journey, goes hand in hand with a radical change in his view of reality. This is especially true in relation to the most important component of American reality: the natives. Columbus had been the first to deprive the American natives of their humanity by reducing them to the category of beasts and merchandise and, as noted indignantly by Las Casas, by using such terms as barbarous, bestial, and "head" to describe them. The protective, paternalistic attitude reflected in Cortés's *Letters* and government ordinances had given back to the natives their membership in the human race. But it did so by depriving them of the privileges of adulthood, as Cortés consistently made them seem vulnerable, infantile, and by implication irresponsible. This set the foundation for perpetuating a protectorate under which the very people whom Cortés claimed he wanted to defend would be forever deprived of their freedom.

In the *Naufragios*, besides the transformation of the conquistador-narrator, that is, of the first aspect of the human model created by the discourse of mythification, there is another equally profound change that shapes a new perception of the natives. The concepts "hero" and "savage" are gradually replaced by the concept "human." This does not mean that the differences between the Spaniards and the natives have been eliminated. But Núñez affirms the fact that human nature is represented by different races and cultures. His account is, in fact, the first ever to present an anthropological view of the American native. He begins his ethnographical presentation by describing the dreadful conditions the natives must deal with to survive, which, according to Núñez, make them primitive but not inhuman. To prove their humanity, the author offers a detailed portrait of their family organization, rites, and customs. "Of all the people in the world, they are those who most love their children and treat them best," says Alvar Núñez. He writes about the natives' matrimonial customs, property system, social relations among groups and clans, religious ideas, scientific concepts, and medicine: "an Indian told me that I did not know what I said by claiming that what he knew was useless, because stones and other things growing out in the field have their virtues"; and "All the medicine man does is to make a few cuts where the pain is located and then suck the skin around the incisions. They cauterize with fire, thinking it very effective, and I found it to be so by my own experience."[92] And he comes to the conclusion that the natives "are well conditioned people, apt to follow any line which is well traced for them."[93]

As an inevitable consequence of his own historical background, the perception Núñez develops gradually throughout his long years with the natives is not without contradictions. One of the survivors, Esteban, is black. Neither Núñez nor the other Spaniards deny his humanity, but they relegate him to a subordinate position. He is the one who obeys orders without question, his surname is never recorded, and he is assigned inferior status precisely because he is "the black."[94] And just as Núñez never overcomes the racism implicit in the image he presents of Esteban, neither his growing understanding of the natives with whom he comes in contact nor his acknowledgment of their humanity really succeeds in erasing the ethnocentric prejudice in him, according to which anyone primitive or different is essentially subhuman. "All over the land," he says, "are vast and handsome pastures, with good grass for cattle, and it strikes me the soil would be very fertile were the country inhabited and improved by rational people."[95] But only myths can be free of any contradictions, and their evidence in the *Naufragios* does not weaken the text's demythifying character. On balance, the extent of the demythification accomplished in the *Naufragios* is revealed by the distance between the conquistador's first perception of the natives and the pacifist philosophy expressed at the end of the text. In the episode in which he first offers an opinion of the natives, Núñez calls them "beings so devoid of reason, untutored, so like unto brutes"[96]—an image perfectly consistent with that of the dehumanized savage presented in Columbus's journal and letters, which was drawn upon to justify conquest by force. But at the end of his report he proposes that violence be replaced by persuasion, and abusiveness by justice: "while it clearly shows how, in order to bring those people to Christianity and obedience unto Your Imperial Majesty, they should be well treated, and not otherwise."[97]

It is the way it questions existing models that gives the discourse of the *Naufragios* its demythifying function. Its critical and subversive nature can only really be accurately measured, however, if it is viewed in relation to the historical context in which it was produced. The perception of the Native Americans formulated by Columbus during his first voyage persisted for many years after Núñez's return to the "civilized world." Ginés de Sepúlveda's *Tratado sobre las justas causas de la guerra contra los indios*, in which the author developed Aristotle's concept of the master and the slave to demonstrate the superiority of the Europeans and the inferiority of the Indians and justify, as consistent with the laws of nature, the conquest and domination of the latter by the former, was written as late as 1547:[98] "It is consistent with natural law that these barbarians must be ruled by the Spaniards. And if they should refuse to be ruled by us, they may be compelled by force of arms to do so, considering that the intelligence, prudence, humanity, strength of body and soul, and all the other virtues of the Spaniards gives them so great an advantage over these little men."[99] The perception underlying this argument equates the natives with "little men, children, barbarians, beasts, and monkeys." Sepúlveda claims that "they are as inferior to the Spaniards as children are to adults and women to men . . . monkeys to humans," and he goes on to say that they "violate nature, are blasphemous and idolatrous," comparing the difference between them and civilized people to the difference between humans and beasts. Sepúlveda's theory, however, was not conceived in a vacuum. He referred to Aristotle and St. Thomas in arguing that Spanish superiority over the natives justified war against them: "This is thus the natural order of things, which we are required by divine, eternal law to observe. . . . This doctrine is confirmed by both Aristotle and St. Thomas."[100] Drawing on these authorities, he posited an extreme version of the philosophy that lay in essence, more or less apparently, at the bottom of the entire enterprise of the conquest.

The first to attack the monstrosity of this perception was Father Montesinos, in his famous Advent sermon delivered in 1511.[101] Bartolomé de las Casas, who gave up his *encomiendas* and devoted himself to defending the natives precisely as a result of this sermon, developed the most passionate defense of their status as human beings, constantly referring to their superior morality compared to that of the conquistadors, who believed they had the right to subject them. In 1527, as Núñez's long journey across the south of the continent was just underway, Las Casas began to write his polemical *Historia de las Indias*, the first critical account of the conquest and colonization of the New World. He stood up for the natives as human beings, defended their right to their land, attacked the violent plans to conquer them and expropriate their territory, exposed the theory concerning a just war for what it was, and held that the only valid way to convert the American natives was by means of peaceful instruction based on persuasion, good treatment, and respect for their life and property.[102]

Núñez's demythifying account of the natives in his *Naufragios* parallels the critical thinking of Las Casas. And the political and ideological implications of his experience were so apparent that Bishop Zumárraga referred to them publicly, in support of his claim that war should be prohibited against the Native Americans, for it was only their souls that needed to be conquered. Marcel Bataillon gives a vivid account of the arrival of the four survivors of Narváez's expedition: "On July 23, 1536 . . . the news spread in Mexico as if carried by the wind: Alvar Núñez Cabeza de Vaca and other men not heard of for ten years had returned.

. . . Not only had this handful of white men, accompanied by a black man, not been eaten by cannibals, but the Indians had treated them as if they were supernatural beings."[103] The ideological significance of the *Naufragios* lay in its implicit criticism and demythification of the prevailing ideology. Its political importance, however, was derived from the fact that it provided crucial support for a current of critical thinking, headed by Las Casas, that had been actively challenging and undermining the imperialistic approach that had shaped the conquest and exploitation of the New World. This challenge, in Núñez as in Las Casas and others, consisted specifically of a rejection of the notion of a just war; a redefinition of the nature of the natives and a defense of their humanity; and an explicit proposal that "peaceful conquest" be made the only just and viable way to relate to them.

Most texts of the discourse of failure confine themselves to a detailed account of the experience of failure. But the *Naufragios* overcomes the rather limited nature of these accounts through its ideological and political implications. Rather than being the end of the account in itself, failure here triggers the awakening of a new consciousness. This new consciousness gradually unfolds a critical demythification of previous models challenged, to conclude with a political proposal whose radical nature would subvert the established order, linking the critical discourse of this new text with that of the other dissidents. An ideological analysis of the *Naufragios* clearly shows its importance in the development of Spanish American consciousness and thinking. But this narrative is no less outstanding from a strictly literary point of view. It stands out among the other narratives of the discourse of failure as a key text in what Raquel Chang Rodríguez calls "the search for the ancient roots of literary expression in Latin America."[104]

In his preface Núñez defines the purpose of his account in terms that clearly set it apart from all those whose declared intention had been to provide information. Cortés, for example, presents his letters as a service, and their value was defined by their informative function: a value derived from the truthfulness of the account and from its usefulness within the context of a general plan of conquest and imperial expansion. It is in the texts of the discourse of failure that the narrative does not rely on the usefulness of the events it narrates or their consequences in order to define its own importance. In these texts the narrative itself becomes the evidence of merit, through the process of definition of the narrator as a selfless, self-sacrificing subject deserving of rewards and recognition.[105] Núñez goes a step further, attributing equal value to words and action. The narrator equates the significance of his account with the *deeds* that distinguished his forebears in the history of Spain, and this equivalence reveals a personal project clearly reminiscent of what Enrique Pupo-Walker has called "an incorporation into history through the medium of writing."[106] The *Naufragios* thus emerges as the expression of a process of self-definition of the narrator in close relation to his historical context and in clear contrast to the political intention behind Cortés's *Letters*, the commercial project informing Columbus's penchant for creating myths, or the simple claim to personal merit that shaped the narrative strategies of the other examples of the narrative discourse of failure.

The literary nature of the *Naufragios* seems limited to a series of structural and narrative elements that organize the material giving it a certain subjective and atemporal character. First, the prophetic structure is retrospectively subordinated to the description of the narrator's misfortunes. This strategy allows the narrator to neutralize any personal responsibility for the events. Any consequent action or failure becomes, rather than the effect of a personal will, the unavoidable fulfillment of a preordained fate, like that prophesized by a Moorish woman from Hornachos to one of the women who had stayed on board one of the ships. According to this prophecy, "neither he nor any of his company would return, and . . . should any come back, God would work miracles through him, as she felt sure that few or none would escape."[107] Framed by this prophecy, which it ultimately confirms, the action takes on the appearance of having been inevitable, and the character seems destined to follow the direction preordained by the prophecy, which fictitiously illuminates the meaning of the discourse and endows it with the consistency found in fiction.

The second element organizing the narrative is the use of prophecy to develop suspense, anticipating the important moments in the action that are thus presented as being extraordinary for the very reason that they have been foretold. The phantasmagoric concert of "bells, also flutes and tambourines" that Núñez and his men hear on a stormy night near Trinidad, about which he says "never has such a fearful thing been witnessed in those parts," making a point that he "took testimony concerning it, and sent it, certified, to Your Majesty,"[108] is an example of the use of such premonition to create suspense, heightening the dramatic character as well as the inevitability of the action that follows. Moreover, the action predicted by the elements that generate suspense is divided roughly into sections: introduction, development, climax, and denouement, in a manner more typical of the novel than of our current notion of a historical essay.[109]

The third element that gives the narrative an obvious fictional character is the use it makes of tales, legends, and fictional or fantastic elements that are woven throughout the entire text.[110] The longest one is the tale of the Bad Thing:

> They said there wandered then about the country a man, whom they called "Bad Thing," of small stature and with a beard, although they never could see his features clearly, and whenever he would approach their dwellings their hair would stand on end and they began to tremble. In the doorway of the lodge there would then appear a firebrand. That man thereupon came in and took hold of anyone he chose, and with a sharp knife of flint, as broad as a hand and two palms in length, he cut their side, and, thrusting his hand through the gash, took out the entrails, cutting off a piece one palm long, which he threw into the fire. Afterward he made three cuts in one of the arms, the second one at the place where people are usually bled, and twisted the arm, but reset it soon afterwards. Then he placed his hands on the wounds, and they told us that they closed at once. Many times he appeared among them while they were dancing, sometimes in the dress of a woman and again as a man, and whenever he took a notion to do it he would seize the hut or lodge, take it up into the air and come down with it again with a great crash. They told us how, many times, they set food before him, but he never would partake of it, and then when they asked him where he came from and where he had his home, he pointed to a rent in the earth and said his house was down below.[111]

As a complement to this tale, which conveys the native view of the fantastic as represented in the *Naufragios*, there are also accounts of miraculous episodes involving the Spaniards. If the supernatural is embodied for the natives in the figure of the Bad Thing, for the Christians it is identified with the figures of God and the Devil. The shift from terms belonging to the native cultural code to terms belonging to that of the Spaniards constitutes an example of an early *mestizaje*, or mingling, of cultures. In this case of the tale of the Bad Thing, this shift is very explicit; when they see the knife marks inflicted by the Bad Thing, the Spaniards can no longer jest over the native legend and feel obliged to accept the fact that it may be authentic. But they do this *after* having reformulated it according to categories that define the supernatural within a Christian ideology. "We laughed very much at those stories, making fun of them, and then, seeing our incredulity they brought to us many of those whom, they said, he had taken, and we saw the scars of his slashes in the places and as they told. We told them he was a demon and explained as best we could that if they would believe in God, Our Lord, and be Christians like ourselves, they would not have to fear that man, nor would he come and do such things unto them, and they might be sure that as long as we were in this country he would not dare to appear again."[112] The Devil is substituted for the "unexplainable," reestablishing the verisimilitude threatened by this latter category—just as in the case of the "miracles" where all the uncanny magic that appears to surround the amazing healing performed by the shipwrecked Spaniards is condensed in the figure of God.

The prophetic structure framing the narrative material, the narrative presentation of the action, the use of prediction as a means of generating suspense and dramatic tension, the introduction of fantastic legends and episodes into the account as if they were factual, all give Núñez's story a "novelistic" cast indeed, if we approach it in terms of contemporary notions of what a historical text should be. However, the presence of these elements does not set the *Naufragios* apart from the other texts of the discourse of mythification, of failure, or from many other accounts and chronicles written at the time, thus making it an exception. Quite to the contrary, these elements make the work perfectly representative of the historical texts of the period. Jacques Lafaye, who has studied the question of miracles in the writing of Núñez, stresses with insight and accuracy the generally literary character of such texts when he says:

> What remains is to consider the history of the period as a literary genre. Its purposes were the same as those of the ancient historians: to put forward edifying examples and glorify individual personalities; and of the moderns, to exalt spiritual values, which were confused with national and political interests; and, finally, to present an elegant version of facts capable of stimulating the spirit. The very notion of objectivity in history was unknown, and the modern historian can use neither the epic, the propaganda tract, natural history, the family chronicle, or the history of the New World as anything other than a history of ideas, not a history of facts.[113]

It is not these elements that make the *Naufragios* a unique and fundamental literary work. Although they would appear to link the text with subsequent literary narrative forms, in fact they anchor it firmly in the old historiographical tradition. Within this tradition, narrative convention had allowed the chroniclers since the Middle Ages the free inclusion, in a historical work, of fantastic occurrences, subjective perceptions and assessments, personal value judgments, and even fictitious or marvelous events. What is specifically literary about the *Naufragios* has to do, rather, with the process of the self-definition of the narrator that shapes the development of the narrative. Ideologically, this self-definition parallels another development discussed earlier: the gradual awakening of the narrator's critical consciousness. In literary terms, this self-definition unfolds through the dynamic interplay of what we might call a double perception of the action; or, more specifically, through the dynamic relationship between the denotative discourse that narrates the events and the complex and sometimes contradictory message connoted by the narrative. A denotative reading of the *Naufragios* reveals a simple narrative of misfortunes like so many other narratives of the discourse of failure. It is an account of daily events that follows the development of the expedition through space and time, from the beginning of Narváez's journey until the arrival of the four survivors in New Spain. Nearly ten years and thousands of kilometers separate the beginning of the narration from its conclusion. At this level of the discourse, the transformation of the character involves several specific physical changes: nakedness replaces European clothing, Núñez's skin undergoes a series of changes and, finally, callouses and other marks develop all over his body as a result of manual labor and constant exposure to the elements. These changes trace his gradual and painful adaptation to the new environment and to the social and nutritional habits of the natives. There is no qualitative difference at this level between the account in the *Naufragios* and those in other texts of the narrative discourse of failure, such as the narratives of Elvas or Castañeda. But in the *Naufragios*, together with the description of the action we find a connotative discourse whose continuity is articulated by the metaphorical projection of a series of key elements. These metaphorical elements provide the underlying structure for the literary presentation of the narrative. Within the literary presentation articulated by this connotative discourse, what the *Naufragios* offers is not a simple narrative of failure but the subjective and personal perception the narrator has of a collective cultural and ideological problematics.

The structure of this connoted discourse is circular. It starts when civilization is left behind and the plans for conquest fall apart (first shipwreck), and it continues with the metaphorical cancellation of the dominant ideology and the symbolic breakdown of European cultural values (second shipwreck). A long period of apprenticeship follows, whose different stages are signalled by the metamorphosis experienced by Alvar Núñez. The circular sequence concludes with a return to civilization. The critical presentation of this return reveals the discoveries and self-discovery of the first-person narrator in the process of redefinition of the self that begins in chapter 12 and concludes in the self-portrait implicit in chapters 32 through 34. In the eyes of this new man, the turn to a "civilization" no longer perceived as such without critical reservations constitutes the last shipwreck in the narrative.[114]

Within this symbolic projection of the narrative, the meaning of the action unfolds and multiplies. When the men kill their horses and melt down their harnesses and weapons, for example, they do so for the practical purpose of obtaining food and the tools they need to build ships. But at the same time, this action expresses the symbolic rejection of a militaristic imperial order that, within the first narratives of the conquest, was consistently represented by the weapons and the horses. Moreover, this transformation foreshadows the substitution of violence by knowledge and the final transformation of the mythical conquistador into a human being. Núñez's nakedness, the result of his second actual shipwreck, makes him more vulnerable to the physical environment. But this physical nakedness also symbolizes his break with the cultural context of Europe, which, in other accounts, was represented by clothing, and it suggests a primeval state of innocence from which the first person narrator begins a spiritual journey that will lead him toward greater humanization and a gradual transformation regarding his initial perception of American reality. Núñez's trek across the land from Florida to Mexico is a great odyssey filled with hardship and suffering, which leads him back to the "civilized" world that was both his point of departure and his final destination. But the radical change in his perception of this "civilized" world separates the Núñez at the beginning of his voyage from the Núñez at the end and, in retrospect, turns his odyssey into the metaphorical expression of a spiritual journey. This spiritual journey leads to the humanization of the conquistador and the critical demythification of the conquest. Through these transformations, the entire ideology underlying the models posited by the discourse of mythification, and so accurately reflected by these models, is thoroughly challenged. At a metaphorical level, the circular trajectory of the journey is an expression of the development of the first-person narrator. It begins with a gradual rejection of the perceptions and values of a sixteenth-century conquistador and concludes with his growing awareness, after his return to the civilized world, of his own final marginalization.

The literary nature of the mode of representation used in the *Naufragios* centers on the problematics of self-definition of the first-person narrator, which turns out to be the central focus of the narrative, and on the emergence of the metaphorical function as the central function of language and discourse. The exceptional nature that makes this work a key text in the early stages of the development of Spanish American literature derives from the central role it assigns to metaphor in the formulation and communication of the main message of the text. What is specifically literary about the narrative is not so much the introduction of fantastic episodes or the fictionalization of particular occurrences, but the fact that, at the level of language, a metaphorical space is created within which a failed expedition is transformed into the subjective expression of a highly personal experience of the ideological and cultural contradictions of an entire historical period.

Guaman Poma de Ayala finished his *Nueva Corónica y Buen Gobierno* around 1615. One of the most complex texts on pre-Columbian America and the conquest, it was not published until 1936. The *Nueva Corónica* is a unique work that combines native languages with Spanish, the written word with drawings depicting major aspects of colonial domination and of the Inca past. It is a work of central

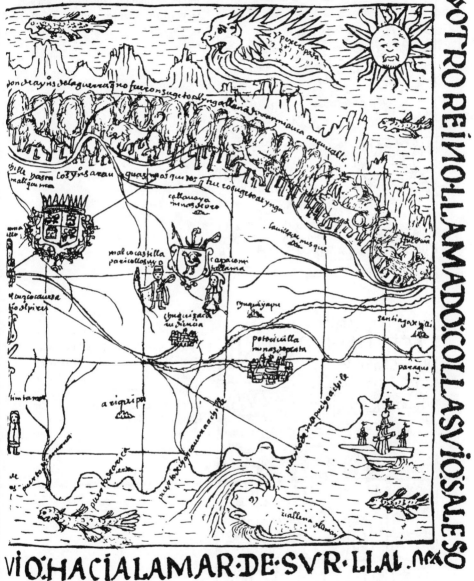

importance for the understanding of pre-Columbian realities and of the natives' experience of the conquest's tragic impact. Guaman Poma de Ayala's map of the world of the Indies incorporates the kingdoms of Antisuyo, Condesuyo, Collasuyo, Chinchaisuyo, and Chaisuyo. All photos from this work are courtesy of the Fundación Biblioteca Ayacucho, Caracas, Venezuela.

"Pontifical world / the Indies of Piru above / and Castile below the Indies." Guaman Poma de Ayala's view of the Spanish empire. From the *Nueva Corónica y Buen Gobierno*.

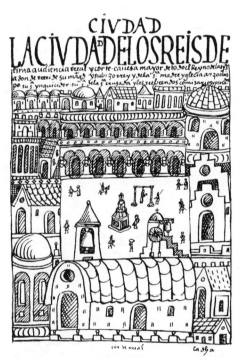

"Lima, city of the kings." Guaman Poma de Ayala, *Nueva Corónica y Buen Gobierno*, from a series of drawings representing important cities and economic centers in the kingdom of Peru.

"Town of Castrovirreina, Coycappallca, Chocllococha, silver mines, Orcoucocha." Guaman Poma de Ayala, *Nueva Corónica y Buen Gobierno*.

"How they mistreat their black slaves, women, and men." From a series of drawings by Guaman Poma illustrating different forms of violence inflicted by the Spaniards on the natives. *Nueva Corónica y Buen Gobierno*.

Guaman Poma's caption reads: "How the friars and officers of the crown mistreat the poor Indian women and men without fear of God or respect for your Majesty's justice / arrogance." *Nueva Corónica y Buen Gobierno.*

Guaman Poma's graphic representation of the plight of the natives. "The poor Indians of this kingdom surrounded by six animals they fear because they devour them: corregidor serpent, Spaniards tiger, encomendero lion, escribano cat, chieftain mouse, fox father of the doctrine / they tear the poor Indians to shreds and it cannot be helped." *Nueva Corónica y Buen Gobierno.*

From a series of drawings illustrating the behavior of the different religious orders toward the natives. "Angry, hot tempered, arrogant Augustinian friar who beats up the poor Indians of this kingdom / without fear of God or respect for justice." Guaman Poma de Ayala, *Nueva Corónica y Buen Gobierno*.

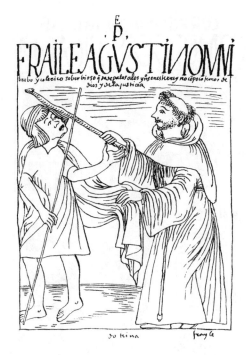

"Father, Franciscan saint who takes care of the poor all over the world and even more so in this kingdom." Guaman Poma de Ayala, *Nueva Corónica y Buen Gobierno*.

"Corregidor de minas / How he punishes cruelly the principal chieftains, governors, and judges without respect for justice, with different punishments, without compassion for the poor creatures / in the mines." Guaman Poma de Ayala, *Nueva Corónica y Buen Gobierno.*

The conquering Spanish fleet according to Guaman Poma. From a series of drawings depicting his view of the conquest. "Conquista / they sailed for the Indies / Juan Diaz de Sole's pilot / Martin Fernández Enciso / Váscones de Balboa / Colón / the Southern sea seven hundred leagues from the río de la plata." *Nueva Corónica y Bien Gobierno.*

Chapter Four

The Models in Crisis

The Search for El Dorado

On the northern continent, territorial expansion had been organized in pursuit of two central goals: the Fountain of Youth and the Seven Cities of Cibola. Every great Spanish expedition to that region had been initially inspired by one of these two mythical objectives. Although these ventures ultimately failed, they never quite succeeded in curbing the mythical impulses of a people who persisted in identifying the unknown with the imaginary things and beings of ancient legends, Native American lore, and the "lying histories" that were the rage of the time.[1]

While expansion continued toward the north, the southern continent was gradually being explored from bases established along the coast in Peru, Quito, and Venezuela. The conquistadors who led these explorations seem to have been just as creative at myth-making as those who had developed and perpetuated the tales about the wonderful fountain and the enchanted cities. Irving A. Leonard notes that:

> There is nothing to indicate that the fantastic notions so prevalent in the earlier years of the century had suffered any appreciable loss of vigor by the time the Spaniards addressed themselves seriously to the almost superhuman task of subjugating the continent of South America. Indeed, as New Spain and its hinterland failed to disclose the location of the enchanted cities, the fountains of youth, the Amazons, and the many other wonders so plainly expected, there was a disposition to shift their locale to the still more

mysterious and forbidding Tierra Firme to the south in which the unshaken faith of eager adventurers would be vindicated.[2]

Actually, more than a resurgence of the specific myths in the southern hemisphere, it was the same collective penchant for fantasy that characterized the exploration of the north that was also present in the south. Except for the story of the Amazons, which persisted for reasons to be discussed later, the myths themselves were not transferred. The conquistadors (including men like Pedro de Alvarado, Diego de Ordaz, or Alvar Núñez Cabeza de Vaca who had gone after mythical goals in the north) were more likely to formulate new myths than to transfer the earlier ones to the unknown territory they were about to explore.

The most important myths during the conquest of the southern continent were grounded on the hypothesis that there was a fabulous region located in the interior along the equinoctial line. Initially this hypothesis did not seem entirely fantastic, for it appeared to be related to one of the most credible cosmographical theories of the time: the theory of the distribution of precious metals over the globe.[3] References to this theory in texts dating from the fifteenth to the seventeenth centuries seem to confirm its importance over a long period. There is an allusion to it in a letter to Columbus from the king and queen, in 1493, in which they consult him regarding the advisability of changing the bull to include more land lying in the tropics. They speak of Portuguese reports according to which "there may be islands and even *terra firma* which, *depending on where they lie in relation to the sun,* are thought to be very fruitful and richer than any other land. And because we know that you know more about this than anyone else, we request your opinion immediately, for if it be advisable and you believe it to be as good a venture as it is thought to be here, the bull will be amended."[4]

In 1495 the prestigious cosmographer Jaume Ferrer wrote to Columbus, telling him that the area around the equinoctial line was especially rich in natural treasures: "Just around the equinox . . . precious stones, gold, spices, and medicinal plants are abundant and valuable; and I can speak of this because of my frequent commerce with the Levant, Cairo, and Damascus, and because I am a lapidary and have always been interested in learning about those places from people coming from there, and in knowing from what climate or province they bring such things. And what I have heard most often from many Indians, Arabs, and Ethiopians is that most of the good merchandise comes from a very hot climate."[5]

Anghiera devoted an entire section of his *Decades* to the subject. The heading of the section reads: "Conjecture concerning the existence of other gold, spice, and pearl producing islands in the torrid zone, besides those already known." He claimed that new lands would soon be discovered "either south of the equator or near by" and that these lands would be "rich in gold sand of the kind already discovered in the Malucas and other previously described islands." Anghiera based his conviction on "the virtue of the effect of the sun on terrestrial matter at the equinox," maintaining that if this virtue had produced such fertile land in the tropics in the area of the Malucas, it was logical to expect similar conditions to have produced similar bounty at other sites along the same latitude: "That circle is greater than all the others. Therefore if in this small area nature is as I have said so great in her art and ability that she can produce in one region the same things that she produces in another subject to similar influences, can there be any doubt that with fragrances likewise there may be somewhere under the great globe of the sky other lands endowed with the same virtues as the Maluca islands and their neighbors, some of them on the equator and others just above or below it?"[6]

The theory regarding the distribution of natural treasures—mostly consisting of precious stones and metals, but also spices in Anghiera's version—continued to be widely respected throughout the sixteenth century. It was used by Father José de Acosta to support his theory on the nature of metals: "Metals are like plants buried in the bowels of the earth and they develop in a somewhat similar fashion, for they too have trunks and branches, meaning the larger and smaller veins, which are likewise intricately coordinated. And in a sense, minerals seem to grow like plants— for they occur in the bowels of the earth as a result of the virtue and efficiency of the sun and other planets."[7] It was referred to also by the chroniclers, from Gómara, who used it to challenge claims that the tropics in the New World were poor, to Herrera, who discussed the influence of the sun and the planets on the region in his *Historia General*.

The theory of the cosmographical distribution of metals provided the scientific foundation for the belief shared by a great many conquistadors that there were fabulous regions in the interior of the continent. But the specific way in which their imagination portrayed these regions, that is, the myths that provided incentives for the explorers, were related to Native American and European legends, historical tradition, and reports by people who had dwelled in the interior or survived one or more of a long series of expeditions that set out between 1530 and 1560, mainly from Peru, Quito, new Grenada, and Paria, to conquer the vast unknown hinterland.

One of the many myths that inspired the exploration of the interior of

South America had already spurred the imagination of a large number of discoverers in the Caribbean and the northern territories (including Columbus and Cortés). It was a new version of a very old legend—the Amazons. Columbus may have been unfamiliar with Herodotus's classical tale, but he did know the version in *The Travels of Marco Polo*. Polo reconstructed Herodotus's myth in his description of two islands and the customs of the inhabitants: "one of which [islands] is inhabited by men, without the company of women, and is called the island of males; and the other by women without men, which is called the island of females. . . . The men visit the island of females, and remain with them for three successive months, namely, March, April, and May, each man ocupying a separate habitation along with his wife. They then return to the island of males. . . . The wives retain their sons with them until they are of the age of twelve years, when they are sent off to join their fathers."[8] The islands appear on Martin Behaim's 1492 map of the world, together with inscriptions describing some of their customs. Both Polo and Behaim refer to an important point that sheds some light on the important role played by the many versions of this myth throughout the conquest of America. According to the medieval version of the myth, the Amazons lived in Far East Asia and consequently were associated with the fabulous treasures presumed to exist there.

Columbus was the first to mention that there might be Amazons living in the New World (on the islands of Matinino and Carib), thus formulating the first American version of the myth and implicitly determining the function it would have for many years after the initial discovery. He did not consider the Amazons an objective as such, but they were an important piece of evidence in his set of identifications, for had he discovered them they would have given him undeniable proof of the proximity of the fabulous regions he was seeking.

After Columbus's first voyage, the Amazons were referred to frequently in narratives of expeditions that sought widely different objectives. Leonard has analyzed the development of this myth, wondered about why it was so persistent and ubiquitous, and noted its function as a means of identifying land containing treasure. He believes, however, that this function was secondary and that the discovery of the Amazons constituted a fundamental objective.[9] It seems likely, however, that the myth's extraordinary vitality and persistence was due primarily to its value as a means of identifying wonderfully rich territory. The Amazons were interesting in that their presence had been associated time and again, since the Middle Ages, with great quantities of gold, silver, and precious stones. Rather than being an objective in themselves as Leonard claims,[10] they were a sign confirming the existence and proximity of certain basic mythical objectives—from Columbus's Cipangu to Orellana's Kingdom of Omagua.

Once transferred to South America, the Amazon myth reapppeared periodically, nourished by native reports consistently misinterpreted by the Spaniards according to the terms of their own versions of the myth.[11] But it was always associated by the explorers with their own imaginary representations of the fabulous treasures of the hinterland. Some of the native reports described the matriarchal organization and customs of certain tribes in the interior, and most of them referred to the Inca virgins (called the wives of the Inca), who had consecrated their lives to the worship of the Sun. The custom attributed to the Amazons in the original myth, of keeping the girls with them while sending the boys to their fathers, became identified with the tribute of young girls and boys demanded by the Inca from his vassals. And the traditional association of the Amazons with rich treasure seemed confirmed by repeated reports of the great wealth that the Incas accumulated in the temples of the Sun—the same temples where the virgins believed by the Spaniards to be the Amazons lived, in close proximity to the fabulous objectives they all coveted.[12] The Inca Garcilaso de la Vega speaks at some length of this treasure in his *Comentarios Reales*, where he says that most of the empire's collected gold and silver was used to serve and adorn the numerous Houses of the Virgins of the Temples of the Sun located throughout the empire.

From the time of Columbus to the eighteenth century there were many versions of the Amazon myth indeed.[13] They ranged from brief references by Columbus, or by Cortés who speaks in his fourth letter of the women who lived "without a single man, and . . . at certain times men go over from the mainland and have intercourse with them; the females born to those who conceive are kept but the males are sent away,"[14] to complex, ornate elaborations as in Gaspar de Carvajal's account of Orellana's expedition along the Amazon. Describing Orellana's questioning of a native who had come from somewhere near Omagua, Carvajal says the latter claimed that there were a great many women "living about seven days inland" in up to more than seventy towns:

> they get together with Indian men when they wish to from time to time, and once they become pregnant send them back to their land without doing them any other harm; and when a child is born, if it is a son he is killed and returned to his father, and if a daughter, she is raised very solemnly and taught the things of war. He said there are enormous gold and silver treasures there, all the important ladies are served exclusively on gold and silver, and

there are many gold and silver idols in the houses with which to serve the Sun.

Carvajal even includes a physical description of what he claims to have seen with his own eyes: "Up to ten or twelve came, which is the number we saw, fighting at the head of all the men, as their captains. . . . These women are very white and tall, their hair is very long and braided around their heads, they are very long-limbed, go naked except for something to cover their private parts, and carry bows and arrows."[15]

Whether in the form of a brief remark or a detailed elaboration, however, every allusion to the Amazons is associated with the existence of fabulous treasures: gold and pearls in Cortés's fourth letter; gold mines richer than any beheld ever before according to Juan de San Martín and Alonso de Lebrija in their *Relación del Descubrimiento del Nuevo Reino de Granada*;[16] a great accumulation of gold, silver, and precious stones in Carvajal's narrative or great quantities of "white and yellow metal," according to Hernando de Ribera who maintained that "the table service and chairs in these houses were all made of this metal."[17]

Throughout the exploration of the southern continent, the itinerary of the Amazon myth was associated with that of several other mythical objectives that embodied in different ways and at different times the fabulous character of the mysterious hinterland. The presence of the Amazons—for Columbus a sign of the proximity of Marco Polo's wondrous Asia—always indicated that the men were near imaginary wonders as diverse as the land of Meta, the hidden treasure of the Incas, El Dorado, the kingdom of the Omaguas—the very mythical objectives that would continue to provide the incentive to keep pushing ahead into the wildernesses and forests of South America.

During the sixteenth century, imaginary representations of the interior underwent several fundamental transformations and reformulations, producing the series of myths that provided the main objectives of the expeditions. In 1516 a caravel in Juan Díaz de Solís's expedition was shipwrecked in the Atlantic, near Puerto de los Patos. Some of the castaways were convinced by native accounts that there was a white king and unbelievable riches somewhere in the interior. They went well into the Brazilian jungle as far as the Charcas mines, where they seized a large amount of precious metal. But only a few native slaves survived the return of the expedition, for everyone else was killed by the Brazilian natives. Those who did return, however, brought back samples of gold and silver, and the castaways who had remained at Puerto de los Patos took this as confirmation that the Silver Mountains and the Empire of the Sun did in fact exist in the interior of the continent. Thus the existence of certain real mines and references to the as yet undiscovered Inca empire provided incentives throughout the first half of the sixteenth century for expeditions into the interior of South America originating on the Atlantic coast.[18]

In 1530 Diego de Ordás was authorized to put together an expedition to the interior along the course of the Orinoco river. His initial objective was the area around the equator, which he assumed to be rich in precious metals. The expedition set out in 1531 and was a complete failure. Diego de Ordás died in 1532 without having found what he was looking for. But one of his men, Gerónimo Ortal, organized another expedition inland in 1533. Here again the objective was land near the equinoctial line, but in this case it concerned a specific, fabulously rich region about which certain vague reports had been heard during Ordás's unlucky venture. This region was the marvelous Land of Meta, in search of which many expeditions journeyed between 1533 and 1538. The final outcome was the confirmation of the existence of this mythical country. Juan de San Martín and Antonio de Lebrija, who took part in these expeditions, wrote to the king listing the many gold and emerald mines they had discovered, describing treasures in precious stones found at the temples of Tunja and Sogamoso and presenting a compilation of native reports that claimed that even more extraordinary treasures were to be had a few days' journey away, and virtually in every direction, from where the men were staying.[19]

When, in 1538, the expeditions led by Benalcázar, Federman, and Ximénez de Quesada converged on the same "six league triangle" from such distant points of origin as Peru, Venezuela, and Santa Marta, the sum of information and proof accumulated by each along the way appeared to provide complete confirmation of incalculable riches in the interior. For Ximénez de Quesada, these consisted of the treasures of the Inca, which since the conquest of Cuzco had been assumed to be distributed in more or less unlimited quantities throughout the empire. The discovery and plunder of Tunja and Sogamoso had confirmed a general belief in these mythical treasures. Moreover, taking as conclusive evidence the discovery of gold and emerald mines in the interior and information from the natives on more and better treasures in the same region, Ximénez de Quesada's expedition also confirmed the existence of the mythical land of Meta. In addition, Federman (whose army included the expeditionaries who had rebeled agaisnt Gerónimo de Ortal) had gathered information from natives all along his route concerning Meta and the vast quantities of precious stones and metals to be found there. And Benalcázar added to all this lore his account of the booty taken at Irruminari and of the existence and capture of the Golden Indian around whom the myth of El Dorado would gradually be woven.

According to Enrique de Gandía, the tale of El Dorado was first heard of in 1534, but the complete version was not put together or passed along until 1538. Gandía claims that it was precisely after the meeting of Ximénez de Quesada, Benalcázar, and Federman that "the fame of El Dorado spread rapidly over the north of South America, then down to Peru, and from there a few years later to the River Plate."[20] The legend that inspired the myth was related to a Chibcha ceremony held in a village on the shore of Lake Guativitá, which had ceased to be practiced even before the arrival of the Spaniards. During the ceremony an offering of gold and precious stones was buried by the chieftain in the waters of the lake. According to the Indian legend, the custom dated back to a time when the wife of an Indian chief who had committed adultery was so fiercely and publicly punished and put to shame by her husband that in her despair, she threw herself into the lake. Filled with remorse, the chieftain consulted his priests, who told him that his wife was living in a palace at the bottom of the lake and persuaded him to make offerings to her in the form of gold. To fulfill the ritual, the Indian chief "covered his naked body from head to toe with a very sticky turpentine, over which he poured a large quantity of fine gold powder . . . and thus bedecked he went to the middle of the lake and made offerings and sacrifices there, throwing gold pieces and emeralds into the water."[21]

Originally the myth focused on two well defined central elements: the offerings thrown into the lake, and the figure of the golden chieftain. But as time went on, "Dorado" began to be used as a preferred synonym for any region gifted with immense treasure. Hence perhaps the importance attributed to this myth by so many chroniclers and historians, who mistakenly claimed it to have been the objective of several expeditions bound for Meta, the House of the Sun, or the Inca treasures, all three of which had developed independently of the legend of the golden chieftain.

Felipe Huten left Coro in search of El Dorado in 1541, when the popularity of the myth was at its peak. He found no trace of El Dorado, but the expedition returned bearing news of another enormously rich kingdom, that of the Omaguas. Gonzalo Pizarro sailed in 1542 in search of the Land of Cinnamon, but upon hearing the latest reports of El Dorado added this objective to his plans. When he came to the Amazon he divided his expedition into two groups, and one, led by Orellana, was the first to sail as far as the mouth of the river. Describing his expedition, Father Gaspar de Carvajal spoke of the presence of the Amazons (always associated with wonderful treasures) in the proximity of the region of the Omaguas. The myth of the fabulous kingdom of the Omaguas, based on an actual province and on the discoverers' determination to find treasure in the hinterland, would later be confirmed with the arrival in Peru of the Brazil Indians. These natives claimed that they had been sailing up the Marañón toward Peru for ten years, and they "said such great things about the river and the provinces through which it passed, especially the province of Omagua; and about the large number of inhabitants and countless treasures there, that many people were inspired to go see and discover them."[22] By the time Pedro de Ursúa obtained authorization to conquer the region in 1559, the myths of Omagua and El Dorado had become fused, both referring to the rich mythical region now thought to lie not in the interior plains between Peru, Colombia, and Venezuela but in the Amazon Basin, which ever since Pizarro's expedition to the Land of Cinnamon had become the main focus of exploration.

The transfer of qualities implied in Ursúa's belief that Omagua and El Dorado were the same place was neither an isolated case nor even an exceptional one. The imaginary representations of the fabulous hinterland that emerged as South America was being explored were highly dynamic. Contacts among the expeditions and the constant dissemination of fantastic reports—absorbed first by one myth, then by another[23]—made the different versions extremely fluid. This extraordinarily dynamic quality was reflected in the way in which some of the conquistadors modified the purpose of their expeditions. Ximénez de Quesada, for example, first set out in 1536 with the intention of sailing along the Magdalena basin in search of an intercontinental connection with the South Seas. Demetrio Ramos notes that "the point was not to carry out Ordás's ideas, in regard to the route along the Gran Magdalena . . . but to attempt to reach the South Seas as proposed by Alvarado, whose purpose must have provided a powerful incentive for Fernández de Lugo."[24] But when in 1539 Ximénez de Quesada led his fourth expedition, he included in its objectives—as recorded by several of the expeditionaries—two of the most important mythical representations of the hinterland, the House of the Sun and the Land of Meta, both of which he associated with the presence of the Amazons, a sure sign of the proximity of any mythically rich territory.[25]

The statements of goals and the accounts of reports gathered during the expeditions eventually became composite formulations that merged various myths of diverse origin and heterogeneous nature with real news of actual treasures, usually from the Inca empire. Hernando de Ribera's report, certified by a notary in the presence of witnesses, on his exploration

of the Igatu River toward the end of 1537, following the orders of Alvar
Núñez Cabeza de Vaca, is one of the best examples of how all the myths
and legends about the interior that circulated at a given time could be
combined within a single account. As if the formal circumstances under
which he dictated his report were not enough to guarantee its accuracy
and objectivity, Ribera begins his narrative with a detailed description of
his careful, objective method for obtaining information:

> And traveling by foot through many Indian villages he heard and took from
> the natives there and from other Indians from places further away who had
> come to see and talk to him, a long and profuse account that he examined
> and attempted to study in detail so as to know the truth from them, as a
> man familiar with the *cario* language, through the interpretation of which
> and statements he communicated and talked with those generations and
> gathered information about the land . . . he stated that to obtain the truth
> from the said Indians and ascertain whether their statements were inconsis-
> tent, he spent an entire day and night questioning each of them in different
> ways, and they in turn all spoke and made statements among which there
> was no disagreement.[26]

The representation of the fabulous hinterland is first introduced in
Ribera's account by a complete presentation of the American version of
the Amazons. All the features to be found in the texts, from Columbus to
Carvajal and even to Herrera's *Historia*, are included: the Amazons are
female warriors governed by a woman; they are hostile toward the neigh-
boring tribes; at certain times of the year they cease their warfare temporarily to have sexual relations with natives from the regions on their
borders, whom they expel once their function has been fulfilled; they raise
and educate their daughters with great care, but send their sons to their
fathers; they possess great wealth in the form of "yellow and white metal,"
which they use to make their chairs and their table service; they live near
very rich land, and "there are very large settlements with a great many
Indians bordering on their territory."[27]

The first item around which Ribera organizes his representation of the
fabulous hinterland (suggested by the presence of the Amazons) is a lake.
In native traditions, lakes were associated with ceremonial rites and the
offering of gifts. The Chibchas and other groups in the interior considered
them holy, and the tradition of casting offerings of precious gifts into their
depths led to the development of legends such as that of the adulterous
wife of the chieftain of Guativitá. With the complex process of generation,
transformation, and reformulation of myths and reports that accompanied
the conquest, lakes also became, from the time of the conquest of Tenochtitlan and the disappearance of the Aztec treasures, a symbol of concealment

for the Spaniards.[28] But there is no question that once the explorers became aware of the Guativitá ceremony and the tale of the golden chieftain, they associated lakes with El Dorado and often thought of them as vast reservoirs of treasures accumulated as a result of long years of Indian offerings. Ribera's version, however, reflects a shift in which the lake changes from being a place where treasures are *buried*, to a natural storage place from which the Indians in the hinterland draw gold and precious stones: "And also toward the west, there was a very large lake . . . and on its borders . . . larger settlements of people who wore clothing and possessed a large amount of metal, and their clothes were embroidered with precious stones, which shone mightily, and they took these stones from the lake."[29] The lake mentioned by Ribera's natives was probably the Titicaca, which according to Gandía[30] was one of the places in South America identified for many years with the mythical El Dorado.[31]

The second central element in Ribera's representation of the fabulous interior is his description of the population living in this unexplored region. Ribera says that "just beyond the women's villages" there were other very large settlements "whose inhabitants were black and who, they said, have beards . . . similar to those of the Moors."[32] By saying that black people and men with Arabic features were living in the region, he repeats the claims of Jaume Ferrer who, in the first account ever written on the wondrous hinterland (his letter to Columbus), identified it with the equinoctial line.[33] Ferrer associated the region with treasures and a hot climate and remarked that the richest regions on the planet were likely to be inhabited by blacks and Arabs or at least be near places inhabited by people like them.

Finally, the last item around which Ribera organizes his mythical representation consists of the legendary echoes of the splendor of the Inca empire. These include references to the Amazons (perhaps a modified version of reports on the Virgins of the Sun) and to the Temple of the Sun at Lake Titicaca. Ribera also refers to the Incas themselves and their llamas: "very rich people who wore clothing, owned a large amount of metal, and raised a large number of animals with very big ears."[34]

Thus Ribera's mythical hinterland contains many features from earlier versions, brought together in a single imaginary representation. The region he describes is located in eastern Peru, but on the basis of native reports he extends it toward the north, so that it becomes necessarily associated with the mythical land of Meta searched for so assiduously by explorers from Peru, Colombia, and Venezuela, and toward the southwest and the territory of Chile, which had barely been explored at the time and was eventually to constitute the last bastion of the myth of El Dorado.

Dictated in good faith—there is no reason to believe otherwise—and based on his interpretation of the natives' replies to his elaborate questioning, Ribera's account formulated a new mythical representation of the nature of the interior. The result of his narrative was not an accurate description of South America but a rather complete synthesis of the central elements shaping the basic myths that had been encouraging the exploration of the mysterious interior. It contains a rather heterogeneous mixture of things taken haphazardly from a variety of occasionally misinterpreted reports of mythical objectives, combined with a number of native reports—some misunderstood or invented—concerning the legendary splendor of the Peru of the Incas. The formulation is interesting precisely because of its synthetic and heterogeneous nature. For in its confusion of sources and objectives, it provides a singular illustration of how these myths were generated and transmitted while the exploration and conquest of the interior of South America was underway. It reveals how extremely dynamic the imaginary component of the experience of the conquest in fact was, and it illuminates the mechanism by which vague knowledge concerning cosmographical theories, geographical descriptions, legends, myths, and personal dreams came together and combined in the minds of the conquistadors, often very subjectively, with the information provided by the natives. The result was that new myths and imaginary versions were constantly being created, of an interior whose marvels had not yet materialized, but whose fabulous nature was not only not questioned but appeared to be reaffirmed with each new formulation. The extraordinary vitality of the urge to create mythical objectives so apparent in Ribera's *relación* provides yet another example of the same process underlying the successive transformations of mythical objectives in Ximénez de Quesada's expeditions. There, a specific if nonexistent geographical objective—the search for a passage to the South Seas—was replaced by a series of increasingly complex mythical goals. In this case the reformulation took place over the course of four expeditions, but there are several instances in which specific geographic or economic objectives were progressively substituted by mythical ones in the course of a single expedition. The expedition led by Pizarro and Orellana toward the end of 1540 is a case in point.

The initial objective of Gonzalo Pizarro's expedition—the Land of Cinnamon—was the same one that aroused the interest of many other discoverers. Its existence had recently been confirmed by Díaz de Pineda.

The first reports of cinnamon in the interior dated back to 1534, shortly after Atahualpa's capture. In May 1540 Sebastián de Benalcázar obtained authorization from the emperor to explore the interior for cinnamon "or any other spice." The terms of his authorization granted him exclusive right to "the profits to be had from this spice."[35] The chronicler Oviedo describes the objectives of the expedition: "And this Benalcázar learned that there was abundant cinnamon, and when he returned from Spain to be governor of Popayan, he told me here in Santo Domingo that he believed he would find it near the Marañón river, and that it was along this river that the cinnamon was to be taken to Castille and Europe."[36]

Fray Gaspar de Carvajal confirms how Pizarro gave top priority to the search for cinnamon while planning his expedition. He states repeatedly that the expedition was inspired by "the many reports about a land where cinnamon was made"; that Pizarro and Orellana met in the province of Motín "to go after this cinnamon"; and that "After the said captain (Orellana) had come to where Governor Gonzalo Pizarro was, he set out personally to find cinnamon."[37] However, Pizarro's letter written to the king after returning from his expedition in September 1542 mentions a second objective that turns up systematically in association with cinnamon. Pizarro says that his objectives are "the province of Cinnamon and the Lake of El Dorado, both very rich and heavily populated." His account of the early part of his expedition to the interior confirms, however, that the initial goal was cinnamon and that El Dorado came later. "I attempted to ascertain where the Land of Cinnamon was from some Indians I had taken from the natives, who said they knew its whereabouts; and because it had been so widely reported and was taken to be so rich . . . I decided to look for it personally . . . and so I searched for cinnamon trees . . . for well more than seventy days."[38] When Pizarro finally reached the cinnamon region he must have been exceedingly disappointed by the land, which turned out to be full of "very rough, uninhabited and uninhabitable mountains," where the highly prized cinnamon trees are "at a very great distance from each other." In the face of such disappointment, he concluded, "Your Majesty will gain no use or service from this land or its products."[39] And it must have been in the light of this assessment that the initial objectives of the expedition were canceled and reformulated to include the mythical El Dorado to which Pizarro would refer two years later in his letter to the king. Carvajal notes the circumstances of the cancellation of the plan to look for cinnamon, in the following brief remark, "He found no land or recourse that might be of service to Your Majesty, and decided accordingly to *proceed onward*."[40]

It is unlikely that when cinnamon failed to materialize Pizarro would not have told his men that his other objective was El Dorado if so it had been. Surely the best means of boosting their morale would have been to offer a valuable substitute. The fact that he presented no more than a vague plan to "proceed onward" would seem to indicate pretty clearly that finding cinnamon had been his sole objective and that it had not yet been replaced by another one, real or mythical.

The goal of discovery soon gave way to the need to find provisions. This seems to be the reason why Orellana left the expedition, and his voyage down the river in search of food to remedy the critical situation of Pizarro and his men implied a second transformation of the original objective. The beginning of this voyage down the Marañón by Orellana and his followers marks the final stages in the cancellation of the initial objective, cinnamon, and the end of the attempt to find it. The valuable objective is first replaced by a somewhat aimless wandering, and then by a search for provisions. The process illustrated by Pizarro and Orellana's change of plans duplicates the development of the action in the narrative discourse of failure discussed earlier. But in Orellana's case, the acceptance of failure is short-lived, for as he sails down the Marañón the impulse to mythify takes over again, resulting in his formulation of a new myth about the fantastic kingdom of the Omaguas.

The first real element on which this new mythical formulation was based was the arrival of natives bearing offerings: "and they came with their jewelry and gold trays," recounts Carvajal. It was the first evidence of gold in the region, and this brief note is followed by a reference to the proximity of the Amazons, associated as always with a region endowed with rich treasure. "Here they told us about the Amazons, and the riches below," says Carvajal.[41] The samples of gold offered by the Indians and the reports confirming its existence that Orellana and his men heard as they sailed down the Marañón were to be interpreted once the expedition reached the coast of the prosperous Omagua settlements as having constituted all along a concrete premonitory sign. "There are many very large settlements next to each other, and the land was very pretty and fertile." According to Carvajal, the natives replied when questioned that "everything made of clay in those settlements was made of gold and silver further inland."[42] The mention of household objects of gold and silver links the representations of the rich kingdom of the Omaguas with the myth of the Amazons who, according to the American version, always drank and ate from bowls and vessels made of these metals. The connection between the Omaguas and other imaginary representations of the fabulous interior is further strengthened by a remark about the llamas, which Carvajal calls "the sheep of Peru" and which are always associated with legendary accounts of the Inca empire. Connected with these signs of premonition, and supported by reports from the Indians, the region of Omagua becomes thus, in Carvajal's account, a new mythical objective combining once again into a new imaginary representation all the treasures presumed to lie in the fabulous hinterland.

But Omagua is not Carvajal's only myth in his *Relación del descubrimiento del Amazonas*. Around the middle of June, Orellana and his men coasted along a region that they later named the province of San Juan, where Carvajal claims they first saw the Amazons. The mythical women are associated here as usual with gold, silver, and other riches, and are described as living in a region in the interior which shares a number of central elements with other mythical formulations. The first of these is again the llama, which Carvajal here calls a "camel." The second and far more important element, since it links Carvajal's version directly to the myth of El Dorado, is a lake, which he locates near Amazons who live near "two salt water lakes from which they produce salt." Later, describing the kingdom bordering on Amazon territory, Carvajal speaks of a land governed by a very powerful man named Arripuna "who was lord of a large amount of land up river requiring an eight days' journey to cross, to the north of which there was a lake in a densely populated area ruled by another man named Tinamaston—said to possess a great quantity of silver."[43]

This representation of the interior, tied by the mention of a lake to the myth of El Dorado, concludes Carvajal's transformation of concrete objectives into mythical ones. The tangible goal of cinnamon, the existence of which had been confirmed by Díaz de Pineda, seems to have been forgotten. Two new mythical constructs emerge to replace it, each confirmed by the nearby presence of the Amazons: Omagua, and a new version of the myth of El Dorado.

The elaborate nature of Carvajal's formulation shows just how far the collective propensity to create myths (already evident in the survival and repeated reformulation of mythical objectives that propelled the spread of the conquest toward the north)[44] encouraged and shaped the exploration of the south. Its dynamism in South America was proof of an intensity that allowed mythical objectives to persist and reemerge—as in Carvajal's account—in the face of new failures and disappointments. And in the south, the mysterious and impregnable character of the hinterland provided an ideal ground for the endless creation of new myths. Leonard refers to the mystery and fascination the unexplored interior held for the conquistadors,[45] and Gil Munilla relates the real difficulties involved in penetrating its domains to the fact that certain myths survived even beyond the eighteenth century: "This vast, hard to explore region was thought of for a long time to come as the inaccessible domain referred to in a variety of fables and myths."[46] There is no doubt that South America offered far more to inspire the creation of myths than the northern continent. Marvel-seekers in the north found themselves more often than not before a reality that left little margin for invention, and they were forced to accept it as it lay before their eyes, with its endless sky, cows, and pasturelands, none of which were very likely to inspire dreams or fables. In South America, on the other hand, the Amazons continued to elude the conquistadors despite insistent reports of their whereabouts; the silver mountains, golden hills, and emerald rocks the natives seemed to be constantly referring to never appeared; and the marvelous kingdom of El Dorado remained undiscovered, amidst a tangle of confusing, contradictory accounts claiming that it lay in the most unlikely places on the continent. But emeralds had indeed been found; mines had been discovered at Charcas; temples dedicated to the Sun by the Inca were a tangible, verified reality, as were the treasures they contained and the virgins who lived there and dined exclusively with tableware made of gold and silver. Legends and facts came together to perpetuate an essentially mythical, imaginary representation of the nature and contents of a mysterious hinterland that was to remain largely unexplored for several centuries.

From Failure to Rebellion

Gandía claims that the history of the conquest of America is the history of its myths and that the poem of that conquest is the narrative of the suffering and illusions of the conquistadors.[47] Writing along similar lines but with greater clarity and precision, Leonard notes the presence of another process that developed parallel to the creation of myths, ultimately prevailing over them: "As the exploring expeditions fanned out in the newly found continents, the resulting discoveries seldom harmonized with the rumors that launched the conquerors so eagerly on their adventures, and the progressive disillusionment slowly overtaking the Spaniards robbed the attractive myths and legends of their earlier validity. The prosaic reality fell far short of the dreams which had stirred their souls."[48]

The emergence of a Spanish American consciousness appears to be more closely connected, historically, with the rejection of myths and models than with the process of generation and formulation of myths that preceded their appearance. Failure, followed inevitably by disappointment, established a foundation for the development of a critical distance from the prevailing ideological and literary models, ultimately eliminating the imaginary structures they reflected. In the north the demythification of earlier models took the literary form of a narrative discourse of failure. This implied a degree of critical distance, from which the models of America and the conquest formulated by Columbus and Cortés were repeatedly questioned, through the narratives that articulated the process of demythification. In the south, however, although examples of this kind of discourse did emerge, there was often an added, explicit element of rebellion associated with the demythification process. Thus while the discourse in the north was organized ideologically and literarily in terms of failure, its counterpart in the south focused on rebellion. And while the former reflected an emerging critical distance and a questioning of earlier models, the latter expressed the disintegration of these models and pointed to their ultimate collapse.

Rebellion was not a new phenomenon, in the context of the conquest of America. In fact, from Cortés to Lope de Aguirre the struggle for power, booty, or survival provoked an endless series of rebellions. Initially the main cause for these rebellions had to do with the distribution of power among the conquistadors themselves. Thus during the clash between Cortés and Velázquez the power of the crown was never in question, and Cortés hastened to emphasize explicitly and repeatedly his unwavering obedience to the king. What was in question was the legitimacy of the crown's representatives, whom the rebels intended to replace.

In Peru the struggle among the conquistadors for more wealth and power led to civil war between the Pizarros and the Almagros. But no sooner had this war come to a conclusion than a long sequence of qualitatively very different rebellions got underway. These showed with increasing clarity that what was at their core was a much deeper crisis threatening the continuity of a social order that centralized all the power in the hands of an absolute monarch. The rebellion led by Gonzalo Pizarro was, among all of these, unquestionably the one with the greatest repercussions. Chroniclers of the day and subsequent historians all agree that the enactment of the New Laws of the Indies was the immediate source of Pizarro's revolt. The rigid intransigence with which Viceroy Blasco Núñez de Vela set about enforcing these laws, and his refusal to entertain any form of appeal, merely exacerbated the *encomenderos'* impulse to reject measures that undermined many of the most important privileges they had so far successfully obtained and preserved as members of the ruling class in the newly conquered territories.*[49]

The chronicler Zárate provides an enlightening description of the *encomenderos'* reaction to the New Laws:

> notification concerning the law was sent to several parts of the Indies, causing a very great disturbance among those who had conquered them, especially in the province of Peru, which is where the harm was most general for there was no one left who did not have all his property taken away from him and find himself forced again to search for food . . . moreover, when they discovered the province of Peru it was stipulated that they were to be given their Indians for life, who would then be passed on to their children or to their wives if they remained childless . . . and that it was not fair for them to have their property taken away from them now that they were old and tired, and of neither an age nor state of health to go out in search of new lands and things to discover.[50]

Zárate's description is interesting not so much for its objectivity—which is extremely dubious in view of his evident sympathy for the *encomenderos*—but rather because it expresses this class's perception of the conquest, of the rights acquired by the conquistadors, and of what they believed the New Laws meant for them.[51] Initially the stated objective of Gonzalo Pizarro's rebellion was to force an appeal of the New Laws and to suspend their application pending a new royal decision that would take into account the claims of the *encomenderos*. Marcel Bataillon notes that the violence of the rebellion was as charged with meaning as it was ambiguous, and he stresses that "the protest against the New Laws, which were rejected by the conquistadors because they represented a denial of their acquired rights and a violation of the agreements reached previously with the monarch, was primarily a legal facade for the crisis."[52] Rather than a clash between the king and the *encomenderos* who opposed the laws protecting the natives, the crisis involved a conflict between the social order supported by the *encomenderos*, and a new one under which the *encomiendas* would be gradually eliminated and the natives would become the vassals of the king. Although Pizarro's rebellion made a point of carefully avoiding any proclamation of its true separatist objectives,[53] the fact that he kept his forces ready for action even after receiving the representatives of the *Audiencia* who had come to advise him that "the King had suspended any application of the ordinances and granted their appeal"[54] amounted to a veiled declaration of a change of purpose. By refusing to lay down his

---

*_Encomiendas_ were awarded in recognition of service in the conquest of new territories, which involved the privilege of collecting tribute and drafting labor among a specified group of Indians.—TRANS.

arms upon the arrival of the *Audiencia* ambassadors, Pizarro's position changed radically. Rather than simply leading a movement ideologically compatible with the established order, he became the head of a rebellion whose decidedly subversive character was a threat to the central pillar of the social and political system represented by the king. This change in the rebellion from a movement in defense of certain claims under the law to a patently secessionist uprising is made perfectly clear in the letter written to Gonzalo Pizarro by Don Pedro de la Gasca, in September 1546. In a masterly presentation of his arguments, La Gasca starts out by discussing Pizarro's revolt in benevolent terms apparently approved by the king himself in his own letters;[55] he goes on to demonstrate the divine origins and natural character of the social relationship that subordinates a vassal to his king and the king only to God; he deduces with impeccable logic that the established order is consistent with the natural order; defines any rebellion against the order presided over by the king as a prelude to chaos; and concludes with a rather explicit warning concerning the harshness of the punishment that will befall anyone who decides to choose so manifestly mistaken a path.

Gonzalo Pizarro was beheaded, Carvajal was drawn and quartered, and the rest of Pizarro's loyal followers were hanged. But rebellions continued to occur in different parts of the territory of South America. Repression of the Pizarro uprising did not solve the problem. Moreover, the distribution of favor by La Gasca at the end of the campaign against the rebels, in strict compliance with instructions from the crown, was yet another aggravation added to the long list of injustices and causes for insatisfaction already afflicting many of the conquistadors. Pero López, who took part in the campaign on the side of the loyalists and benefitted from the distribution of favors, remarks that "Gasca treated His Majesty's servants badly. He left them all poor, and to many who had been on Pizarro's side he gave what they had and a lot more. So that what he took from us he gave to them. He satisfied everyone: His Majesty's servant with words; his enemies with deeds;"[56] and this appears to have been confirmed by several contemporary chroniclers.

The reports, dispatches, and chronicles show that it was no longer disillusionment that prevailed among the Spaniards in South America after the Pizarro rebellion. Disappointment over the unjust distribution of favors by La Gasca was reinforced by the negative implications—in regard to the prerogatives of the *encomenderos*—of the final victory of the loyalists. Bataillon maintains that "it can be held without undue oversimplification that the most patent result of La Gasca's victory was that it firmly established the King of Castille as the sole authority with regard to the distribution of Indians among the Spaniards in the lands already conquered, and to the concession of any territory conquered in the future. The latter would, henceforth, no longer be referred to as 'conquests' but as entries or 'discoveries.'[57] Unlike what happened in the north, disillusionment soon ceased to be the prevailing sentiment in South America and became merely one of the many sources of general growing discontent, which took the form of endless rebellions and uprisings during the period from 1544 to 1559.[58]

The specific objectives of each rebellion provided a catalyst for the increasingly active dissatisfaction stemming from the growing frustration felt by most of the conquistadors as they came in contact with American reality and gradually lost any hope of seeing their fantastic expectations materialize. As the objectives of the rebellion were redefined, they moved further away from the simple goal of distributing power more equitably among the conquistadors (which would not have necessarily affected the foundation of the established order) and began to indicate an increasingly clear intention to secede and break the ties with the power structure embodied in the figure of the king. And while Pizarro never dared to be entirely explicit about the real purpose of his revolt,[59] when the Contreras brothers' rebellion erupted in Panama shortly thereafter, the shout that rallied the followers, "Liberty, liberty for Hernando de Contreras, Captain General of Liberty!," left no further doubt regarding the character of a movement that had come to equate its program with a global rejection of a political system no longer considered acceptable. The chronicler Juan Calvete y Estrella summarizes the rebels' intentions:

> they designed to kill the Bishop of Nicaragua in his home . . . and steal the royal property and rise up with as many people as possible; and go together to the mainland where they knew there was a large quantity of gold and silver belonging to the Emperor, and steal it and occupy the province; and build ships and set sail in them in January of the following year, 1551, and pillage and put fire to Panama, Nombre de Dios, and Nata, and destroy all the livestock there, to prevent the Emperor from being able to send people against them; and take the ships and go to Peru with everything they had stolen, and with the additional people who joined them rise up in the province of Peru and make Hernando de Contreras king and lord thereof; and they would build two galleys and man and arm them with blacks amounting to more than six hundred men from the three above towns; and with these galleys and other ships they would sail along the coast of Nicaragua, Guatemala, and New Spain, allowing no vessel there to escape being burned and sunk to the bottom.[60]

The general feeling of discontent reflected by the rebellions led the authorities to take a measure that was to modify the character of the new expeditions and profoundly alter the composition of the armies sent to explore the interior. The measure came to be referred to as "the unburdening of the land."* Zárate refers in his chronicle to the application of this practice after the Salinas war and discusses the rationale behind it: "And seeing that there was no way of satisfying those who had served him, because each of them believed that an entire governorship was not sufficient payment, he decided to disassemble the army and send the people off to new places that were known to have been discovered, by which means he accomplished two things: his friends were remunerated and his enemies banished. And so he sent Captain Pedro de Candia off with three hundred men of his own and those of Don Diego to conquer land whose treasures were much discussed."[61] In Candia's case, as in many others, the expedition was a failure and Candia returned with "all the people on the verge of mutiny."

It is easy to imagine how explosive the mood in the colonies was becoming as a result of the accumulation of frustrated expectations and failures. It was not simply that the failure to locate certain specific mythical objectives forced the men to reconsider their mythical view of American reality, as had occurred in the north. Here the expeditions were already seen as a compensation for earlier disappointments, and the personal implications of failure went beyond the disappointment of expectations related to "treasures": they added to a vicious circle of frustrations and disenchantments that was bound to explode into a radical challenge of every aspect of the conquest—economic, political, and social. La Gasca refers over and over again, in his correspondence with the Council of the Indies, to the danger represented by the presence of so large a number of unsatisfied, idle conquistadors in Peru, and he reiterates the pressing need to "unburden the kingdom" of people for whose just compensation there were no means, by sending them off on a variety of exploratory expeditions.[62] The result was, however, that from that time on the people from the most unsatisfied, explosive sector of the population were likely to be the ones sent out on missions of discovery, making the composition of the expeditions very different from those in the north. Their members were those "disruptive men," that "unruly phalanx," mentioned by Aristides Rojas in his *Historia de Venezuela*. This change in composition produced in the expeditions a tradition of uprisings similar to the ones that were shaking the colonies.

Basing his analysis mainly on Martín de Guzmán's uprising against

* "*La descarga de la tierra*"—TRANS.

Governor Heredia in Cartagena de Indias, Demetrio Ramos Pérez emphasizes that economic factors motivated most of these uprisings and rejects the notion of any important ideological goal. He notes the connection between failure and rebellion characteristic of so many unsuccessful expeditions in the south, as opposed to the simple recognition of failure in the north. And, indeed, in the south failure does appear to have been the direct cause of rebellion. Ramos summarizes the circumstances of the Heredia expedition just before the revolt: "Martín de Guzmán and his companions have taken part in a venture that has failed: their search for the source of the gold found buried in the graves at Cenu has been futile."[63] A failure of this nature was complicated by the way in which the expeditions were funded. The conquistadors usually incurred heavy debts in order to finance their participation in an expedition. Consequently, besides their disappointment at not finding the wonders they expected, failure often signaled total bankruptcy. This meant that they could not join another expedition that might help them, through the discovery of treasures, to remedy a situation that for many had become quite desperate. Within this context the increasing confusion between the economic and political motives that fueled individual uprisings was inevitable. Ramos Pérez sheds some light on this issue: "the confusion between political and economic motives arises from the fact that, in the context of the economic organization of the expeditions, and because the governor in charge of them identified his interests with those of the manager of the company formed with his own soldiers, any internal economic opposition or disagreement was seen inevitably as a political move against authority."[64]

Uprisings became frequent enough to establish a tradition, which foreshadowed certain aspects of the rebellion of the *Marañones** against Pedro de Ursúa. They became so widespread that even Francisco de Orellana was harshly accused of having planned to "rise up and take off with the brigantines"[65] when in fact he had started down the Marañón under express orders from the governor of the expedition, Gonzalo Pizarro. This accusation was even supported by Fernández de Oviedo, who claimed that although Orellana had told him personally that "he could not return because the river he had sailed into was so cold . . . others say that had he wished to he could have come back to where Gonzalo Pizarro was waiting; and I too believe this"; he adds, "for reasons to be seen further ahead."[66]

Of this long sequence of rebellions, the one known as the rebellion of

---

*Name given to the rebels who joined with Lope de Aguirre against Pedro de Ursúa, killing him and proclaiming as prince of Peru Fernando de Guzmán, whom they subsequently killed also.—TRANS.

the *Marañones* is especially interesting. This is not just because it represents the historical convergence of the two central manifestations of the general mood of discontent in Peru: uprisings and revolts seeking primarily economic objectives on the one hand, and rebellions related to fundamentally political goals on the other. The revolt of Lope de Aguirre and his *Marañones* provides a particularly illuminating illustration of the crisis of centralized power that was shaking the colonies and of the revolt against the dominant economic and political system. In this uprising, the crisis that was at the core of increasingly strong secessionist tendencies manifested itself with a complexity and clarity that revealed and summed up most of the central elements of previous uprisings. Its condensed quality gives it a particular ideological interest, for it is as if this single, clearly defined episode contained all the complex problematics that had exploded with periodic futility into all the rebellions and uprisings that shook South America from the time of the first civil wars in Peru: perpetual hunger, debt, the desperate circumstances of the expeditionaries; their drastically harsh living conditions; the progressive disappearance of the illusions embodied in their imaginary representations of the hinterland; the cancellation of their mythical objectives; social inequality, leading to growing opposition between the privileged class of victorious conquistadors represented by Ursúa and the multitude of obscure, dispossessed hidalgos represented by Aguirre; constant injustice in the distribution of favors and positions; and the increasing discontent felt by many expeditionaries who, like Aguirre, had already participated in other revolts.[67] All these elements, which had been associated individually with various earlier uprisings, came together in Ursúa's expedition, where they provided the foundation for the formulation and development of the program of the revolt up to the time of its final defeat.

Quite a few documents narrating Ursúa's expedition and the uprising of Aguirre and his *Marañones* have been preserved. There are at least ten accounts written by participants in the expedition. To these one should add numerous statements and reports presented to various legal authorities by eyewitnesses to the events on Margarita Island and the mainland. Finally, we have several letters written by the local authorities in reference to the events and three letters from Aguirre himself: one to Father Montesinos, another to Governor Collados, and a third to King Philip II.

In addition to sharing the same subject, the ten main accounts also share certain structural features that define them as different voices within a single narrative discourse. Unlike the narrative discourse of failure exemplified by Alvar Núñez in the north, this discourse does not confine itself to recognizing the inadequacy of the earlier models and developing a critical distance. It is a new narrative mode that essentially takes up where the discourse of failure left off. Its representation of reality is grounded in a radical subversion of the ideological models rejected by the discourse of failure. The criticism and rejection developed gradually by the discourse of failure reaches its final and irrevocable stage in the discourse of rebellion.

In the context of this new mode—the discourse of rebellion—the point of departure in the cancellation of the American myth formulated by Columbus is the same as in the narrative discourse of failure: a rejection of the expeditionaries' mythical objectives. All the *relaciones* state that the mythical kingdoms of Omagua and Dorado (occasionally referred to as one and the same) were the objectives of the expedition, and most claim as their source of information on these mythical objectives the famous "Brazil" natives who had come to Peru a short time earlier. According to these natives, the two fabulous kingdoms were located in the region of the Amazon basin. They were associated with other reports of great amounts of gold, silver, and other treasures, and large areas densely populated by natives. The identification of El Dorado with Omagua was generally believed to have been confirmed by reports from the expedition of Governor Juan de Salinas. This recent expedition had failed to explore the area because of the rough slopes leading down to the North Sea, but the expeditionaries intended to return there "because of all the reports of people, gold, and silver that [Salinas] had heard [while sailing] downriver along the Marañón."[68]

In contrast to the discourse of failure, mythical objectives in the discourse of rebellion are rejected very quickly. Any brief initial mention of such objectives is soon displaced by a detailed critical description of an intolerable reality. The experience of this reality makes it very difficult to fantasize, and pushes the men toward rebellion. American nature, which turned out to be much harder to withstand in the Amazon basin than anywhere else on the continent, overwhelmed the expeditionaries with its multitude of tributaries, lakes, marshes, estuaries, and immense quantities of rainfall. Even while at the camp where the sailing vessels were being built, those who wrote about the experience refer over and over again to the swarms of insects, the stifling heat, the constant rainfall, the rot that decays everything: clothes, food, and even the hulls and lines of the newly built brigantines and barges. The presence of nature as a hostile force to be reckoned with obsesses the men from the outset, and the intensity of this obsession prevents them from focusing on anything else. In the face of this daily torment, made even worse by the miserable living conditions and the brutality that marks all interaction among people in an expedition consisting of, as they were called, men (Spanish and white), blacks (all of them slaves), and pieces (native), the "best and richest land of Peru"[69] presumed to lie downriver begins to seem unreal. This reversal of the relative weight of fact and myth in favor of the former is reflected by the way in which the texts very briefly mention the original mythical objectives—in a rather formulaic and introductory fashion—and then immediately detail daily reality in all its unendurable dimensions. It is the experience of this reality that determines the ultimate transformation of the objective from the discovery of Omagua and El Dorado into a plan to secede through the conquest and emancipation of Peru.

The detailed description of the experience of the environment now becomes—for the first time in the development of the discourse of the conquest—a primary, as well as typical, aspect of the narrative discourse of rebellion, canceling for good the model of reality formulated in the *Letters* of Cortés. In the latter, reality was always presented in flattering Utopian terms. The idealized character attributed to the Spaniards in the epic struggle was heightened by a complete silencing of any conflict that could not be considered appropriate in terms of the "just war" against the Aztecs. Cortés presented himself as a model among vassals; his army as an extension of his attributes and the agent of his power; and the entire Spanish side as a monolithic body united by its epic goal, an orderly, harmonious unity up against an enemy divided by conflict, betrayal, and intrigue. Anything that might be considered conflict-ridden or problematical was associated in his letters with either the natives or the invaders who—like Narváez or Velázquez—sought to threaten the order created and held together by his mythical self-characterization. The narrative discourse of failure, on the other hand, canceled this epic model through a representation that involved a gradual redefinition of objectives and functions. But the collapse of the Spaniards as an organized, disciplined force always appeared to be a result of the disappointment of mythical expectations and the realization of the unreal nature of Cortés's models. In the presence of an antiheroic daily reality composed of hunger, mosquitoes, swamps, and buffaloes peacefully grazing on limitless pasturelands, mythical objectives and epic models lost their meaning. Thus the narrative discourse of failure reflected the need to come to terms with a reality different from the one anticipated, and it portrayed the growing humanization of the conquistador as he adjusted to his new situation. The key demythifying element was reality. Its effect was to reveal the fictional nature of the epic model. The discourse of failure did not engage in a systematic critique of the harsh realities of the conquest so successfully idealized in Cortés's writings, but simply pointed out the inaccuracy of this idealization.

In the discourse of rebellion, on the other hand, recognition that the models have failed is a starting point toward a qualitative change in perception. These texts do not simply question the inadequacies of the earlier models. They also reveal the complex reality underlying them and are openly critical of the ideological, political, social, and economic order they have served to mythify. Conflict is presented from the very outset as existing among the Spaniards themselves rather than just between the Spaniards and the natives. The *Relación anónima* makes this explosive atmosphere evident, referring over and over again to the "gossiping," "friction," and tension that characterized the relationship among the Spanish members of the expedition.[70] Custodio Hernández discusses the question of gossip and rumors obsessively in his *Relación*. He confirms the remarks in the *Relación anónima* concerning the "considerable gossip" caused by the arrival in the camp of Inés de Atienza and adds that her presence there was yet another source of conflict, for "Ursúa loved her so much that he clearly lost his head over her, and the soldiers said that he must have been bewitched. The most malevolent among them gossiped a great deal about this and other things, while others didn't care one way or another."[71] Hernández actually comes to replace altogether the word "speak" by "gossip," an effective stylistic means of conveying the dissatisfied, even conspiratorial atmosphere at the camp. It is Francisco Vázquez and Pedrarias de Almesto, however, who capture this atmosphere most thoroughly. Pedrarias speaks of "tumultuous, licentious behavior and above all, the neglectful way in which the camp was governed," of the constant "lies and inventions" spread about by "evil men desirous of causing a mutiny."[72] Vázquez refers to the "great enmity" provoked by envy over any differences in the assignment of positions or duties.[73] Both men relate all this to the mutinous atmosphere prevailing in the camp: "we set out downriver exceedingly dissatisfied . . . and also as we were leaving, there were some mutinies, aside from the fact that the men wanted to return to Peru; realizing this, the Governor made some arrests and, disguising his intentions, set sail without giving anyone a chance to escape."[74] And Vázquez mentions that differences of opinion with Don Juan led to "some mutinies" against him.[75]

Pedrarias and Vázquez are the only expeditionaries who make any explicit connection between the rebellious atmosphere of Ursúa's expedition from the start and the policy of "unburdening the land" mentioned earlier:

> There were at his camp some soldiers who had wanted to revolt and return to Peru; also, certain frustrated traitors who had taken part in several riots in Peru against His Majesty's service, some of whom had fled here as a last resort to hide from the authorities who were looking for them because of their crimes and treachery. Other would-be rioters had come because it was said publicly in Peru that Governor Pedro de Ursúa was gathering men together not for an expedition but to fall upon Peru, and that the Viceroy supported this plan.[76]

Everything that is associated from the beginning of the discourse of rebellion with a rejection of the Cortés model is covered in this passage. The dispute has occurred within the Spanish camp, which has become fragmented, its members divided and in conflict; the model centered on the vassal relationship is crumbling, in the face of revolts against the king and evidence that a tradition of discipline and obedience is giving way to rebellion and insubordination; and the expedition's mythical objectives appear to have been intertwined from the outset with a design for political insurrection. (According to Vázquez the rumors that openly attributed this design to Ursúa and Cañete were precisely what attracted many of the participants to Ursúa's expedition.) Thus two traditions converge here, one related to the search for mythical objectives in the interior, the other to rebellions reflecting a general sense of dissatisfaction over the economic and political situation in the colony. And the issues at the source of these rebellions appear to have been transferred to the expeditionary forces as a result of the policy of unburdening the land, which continued to channel the energies of those most likely to cause social and political conflict toward the discovery of the interior.

In the narrative discourse of rebellion, the rejection of the system of vassalage and the substitution of the mythical objective of discovery and conquest by revolt and secession provide the point of departure for a qualitatively different representation of the social reality of the conquest. The first effect of this substitution of goals is the unleashing of violence. In Cortés's model, violence had been conceived as a controlled, necessary instrument in the epic effort to conquer the natives and had been channeled accordingly. It was directed outward, never against the members of one's own camp. In the narrative discourse of failure, violence became a mere defense against a hostile environment. By the end of the *Naufragios*, moreover, the use of violence had been radically questioned as Núñez proposed that it be eliminated altogether in favor of a more civilized means of establishing a relationship with the natives—a relationship that did not need to be inherently conflictive. But in the narrative discourse of rebellion, violence is unleashed. It is directed against everything and everybody, and the systematic, constant use of it is both an expression and an instrument of discontent and of the desire to reject everything and everybody who supports the established order. In a situation in which all relationships appear alienated and corrupt, it becomes impossible to reach any compromise or to establish any sort of pact, commitment, or bond of loyalty.

The destructive and at the same time revealing character of this violence is apparent in the pattern of its use throughout the discourse of rebellion. First, it is directed against the authority of the king in the person of Ursúa: Ursúa is assassinated, and replaced by the liberator, prince Don Fernando, a new authority chosen by the rebels. But this second authority figure is likewise assassinated, and violence becomes fratricidal, remaining thus throughout the long period during which the *Marañones* systematically assassinate one another. In the last stage, Aguirre takes almost exclusive control of the expedition, and his violence is in the end directed against himself through the murder of his own daughter Elvira.

The solidarity that characterized the army in Cortés's model is progressively turned by this violence into intimidation, blackmail, aggression, and fear. These come to shape all human interaction once the ideological structure underlying the discourse of mythification has been implicitly destroyed by injustice, violence, and oppression. In this last form of the discourse of demythification, the epic order fictionalized by Cortés is replaced by the chaos of terror; his Utopian representations of a world organized in terms of an idealized concept of honor, justice, discipline, and obedience under the law are challenged here by a critical presentation of violence, rivalry, injustice and corruption. This view both cancels Cortés's model and reveals the irreversible decadence of the chivalrous medieval ideological model he implicitly invoked in his mythifying discourse. The fact that the center of the conflict lies in the Spanish camp itself, and that violence is directed by the conquistadors against one another instead of toward an external enemy, implied a final rejection of the epic model of action. In the narrative discourse of failure, this form of action had already been forced to give way to a struggle for survival, as it led to the consequent redefinition of incentives, objectives, and functions. This redefinition, on the other hand, had led to a progressive replacement of the heroic model by a humanized image of the conquistador as a vulnerable being, a castaway lost and unable to adapt to an unknown and hostile land.

Some of these elements persist in the discourse of rebellion, but their relative importance in the redefinition of the original enterprise changes drastically. The narrators refer incessantly, from the outset, to the hostility of nature; the harsh living conditions; the lack of water, provisions, and ships; and to hunger as a daily affliction that, to a degree, determines the very development of the expeditions. Custodio Hernández notes that even before setting out downriver, "the men working on the brigantines had eaten the horses, and people were suffering from great hunger and a lack of salt."[77] Pedrarias says that "there were many who had nothing to eat but some reeds they found along the beach,"[78] and Gonzalo de Zúñiga describes his anxiously awaited meeting with Juan de Vargas, who had sailed off in search of food to remedy the critical situation of the members of the expedition: "And we each had so little to satisfy our hunger that we walked all over the wilderness, eating turtle eggs and an occasional bit of fish; and the camp lived mostly on alligators, which we shot with our harquebuses."[79]

Rather than a primary incentive, however, necessity appears to have been simply one more factor reinforcing the real motive of the action described in these texts: *discontent*. In fact, the discontent is discussed by all the chroniclers as an overriding sentiment among the Spaniards even before their physical needs became a problem. According to the accounts, it is constant from the very beginning, leading to diverse forms of indiscipline, violence, and rioting. Any single incident appears to warrant an eruption: the arrival of Inés de Atienza; disappointment over the distribution of positions; the loss of horses and stores abandoned because the ships were riddled with rot; or the failure of the expeditions' mythical objectives to materialize. And discontent progresses from indiscipline to rebellion, gradually becoming the bond that brings the rebels together and impels them to action. Not a trace is left of fame and glory as the goals for action and, with their disappearance, the projects traditionally associated with them vanish likewise. There is no room in the critical context of the discourse of rebellion for an epic plan designed to glorify the values of the established order. Instead, action is directed precisely against this order, with the ultimate intent of destroying it.

The formulation of this plan for destruction comprises three clearly differentiated stages. The first runs from the beginning of the expedition to the death of Ursúa: the rebellion against Ursúa focuses on a redistribution of rights, privileges, and benefits, without necessarily implying a change in the foundations of the established order. The point is not to eliminate authority, but to replace a king's representative whose reliability is considered questionable by another considered more just. In this regard, the first phase of the rebellion may be compared to that of Pizarro's insurrection. Its reformist character is explicitly noted in the accounts: "they had not yet declared themselves unwilling to serve the King; rather, they believed that by looking for land in the service of His Majesty, they would be pardoned. Most of the officers and captains at the camp, including the other allies as well as those who had killed the governor, agreed that they should search for the land referred to in Pedro de Ursúa's instructions and settle it, and that for this service His Majesty would forgive those who had killed the good Pedro de Ursúa."[80] Up to this point, the goals of the uprising appear to be limited to a reformist program. The plan for the discovery remains unchanged, as does the recognition of royal authority; and this may explain why during the distribution of positions following the assassination of Ursúa (the only practical measure resulting from the first stage of insurrection), Diego de Valcázar should have stated publicly, upon being appointed chief justice, "that he accepted the office in the name of King Philip, our lord."[81]

The second stage begins with the election of Don Fernando who, after being confirmed in his new role as leader of the expedition by most of the soldiers refers for the first time to the replacement of any mythical objective by a design to secede: "he said that anyone wishing to continue fighting the war against Peru, as he and his companions were determined to do, should sign and swear to follow him . . . and, unanimously in agreement about the war in Peru they were engaged in, they swore to help and favor each other, and promised that there would be no rancor or revolts among them nor would they oppose the others."[82] This is the first time since the beginning of the expedition that the conquistadors appear to be united in a common cause, but this cause is no longer concerned with the epic design to discover and conquer. On the contrary, its goal is to destroy this design and to "reconquer" Peru and free it from the sovereign power of Spain. The action in this second stage reaches its climax with the proclamation of Don Fernando de Guzmán as, "by the Grace of God, Prince of the Mainland and Peru and Governor of Chile." The implications of this proclamation, which absolutely destroy the ideological and political model underlying the discourse of mythification, become explicit in the following statement by Lope de Aguirre to his soldiers, included in the various narratives of the rebellion: "the best means of giving the war a better foundation and more authority would be to take Don Fernando de Guzmán henceforth for their King. For the purpose, they would have to relinquish their bonds with the kingdom of Spain and refuse to serve as vassals to King Philip; and he himself declared that he had never seen the latter, did not know him, and neither wanted him for his King nor held him to be so."[83] This second phase, with its clear plan to reject royal authority, break off the vassal relationship, emancipate Peru and the mainland, and establish an independent parallel monarchy in the emancipated territory, ends with the assassination of Don Fernando de Guzmán.

Don Fernando's death at the hands of Aguirre and his followers—which implies the elimination of the political model centered on the figure of a king and an end to the plan to establish an independent parallel monarchy—introduces the third stage. What the rebels now envisage is a form of government led jointly by an aristocratic group of conquistadors, which Aguirre considers himself to represent. This is the aristocracy that is to occupy and control all positions of power in the colony. With all forms of established authority symbolically liquidated as a result of the death of Don Fernando, what follows is a proposal for the egalitarian distribution of booty among this group of marginalized conquistadors, a dramatic reversal from their earlier deprivation. This is to be the first measure implemented following the institution of a government of *Marañones*: "It is my wish to see you all very prosperous, with Peru in your hand to divide as you desire. Leave things to me and Peru will be ruled and governed by *Marañones*, and there will be not a one among you who is not a captain in Peru ruling over other men . . . all I ask is that no one conceal anything or spread secrets, so that we may live safely and free from insurrection. And if you will be my friends, I will see to it that new Goths like those who ruled in Spain arise from the Marañón to govern Peru."[84] Aguirre's stated intention followed by his appeal for solidarity to the rebels, who appear united in their plan to destroy the established order and liberate Peru and the mainland, his call for harmony and the cessation of rebellious action conclude in this speech with the formulation of an unmistakably reactionary, anachronistic political plan, made more explicitly so by his allusion to the Goths as the models that have inspired it.

The last step in the demythification process carried out in the discourse of rebellion involves the elimination of the heroic model of the warrior-hero created by Cortés. Cortés's had emerged in his letters as an absolutely flawless, invulnerable mythical figure: a perfectly consistent human representation of the prevailing ideological and political order that the writer proposed to expand and glorify. In the narrative discourse of failure, on the other hand, this mythical figure had become increasingly problematical: his invulnerability and coherence were gradually replaced by frailty. The demythifying process showed his increasing humanity, and his experience of doubt, indecision, and suffering. By the end of his ordeal he had come to symbolize the displacement of aggression by understanding. In the discourse of rebellion, the model of the conquistador is eventually banished once and for all. This final elimination continues the demythification of the narrative discourse of failure, but rather than simply portraying the conquistador's progressive humanization, it goes on to redefine him as a reflection of the problematics that shaped the enterprise of the conquest. There are two sides of this redefinition. The first has to do with the degradation of all the representatives, within this discourse, of a class of conquistadors consistent with Cortés's model; the second, with the characterization of the figure of the rebel.

In the accounts of the Marañón rebellion, the disintegration of the model of the conquistador centers on the characterization of Pedro de Ursúa and Fernando de Guzmán. From the beginning, there is an implicit contrast established between the characterization of Ursúa and earlier portraits of the same man. Custodio Hernández remarks on the difference between Ursúa as he was *before* the expedition and what he has become *now*, claiming that he has been bewitched by Doña Inés. Francisco Vázquez refers to the change in similar terms, saying, "and they meant that his friend Doña Inés had somehow made him change and had bewitched him."[85] Gonzalo de Zúñiga says that before going to Omagua, Pedro de Ursúa "had been the captain best loved by all his soldiers and everyone else than any man could be, everywhere he went."[86] And Francisco Vázquez is even more explicit in his characterization of the early Ursúa, providing a model and yardstick against which all the accounts of the expedition implicitly contrast his subsequent decadence. "He was very kind, good in his actions and in his conversation, and a very affable companion to his soldiers . . . he treated his soldiers well and very politely. He was more merciful than strict. He was extremely skilled at horsemanship . . . above all, he served His Majesty faithfully and well. . . . As long as he had these qualities he was always well liked and loved by everyone."[87]

Until he set out on the much coveted journey to Omagua and El Dorado, granted precisely in recognition of his outstanding service record, Pedro de Ursúa's life had indeed been that of an exceptional man, a model among conquistadors. Thirty-five years old at the time, he was considered one of the most prestigious conquistadors of his day. This was owing as much to the personal qualities referred to by Vázquez as to his military and political background, which included pacifying and conquering the hostile Muso Indians and the natives in the hills of Tairona; quelling the black revolt in Panama in 1556, by order of the Marquis of Cañete; and founding the cities of Pamplona and Tudela in the territory he had conquered and pacified. The *Relación anónima* states that "he was of very good appearance, 35 years of age, a man of a very good family, and very skilled at war," adding that the Viceroy had granted him so desirable an expedition because of his "great good will toward him, realizing that this gentleman from Navarre would be up to even greater ventures."[88] The disintegration of this model figure is apparent from the outset in the texts of the discourse of rebellion, which consistently point out the lack of correspondence between the Ursúa everyone had expected based on his excellent reputation and the man they actually met. All agree in noting a change so evident and so inexplicable that they attribute it either to the spell of Doña Inés (Hernández) or to a possible illness (Pedrarias and Vázquez). Vázquez is as usual the most explicit in his rendering of the difference between the real Ursúa and the model:

> He indulged in certain vices and bad habits, although it was believed that it was mostly his friend Doña Inés who made him do so . . . from having been very affable and full of conversation for everybody, he had become rather serious and dull and avoided all conversation . . . he had begun to keep to himself and lived alone with Inés as far away as possible from what was going on in the camp, with the sole purpose, so it seemed, of preventing anyone from disturbing his love affair, which appeared to have him so entranced that he had forgotten all about the matters of war and discovery.[89]

The last sentence summarizes the fundamental change in Ursúa. Not only does he no longer fit the model of the conquistador, since he has put aside war and exploration (the activities that perfectly embody the two basic aspects of the epic venture), but he has chosen to devote himself to the satisfaction of his personal desires (thus breaking another basic rule associated with the model, whose interest was always to be subordinated to that of the community and identified with the will of the king). In the discourse of rebellion the destruction of the model of the conquistador begins with a "spell" or "change in condition" and follows the lines of the increasingly negative characterization of Ursúa. The mythical warrior vanishes, giving way to a figure that is temperamental, arbitrary, sensual, selfish, unskilled, arrogant, inconsistent, and irresponsible: the opposite of the qualities posited by the myth. The *Relación anónima* remarks on Ursúa's abusiveness and disposition to deceive people; Gonzalo de Zúñiga criticizes his lack of foresight and his arrogance, noting his "kind words" as a sign of an inclination toward manipulation and deceit. And even Vázquez, more favorably disposed toward him than the others, acknowledges that he is uncharitable, ungrateful, false, and neglectful in his management of the camp. Ursúa's new personality represents a violation of the rules defining the character of a warrior, a Christian, and a leader that had shaped the hero of the discourse of mythification; his behavior represents a betrayal of the ideological code governing the comportment of Cortés's mythical vassal and discredits the model that had guided the epic warrior in all his designs and modes of action.

The last stage in the liquidation of the model of the conquistador is the grotesque characterization of Don Fernando. There is no question here of an inexplicable change or spell; Don Fernando is simply the very embodiment of degeneration with very little to redeem him. Zúñiga, the most benevolent of these narrators, finds in him a certain quality of innocence, but this is in a context that shows this innocence to be immature and simplistic. Don Fernando is the quintessence of the most negative aspects of the conquistador, embodying the degeneration and perversion of every heroic virtue. He is selfishly incapable of delegating authority, ambitious yet without the initiative required to fulfill his ambitions, kind only as a function of his extreme weakness, ungrateful and treacherous to a degree matched only by his cowardliness and indecision. While Ursúa's decadence elicits a measure of forgiving perplexity among those who write about him, apparent in the excuses they make for him by referring to illness and witchcraft, the degradation of the heroic ideal in the person of Don Fernando causes them to despise him without mercy, as is clearly evident in the following fragment:

> He was full of corrupt habits, a glutton who loved to eat and drink, especially fruit, fritters, and pastries, which he was always anxiously on the lookout for; and anyone who wished to have him as a friend could win his favor and support by providing any of these things for him. He was extremely ungrateful to his Governor . . . he killed him out of sheer ambition. He remained in his tyrannical position of command first as General and then as Prince for almost five months. And this was not long enough for him to gorge himself on fritters and other such things on which his happiness depended.[90]

The description is obviously grotesque, and what is involved is no longer a question of simply demythifying models of human conduct that had led to an inaccurate representation of reality but of explicitly revealing the actual degradation and corruption concealed in the past by the fictions and heroic models of the discourse of mythification.

In the discourse of rebellion the destruction of the model of the conquistador, implicit in the characterization of Ursúa and Don Fernando, is complemented by the presentation of the figure of the rebel. The main difficulty in analyzing this figure is that its characterization is linked to each narrator's need for self-justification—a need that shapes to a considerable extent the very nature of the discourse. The true function of Cortés's *Letters* was not, as he claimed, to provide information, but to transform the nature of the conquest in such a way as to adjust its representation to the demands of his desire for power and glory. The function of the narrative discourse of failure, on the other hand, was to replace service in action by a text describing an expedition that could not be glorified because it had failed, but whose description was presented as being just as valuable as any other type of successful action. In the discourse of rebellion, the primary function is to justify one's highly questionable involvement or direct participation in the uprising. The purpose of the narrator in each of these accounts is to reiterate his unconditional loyalty to the king and to prove his innocence in the event of any future accusation of complicity or involvement in rebellious activities against royal authority and the established order. The most direct means of accomplishing this is by showing that one radically repudiates and condemns the rebellion and its participants, and this is precisely the approach adopted by all the chroniclers of Ursúa's expedition. Aguirre and his followers are characterized in absolutely negative terms, to the point of being portrayed as beasts. The rebels are described as seditious, cruel, ambitious, treacherous, or even worse. Their rebellion is clearly associated with bestial degradation as in the episode involving Antón Llamoso. When Aguirre calls his loyalty in question, Llamoso "strongly denied this, swearing that it was not so; and believing that it would give him greater satisfaction, he threw himself upon the field officer's body in front of everybody, and lying on top of him sucked the blood oozing from his head and then part of his brains, saying 'I will drink this traitor's blood.' "[91]

As a result of a characterization of people and events that is subordinated to an individual need for self-justification, the rebels are portrayed in these narratives as the very embodiment of all the negative qualities associated with treason. But there is something else common to all the accounts that is consistent with their exculpatory function: their claim that the order instituted by the rebels is based on terror, and that any possible form of relationship between Aguirre, the rebels, and the rest of the expeditionaries is based on fear. Vázquez, Pedrarias, Gonzalo de Zúñiga, and Custodio Hernández are the only narrators who recognize Aguirre's popularity, although they dissociate themselves from it by adopting a strongly critical attitude. In all cases, the way the rebellion is presented is primarily determined by the author's need to justify his own passivity or complicity, and all rebel activity is described as having involved coercion, intimidation, and threats, so as to exempt the narrator from any responsibility or blame for the development of the events.

The ideological perspective underlying the rebels and their rebellion in all the descriptions of the *Marañones'* insurrection is thoroughly consistent with that of the dominant order whose mercy the narrators hope to win through their account of the events. This means that every aspect of the rebels' program must be misrepresented in a way that will allow the narrator to dissociate himself from it while hiding its deeper sociopolitical implications. Shaped by these constraints and hidden motives the characterization of the rebellions becomes meaningless, a mere representation of the evils of transgression. Paradoxically, however the depth of the crisis affecting the social order and the scope of the implicit challenge to the values represented by that order are reflected very intensely by the tension in the discourse of rebellion between a willful insistence on the purest ideological orthodoxy and the undeniable presence of certain facts that reveal the final collapse of the order fictitiously represented by the models of the discourse of mythification.

In this new representation of fragmented, conflict-ridden reality of the conquest, the epic order has given way to the chaos of terror, harmony to conflict, unity to division, justice to arbitrariness, obedience to indiscipline, and conquest to sedition. No longer governed by the myth of the warrior, vassal, and Christian, the problematical figure who now holds sway over this reality is that of a traitor whose characterization is grounded in the global and uncompromising rejection of the ideological, political, and social order symbolized in the figure of the king and presided over by him.

Rebel and Madman: The Pilgrim

Among the accounts of Ursúa's journey belonging to the narrative discourse of rebellion, there is one that clearly reveals a transition from historiography to literature similar to the one I referred to in my analysis of Alvar Núñez Cabeza de Vaca's *Naufragios*.[92] In Núñez's case, the text was distinguished by its organization in discursive and narrative terms that went beyond the merely documentary and informational, linking it with literary forms of representation. The semantic and structural transformation involved in this development shaped a process of self-definition of the narrator. It began with his realization of the failure of previous models and concluded with Núñez's formulation of a critical perception of the reality of the conquest, a first step toward an expression of a new, Spanish American consciousness.

Francisco Vázquez's *relación*, which goes beyond a strictly documentary presentation of the events, reflects a somewhat similar process. But unlike the *Naufragios*, rather than being focused on the narrator this text reflects an effort to explicitly dissociate him from the action and keep him outside of the narrative. The literary nature of Vázquez's narrative derives from the selective elaboration and restructuring of the material. The development of the action follows the psychological development of three main characters, whose trajectories exemplify different aspects of the most serious ideological, social, and political problems lying at the heart of the crisis.

The central theme of the narrative is the transgression of the established order and its consequences. Structurally, the narrative is divided into three main dramatic acts. Within each act, the action is organized around a central figure representing the main aspects of the problems dramatized by the action. The first act centers on the decadence of the conquistador. It begins with a portrait of Ursúa as model warrior, Christian, and vassal. But the journey to Omagua, granted to him by the viceroy in recognition of his outstanding conduct, marks the beginning of a process of decay whose causes appear to be, not surprisingly, incomprehensible from the perspective of the narrator, who identifies them with illness and witchcraft.[93] This decadence turns the former heroic conquistador into an indolent lover who exchanges the glories of "the affairs of war and discovery" for the pleasures of the bed he shares with Inés de Atienza. She is in the opinion of the narrator the "principle cause of the death of the Governor and our total destruction." The first act ends with a dramatic presentation of the inevitable consequences of this transformation: the warrior's loss of authority and power and his assassination at the hands of his own soldiers, who decide to kill him, "because with Don Fernando as their general and leader they would be able to go in search of land to settle, which would in fact be a service to the King and not the opposite, in view of how the Governor had been neglecting the enterprise of discovery."[94]

The second act focuses on Don Fernando de Guzmán as it explores the political alternatives of a parallel monarchy in America. But Don Fernando's "kingdom" is exposed as a farce, without a trace of seriousness or substance. Vázquez refers laconically to this pathetic kingdom, saying that "the madness and vanity of his Principality [finally] came to an end." The "prince" is a decidedly grotesque character. Vázquez calls him a straw man, stressing that he bore the "name" of general and then of prince— thus implying that he had the makings of neither—and mocks his pretensions to dignity when he sums up his death by saying "there perished his assumed gravity." In Vázquez's dramatization of the political alternative of a parallel monarchy—roughly representing the designs that motivated Pizarro's rebellion—the reign is presented as a caricature, and its central figure is rendered as unmistakably grotesque. Sarcastically emphasizing the prince's highest aspirations, Vázquez says that his only desire was to gorge himself on fruit, fritters, and pastry; that everything he did was aimed at this purpose; that to offer such things to him was all it took to gain his support and favor; and that his greatest failure as a governor was that he had not had time to eat his fill.⁹⁵ The second act concludes with the assassination of Don Fernando de Guzmán, the last of the degraded representatives of royal authority.

The following act focuses on the figure of Lope de Aguirre. Aguirre starts his rule as governor with a speech that lays out the main points of his program, symbolically liquidating the order implicit in the discourse of mythification. The first thing he does is to appoint himself general. By so doing, he explicitly dissociates himself from the authority of the king and his representatives and presents himself as the legitimate representative of the interests of the *Marañones*. He stresses the democratic nature of the power thus constituted, reminding his soldiers that they must continue to consider him their "friend and companion."⁹⁶ Then he states as his true objective the seditious plan to conquer and emancipate Peru. Aguirre assures his men that there will be no further interference, riots, or insurrection; and that "henceforth the management of the war will be straightforward."

This confirmation of a design to proceed toward a war of independence, so contrary to the epic model of action, is dramatized shortly thereafter in an incident during which the initial objective of Ursúa's expedition is explicitly rejected: when the ships reach the Omagua region, two days after the death of Don Fernando, Vázquez writes: "A rather low-lying range of huts and barren hills appeared on the right. There was a lot of smoke, and some settlements could be seen along the edge of the river. The guides said that that was where Omagua was, and also the good land they had talked to us about so often. [Aguirre] gave orders forbidding anyone to speak to the guides. We drifted toward the other branch of the river, following the direction taken by the tyrant."⁹⁷ This other branch of the river chosen by Aguirre, a symbolic deviation from the route that led to the original objectives of the expedition, suggests both a geographical distance from the original goal of the expedition, and an ideological deviation separating Aguirre and his followers from the path drawn up earlier by the representatives of the dominant ideology. This symbolic deviation sets the stage for the terms of the order established by the rebels—an order firmly based on their rejection of the authority of the king and the sovereignty of Spain—and for their single-minded commitment to emancipating the kingdoms of South America.

As in the first two acts, the action through which Vázquez dramatizes the order created by the rebels is an exact projection of the characteristics and personality of a central figure. The figure here is Aguirre, and the development of the action runs parallel to that of his psychological characterization. Aguirre is initially portrayed as a popular man, with a great ability to use his cunning, gift with words, and power to persuade, to influence his discontented companions. But his character changes radically immediately after he takes power, and his qualities become reduced to one alone: cruelty. From then on, the action is a constant reflection of this trait, as he subjects his men to arbitrary killing, torture, and every kind of abuse and punishment. In the final stage, and as a result of the sheer accumulation of the horrors he inflicts on everyone, the apparently demented Aguirre comes to be known as "Aguirre the madman."

Throughout the development of the action in the third section of Vázquez's account, Aguirre and his abuse of power dramatize the danger of putting power in the hands of a "friend and companion of men who are low and wicked." His image stands in implicit contrast to that of the model conquistador: the mythical conquistador had always been a good vassal, whereas Aguirre is "agitated, boisterous, a friend of revolts and riots"; the conquistador was a model Christian: Aguirre is a "bad Christian, even a Lutheran heretic or worse . . . one of his habitual vices was to commend his body and soul to the Devil. He never spoke without profanity, always swearing against God and the Saints."[98] And whereas the model conquistador had devoted his life to furthering the glory of the established order and increasing the possessions of the empire, Aguirre is a man bent on undermining that order and breaking up the territorial empire won by the efforts of so many illustrious vassals, to whom he would refer only in order to curse them.

Vázquez's characterization of the figure of the rebel involves a systematic reversal of the traits of the model. The reality he presents reveals a chaotic situation that illustrates, through all the elements that shape the action, the hideous character of this reversal. It should not be forgotten, however, that the monstrous nature of Aguirre's character as the very incarnation of evil in all its manifestations ("he was so evil, cruel, and perverse that nothing good or virtuous may be found or noted in his person") is largely determined by the exculpatory function of Vázquez's account. It was crucial for the author to make Aguirre's perfidy, cruelty, and corruption sufficiently acute if he was to justify his own responsibility in allowing him to exercise unchallenged, absolute power for almost six months. Only the superhuman nature of Aguirre's perfidy could absolve from any guilt or responsibility those who, like Vázquez, chose to protect their own lives rather than defy the very insurrection they came later to so openly condemn.

All three acts in Vázquez's text end with a portrait of the figure on which the drama is focused. This narrative strategy stresses structurally the importance of this figure within the development of the episode and implicitly subordinates the action to the psychology of the central character. The portrait of Ursúa is a synthesis of the trajectory of the conquistador and the degradation of his heroic values. It reveals his progressive contamination by the violence and corruption of a society in crisis, his ultimate transformation by bewitchment, and his utter loss of control over reality. The portrait of Fernando de Guzmán sets the conflict-ridden but legitimate order of the monarchy against a farcical parallel monarchy characterized by petty personal interests and a project of political disintegration. Finally, the accumulation of negative features that shape the devastating portrait of Aguirre provides a mirror image of the destructive nature of rebellion as an alternative, an alternative that Vázquez's narrative identifies with terror, chaos, and destruction. Rather than responding to strictly objective, informational criteria, the narrative components of each episode dramatize the problems exemplified by the psychological portrait of the central character and illustrate their implications, and it is this approach that gives Vázquez's manner of presenting his material a fictional quality. By means of a literary reconstruction of actual events represented with clear fictional overtones, his account explores the profound crisis that was severely undermining the ideological, political, and social order represented by the earlier mythical figure of the conquistador. It also dramatizes the potential alternatives explored historically by previous uprisings through the development of the three stages of Aguirre's insurrection and his *Marañones*. The catharsis produced by the tragic developments of the third act is reinforced by an explicit reference to the reinstatement of the same order challenged at the beginning of the text: "Once the destruction caused by this cruel and evil tyrant was over, the Governor and Captain General and other captains withdrew to Tocuyo where they were residing; and the people of Barquicimeto and Mérida left to rebuild their villages; and so it was that with the death of that evil man, the land became calm; and the tyrants who had come with him went off to seek their fortune . . . and there was peace."[99]

In the literary representation of the crisis of central power, the death of the traitor Aguirre is equated with the final elimination of rebellion in all its forms and the replacement of rebellion by peace and tranquillity. This restoration successfully turns the history of a rebellion into a moral tale.

The specifically literary, linguistic, and structural features of the *Naufragios* had been consistent with the design to convey, through a qualitatively different mode of representation, an increasingly critical attitude toward conquest and its myths. And this critical attitude is at the very roots of the gradual historical development of a Spanish American consciousness. The literary structure that shapes representation in Francisco Vázquez's text, on the other hand, reveals no desire whatsoever to dispel myths or question the prevailing ideology. In fact, its function is to reassert the values of the established order and ward off any possible transgression. Paradoxically, it is precisely this function that singles out this text as a key literary work in the same process of development of a Spanish American consciousness. In his analysis of Gonzalo Pizarro's rebellion, Marcel Bataillon remarks that the period of great insurrections ending with that of Aguirre led to a reaffirmation of the values of the metropolis; and he draws a specific connection between this process and the development of a Spanish American consciousness: "It was precisely in the wake of the Pizarrist rebellion which had shaken its very foundations that America became truly Spanish, internalizing and defending for the first time the values and culture of Spain both as a justification for the conquest and as an antidote in the face of growing anarchy among the conquistadors. And, simultaneously, that new colonial America would become conscious of its solidarity, from Mexico to La Plata and to the Strait of Magellan."[100] The historical context described by Bataillon reveals the historical meaning of the fictitious restoration of order portrayed by Vázquez: it is the dramatization of a period of growing conflict and disorientation brought symbolically to an end with the return of harmony. This harmony appears to be the result of a peaceful political solution that in fact restores all the central foundations of colonial America. Vázquez's literary representation of the Marañón uprising exorcises both the crisis and the rebellion, fictitiously circumscribing all the problems of the period within the figure of a single central character, who is presented as the embodiment of every kind of evil needed to justify by itself the violence and transgression involved in the action.[101]

The hero of the discourse of mythification had been the sum of every quality demanded by his epic purpose: he was a man chosen by God as the agent of History. The central characters of the main texts of the discourse of demythification—the narratives written by Alvar Núñez and Francisco Vázquez—mark the beginnings of a transition from an epic mode to a novelistic approach to the representation of reality. No longer the instrument of God or the agent of History, the main character is portrayed as a complex individual, placed at the very center of the conflict and torn by all the contradictions that surround him. But while the narrator in the *Naufragios* had grown ever more complex and problematic, illuminating in the process the demythification of American reality, Aguirre's characterization becomes increasingly schematized and oversimplified in an attempt to hide the true meaning and implications of his rebellion. The entire narrative revolves around his figure, the key element in the narrator's self-justification. The primary function of a characterization that turns Aguirre into the very embodiment of evil is to hide the widespread overarching implications of the uprising. By presenting him as an insane, evil maniac, Vázquez instrumentalizes the characterization of Aguirre, rendering him meaningless and deeply misrepresenting the meaning of his rebellion.

The critical reassessment of the figure of Lope de Aguirre is relevant, however, from both a historical and a literary point of view. He is important historically because he led an episode that had major political and ideological significance, whose outcome is relevant to the process of defining a Spanish American identity.[102] From a literary perspective, his significance comes first of all from a series of elements that tie his perception and representation of the realities of the conquest to certain aspects of baroque thinking and aesthetics which, in many ways, his discourse anticipates; and second, from the lasting influence of his image on a number of literary works in Spain and Spanish America.[103]

Traditionally, there have been two main lines of interpretation concerning Aguirre as a historical figure. The first, led by Segundo de Izpizúa's interpretation,[104] attempts to vindicate the questionable leader of the *Marañones* and portrays him as a worthy and glorious forerunner of Latin American independence. The second, closer in intent to the official accounts of the period, shows him as a horrible tyrant, bloodthirsty and cruel. The first position is consistent with Aguirre's own self-definition: he was a rebel, a pilgrim, a prince of freedom. According to the second, developed in a critical study by E. Jos, Aguirre was a "madman," just as he was called by some in his own time.[105] The striking difference between these two perceptions can be explained in terms of their different approach to the use of sources. In the first, much of the actual material in the reports on the expedition is ignored in favor of a mythifying version constructed by the author. In the second, these reports and the condemnation they express are taken to be accurate and reliable.

There exists, however, a voice of Aguirre that all the accusations and judgments in the accounts could neither obliterate nor silence. The few documents that have preserved this voice provide a sufficient as well as authentic foundation for analyzing and reinterpreting his character. This is the voice that speaks in sentences, remarks, speeches, and transcriptions, repeated literally or with minor variations in all the different accounts of the expedition. It is the voice that speaks in the three letters written by Aguirre that have been preserved: one to Provincial Montesinos, one to King Philip II, and one to Governor Collado. A comparison between his letters and his quoted speeches reveals their linguistic and ideological consistency, aside from possible minor variations introduced by the narrator because his memory failed him or because he wished to use them in portraying his character. Both in the letters and in the speeches we find essentially the same ideas expressing Aguirre's perception of the crisis and of a possible alternative. The same definitions, values, view of reality, ideological and practical designs appear in similar or equivalent terms in the letters and speeches alike. There is an unquestionable inner coherence in their discourse. This discourse revolves obsessively around the crisis of the centralized power structure, a crisis that Aguirre identifies with three fundamental developments: the decadence of existing political structures, the disintegration of the vassal relationship, and the corruption of traditional ideological values.

For Aguirre, the decadence of the political structure is a reflection of a general state of corruption that affects everyone in a position of authority. All these people are covetous, venal, liars, thieves, pernicious, and even idolatrous, for "like Nebuchadnezzar, they expect us to kneel down and worship them." He advises the king not to trust these people who "spend all their time arranging marriages for their sons and daughters and care about nothing else, a very frequent saying among them being 'A tuerto o a derecho nuestra casa hasta el techo' ["by whatever means, crooked or honest, we must promote the interests of our own people all the way"]."[106] They serve the king "by the sweat of the brow of the *hidalgos*" and "eat the bread of the poor" without contributing any effort of their own.[107]

The disintegration of the vassal relationship is the result, according to Aguirre, of the king's betrayal of his vassals, which has left them at the mercy of the injustice and corruption of his representatives. No longer "just," this king is "cruel and ungrateful"; he has forsaken his men and neglected to compensate them for their service. From the authoritarian, paternalistic figure he once was, a figure whose actions were endorsed by God and whose behavior exemplified medieval ideological models, he has turned into an irresponsible monster motivated only by "ambition and by a hunger for human flesh."[108] No longer associated with the function assigned to him by the dominant ideology—that of the most illustrious representative of Christian values and a guarantor of the protection and welfare of his subjects—the degraded figure of the monarch presented by Aguirre in his texts and speeches implicitly invalidates the ideological model that had provided the foundation for both the discourse of mythification and the political structures of the period.

The degeneration of traditional values, the last element shaping Aguirre's perception of the political crisis of his time, has two aspects. One concerns the decadence of the church, evident in the dissipation of the clergy and the influence in America of the Lutheran schism. "The friars have become so dissolute here that I believe they deserve your wrath, for not a one among them considers himself less than a Governor." This perception of the religious aspects of the ideological crisis already reveals a xenophobic streak that links Aguirre's thinking to that of the *comuneros*.[109] One of the main sources of the general decadence in his opinion is the "foreign element present" in Spanish society. "All of us here know, most excellent king and lord, that you have conquered Germany by means of weapons, and Germany has conquered Spain by means of vice," says Aguirre in his letter to Philip II,[110] in a passage reflecting not only his own xenophobia but the existence in his mind of an essential opposition between *weapons* and *vice*. This opposition articulates the second aspect of his perception of the crisis. For Aguirre, weapons and warfare always represent the heroic values of a mythical era associated with the *Reconquista*. The decadence of these mythical, heroic values of chivalry can only result in vice and degeneration for Aguirre. Ideologically, in Aguirre's perception, Spain's decadence is a direct result of the displacement of the medieval heroic values by the vices of foreigners. From the standpoint of religion, this same decadence is identified with a foreign development: the "great Lutheran schism," which has inspired in Aguirre such "terror and fear."[111]

Ideologically Aguirre's rebellion expresses his emotional response to a political and social crisis that he interprets in the irrational terms just discussed. His uprising against constituted authority is above all a matter of honor. In his first statement to Philip II explaining what has led him and his followers to wage against the king "the most cruel war our strength is able to withstand," he states categorically that resignation and obedience in the face of such injustices would amount to loss of honor. "And you must believe, King and Sire, that we have been forced to do this because we could not withstand the great and unjust tributes, levies, and punishments inflicted upon us by your ministers who . . . have usurped and taken from us our reputation, life, and honor."[112] If passive acceptance of the shift from a society that upheld faithfully the values of the medieval warrior to a society riddled by vice means for Aguirre giving up his honor, he has no alternative: he must resort to rebellion in order to recover the values threatened by the new society. This new society is associated in his mind with the triumph of the "civilian" over the "military man"; of the "tapioca and corn cake" people or the "mattress makers," as he sometimes calls them, over the warrior; of the government official and the bureaucrat over the conquistador. In the program of his rebellion, Aguirre targets all of these, and he is determined to eliminate them without exception, just as he ordered a German torn to bits when he learned of the Lutheran schism. "Likewise," he says, "all the presidents should be killed, and all the judges, bishops, archbishops, governors, lawyers, attorneys, and any-one else we can lay our hands on, for . . . they and the friars have destroyed the Indies."[113] In Aguirre's rebellious discourse, the figure of the rebel, unlike the "mattress makers," bureaucrats, and friars, is "generous, great of spirit," a Christian and a warrior. Standing in clear opposition to a vice-ridden society organized and controlled by *bachilleres** and people in "low professions," he is a reincarnation of the crusader. His mission is to accomplish, through his rebellion, the military and spiritual reconquest of a society threatened by foreign infidels and base men without honor. It is the *Reconquista* that Aguirre has in mind when he equates the political and social crisis he attacks with heresy, and compares the king to Luther: "we in this kingdom now realize how great is your cruelty, and how badly you have broken your faith and your word, and we give your promises less credit than the books of Martin Luther."[114] And the presence of this reference is made more explicit when, in several of his talks and speeches, he details his plans to reconquer and govern Peru: "Give me your friendship and I will see to it that new Goths like those who ruled in Spain arise from the Marañón to govern Peru . . . and I must see to it that the kingdoms of Peru are governed by Marañones, just as the Goths governed Spain."[115] In Aguirre's mind, it is the historical destiny of his Marañón Goths to reconquer Peru from its corrupt, heretic rulers, and restore spiritual purity in the colonies, just as the Goths did before them when, by means of a war of reconquest that lasted eight centuries, they succeeded in winning back from the Moslems their occupied peninsula. Aguirre reinforces the predestined character of this new holy war by alluding to a native prophecy

---

*From the fifteenth to the seventeenth century, a *bachiller* was the holder of the first or lowest level university degree awarded for the study of literature.—TRANS.

concerning the reconquest of Peru: "Witchdoctors all over Peru claim that people will come from certain hills and hidden lands to rule over Peru, and I know for a fact that they are referring to us."[116]

From an ideological perspective, Aguirre's rebellion is unequivocally reactionary and anachronistic. It contains not a single progressive—let alone revolutionary—element. Its goal is to defend the idealized values of a mythified past, and it rejects any change in the obsolete medieval military society Aguirre wishes to perpetuate. In his perception, the military-Christian values of the Crusades are the very essence of the spirit of Spain, and any change means degeneration and corruption. He proposes to restore the purity of this spirit by eliminating all those representatives of the civilian order who do not understand the higher value of war. For him, a life dedicated to war is the highest possible human aspiration, and he documents his position with a very personal reading of previous history: "they were timid and cowardly, worse than barbers . . . how could it be that no one had come over to his side and that they all refused to take part in war, when men had loved war and followed it since the beginning of time, . . . even the angels in Heaven had engaged in war when they expelled Lucifer?"[117] From the expulsion of the rebel Lucifer to the expulsion of the Arabs from Spain by the Goths, Aguirre identifies all warfare with his plan to restore Christian orthodoxy by means of a process of purification. Thus, every member or accomplice of corrupt civilian society must be eliminated at the hands of his Marañón Goths, whose "faith in God's commandments is absolute and without corruption, as befitting Christians" and who are prepared to "become martyrs" if need be to defend them.[118]

The deeply reactionary character of Aguirre's ideology in no way diminishes the subversive importance of his rebellion. Within the political context of his time, the mere act of rising up against the authority of the king and the integrity of the empire had revolutionary implications. The extreme seriousness of these implications was made quite clear by the nature of the punishment the law contemplated for the charge of rebellion. By law, a rebel was sentenced to be beheaded, drawn, and quartered. But all the legal documents of the time reveal an intolerance that takes his destruction one step further. They define a rebel as a traitor to the natural order, who not only deserves to be executed but obliterated from the memory of history, with his house torn down, his fields laid waste, his children dishonored, and his reputation and memory condemned forever. An excerpt from the sentence passed against Aguirre by His Majesty's governor and judge of the *Audiencia*, Licenciado Bernáldez, provides a good illustration:

> I declare the tyrant Lope de Aguirre guilty of the crime of lese majesty against His Royal Majesty King Philip our Lord, and of having committed treason against him on many occasions; in consequence of which I condemn his reputation and the memory of his name to be taken for those of a tyrant and traitor against his king and natural lord, from the time he first planned his tyrannical treason forward; and I declare him to have been justly beheaded, drawn, and quartered. I further declare that . . . all his property will henceforth belong to the chamber and treasury of His Majesty; and I order that any houses belonging to the said Lope de Aguirre be razed to the ground so that neither they nor their memory will remain, and the land on which they stand ploughed and covered over with salt, and this sentence is to be proclaimed to the public. I further declare that any sons left by the said Aguirre, either legitimate, bastard, or adopted, are to be considered the children of a tyrannical traitor, forever infamous, unworthy, and unfit to be knighted, hold public office, or be given any other position forbidden in such cases under the law; nor shall they receive any inheritance or legacy from any person, relative or stranger alike. And I order this sentence against the memory and property of the accused to be executed without recourse to appeal by any person whatsoever.[119]

An analysis of the ideology underlying Aguirre's rebellion will elucidate only part of the complexity of its significance. Taken as the expression of the awakening of Aguirre's consciousness, however, his letters formulate a complex perception of the crisis of his time. Moreover, the analysis of these letters also reveals certain elements that, through the desperate nostalgia that shapes his design of spiritual "reconquest," clearly anticipate the earliest forms of the problematics of Spanish baroque thought. This is especially true of his letter to Philip II, where he expresses his personal experience of the conflict-ridden reality of America and its conquest, through a representation of a spiritual journey that ends with the transformation of Aguirre, the perfect hidalgo, "old Christian," and vassal portrayed in the first paragraphs, into the "rebel unto death" who signs the letter. His transformation is presented as the result of social changes that have invalidated the ideal terms of the relationships of knighthood and vassalage. As an hidalgo, old Christian, and vassal, Aguirre has lived up to the medieval code of chivalric honor: "as a young man I went by sea to Peru, to become a better man by the use of my lance, and to fulfill the debt owed by all men of good breeding . . . I have rendered you many services."[120] But the king has not fulfilled his part, and his "cruelty and ingratitude" reflect the deep crisis of the medieval order that Aguirre proposes to reinstate. His emotional response to the obvious changes revealed by the transformation of the vassalage system and the religious pluralism of the Lutheran schism is one of "fear" and "terror." His response to the crisis is to call for a plan for spiritual restoration involving a denial or destruction of the reality of his time. His anguish and confusion and the anachronism and nostalgia of his perception materialize in his plan to return to a mythical past, while his intermittent awareness of the impossibility of such a return leads him to despair. Within Aguirre's discourse, despair is all he has left to replace his lost innocence, the only yield resulting from his personal experience of the conquest.

Aguirre's description of his journey down the Marañón River becomes a symbolic representation of a spiritual journey that leads to a growing awareness of his irrevocable marginalization. In his letter to the king, Aguirre describes the expedition down the Marañón as an emotional rather than spatial journey, when he says: "We continued ahead on our path through all this death and ill fortune, along the river Marañón."[121] He develops this metaphorical representation even more explicitly in his letter to Father Montesinos:

> I do not deny . . . that we left Peru and followed the Marañón to discover land and settle there, some of us lame, some of us well enough considering all our hardships in Peru; and had we found land no matter how miserable, we would have stopped there to rest our forlorn bodies, which are more torn than the clothes of a pilgrim. And considering our deprivation and hardship, and the way our lives have been threatened by the sea, the river, and by hunger, we believe we are alive by the grace of God, and if anyone has in mind to attack us they should be aware that they are coming to fight against the spirits of dead men.[122]

In this paragraph, the journey starts out with the usual project of discovering and settling new land. But almost immediately it becomes a quest for a place where the men can rest and take refuge. The journey concludes with symbolic death brought about by hardship and by the final failure of the quest. This death is expressed by a sequence of substitutions that parallel the transformation of the epic design. First the conquistador becomes crippled and then, in succession, a "forlorn body," a "pilgrim," and, finally, a "dead man." His final transformation into the "spirit of a dead man" illustrates very clearly Aguirre's tragic view of the irreversible crisis of medieval heroic values. It also highlights his emotional perception of his own plight and of the situation of his fellow rebels: the spirits of dead men are the final metamorphosis of a human type—the heroic warrior who has become obsolete. In his letter Aguirre returns over and over again to the idea of death in life, linking it to the desperate, irreversible character of his own rebellion. He believes that he and his men "have little wish to live" and that they would all rather die than give up their attempt to bring back the past. The relentless, suicidal character of Aguirre's war against his king—who stands for the decadent order he hates so fervently—is explicit in every letter. "I swear to God that I will leave nothing alive on this land," he says to Collado; and to the king: "Together with my companions, whose names I will give you later, I have removed myself from my debt of obedience to you; and we have broken our bonds with our country, Spain, to wage the cruelest war against you our strength can suffer and sustain." Here, the statement is signed "a rebel unto death," reinforcing the same message.[123]

The literary representation of this voyage of discovery unfolds a metaphorical journey leading from a state of innocent acceptance of the traditional epic order to an experience that renders the earlier models obsolete, leaving only despair, isolation, and death. The existential definition of the rebel presents him as the spirit of a dead man. And the characterization of rebellion shows a desperate, suicidal struggle to the end. All these narrative elements reflect a single reality: the impasse reached by the tragic consciousness of a man who identifies totally with a mythical past and who is completely unable to come to terms with the present, even though he obscurely realizes that his design for spiritual restoration is an impossibility.

In Lope de Aguirre's narrative discourse, the presentation of *experience*, illustrated through the metaphorical transformation of the Marañón journey, is consistent with his personal experience of the crisis; and this correspondence provides an early indication—as does the narrative structure in Vázquez's account when he develops the action as a projection of the psychology of his three central characters—of the increasingly anthropocentric perception of reality that was to become one of the most fundamental characteristics of the Baroque. In the words of José Antonio Maravall: "I have said that Velázquez paints in the first person. This is entirely consistent with the change in the notion of experience that occurred between the Renaissance, for which the phenomenal world was a manifestation or reflection of objective reality, and the baroque period, for which experience was the translation of an earlier perception: 'The world that I regard is my self.'"[124] Such a perception, which, like Aguirre's, equates reality with personal consciousness, radically undermines the very notion of experience. The problematical nature of experience is further developed in a paragraph that could easily be one of the most obscure and contradictory in all Aguirre's letters:

It is a large and fearful river, and contrary to what they say, at its mouth it measures an expanse of eight leagues of fresh water. Many of its branches contain large shoals, and it runs for 800 leagues along a desert area where there is absolutely no settlement to be seen, as your Majesty will find stated *in a true account we have made.* There are over 6,000 islands in the stretch we covered. God only knows how we managed to get out of so fearful a lake! Let me advise you, my king and lord, neither to authorize nor provision a fleet to enter this unfortunate river, for I swear to you by my faith as a Christian that if 100,000 men were to come here not a one would escape, *for the account is false* and the journey down the river leads to nothing but despair.[125]

The paragraph is organized around two central points: the geographical journey is transformed into a spiritual one, and the true account becomes a false one. The first transformation follows the gradual replacement of an objective geographical mode of characterization by one that is subjective and emotional. Aguirre begins with a description of islands and currents, distances, accidents of the terrain, and then, suddenly, reduces the reality of the Amazon to a single element, despair. And this shift is linked to the second point: the geography of the place has been described, says Aguirre, in a "true account" that he immediately goes on to call "false." Why does this initially true account suddenly turn out to be false? Because it obscures the true nature of what he is trying to describe. For Aguirre, the reality of the journey along the Marañón does not lie in its length, its islands, the nature of its geography but in the unbearable despair that shapes the spiritual journey of the conquistador who, sailing down its waters, is transformed into the specter of a dead man. Truth lies not in the geographic details of a "true account" but in an inner journey of discovery that leads to a tragic realization of the irreversible crisis of the heroic values of medieval times.

In Aguirre's discourse external reality is a lie, and only the subjective experience of reality can legitimately be called true. The result of this perception is the proliferation of "worlds," theoretically as numerous as the minds that observe them. Everything becomes unstable, changeable, varied, in total contrast to the more immutable, uniform world of the Middle Ages. At the same time, the attribution of value to subjective experience versus objective reality signals a central change in the transition from the Renaissance to the baroque, a change that modifies the very concept of human nature. Since the Middle Ages people had been seen at the center of the social order, firmly grounded in the social values of a communal organization. Now individuals become aware of their solitude and isolation. "Baroque man," says Maravall, "is constitutionally alone, and closed off from the world. He relates to others for tactical reasons only; his inner self is like a fortress or a prison."[126] Aguirre's self is both. Everything about his discourse reveals the awareness of his solitude as an essential feature of his personality: from the manner in which he uses the pronoun *I*, which distinguishes and separates him from his ancestors and followers, to his design for a suicidal, destructive enterprise that isolates him progressively from his men, in whose mind rebellion had always been of essentially secondary importance compared to the acquisition of power and booty. Aguirre's sense of his own solitude and isolation in the realization of the tragic collapse of his world ties him unequivocally to the ideas and values that would be formulated in baroque thought a few decades later.

Aguirre's letters and speeches reveal that he was an anguished, anachronistic rebel, not a madman.[127] The source of his rebelliousness was a subjective, irrational perception of the irreversible *crisis* of an order with which he felt completely identified. His plan was a desperate, nostalgic attempt to restore the spiritual values of a time that was no more. Despite the politically subversive nature of his rebellion, one can hardly claim that Aguirre's ideology and worldview anticipated the ideas that shaped Latin America's struggle for independence. His rebellion was an anachronistic flight toward a mythified past, not an anticipation of future forms of freedom.

And yet, this reactionary rebel and traitor who was known to his contemporaries as "Aguirre the madman" signed his letter to Philip II as "Lope de Aguirre the Pilgrim," reflecting a view of himself suggested by his earlier comparison of "rebels" to "pilgrims."[128] Was Aguirre truly a pilgrim, and if so, what was the nature of his pilgrimage? His rebellious ideology was clearly reactionary, and in this sense, his pilgrimage should be considered nostalgic, regressive, and anachronistic. But in spite of his reactionary ideology, in spite of an irrational perception of reality that proposes as the only alternative a return to the past and death, there are several aspects of his discourse that reveal the fundamental ambiguity and contradictions of Aguirre. And both his ambiguity and contradictions signal the transition toward a baroque consciousness. Aguirre chose anachronism as a means of escape, and his choice expresses his lack of understanding and radical rejection of the times he lived in. But it should not be forgotten that nostalgia for a Golden Age, and the anachronistic fascination with obsolete values identified with a past always imagined to be radically different from the decadent and uncertain present, was a constant theme for Spanish writers from Cervantes to Calderón. It was a theme that consistently expressed the subjective perception the people of the baroque period had of Spain's major historical crisis at that time. Aguirre's anachronism thus ties him emotionally to the medieval past, but philosophically it links him to the worldview of the baroque, which in many ways he anticipates. He did not have a rational understanding of the crisis, and he could not reconcile himself to the instabilty and multiplicity of the world around him. He did not have a clear sense of the meaning of his own increasing marginalization, which he experienced merely as an intense feeling of isolation and solitude. Such forms of rational understanding were not part of what his writings show to have been a rather more intuitive and disjointed sense of the world and of his own self. But one can certainly speak of his tragic sense of the crisis undergone by a number of central concepts—experience, reality, humankind—that signals the beginning of a baroque worldview. In this sense, Aguirre's tormented trajectory can indeed be equated with a spiritual pilgrimage. In its continuous shifting from one contradictory intuition, disconnected perception, or categorical denial to the next, his problematical figure expresses the emergence of that tormented being Baltasar Gracián would call, many years later, "the pilgrim of being."[129]

Aguirre's terrible actions exemplify in a condensed, intensified way all the forms of violence that characterized the period of the conquest. This is not to say that he was typical of the average sixteenth-century conquistador, but to stress that the difference between his cruelty—so often labeled insane[130]—and the forms of institutional violence that shaped the conquest as a whole was only a matter of degree. Rather than isolating him from his historical context as some authors who have used his "madness" to disqualify him would claim, his appalling behavior during the Marañón journey and the occupation of the island of Margarita show him as a key historical character. His actions unmask and reveal the true nature of a conquest founded on systematic violence and on the abuse of power. And his obscure, tormented discourse reflects his anguished perception and his desperate nostalgia for a mythical lost world. His words trace the hopeless awakening of a man caught between his nostalgic flight and his inability to reach a clear understanding of his own historical situation.

From a modern perspective Aguirre's importance is twofold: historical and literary. His conflictive and contradictory figure illuminates some of the major changes that shape the transition between a worldview grounded in medieval ideological structures and the aesthetic and philosophical values that shape the beginnings of modern thought during the age of the baroque.

Part Three

*A Literary Expression of the
Unfolding of a New Consciousness*

Chapter Five

Alonso de Ercilla and the Development of a Spanish American Consciousness

Characterization of the Native American: Dehumanization and Mythification

Columbus's journal entry for October 12, 1492, reads as follows:

> They all go naked as their mothers bore them, and the women also, although I saw only one very young girl. And all those whom I did see were youths, so that I did not see one who was over thirty years of age; they were very well built, with very handsome bodies and very good faces. Their hair is coarse almost like the hairs of a horse's tail and short; they wear their hair down over their eyebrows, except for a few strands behind, which they wear long and never cut. Some of them are painted black, and they are the colour of the people of the Canaries, neither black nor white, and some of them are painted white and some red and some in any colour that they find. Some of them paint their faces, some their whole bodies, and some only the nose.[1]

This is the first written characterization of an inhabitant of the New World from a European perspective, and the visual image it provides in a rather rough and rudimentary way conveys two central impressions: *primitivism*—the Indians are naked—and *exoticism*—their bodies are painted. This characterization has the immediacy of a snapshot, an effect that is reinforced by the multiplicity of visual elements and the absence of any kind of interpretation, evaluation, or judgment on the part of the narrator.

But even at this early stage, Columbus's subjective perceptions soon begin to distort the nature of the inhabitants of the Antilles. His characterizations always appear to waver between two poles. The first reflects his desire to identify America and its inhabitants with the lands in Eastern Asia described by Marco Polo;[2] the second, his need to assess their utility within a project of commercial exploitation of the new lands and, later, for commercial exploitation and organization of a slave trade.[3] Rather than exploring and revealing the specific nature of the American natives, Columbus's discourse reduces and alienates their humanity, using their personal and cultural attributes to disqualify them to be anything other than serfs, beasts, or things.[4]

The ultimate consequence of this characterization is the establishment within Columbus's narrative discourse of a fictitious equivalence between identity and function—a function based on needs and criteria that have nothing to do with the human reality they have come to define. The human nature and cultural identity of the natives are radically undermined in a representation that gradually reduces them to what can be profitable in terms of the ideological and economic context of the discovery and exploitation of America. The American natives become a commodity. The implications of this first European characterization of the American natives are reinforced by a parallel process that symbolically deprives them of the right to speak.[5] Columbus's gradual questioning of the linguistic abilities of the natives, ultimately claiming them to be verbally incompetent, reflects the same ignorance and callousness apparent in other aspects of his characterization. The result of this second misrepresentation is Columbus's implicit claim to an exclusive right to language, culture, and humanity. In the context of this claim, Columbus's perceptions of the natives become, in the absence of any cultural pluralism, absolute and unquestionable realities. Columbus's double misrepresentation anticipates the broader process of cultural deprivation that shaped the official view of the conquest of America and resulted in the perpetuation of the stereotype of the natives as an intermediate category somewhere between beast and object.

Columbus's characterization of the native as commodity was the first stereotype formulated by the discourse of mythification, but not the only one. Cortés rejected this characterization just as he rejected the entire economic model of plunder associated with it. In his *Letters* and government ordinances he proposed an alternative perception and characterization. Cortés realized that the level of civilization of the Aztecs ruled out any characterization that, like Columbus's, would equate the absence of European values and customs with "bestiality" and "inhumanity." Even though it retains implicitly some of the basic aspects of Columbus's characterization, Cortés's version is more subtle. What is specific to

Cortés's presentation of the natives is its ambiguity. From his first overall assessment of the Aztecs and their society in his second letter, this ambiguity defines a characterization that is full of contradictions. After explicitly stating that "these people live almost like those in Spain, and in as much harmony and order as there," Cortés expresses surprise that such a civilization could be created by people "barbarous and so far from the knowledge of God, and cut off from all civilized nations."[6]

The contradiction between the barbarous and the civilized in this paragraph suggests a displacement in the meaning of the word "barbarous." In Cortés's discourse the word comes to mean "infidel" and "different" rather than "savage" or "lacking in culture." It was their ignorance of God and of the culture of the West as Cortés knew it that led him to call the Aztecs barbarous, not their civilization, whose value and refinement he stresses in wonder. In a sense the way Cortés uses the word "barbarous" to characterize the natives is similar to the way the word "infidel" was used in medieval times throughout the long struggle against Islam in the *Reconquista*. Like the Moor, the Aztec represents an advanced civilization whose refinement is comparable to that of Spain—we need only recall Cortés's description of the houses of Moctezuma. The insulting epithets used to depict both the Arabs and the American natives ("dog" being the most frequent) express not so much an assessment of character as a typical label routinely applied to a non-Christian enemy. When Cortés calls the Aztecs "dogs" after the *noche triste*, he is merely using the same conventional term to represent the enemy that was developed by the Iberian literary tradition throughout the long years of the *Reconquista*. The term does not imply a dehumanized perception of the native equal to that reflected by the use of words such as "heads," "beasts," and "pieces" in the discourse of Columbus. Cortés never questions the humanity of the Aztecs, or of the other far more primitive groups with which he came in contact in his later expeditions to the mainland. In the final balance, however, their humanity is never quite comparable to that of the Europeans. His favorite name for the natives is *naturales*, a term that of itself provides a foundation for the distinction he develops between the Americans and the Europeans, to justify the Spaniards' domination and subjugation of a people so highly civilized as the Aztecs. The term contains two immediate semantic components. The first involves the notion of "innocence" and primeval simplicity, and is contrary to anything contrived or artificial. The second is related to "source," expressing a natural relationship between human beings and their place of origin. The natives as portrayed by Cortés belong to the New World, being *natural* to it, but the

New World does not belong to them precisely because of the innocence attributed to them in his discourse. Innocence is incompatible with the exercise of power, and on this notion Cortés builds his implicit justification of the conquest of America and the subjection of its inhabitants to a paternalistic system of organization. In such a system, Cortés is an authoritarian, wise, and benevolent father, and the natives he has conquered are defenseless and vulnerable children. He assumes the obligation of defending them from the king, the conquistadors, the corrupt friars, and themselves: "I place them in *encomienda*," says Cortés, so that through his paternal supervision "they are released from captivity and given their freedom." And he adds: "I will not allow them to be used for mining gold, or to be removed from their homes and obliged to work the land, as was done on the other islands."[7] His numerous governmental decrees repeatedly and explicitly confirm this notion of the native as a minor who owes him complete obedience in exchange for protection. In fact, it is the very helplessness and vulnerability of that essentially immature being that makes Cortés's protection necessary and justifies his paternalism.

But despite obvious differences, a number of similarities remain in Columbus's and Cortés's characterizations. The paternalistic model of interaction proposed by Cortés in his letters and decrees does not entirely obscure the true function he assigns to these "immature" natives in his Utopian version of the new society. In his letter to the king written on October 15, 1524, Cortés describes this function as follows:

> the Spaniards here have no other means of profit or support than the *assistance* they obtain from the natives. Without this they would be unable to live, and those here would be obliged to leave the land and no others would come with the new. This would cause no little harm. It would put an end to conversions, thus affecting service to Our Lord. Furthermore, it would decrease Your Majesty's royal income and reduce the extent of Your Majesty's dominion over these lands as well as others to be had that entail more than the world now knows of.[8]

The message could not be clearer: the natives are children and Cortés a wise, benevolent father who is determined to develop and educate them. But until they reach adulthood, a possibility that Cortés's characterization does not really seem to contemplate, they are eligible for none of the rights that come with it. The position of the natives on the social scale is that of serfs, and all the sustenance of the colonists and the prosperity of the colony depends on the ruthless exploitation of their labor—"assistance" as Cortés puts it. The figure of the serf reveals all the limitations of Cortés's "humanization" of the natives. They are no longer called "pieces" or "things" as in the texts of Columbus, but the humanity that Cortés so generously grants them is very narrowly conceived, both in his *Letters* and in the ordinances proclaimed regularly for their protection. None of these texts attempted to promote a prompt emancipation of the natives. They never express a full recognition of their human and cultural identity. Their true objective is to define the perfect conditions that would allow for the institutionalization of the natives' status as perpetual servants within colonial society.

The limitations of the humanity attributed to the natives in Cortés's discourse are obvious. And yet, when compared to the monstrous portrait of the native as object in Columbus's account, and the impressions expressed by Cortés's companions, Cortés's presentation constitutes a clear improvement. Andrés de Tapia's appalling descriptions of the great temple at Tenochtitlan, with its gruesome details, implicitly portrays its creators as incomprehensible savages—terrifying, cruel, and bloodthirsty.[9] Bernal Díaz focuses on a single central quality, monstrosity, by isolating and concentrating on certain features and forms of behavior "against nature." Two in particular recur obsessively in his account: cannibalism and sodomy. Sodomy according to Díaz (who seems determined to attribute the practice of sodomy to all the inhabitants of America) places the natives outside the realm of humankind. It is a practice defined as "against nature" in Díaz's own culture, and its attribution implicitly opens the way to the transformation of the natives into monsters. Díaz also systematically attributes cannibalism to the natives. But more shocking than the act of cannibalism itself is the way in which it is perceived and portrayed in his account, revealing once again the ideological mechanism by which the unfamiliar is identified, through fear, with the monstrous. His approach is both ignorant and childish, and his descriptions far more suggestive of the child-eating ogres and witches in fairy tales than of the complex reality of ritual sacrifice and cannibalism practiced by the Mexican Indians. Hansel and Gretel come easily to the mind of a modern reader when reading in Díaz that the people of Cempoal kept captive Indians in wooden cages to fatten them before sacrificing and eating them. Díaz's explanation of the plan for the Cholula rebellion as part of a great design to stew the Teule warriors is grotesque. He asks himself—attributing the question to Cortés—why "in return for our coming to treat them like brothers and tell them the commands of Our Lord God and the King, they were planning to kill us and eat our flesh, and had already prepared the pots with salt and peppers and tomatoes."[10] Díaz's perception would be merely ridiculous were it not that, as grotesque and monstrous as it seems, it is used a few lines further on to justify the appalling Cholula massacre, which he summarizes laconically as follows: "and they received a blow they will remember forever."[11]

On November 30, 1511, Fray Antonio de Montesinos gave an Advent sermon in Santo Domingo that, among other things, changed the life of an *encomendero* called Bartolomé de Las Casas. This was the first time anyone in America had spoken out against the shared dehumanizing perception of the natives that shaped all interaction between Spaniards and Native Americans, between the colonizers and the colonized. Every question raised by Father Montesinos was an accusation against one form of deprivation or another inflicted on the Native Americans. When he asked from the pulpit whether the Indians were human and whether they had rational souls, there was nothing rhetorical about his questions: he was denouncing a society that perceived and treated the natives precisely as if they were *not* human and did *not* have rational souls.

Montesinos's denunciation gave rise to a new awareness of the plight of the natives and to ways of thinking that changed how the American Indian was perceived. The new perceptions shaped the characterizations of Las Casas and the more humane presentations in some of the texts of the narrative discourse of failure. They also challenged the ways in which the discourse of mythification had deprived the Native Americans of their responsibility, freedom, and humanity by either reducing them to the category of an object or identifying them with the monstrous. The new perception of the natives, based on a radical redefinition of their nature, stood in opposition to a line of thinking that attempted to justify the conquest by referring in a particular way, in its discussions of the natives, to the Platonic notion of the slave as a body without a soul, and to the Aristotelian concepts of the natural slave and master.[12]

In contrast to the official perception, Las Casas's characterization was the first serious attempt to reclaim for the natives the humanity that, from Columbus on, so many colonists were determined to deny them. Las Casas focuses on one fundamental element: innocence. Everything else in his characterization of the native is related to this central idea of primeval innocence, which both illuminates the difference between the Europeans and the Americans and stands in explicit opposition to the corruption and violence that shape, within Las Casas's discourse, the characterization of the conquistador. Las Casas's natives are innocent, candid, gentle, and trusting. Their portrayal as "good savages" constitutes, in fact, a systematic inversion of the terms of his characterization of the conquistador: "we know them to be good by nature, simple, meek, gentle, vulnerable, virtuously inclined, intelligent, quick, and extremely willing to receive our holy faith and be persuaded by the Christian religion."[13]

To avoid suggesting a subjective appreciation, Las Casas carefully supports his authority in two ways. First, he provides an ethnological description of the customs of the inhabitants of the Antilles. He discusses the values they share and points out that their society is better governed in some respects than European societies. Second, he relates their social and cultural organization to ancient Western traditions, specifically to the myth of the *Beings*:

> And truly, to describe briefly the good habits and qualities of these *yucayos* and the inhabitants of these small islands . . . I find no people or nation to whom I can better compare them than those oriental people of India called the Beings both today and by the authors of antiquity who claimed them to be extremely tranquil and gentle. . . . I believe the people living on the Lucayo islands lacked few or even none of the qualities of the Beings; and if we were to look back to those times we might find that in fact they were even superior.[14]

The trend initiated by Montesinos and Las Casas was echoed by Alvar Núñez Cabeza de Vaca in his *Naufragios*. His characterization is somewhat less idealized and more empirical than Las Casas's. But it contains many of the same features. Throughout the long period during which he lived with the natives in the south of the North American Continent, Núñez learned to understand their customs and came to challenge the equivalence assigned to *difference* and *inferiority* in the discourse of mythification. His descriptions offer the first detailed account of the social and cultural organization of people who might be *primitive* but are no less human for that reason. They are not *rational beings*, that is, civilized, but they "are well conditioned people, apt to follow any line which is well traced for them."[15] Because the natives are ignorant of the Christian religion, Las Casas calls them "infidels"; because they are ignorant of Western civilization, Núñez considers them "people without reason"; but both men regard their ignorance not as a lack of humanity but as a problem to be overcome by learning. The natives described by Las Casas do not know because they are *innocent*; those described by Alvar Núñez do not know because they are *primitive*. But both authors reaffirm their humanity explicitly, and they support their position on the grounds of native values and forms of civilization that clearly differ from the values of the conquistadors. This difference often reveals for both authors a superiority in native values that amounts to a direct challenge of Western culture.

Las Casas's voice made itself heard in America and also in Spain, where he played a decisive role in the drafting of the New Laws of the Indies decreed in 1543. And Núñez's account became familiar all over Mexico, through the sermons of Bishop Zumárraga. But neither Las Casas's indignation nor Núñez's insight were enough to put an end to the stereotype created by Columbus, rationalized by the neo-Aristotelian current of official ideology, and reinforced daily by the practice of exploitation in the colonies. The New Laws did not measurably improve the lot of the Indians in any significant way. They did not change the way they were perceived by *encomenderos* whose wealth depended on exploiting them mercilessly and treating them like slaves or beasts of burden. One need only glance at the statements and texts produced by the many rebels who rose up against the king to realize that none of the plans to liberate America from Spanish sovereignty involved freeing the natives from exploitation. From Gonzalo Pizarro to Aguirre, all the rebellions in the sixteenth century involved a plan to emancipate America. But they were all organized in defense of the interests of the *encomenderos*, and never even suggested a social revolution that would change the way the natives were perceived, or put an end to their exploitation—an exploitation that in some places had already caused their complete extinction. Quite the contrary: because the *encomenderos* were completely dependent on native labor—despite the massive number of African slaves brought over to compensate for the drastic decrease in the native population during the first decades of the conquest—any measure designed to free the Indians, recognize their humanity, or give them social equality, would have thoroughly jeopardized the interests and privileges of the *encomendero* class, which every one of these rebellions had sought to defend.

In the narrative discourse of rebellion, the natives are characterized in virtually the same terms as in Columbus's discourse. According to the accounts of the expeditions, their social position was even lower than that of the slaves imported from Africa. The latter are always called "blacks," whereas the natives are systematically referred to by the dehumanizing term coined by Columbus: "pieces." Describing the expedition of Juan Vargas, Francisco Vázquez says that "three Spaniards and many pieces died," thus making explicit their difference in his mind: the former are human beings, the latter are animals. Further on, he refers to Aguirre's decision to abandon "almost one hundred *ladino* and Christian pieces" in one of the villages along the Amazon; and he uses similar language in his account of the execution of Diego Palomo and Pedro Gutiérrez:

> The tyrant killed two soldiers here, one called Pedro Gutiérrez and the other Diego Palomo, because in a conversation between them they had said: 'Leave the pieces here with us and let whatever has to be done be done . . .' and

Diego Palomo begged the tyrant for God's sake not to kill him but to leave him with the pieces from Piru who remained there, and he would become a hermit and gather them together and give them religious instruction.[16]

In his plan to emancipate Peru and create an independent kingdom governed by an aristocracy of *encomenderos*, Aguirre made provisions for the black slaves, but he never once refers to the natives whom he unhesitatingly abandoned without food as soon as they were no longer useful or necessary for the expedition. And even if we assume, considering the nature of his plans for rebellion and emancipation, that his repeated promises to liberate the black slaves "to whom he said that they were free and that he would give any of those who followed him their freedom"[17] were entirely motivated by his need for them, the fact that he made no such promises to the natives is not without significance. All of this—the absence of references to the natives by Aguirre, the claim by Vázquez and other expeditionaries that Aguirre habitually abandoned the "pieces" at the first opportunity—shows that the term was by no means a meaningless one, but conveyed a rather generalized perception of the American native as a beast inferior even to the black slaves, perpetuating the view developed in Columbus's discourse.

Meanwhile, the crown's suppression of rebellions such as Aguirre's strengthened its power and placed some limits on the enormous privileges of the *encomenderos*. The difference in the legal status of the natives, however, who by virtue of the New Laws had become dependents of the crown, produced no real change in their estimation by the ruling class nor in their intolerable exploitation.

Against the background of an ideological perception of the Native Americans as objects, pieces, or serfs, and a narrative tradition that first characterized them as merchandise and then as primitive beings "without reason" (Alvar Núñez) or as "gentle savages" (Bartolomé de Las Casas), the characterization of the Araucan Indians in Alonso de Ercilla's epic poem on the conquest of Chile, *La Araucana*, is particularly noteworthy.

The importance Ercilla attributes to the Araucan people and the highly positive, admiring light in which he casts them are the source of a very old controversy.[18] In a humorous summary of the most common attitude among members of the critical establishment in Spain since the poem first appeared, Fernando Alegría says: "Spanish critics seem to have spent centuries looking for a better epic poet than Ercilla, to avoid the embarrassment of having to recognize that the best epic poem in Spanish is a work that conventional theorists claim is not an epic at all and that Spaniards themselves feel does not really belong to them."[19] Alegría's remark indicates two aspects that have made *La Araucana* problematical and controversial from the start, one aesthetic and the other ideological. In regard to the first, there has been much discussion as to the genre of the work; its connection with Classic and Renaissance epic poetry; the influence of Boiardo, Ariosto, and Tasso; the many ways in which Ercilla at times followed, and more often broke with, rules of composition, structure, and characterization traditionally held to be mandatory. As to the ideological aspect, although not generally acknowledged as such, it lay at the heart of the uncomfortable feeling on the part of a large number of Spanish critics that the poem was strange, that it did not "belong to them." It was also connected with many aesthetic reservations expressed in both Spain and America regarding a poem whose atypical form conveyed a consistent point of view, but one that was *different* and for that reason, frequently misunderstood and poorly analyzed.

At the very center of the controversy is the characterization of the Araucans, which breaks with two fundamental aesthetic rules of traditional Spanish epic poetry. One of these stipulates that the action must be focused on and led by a hero representing the values of the victorious side; the other, that all action and characters must be portrayed in such a way as to glorify the victor's position. Not even the most obstinate voices of the critical establishment in Spain have succeeded in denying that the work's narrative structure and character portrayal do exactly the opposite. The figure of the native is praised and glorified in *La Araucana* by a narrator whose admiration for the defeated is maintained throughout the entire poem. Moreover, the victors are not only not exalted but questioned and at times openly criticized, through portraits presenting them in terms that range from anonymity to caricature.

The Araucan people—collectively, or in the individual portraits of such representative figures as Caupolicán, Tucapel, and Rengo—are more than simply prominent in the work; their characterization constitutes one of the two centers around which the poem is structured, the other one being the presentation and development of the narrator. Let us begin with an analysis of the characterization of the natives, before attempting to show the ideological importance and the aesthetic implications of this characterization. The characterization of the Araucans begins early in the first canto, with a brief summary of their outstanding qualities:

> la gente que produce es tan granada
> tan soberbia gallarda y belicosa
> que no ha sido por rey jamás regida
> ni a extranjero dominio sometida.

> This land produces people
> of such outstanding disposition
> so bellicose, so full of pride, so brave
> that no king could ever rule over them
> nor could any foreign nation ever conquer them.[20]

These four lines introduce most of the main attributes that will shape the development of the characterization: pride, bellicosity, courage, and an unbreakable will to be free. At the same time, they reveal the narrator's attitude right from the start: although it might be argued that the descriptive value of *soberbia* (proud) and *belicosa* (bellicose) is relatively neutral, the choice of two such obviously complimentary terms as *gallarda* (dauntless) and *granada* (noble) expresses an undeniably positive evaluation. Moreover, the very fact that this initial characterization is presented in what is, properly speaking, the beginning of the narrative following a general introduction, similar to the ones we find introducing each canto, clearly underscores its importance.

The first physical description of the Araucans also appears in the first canto. It stresses one fundamental quality: strength, one of the attributes most frequently reiterated throughout the poem. The significance of this strength, from the time it first appears as a distinguishing trait, is worth discussing. Physical strength and violence are, on the one hand, qualities that make the Araucans outstanding in war, and all the male figures in the poem are characterized in this context. At the same time, however, they express their natural harmony with their environment and introduce the poet's perception of these natives as the very embodiment of American nature. The Araucans are, says Ercilla:

> . . . de gestos robustos, desbarbados
> bien formados los cuerpos y crecidos
> espaldas grandes, pechos levantados,
> recios miembros de nervios bien fornidos,
> ágiles, desenvueltos, alentados,
> animosos, valientes, atrevidos,
> duros en el trabajo, sufridores
> de fríos mortales, hambres y calores.[21]

> Their shapely, hairless bodies
> reveal their inner strength
> in the breadth of their shoulders, in the power
> of their chests, and in the iron of their limbs.
> They are agile, dynamic, brave and daring;
> resilient and hard working they withstand
> with equal fortitude

the deadly cold and heat
and thirst and hunger.

This description is a perfect expression of an aesthetic of war. The features chosen by the author for his portrait constitute all the optimal qualities that ideally befit a model warrior. But the two stanzas that frame this first portrait, one at the beginning of the canto and the other at the end, make its implications quite clear: according to the initial stanza, it is their *hado y clima* (fate and environment) that has made the Araucans ferocious and free. In the final stanza, these *gente libertada* (fiercely independent people) appear as the very incarnation of freedom and independence.

The first definition of the Araucans as freedom personified has a fundamental significance that will be analyzed in detail. But the specific context of this definition is the first description of Chile's natural environment. Most important, it is also the physical description of the natives as the embodiment of that environment with all its ferocity, relentlessness, and violence. Ercilla's presentation of the physical and moral characteristics of the Araucans as a projection of the nature of the land suggests a belief in the natural harmony between this people and their environment, and the very notion of this harmony is a new development in the characterization of the American native. Elvas had repeatedly pointed out the Spaniards' inability to adjust to the new surroundings.[22] He showed their clumsiness and awkward incompetence in an environment they could neither understand nor control. But this did not prevent him from describing the natives as bestial savages. Cortés had gradually learned to think of the natives in relation to their own physical and cultural environment, especially after his third letter. But Ercilla goes much further, when in *La Araucana* he creates a characterization that attempts to convey an American view of the native. His presentation shows Araucan values not as an *absence* of Western values and attitudes but as an expression and projection of the different nature of American reality. In his characterization, the natives are defined in terms that implicitly reject the use of Western referents to relate the values and culture of the Araucans to their environment. Only in this manner can the identity of the Araucans be revealed. In harmony with the American environment that is his own, the native is no longer a serf, a piece, or an object: he is a natural aristocrat, the model of all the best values and qualities required by the natural and social environment within which he has developed.

The implicit elimination of an ethnocentric perspective in the three stanzas discussed above sets the stage for the way in which the Araucans are characterized throughout the entire poem. In his characterizations,

Ercilla uses portraits, comparison, and descriptions of the action. He dramatizes basic values through native speeches and traditional events such as native assemblies. Occasionally he inserts an explicit judgment or evaluation by the narrator or some other character. Through these narrative strategies, Ercilla creates the first representation ever of the Native American as a mythical, free, and superior human being.

In *La Araucana* the action revolves around war. The first characterization of the Araucan presents him as an outstanding warrior, pointing out first his violence and courage. Violence is conveyed by a series of adjectives associated in particular with physical strength (the natives are large, strong, robust, gigantic, etc.) and aggressiveness (they are fierce, audacious, ferocious, daring, brave). Ercilla offers many descriptions of the physical strength and uncommon courage of the Araucans. And he also dramatizes their importance through his representation of battles and duels. In battle the Araucan army moves in unison to cut its enemies down, slash their throats, dismember them, and rout them, and this is repeated over and over again. In duels the individual fighters will illustrate the same values and attributes in amazing performances. One of these duels, between Tucapel and Rengo, is perhaps the most hyperbolic representation in the entire poem of the aggressiveness and physical strength of the Araucans.

The next attribute that makes the Araucan superior in the art of war is courage. Courage is at the very core of Araucan philosophy. People's honor and their sense of self depend on this quality. In the Araucan worldview, to be an Araucan and to be brave mean one and the same thing. The absence of courage implies (as it did for the Spaniards) a loss of honor, but also a loss of cultural identity. An Araucan is not only brave but holds himself to be an Araucan precisely because of a virtually mythical valor that sets him apart from all other peoples, in Europe or America. Each character in the poem proves his extraordinary valor time and again. Lautaro, the greatest hero of all in the first part of the work, becomes so by virtue of an act of courage in which he defies Fortune herself: impressed by his superhuman valor and effort, Fortune revokes her decision to grant victory to the Spaniards in the battle described in Canto 3. In the episode involving the log contest, Colocolo's proposal is offered as a peaceful solution to a struggle for power among the Araucan chieftains, who cannot agree on who is the bravest and therefore the most worthy among them to be their governor. Courage is thus once again presented as the fundamental quality, and the degree to which a man possesses it determines his prestige in Araucan society.

The characterization of the Araucans revolves around their violence and openly stresses their physical strength, valor, aggressiveness. But this violence is never presented as a form of bestiality or barbarism. On the contrary, violence is incorporated in a variety of ways into a context that makes it consistent with civilization. The crucial mechanism in this incorporation is the use of the concept of honor. The poet refers to it repeatedly as an explanation for the Araucans' use of violence. Its importance is dramatized in a number of episodes involving bets, duels, and other challenges, where the main theme is the loss or gain of honor. What is in question in the episode of the log, for example, is who will be the next governor of Arauco. But the ritual clearly duplicates many elements typical of such contests among the medieval knights of chivalry, where the issue was not so much the acquisition of power but the demonstration of one's honor, directly related in both cases to personal valor. The dispute between Tucapel and Rengo that continues through the three sections of the poem is likewise an expression of the central importance of honor, and the challenges that precede each of their fights make it clear that honor is what is at stake. All the rhetorical language of Tucapel's challenge and the account of his differences with Rengo's uncle focus on honor.[23] The same is true of the description of the celebration of victory in Canto 10. The challenges among the best warriors do of course concern the prizes offered: the sword, the helmet, the greyhound, the bow, and the horse are central to the challenge. But just as with a joust or tournament in medieval times, what really matters is the honor of the participants.

Ercilla's literary representation links violence to honor, thus justifying it and making it part of a value system directly associated with the canons of medieval chivalry. In this context, and in the presence of a constant confrontation that makes the use of force essential and unavoidable, violence and aggression express courage and dignity, not bestiality. Here the violence of the Araucans appears to be one manifestation of a set of ideological values very similar to those of Europe. The similarity is reinforced by means of a second narrative strategy that attributes the same forms of violence to the Spaniards, and that associate them again with honor. The Araucans and the Spaniards display equal violence and aggressiveness, and just as the Araucan warrior "rompe, magulla, muele y atormenta / desgobierna, destroza, estropia y gasta" ("breaks, bruises, grinds, and twists / wears out, damages, tears out, and destroys"),[24] the Spaniards "hieren, dañan, tropellan, dan la muerte / piernas, brazos, cabezas cercenando" ("wound, hurt, trample, and kill / mutilating arms and legs, cutting off heads").[25] The function of Andrea in the structure of the poem illustrates precisely that the forms of violence portrayed are applicable to all and do not imply a negative characterization. Araucans and Spaniards are equally violent, ferocious, aggressive, and destructive; in their confrontations, the man who displays these attributes to a higher degree is the better warrior, not the most bestial—and this better warrior usually turns out to be an Araucan. Andrea is a Spanish version of the Araucan warrior. He exemplifies on the side of the Spaniards the ideal qualities, just as Tucapel and Rengo do for the Araucans. And the behavior of the Spaniards in battle is on every occasion the exact counterpart of the destructive fury of the native warriors who, by virtue of this equivalence, can be called neither barbarous nor bestial.

In *La Araucana* violence is always subordinated to a set of shared social values. In terms of the war between the Spaniards and the Araucans, it becomes unavoidable, a positive quality for any warrior rather than a sign of bestiality. But this transformation of the meaning of violence is not the only process that gradually shapes Ercilla's characterization of the Araucans as the representatives of a different kind of civilization. Araucan society is entirely oriented toward war: "Venus y Amor aquí no alcanzan parte / sólo domina el iracundo Marte" ("Venus and Love have no role to play / where only angry Mars prevails").[26] Its military, social, and political organization is complex, however, and Ercilla devotes a good portion of the first canto to its detailed description.

Araucan society is a feudal organization ruled by sixteen lords and chieftains, whose prestige derives from their being "en militar estudio los mejores / que de barbaras madres han nacido y por valientes / son estos en mandar los preeminentes" ("among those born from barbarian mothers / the most oustanding in military skill whose courage / makes them natural leaders").[27] The heroic nature of this society's most fundamental values— bravery and military talent—is stressed from the very beginning. Each chieftain has several vassals. He provides them with a military education, and in return, they are at his service whenever required—an exchange consistent with European feudal tradition. The warlike orientation of Araucan society is also manifest in the education of its children. They are carefully trained in everything needed to make them excellent warriors. Their position in society will be determined later precisely by their military abilities:

> Y desde la niñez al ejercicio
> los apremian con fuerza y los incitan
> y en el bélico estudio y duro oficio
> entrando en más edad los ejercitan;
> si alguno de flaqueza da un indicio
> del uso militar lo inhabilitan

y el que sale en las armas señalado
conforme a su valor le dan el grado.[28]

And from early childhood
they are rigorously initiated in the military skills
which they perfect through hard training
and warfare exercises as they grow up.
Whoever shows any weakness
is eliminated from an elite
in which rank will always be determined
on the basis of courage and skill.

In Arauco, the most outstanding warriors constitute a genuine aristocracy, based on merit, not on blood lines. In Araucan society "a person's worth / . . . is determined by his skill and accomplishments as a warrior. A warrior is exempt from manual labor or any other service involving nonmilitary activities. Farming and other similar pursuits are considered the responsibility of low people, "la gente baja." The degree of sophistication achieved by this society is exemplified by the variety and perfection of its weapons. These, together with the complex and diverse military tactics of the Araucans, the strategies they apply to the art of war, the architecture of their fortresses surrounded by ditches and palisades, are enumerated in detail, illustrating the considerable level of sophistication they reflect.[29] Legal and juridical power lies with a senate formed by the chieftains and lords of the state. These leaders make all the political decisions, which are then conveyed to the common people, "la gente común y de canalla." Finally, the Araucans have a religion, centered on the figure of Eponamon to whom the people appeal and with whom they communicate during their rites. They also possess a system to predict the future that involves magicians and auguries.

Ercilla's characterization of the Araucans presents a political and social reality different from that of Europe in the sixteenth century, but comparable to it concerning basic values. Differences between Arauco and any European war-oriented civilization are a matter of degree, and they are attributed implicitly to the respective society's stage of development. Where the differences are in fact irreconcilable—for example, in the matter of religion—regardless of how erroneous he may think the Araucan conception to be, Ercilla puts the two models in relative perspective instead of ethnocentrically rejecting out of hand the view of the other.[30] Moreover, the narrator always goes out of his way to explain, from an American perspective, the true meaning of the attitudes or the forms of behavior that might seem barbarous to a European. A case in point is his commentary on the struggle for power that takes place among the Araucan war leaders in Caupolicán's absence; or the episodes concerning the log contest where, anticipating his Spanish reader's objections ("pues en razón no cabe que un senado / de tan gran disciplina y pulicia / pusiere una elección de tanto peso / en la robusta fuerza y no en el seso" ["since one could well question the discipline / and sophistication of a senate / that would trust an election of such importance / to muscle rather than to brains"]),[31] Ercilla hastens to remark that this was a mere stratagem prudently designed by Colocolo to prevent a fratricidal struggle for control in the absence of Caupolicán.

Araucan society is centered on war but governed by law. Some of the characters in Ercilla's long gallery of portraits personify brute force, such as Tucapel or Rengo. But this force is always controlled by the law embodied in the senate and by the intelligence and good judgment of other characters who excel in political, not just military, affairs (in particular Caupolicán and Lautaro) and by the authority and wisdom of such venerable and respected persons as Colocolo. In this way Ercilla's characterization of the Araucans places violence within a human and social framework that distinguishes it from brutality, transforming it into a valuable instrument, an attribute of war, and a measure of human worth. In this context, the interminable descriptions of the Araucans' use of force and violence and its effects, in all sorts of individual and collective challenges, battles, and confrontations, convey a view of the native not as a savage beast but as a representative member of a nation greater in warfaring virtues than any other: "que . . . cotejado / el valor de las armas y excelencia / es grande la ventaja y diferencia" ("for it is clear that in terms of courage and warfare skills / this nation far surpasses any other").[32]

The male warrior is the central figure in the poem, and in relation to him female characters always take second place. These include the individual portraits of Guacolda, Tegualda, Glaura, Lauca, and Fresia; a couple of group descriptions of native women; and the Dido episode, which although not focused on any of the heroines, sums up the main virtues of all Araucan women. The images projected by the individual and group portraits are qualitatively different. Group characterization follows more closely the attributes of male characterization. It is shaped by the virtues of the warrior. Ercilla emphasizes explicitly the manly character of these women "a quien la rueca es dada" ("who were meant for the spinning wheel") but who in battle:

> con varonil esfuerzo los seguían . . .
> el mujeril temor de sí lanzando

y de ajeno valor y esfuerzo armadas
toman de los ya muertos las espadas . . .

de medrosas y blandas de costumbre
se vuelven temerarias homicidas.[33]

curbing their natural fear . . .
followed them with manly determination
and, armed with unnatural drive,
they would take the swords from the fallen ones . . .

their sweet and gentle natures giving way
to homicidal violence.

These lines, from the first portrait of women in the poem, indicate a
problem of which the author was clearly aware. Any realistic characterization of the Araucan women as warriors was bound to deviate considerably from European aesthetic criteria concerning acceptable female
literary models. In fact it would be almost a complete reversal of those
models. According to Western literary tradition, one of the symbols of
womanhood was the spinning wheel, and weapons and violence were
typically associated with the male stereotype. To give a female figure the
same attributes as those of the male would mean turning her into an
inconceivable monster from the perspective of European culture, which
would consider antiaesthetic and barbarous rather than heroic any female
character who "no sienten los pechos al correr ni las crecidas / barrigas
de ocho meses ocupadas / antes corren mejor las más preñadas" ("in the
chase do not feel the weight of their breasts / nor are they hindered by
their pregnant bellies").[34] These lines represent Ercilla's last attempt to
provide a realistic characterization of the Araucan women in terms of
warlike attributes, and from then on his female characters will for the
most part conform to the models of Europe. But here his use of adjectival
forms that stress the unnatural, "foreign" character of the women's behavior reveals how conscious he was of the problem posed by any deviation
from accepted female models. It also reveals that realism and verisimilitude
were not the criteria that shaped his characterizations of people and events.
La Araucana was a literary project that had little to do with an ethnographical presentation of the Araucans or with an accurate historiographical narrative of their wars.

Only one of the five individual female portraits—that of Fresia—contains
any of the warlike features discussed above, and even here the style chosen
dilutes these features and makes them more acceptable from a European
perspective. The other four are entirely different: they follow accepted

models from European literary traditions.[35] If the characterization of the Araucan warrior may be associated with the medieval knight because, like him, he personifies honor and such fundamental warrior virtues as physical strength, personal courage, and military talent, the images of Araucan women projected by the portraits of the five heroines recall the person and values of the "lady" in the literature of chivalry and are shaped primarily by the attributes of love. The first description of Guacolda presents her in terms of her love for Lautaro: "la bella Guacolda enamorada / a quien el de encendido amor amaba / y ella por el no menos se abrasaba" ("she was the beautiful Guacolda / in love with Lautaro, who adored her with a love / which she returned with equal passion"). Love is likewise central to the characterization of Tegualda, about whom the poet wonders:

> ¿Quién de amor fizo prueba tan bastante?
> ¿Quién vió tal muestra y obra tan piadosa
> como la que tenemos hoy delante
> desta infelice bárbara hermosa?

> Who would surpass her in passion?
> Whoever felt a bond of burning love
> as overwhelming as the love
> of this unfortunate, beautiful barbarian?

In *La Araucana* the presentation of love and the relationship between lovers follows all the conventions of the literary tradition of chivalry. In the story of Tegualda, for example, we find a beautiful, arrogant princess who rejects all her suitors; a tournament in which the most valiant and distinguished men of the kingdom compete for her favor; an unknown figure who appears and defeats them all, and with whom Tegualda falls madly in love; a garland and a ring given as prizes to seal a bond of love, described as a relationship similar to the one between a knight and his lady. Nothing distinguishes Crepino from the knights of the "lying stories" of chivalry when he declares his love in terms that duplicate the motifs of that literary tradition:

> Señora una merced te pido
> sin haberla mis obras merecido:
> que si soy extranjero y no merezco
> hagas por mí lo que es tan de tí oficio,
> como tu siervo natural me ofrezco
> de vivir y morir en tu servicio.[36]

> Milady, I ask only one mercy, though I deserve none:
> if, being a foreigner, I cannot aspire to your favors

I only ask that you accept me as your natural serf,
and that you allow me to live and die in your service.

Each episode focusing on a female character revolves around love. Ercilla points out the need to switch to a different poetic mode replacing the language of Mars with the language of Venus. And by consistently associating women with love—just as he repeatedly associated men with war—Ercilla implicitly follows a literary tradition for which love is the privileged space of female characterization. Traditionally feminine virtues (beauty, gentleness, chastity, fidelity) are all related in the poem to the role assigned to women in love relationships. In fact, it is primarily within these relationships that women achieve any relevance at all. But the women in *La Araucana* possess another central attribute, related to love but distinct from it as well: a sense of honor. While the primary focus of the characterization of the Araucan heroines is on love and fidelity, honor and chastity are given importance as well. The first two virtues establish a link between this characterization and the medieval tradition of chivalry, with its conception of courtly love and of love more powerful than death. The second two suggest something far more contemporary: the Spanish obsession with *honra*, which would lead, during the Golden Age, to the development of an entire dramatic genre, the *drama de honor*.* The episode of Glaura is organized around this issue, of which in his introduction to the defense of Dido Ercilla says: "una ficción impertinente / que destruye una honra es bien oída" ("an impertinent tale is always welcome / when it destroys someone's honor"). The literary nature of the story of Glaura is apparent from the very beginning of the episode. The first stanza offers a portrait that includes the primary aesthetic criteria and descriptive rhetoric of the time:

> Era mochacha grande, bien formada
> de frente alegre y ojos extremados
> nariz perfeta, boca colorada,
> los dientes en coral fino engastados
> espaciosa de pecho, y relevada,
> hermosas manos, brazos bien sacados
> acrecentando más su hermosura
> su natural donaire y apostura.[37]

> She was tall and shapely, her forehead was high,
> her eyes most radiant.

Honra and *honor* here refer especially to the more narrow definition of a sense of what is correct and in accordance with high standards and rules of conduct requiring integrity in men, and discretion, modesty, and chastity in women.—TRANS.

> She had a perfect nose, red lips,
> and teeth like pearls on soft pink coral.
> Her shoulders were broad, her waist was narrow,
> her bosom generous
> Her round strong arms and beautiful hands
> completed her proud, graceful figure.

Starting with this portrait, the text goes on to describe Glaura's history as a succession of struggles to defend her honor from the most diverse and, at times, rather picturesque attacks. The first offender is her uncle, Freolano, "que ingrato al hospedaje del amigo / del deudo y deuda haciendo poca cura / me comenzó de amar y buscar medio / de dar a su cuidado algún remedio" ("who began to court her / in total disregard of his obligations to the relative and friend / who so generously had given him shelter"). Glaura defends herself from his dishonest proposition in the most elaborate rhetorical language, saying: "Oh malvado / incestuoso, desleal, ingrato / corrompedor de la amistad jurada / y ley de parentesco conservada" ("Oh you, incestuous, ungrateful, evil one / who would not hesitate to violate / the sacred bonds of family and friendship"). Rejected, Freolano throws himself into battle and dies at once.

The second attack comes from some black men who, finding Glaura lost in the woods, attempt to rape her. She is saved by Cariolán, but not before expressing her thoughts on the momentous importance of that honor which she is so often on the verge of losing:

> Fui dellos prestamente despojada
> de todo cuanto allí venía vestida
> aunque yo, triste, no estimaba en nada
> el perder los vestidos y la vida
> pero el honor y castidad preciada
> estuvo a punto ya de ser perdida.[38]

> They quickly stripped me from everything I wore
> and I would not have cared about losing my clothing
> had it not been that my very honor
> and precious chastity
> were now in danger of being lost as well.

Once Cariolán has disposed of the last of her assailants, Glaura recovers her honor in the manner prescribed in such cases: by washing the offense clean with blood. The dramatic nucleus of the episode is the attempted rape, but once this is over, Glaura's concern with honor continues to be the focus of her characterization. She claims that she married Cariolán because she was "medrosa de andar en opiniones" ("afraid of gossip"), and that ever since Cariolán left her in the woods because he feared "mucho mas mi deshonra que su muerte" ("much more my dishonor than his death"), she has been wandering about in the neighborhood of the Spanish camp concealed "por el honor que mal me le asegura / mi poca edad y mucha desventura" ("to save an honor that I can barely defend, given my youth and great misfortune").[39]

The central importance of these elements in Ercilla's characterization of women is heightened by the only episode about a woman who is not an Araucan: the story of Dido. Dido is the implicit model for all the native heroines in *La Araucana*, all of whom share with her such essential qualities as "steadfastness in love," "great perseverence," chastity, and honor. Dido excels in cleverness and prudence, but her most fundamental virtues are her faithfulness to her dead husband, her steadfast chastity, and her sense of honor. What makes this Dido memorable is her determination to "acabar la vida miserable / primero que mudar la fe inmudable" ("end her own life / rather than betray her dead husband"). Instead of remarrying, and thus betraying her first husband, Dido chooses to "spill her pure blood" by plunging a dagger into her "chaste bosom." The use of such terms as "pure" and "chaste" ties this description to the stylistic terms of the representation of honor that developed in Spanish literature during the sixteenth and seventeenth centuries. It is also consistent with the attitude of the Araucan heroines. This close correspondence is another indication of the fundamental problem involved in the way native characters are portrayed in Ercilla's poem.

Linked to the model personified by Dido, the characterization of the Araucan heroines consists of a systematic transposition of the ideological values of sixteenth-century Spanish society, and it conforms with the canons and conventions associated with female figures in the European literary tradition. Guacolda is the prototype of the woman in love and as such the rhetoric and motifs of her speech echo those of traditional Italian Renaissance poetry. Tegualda's story follows the chivalric model of representation, and her image is that of a lady in love in the manner of the courtly tradition. Glauca and her story personify and dramatize the issues of chastity, honor, and honor offended that were so prevalent a concern in sixteenth-century Spain. Lauca, briefly appearing as the prototype of the faithful woman, represents yet another central value of the ideology and culture of the period. And Fresia, the only character who retains some of the violence and heroism depicted in Ercilla's initial problematic representation of Araucan women, is also related to the European ideal of womanhood through the use of a high style and elaborate rhetoric that reveals the literary and ideological clichés current at the time.

Existing scholarship on *La Araucana* has devoted a great deal of attention to a set of questions that are only of secondary importance to this analysis. These questions include whether there actually ever was an Indian woman by the name of Gualda, whether Ercilla invented the relationship between Tegualda and Crepino, and whether the narrator's encounter with the badly wounded Lauca was imaginary or real.[40] An analysis of each of the portraits of these female characters reveals them to be purely fictional creations idealized according to the terms of contemporary literary and ideological models. Lía Schwartz clearly summarizes the essentially literary character of Ercilla's heroines:

> Ercilla leaves to one side any possible documentary purpose here, and creates literary figures inspired by passages and episodes from Ariosto's *Orlando Furioso*. Guacolda, Tegualda, Glaura are fictitious beings acting under names presumed to be Indian, in an idealized environment that has nothing in common with that of Chile. The characters express themselves in elaborate, rhetorical language, and become involved in adventures that are literary in tone and in no way reflect historical reality.[41]

Schwartz also points out two important additional elements: that the presentation of nature and the use of language are subordinate to the idealized characterization of the female figures. We might add that this applies likewise to the male characters, for Ercilla clearly leaves any documentary accuracy aside in the characterization of male Araucans. They too are idealized and mythified. This does not seem so striking in their case, however, because what is involved is mainly a magnification of authentic attributes—valor, strength, pride—rather than the qualitative transformation implied when a character who has been a woman warrior in Canto 10 appears as a Renaissance lady in the intercalated episodes.

The idealized characterization of the Araucan woman is not shaped by accuracy or realism but by the conventional elements of European literary models. On the other hand, the idealization of Araucan male characterization is a result first of a magnification of their warrior virtues, which take on a mythical dimension in the poem, and second of the author's decision to attribute to them a philosophy and a set of values that link them to the chivalric model. This philosophy is presented in a series of speeches by Araucan chieftains. Their rhetoric is that of a sixteenth-century Spaniard, and their characterization as heroes follows an unmistakably European mode of representation. Unlike the characterization of the Araucan women, that of the men is centered on physical and moral qualities that reflect their harmonious relationship with the environment and that have made Arauco the most feared and respected warrior nation in America. (The poet stresses in the first canto that the prestige of the Araucans as warriors is absolutely real, and he carefully lists the most noteworthy peoples defeated by them or placed under their control—the last name on the list being that of the Spaniards.) It is the *manner* in which their true qualities and fundamental values are represented that turns the Araucans and their world into an idealized fiction. Physical strength, valor, fortitude, and independence are all placed within an ideological framework that makes them, fictitiously, a part of Europe by subordinating them to European philosophy and values. The result is the transformation of a struggle to the death, undertaken by a nation determined to die in defense of its independence, into the dramatization of a set of ideological values— honor, fame, glory, and so on—conceived and formulated in terms that cannot be dissociated from the European worldview they express. This Europeanization of the Araucans' qualities, values, and customs is especially apparent in the speeches and exhortations made by the central characters: Colocolo, Caupolicán, and Lautaro.

Taking as its point of departure real warrior virtues and the extraordinary valor of a nation respected all over America for its military might, the poem creates a mythifying structure that glorifies the men and women of Arauco through an idealized mode of representation that clearly transforms them. The specific elements of this structure (the rhetoric of the Araucans, the subordination of their personal and social qualities to the European ideological parameters, the transformation of women warriors into Renaissance ladies and of the Chilean environment into a pleasant landscape in the style of Garcilaso) all perform the same function: the insertion of the world of Arauco into the cultural context of Europe.

Structures of Integration

Most critics agree that the nature of the heroines in *La Araucana* is thoroughly literary and idealized, and that of the male figures clearly mythical. Fernando Alegría states with good reason that Ercilla created *myths*, not *characters*, in his poem, and he points out accurately the deceptive nature of the author's "realism." But his interpretation is far more open to question when he refers to the meaning of this "deceptive" realism, as it appears specifically in the work. And when he considers the function of the idealization of the Araucan heroines, he dodges the issue, claiming that it does not alter their condition as women, and that this is what really matters.[42] Lía Schwartz acknowledges that the female characters are drawn artificially and unrealistically, making any analogy with the world of the Araucans "highly questionable." At the same time, however, she explains their function in the poem in terms similar to those of Ercilla's own statements: "Wishing to give his poem diversity and balance, Ercilla breaks the monotony of the military episodes by inserting, in the style of the epic, love scenes and characters reflecting literary rather than real life experiences."[43] In fact, there is no more reason to accept the poet's explanation concerning the function of his female characters than there is to believe his constant lamentations over the dryness of his subject, war—which was obviously not only *not* dry to him but a source of great enthusiasm. Schwartz's explanation is not satisfactory, for Ercilla's need to diversify his material would appear to be related to only one of the minor functions of the idealized representations of the episodes inserted in his war narrative, an idealization that affects all characteristics of Araucan men and women, even if not to the same degree. A more clarifying approach to the problems posed by Ercilla's characterization would be an analysis of specific idealizing and mythifying strategies that illuminates the dual function they perform within Ercilla's poetics in *La Araucana*. This dual function derives from their subordination to the two distinct but complementary thrusts that shape Ercilla's characterization: mythification and integration.

In contrast with the earlier forms of narrative discourse that had presented American natives as objects, animals, slaves, noble savages, or minors, Ercilla's starts out affirming their superior humanity and ends up creating a myth. In a manner consistent with the epic mode of representing a warrior, the poem illustrates the superiority of the Araucans by systematically magnifying their military virtues (strength, valor, fortitude, daring, military spirit, etc.) in terms so superlative that they border on the unbelievable. Beginning with this superlative characterization, the mythifying characterization of the Araucans gradually subordinates everything about them to the central cultural values of Spain at the time. Aggressiveness, strength, violence, and so on, rather than signs of a bestial or primitive condition, become the qualities most appropriate and necessary for the defense of certain ideological values wholly accepted by Europe (honor, dignity, nationhood) that the Araucans appear to share. I do not wish to imply that the Araucans were without honor, dignity, or a sense of nationhood, but the poem presents these virtues in unmistakably European terms. What is involved is not honor or fidelity per se, but a concept of honor and fidelity inseparably associated with the European tradition of chivalry and the codes of sixteenth-century Spain, and the same holds true for all the other ideological values attributed by the author to his Araucan characters. The idealization that results from implicitly subordinating all the specific aspects of the characterization of the natives to the fundamental values of European ideology is complemented in the text with a parallel process of selection and elimination that has the effect of masking *difference*. Just as it includes no female traits (other than its initial problematic representation of the women warriors) that cannot be associated with the Renaissance model personified by Dido, the poem eliminates from its male portraits anything that might appear inconsistent with the mythical figure on which these portraits are based: the model warrior associated with the tradition of chivalry. Regardless of any superficial differences, the ideological and aesthetic referent that informs the characterization of the Araucan nation and its individual representatives is European, and anything that cannot somehow be reconciled with this framework must be rejected or transformed.

This subordination of the characterization of the Araucans to the ideological and aesthetic values of Europe is dramatized in the text in a number of episodes. One of the most revealing occurs in Canto 8. It follows the Araucans' overwhelming victory of the capture of the city of Concepción, when the "most important men in the land" convene a council of warrior chieftains to determine how to proceed against the invaders. The text describes the arrival of Caupolicán as follows:

> Llevaba el general aquel vestido
> con que Valdivia ante él fue presentado,
> era de verde y púrpura tejido,
> con rica plata y oro recamado,
> un peto fuerte, en buena guerra habido
> de fina pasta y temple relevado
> la celada de claro y limpio acero
> y un mundo de esmeralda por cimero

> The general wore now the same green and red dress,
> embroidered in gold and silver, that Valdivia himself
> wore when they first met.
> And he displayed Valdivia's own steel armor and his
> finely wrought helmet, with the round emerald.

But Caupolicán is not the only chieftain who appears dressed up as a conquistador, and the text notes that:

> Todos los capitanes señalados
> a la española usanza se vestían;
> la gente del común y los soldados
> se visten del despojo que traían;
> calzas, jubones, cueros desgarrados
> en gran estima y precio se tenían

por inútil y bajo se juzgaba
el que español despojo no llevaba.[44]

And all the other captains were, likewise,
dressed up like Spaniards.
They wore the clothes and suits that they had won
as spoils after the battle
and anybody who had any pride at all made sure to wear
some Spanish spoil or garment.

These detailed descriptions reveal a dual signifying process. On the one hand, they allude—at the more immediate level of representation—to the celebration of victory ("A manera de triunfos ordenaron / el venir a la junta asi vestidos" ["thus clad in triumph / they convened for the meeting"]), and to the plunder that traditionally follows such a victory, of which examples abound throughout the text. But the specific manner in which tradition and celebration converge, in a scene describing in the most theatrical and visual terms every detail of a disguise that connotes a fictitious transculturation, points toward a second signifying process that links the representation to the more general problem of Ercilla's characterization of the natives. The costumes worn by the Araucans, besides transforming them fictitiously into Spaniards, allude to another disguise more subtle and complex. The figure of Caupolicán, invested with all the attributes of the conquistador, a perfect semblance of the unfortunate Valdivia, foreshadows Caupolicán's own final integration into the Spanish camp through his baptism, his acceptance of the ideology of the Spaniards, and his wretched death, which will turn out to be no better than Valdivia's.

The main action described in the stanzas quoted above is conveyed by the use of four verbs. "Llevaba/Vestían/Visten/Llevaba" all describe the same operation—that of *wearing, being clothed in,* a costume—and the two verbs repeated symmetrically at the beginning and end of the passage clearly frame the picture within the context of the other stanzas. Moreover, these four verbs also express the Araucan's temporary concealment beneath a Spanish appearance. This notion of concealment relates metaphorically to the process of idealization that shapes an array of characterizations drawn in terms of aesthetic and cultural points of reference that are no less Spanish, no less foreign to the identity of the Araucans, than the clothing worn by Caupolicán in the first stanza quoted.

Throughout a process of mythifying characterization of the Araucan people, which ranges from the exaggeration of their warrior virtues to their ultimate transformation into a symbol of freedom, the cultural referent is always Europe. This idealization in terms of European values and aesthetics poses two immediate problems. First, it creates an apparent contradiction between the distortion of reality implied by this idealization and the poet's intention, stated from the very beginning, to tell the truth. In his prologue to the first part, Ercilla declares that the poem is "the true history," and he returns to this definition in the first stanzas of the first canto, claiming that what he writes is "relación sin corromper sacada / de la verdad, cortada a su medida" ("an accurate account / that conveys nothing but the truth"). Second, the fact that this idealization should reflect Spanish ideological and aesthetic models would initially seem to indicate the presence of an ethnocentric attitude that, if actually there, would thoroughly transform the work's value and significance. It would also contradict my earlier assertion regarding the presence in *La Araucana*, for the first time ever in the narrative discourse of the conquest, of a perception of the natives that attempts to present them in harmony with their own natural and cultural environment rather than isolating them from their context in order to measure them by the standards of Europe. How are we to reconcile a characterization that presents the natives as representatives of the natural order they inhabit, in complete harmony with the American environment to which they belong, with a parallel process of idealization that implicitly but consistently subordinates all the qualities that make them superior beings in America to European ideological structures?

The answer to this fundamental question lies in the tension between the two conflicting cultural contexts that frame the characterization: Europe and America. In the world for which Ercilla was writing, humanity, civilization, and culture were associated almost exclusively with European models, that is, with the models of the dominant society. Everything to do with America, on the other hand, was thought of in terms of categories similar to those created or imagined by the ancients to describe the unknown. These frequently identified the New World with things fantastic or monstrous. Within the narrative discourse of the conquest that starts with Columbus and culminates in Ercilla, American reality is first associated with the fantastic and then perceived increasingly as primitive, savage, or barbarian. Ercilla, however, focuses his mythifying characterization of the Araucans on all the qualities—such as strength, valor, pride, independence—that express the natives' harmonious relationship with their natural environment. But from the perspective of the Spanish cultural assimilation and military domination of America, these same qualities also represent a source of potential conflict. Grounding his characterizations in these qualities, Ercilla portrays the Araucans as representatives of a superior civilization of warriors and as the very embodiment of freedom. In what would appear to be a contradiction, however, he subordinates the specific presentation of their qualities to an ideological superstructure and a set of models that assimilates them into Spanish culture, undermining their identity as Americans. And yet this subordination of presentation and characterization to European cultural and ideological models is not, within this poem, a sign of an ethnocentric inclination to ignore or undermine things American. On the contrary, it is a literary strategy that expresses Ercilla's determination to defend the superior nature of a different people and the value of their culture, by fictitiously assimilating them into the literary and historical traditions of Europe.

The image of the Araucans as a people outstanding in war and determined to be free, which not only humanizes them but gives them a mythical dimension, implicitly challenges the validity of the earlier stereotypes created by the different versions of the narrative discourse of the conquest. There is, however, a subversive potential in a representation that transforms "pieces" into "models." The threat implicit in that transformation must be neutralized if its message is to be intelligible and acceptable to the culture to which it is addressed. The idealization that results from Ercilla's subordination of the warrior virtues of the Araucan men and the personal qualities of the women to the ideological parameters of the West fulfills this function precisely. Agustín Cueva remarks on this as follows: "What must be stressed is that in a period manifestly ethnocentric, made even more extreme by its colonialism, to ascribe European traits to American characters was tantamount to erasing the mark of absolute otherness dividing the conqueror from the conquered."[45] To erase otherness becomes in fact essential, if the humanity of the native is to be accepted in a world for which *human* means *European*, and culture and civilization are systematically denied to any aspect of American reality. In this context, the idealized transformation of the Araucan warriors into Spanish knights, and of the women into perfect Renaissance ladies, indicates neither superficiality nor blind ethnocentricity on the part of the author. I mentioned earlier in this chapter that Ercilla's decision to give up any attempt to characterize the women of Arauco realistically reveals his awareness that as such, they would have been unacceptable to the culture he was addressing, and that his decision, after the first experiment in Canto 10, to replace his realistic characterization focused on *difference* by another that equated the natives with the women of Europe, revealed an important fact: that documentary and descriptive accuracy were not the author's main objectives. On the contrary, historiographical accuracy and descriptive verisimilitude in *La Araucana* appear to be subordinated to a project that is quite different from a documentary account of Araucan reality. This project is a literary creation that asserts, defends, and demonstrates the superior humanity of these American natives. But paradoxically, this humanity can only be conveyed to a Eurocentric audience by rejecting all problematic aspects of the new reality and by replacing accurate or realistic characterizations by idealized models.

Because of the thoroughly ethnocentric worldview of sixteenth-century Spain, the culture for whom the author was writing would almost assuredly have interpreted the distinctions between Americans and Europeans as clear indications that the natives lacked humanity altogether, or possessed it to only a minor degree. To have chosen an idealizing Spanish model against a potentially more realistic one does not mean that the author was blinded by his own ethnocentric views. It indicates, rather, that he was determined to challenge the view that "natives" were not "human" and that everything civilized could only be identified with Europe, proposing instead the notion that the natives were equal to the Europeans in that both groups shared a common human condition. Given Ercilla's historical and literary context as a writer, what he claimed for the natives could hardly be accepted without a mythification of America that fictitiously placed it within the ideological parameters and literary traditions of the West. Ercilla's constant remarks on the Araucans' preoccupation with European notions of honor; his presentation of the feelings and emotions of the Araucan women similar to those of heroines of Renaissance literature; his attribution to the natives of an impeccable rhetorical style, which they use to assert the fundamental importance of the same Western values that shape their own characterization; and his subordination of every personal and social relationship to these values—all perform an identical function, however different the tactics involved: they show that "these proud, free people" are neither a herd of primitive savages, equipped only with the brute force needed to harass and hold at bay the technically superior army of the Spaniards (as the official version of the Araucan war claimed) nor bestial beings whose strange habits have made them sufficiently exotic and interesting to warrant being observed, more or less curiously, from the Olympian heights of the metropolis. They are a warrior nation whose dignity and determination to be free reflect a superior degree of humanity, and whose level of civilization may be compared to that of the most famous warrior nations of antiquity.

To defend the natives' humanity and excellence, the poet developed a series of textual strategies that represented Araucan reality as wholly consistent with the ideological and literary contexts of the West. An analysis of the text will show, however, that this idealization is not an isolated element but only one aspect of a central signifying structure that shapes the poetics of *La Araucana*. It is a structure of integration, primarily designed to authorize the narrative material as well as the perception it reflects and the proposals it contains.

This integrating structure defines the precise function of diverse textual elements, which have often irritated purists and provoked many of the most enduring criticisms against the poem since it first appeared. These criticisms have focused mainly on three "problematical" aspects of the poem. All three result precisely from the presence in the text of that integrating structure. The first aspect is the idealized characterization of the natives discussed earlier; the second is the unorthodox development of the poem as a literary composition; the third is the poet's frequently conventionalized representation of the natural environment.

The idealized characterization of both the natives and their surroundings has been considered problematical for two reasons. First, there is a contradiction between this idealization and the poet's initial claim that his text contains nothing but a truthful account of objective events, making this objectivity and truthfulness a fundamental principle of the work's composition.[46] At the most literal level, it is difficult to reconcile the poet's claim with the evident fictionalization of many of the elements of American reality present in the poem. This apparent contradiction disqualifies *La Araucana* from the perspective of "*verista*" critics, who believe that epic poetry should concern itself strictly with historical truth.[47] Likewise, the ambiguous coexistence in the poem of actual historical events, ideal characters, and totally invented episodes also makes the text problematical for those who expect "verisimilitude." According to the "*verosimilista*" critics, rather than narrating particular concrete realities, epic poetry should convey through its inventions a more generally conceived "poetic truth." The problem is that Ercilla's poetic verisimilitude is inconsistent, for there are instances in the text where it is undermined by episodes whose documentary accuracy challenges, from within the text, the kind of poetic verisimilitude demanded by this latter aesthetic school. We need only compare, for example, the first portrait of the Araucan women in the guise of warriors with their later characterization in the idealized episodes of Tegualda and Guacolda to feel skeptical about the verisimilitude of the latter. José Durand refers precisely to this constant tension between objectivity and idealization in the poem when he comments: "We may catch Don Alonso inventing a woman's name, or just as likely being absolutely accurate."[48]

For critics who demanded verisimilitude, this dual manner of representation constituted one of the poem's main flaws. It implied a lack of poetic skill and creative talent on the part of the poet. This led them to criticize the work's method of composition just as harshly as did the critics devoted to the communication of "historical truth." Both schools, however, might have agreed with the first part of Voltaire's cutting remark, in the conclusion to his critique of *La Araucana*: "there is no power of invention here, no plan, no descriptive variety, no unity. This poem is more savage than the nations that have given it its subject."[49] Besides rejecting the work for reasons related to historicity and verisimilitude, Voltaire directs an explicit criticism precisely against the second "problematical" point I have mentioned: the poem's design or composition. He states categorically that the poem is thoroughly defective from this point of view because it lacks inner coherence as well as an overall plan. Few critics have gone so far in their disqualification of the poem, but most of them, from the seventeenth century to the present day—including those who have recognized several merits in Ercilla's work—have challenged its manner of composition. Conservative theorists questioned its validity in terms of the models followed by Spanish and Italian epic poetry; nineteenth-century critics faulted its lack of a proper beginning and an end, its development, and the insertion of the intercalated episodes in the body of the text. Only a few—Martínez de la Rosa among them, as noted by Alegría—sensed that there was a close connection between the work's "problematical" design and the author's complex intent.[50] Aside from the reaction of this small number of critics, the poem's composition has until very recently been considered contradictory and questionable.[51] This explains why, as Cueva points out, *La Araucana* has consistently been regarded as a "permanent source of aesthetic scandal."[52]

Throughout the poem, Ercilla frequently explains the insertion in the text of certain passages—specifically the love episodes—that might appear to break the unity of his composition. The context of such explanation is provided by his own frequent lamentations concerning the aridity and monotony of his subject:

> haber de tratar siempre de una cosa:
> que no hay tan dulce estilo y delicado,
> ni pluma tan cortada y sonorosa
> que en un largo discurso no se estrague
> ni gusto que un manjar no lo empalague[53]

For no style, no matter how sweet or subtle
can overcome forever the dullness of a single subject.

Thus the purpose of the episodes involving women is to open up a space for love, without which according to the poet "no puede haber verso bueno ni materia llena" ("there can be no good verse, no enjoyable subject"), or to weave into the poem one of the "mil fábulas y amores" ("thousand loves and fables") that other poets are accustomed to include in their works. Ercilla states that he knows how dry his subject is and how boring it may become to the reader, and that this has moved him to seek a remedy for both difficulties:

> Que el áspero sujeto desabrido
> tan seco, tan estéril, y desierto,
> y el estrecho camino que he seguido
> a puros brazos del trabajo abierto
> a términos me tienen reducido
> que busco anchura y campo descubierto
> donde con libertad, sin fatigarme
> os pueda recrear y recrearme[54]

> My subject is so harsh and stern
> the path I choose to follow is so narrow
> that I long and search
> for the expanses of an open field
> where I could find relief and enjoyment
> without further hardship.

But his many explicit claims as to the true function of these intercalations or of any other "strange" or questionable elements in the poem are not very useful. First, there is no reason to accept his explanations, and if there were, the diversification he claims to be their purpose would not be sufficient cause to justify the presence of so large a number of "digressions," as he calls them, or to excuse their apparent lack of connection with the declared purpose of the work. Second, quite aside from these reservations, the poet's explanations refer to only one of the problematical aspects of the composition of *La Araucana*—the intercalated episodes. However, if all the extraneous elements (the intercalated episodes, the digressions and fantastic episodes, the idealized or stereotyped representations of characters or nature, etc.) are analyzed as organic components of the integrating structure I have referred to earlier, their function in the text becomes clear as part of the design that shapes the work. They are all subordinate to the need to authenticate and authorize in terms of the historical and literary traditions of the West, a representation of America and the conquest that challenges with increasing lucidity the official account of the conquest, and of its ruthless colonization of the natives.

Besides the poem's idealization of the natives and its unorthodox composition, there is a third aspect of the poem frequently considered to be problematical: its representation of American nature, which many critics find inconsistent. The most common criticism has been directed at his frequent use of landscapes typical of the Renaissance to describe America. But even the most critical analyses have acknowledged that while nature is sometimes unmentioned and often transformed according to unmistakable Garcilaso aesthetics, the description of American nature in some stanzas is strikingly realistic. Fernando Alegría refers to these realistic passages in response to critics who have challenged the artificial quality of the poem's idealized descriptions, although he acknowledges that it is the latter that occur most frequently: "Nor is there any lack of realistic descriptions in *La Araucana*. True, the landscape described by Ercilla is in general conventional; the classical stream that winds a crystalline path through his pasturelands is much the same as those to be found in Virgil, Petrarch, and Garcilaso. At times, however, a tale takes a powerful hold on the poet's memory, and he recalls it later with admirable lucidity."[55] Alegría offers no explanation, however, for the presence in the poem of two such contradictory modes of representation.

One need only examine Ercilla's realistic descriptions of nature to realize that it makes no sense to attribute the scenes in which nature is presented in the archetypical manner of the Renaissance to a limited talent for observation of creativity. We might recall, for example, the description of the marshlands in Canto 12, reminiscent of some texts of the narrative discourse of failure, particularly those of Elvas and Cortés; or the storm unleashed in the last canto of Part 1 and brought to an end years later in Canto 16 at the beginning of Part 2; or finally, the craggy, thickly overgrown, inhospitable terrain traversed by the narrator during his expedition to the south of Chile, which he describes in detail on several occasions. Conventional descriptions of nature in the text, therefore, seem to reflect a specific choice, not a lack of skill. And if we reflect upon the meaning of this choice, relating it to the structure of integration we have been analyzing, its purpose within the poem becomes increasingly clear. From this perspective, the frequent replacement of American landscapes by those typical of the European Renaissance no longer appears to reflect a lack of poetic ability or sensitive discernment. The idealized landscape becomes an analogical construct designed to give authority and prestige to the elements contained within its stereotypical frame. An examination of some of the specific instances when these stereotypical descriptions appear will confirm this hypothesis. The Chilean landscape takes the form of a perfect, Garcilaso landscape at strategic points in the text that introduce fundamental aspects of the world of the Araucans. The section describing Araucan society provides a good example. Explaining the Araucan people's legal organization—whose validity and seriousness are crucial if he is to prove that the Araucans are civilized and have a culture—Ercilla frames his description of the council in the following stanzas:

> Hácese este concilio en un gracioso
> asiento en mil florestas escogido,
> donde se muestra el campo más hermoso,
> de infinidad de flores guarnecido:
> allí de un viento fresco y amoroso
> los árboles se mueven con ruido
> cruzando muchas veces por el prado
> un claro arroyo limpio y sosegado
>
> de una fresca y altísima alameda
> por orden y artificio tienen puesta
> en torno de la plaza y ancha rueda
> capaz de cualquier justa y grande fiesta
> que convida a descanso y al sol veda
> la entrada y paso en la enojosa siesta:
> allí se oye la dulce melodía
> del canto de las aves y armonía.[56]

> The council takes place in an idyllic setting
> amidst rolling fields covered with wild flowers.
> The trees sway gently under a soft, cool breeze,
> a crystal clear spring
> winds through the rolling meadows.

> With artifice and vision they have designed a round,
> wide square
> surrounded by tall poplar trees
> and it is in such pleasant surroundings, enjoying the
> cool shade and the clear singing of the birds
> that they carry out their debates,
> and tournaments, and contests.

The enumeration here of almost all the features of a conventional Renaissance landscape has the same function as the specific mention of the words *orden* (order) and *artificio* (design) in the second stanza: it shows that the Araucans are a civilized people.

The symbolic characters of these stereotypical descriptions is reinforced by their appearance in another context, that of certain imaginary episodes such as the poet's dream, recalled in Canto 18. Here the description evokes, with utmost lyrical economy, a reality symbolized by the model of representation in question.

> En un asiento fértil y sabroso
> de alegres plantas y árboles cercado
> do el cielo se mostraba más hermoso
> y el suelo de mil flores variado
> cerca de un claro arroyo y sonoroso
> que atravesaba el fresco y verde prado
> vi junta toda cuanta hermosura
> supo y pudo formar acá natura[57]

> And in that place, where all manner of plants
> and trees grew lusciously
> and where the ground was covered by countless
> wild flowers under the bluest sky
> where the clear spring wound its course
> through the gentle meadow
> I saw, with my own eyes, all the beauty
> that nature can ever offer in this world.

Its specific components are an almost exact duplicate of those in the two previously quoted stanzas. In both cases, the referent is "happy Spain." But the function of this second passage is different: that of simply invoking the cultural context of the action developed in the stanzas that follow. In the first two stanzas quoted, on the other hand, the replacement of concrete American reality by a Renaissance model has a dual purpose. It serves to erase the connotation of barbarism inseparably associated at the time with America. And, by symbolically equating the natural environment of the Araucan and European civilizations, it also makes the character of the two appear analogous. The symbolic landscape that introduces the episode concerned with the council has then an integrating function designed to associate the Araucan and European civilizations, fictitiously equating them, and to attest to the dignity of what is being narrated by placing it within the formal structure required for its incorporation within the literary tradition of Europe.

Another form used to portray nature in *La Araucana* is mythological representation, and its function is identical to the one we have been discussing. The personification of the elements—wind, dawn, sun, sea—was not new to either the classical or the Renaissance epic tradition. And if we compare Ercilla's poetry to that of Camoes, for example, we find Ercilla to be very spare in his use of mythological references. But here again, what characterizes his approach is not only the form selected as such, but the specific manner in which he uses it and the specific function it fulfills within the text. When narrating one of the most important episodes concerning the Araucan people and their customs—the contest involving the log—Ercilla uses mythological representation almost throughout. Dawn becomes "Triton's wife" who "ya parecía / los dorados cabellos esparcidos / que de la fresca helada sacudía" ("seemed / to be shaking off the frost / from her spread out golden hair"), and the sun, "El carro de Faetón sale corriendo / del mar por el camino acostumbrado" ("racing out of the sea in Phaeton's cart / following his customary path"), is represented as Apollo, of whom Ercilla says, "en seguimiento de su amiga / tendido había los rayos de su lumbre" ("he, likewise, was spreading out / the gold of his warming rays").[58] Here the mythological representation of natural elements lends dignity to a key episode that might otherwise be perceived as no more than a struggle for power among a group of barbarians. The lyrical presentation of the contest based on mythological personification as a fundamental aesthetic code gives it a mythical character by associating it with a heroic literary tradition, of which both the Araucan's actions and Ercilla's poem become implicitly an example.

The stanzas just quoted illustrate only one of the important functions of mythology in *La Araucana*: that of giving authority to American realities by establishing a formal connection between this material and a previously canonized literary tradition. This is not, however, the only function of mythological references within the poem. They tie together the two major aspects of Ercilla's project to represent American reality in a way that validates it in the eyes of a strongly Eurocentric audience. The first aspect is the symbolic integration of this material within an existing literary tradition. The second is the legitimation of American material through its symbolic inscription in the history of the West. Famous gods, heroes, and warriors from classical antiquity share center stage in the pages of *La Araucana* with the natives, to whom Ercilla compares them explicitly. Rengo's immense strength, for example, is compared to that of Antheus, the mythical giant of ancient Greece, son of Poseidon and Gaea, who could recover his prodigious and inexhaustible strength simply by touching the earth with the soles of his feet. Thus a parallel is established in the poem between the two figures. The war between the Spaniards and the Araucans is compared to warfare in classical antiquity—more specifically, to the wars between the Greeks and the Trojans, with the sacking of Concepción likened to the plunder at the end of the siege of Troy.[59] Finally, the Araucans are compared to numerous heroes in European history, whose extraordinary deeds are shown to have been even surpassesd by those of the native warriors.

> No los dos Publios Decios que las vidas
> sacrificaron por la patria amada,
> ni Curcio, Horacio, Scevola y Leónidas
> dieron muestra de sí tan señalada:
> ni aquellos que en las guerras tan reñidas
> alcanzaron gran fama por la espada,
> Furio, Marcelo, Fulvio y Cincinato,
> Marco Sergio, Filón, Sceva y Dentato.
> Decidme: estos famosos ¿Qué hicieron
> que al hecho de este bárbaro igual fuese?[60]

> Not even the two Publio Decios who sacrificed
> their lives for love of country
> had a higher claim to glory.
> Nor did Curcio, Horatio, Scevola, or Leonidas
> for all their exploits
> nor all those who in so many ways lived by the sword
> and by the sword became famous
> like Furio, Marcelo, Fulvio, and Cincinato,
> Marco Sergio, Filon, Sceva, and Dentato.
> Just tell me one thing they accomplished
> that has not already been surpassed
> by these barbarians.

Thus by means of equivalences, comparisons, and parallels drawn between the Araucans and the heroes of European tradition, the former are assimilated into Western history and dignified according to European cultural and ideological codes.

One last element completes the fictitious integration of Arauco: the implicit parallel that Ercilla draws between the Araucans' military campaigns and some of the most notorious battles of Ercilla's own time, especially those of San Quintín and Lepanto. In regard to the latter, the equivalence arises essentially from a representation of military violence that implicitly puts Christians and Araucans on an equal plane. The function of this equivalence in the text is stated clearly by the magician Fitón:

> que pues en nuestro Arauco ya se halla
> materia a tu propósito cortada,
> donde la espada y defensiva malla
> es más que en otra parte frecuentada
> sólo te falta una naval batalla
> con que será tu historia autorizada[61]

Since you have already found in Arauco
an ideal ground to treat your subject
better than anywhere else
you only need to add the account
of a great naval battle
to make your story complete.

The parallel drawn with the battle of San Quintín links one of the most problematical scenes in the first part of the poem (the sacking of Concepción by the Araucan warriors) with a similar scene where the agents of aggression, rape, and plunder are Christians. The identical behavior of Araucans and Spaniards in the two scenes has the effect of revealing Araucan violence not as a sign of primitive barbarism, but as an element that identifies them with a historical tradition that, from the time of the wars of the ancients up to the conquest of America, had always acknowledged that plunder was a warrior's legitimate reward.

Besides the legitimizing function just described, Ercilla's inscription of the Araucans within European tradition has another important meaning. It is a symbolic restitution of history. Through this inscription, Ercilla fictitiously fills the actual historical void created for the natives by the conquest and the official Spanish accounts of their cultures. It is important to stress the symbolic and fictitious nature of this restitution: what is involved is by no means a true *recovery* of the past, but its replacement by a version of history borrowed from Europe. Hence Ercilla's "restitution" is a very limited one. But it is equally important to remember that beginning with Columbus a number of narrative discourses had, by means of different strategies, deprived Native Americans of their speech, culture, and history, and to note that comparatively speaking, all three of these are symbolically restituted in *La Araucana*, regardless of the highly questionable form taken by such restitution. Ercilla never attempted to convey an authentic rendition of the native past. This would be closer to the goals of the Inca Garcilaso de la Vega in what Pupo-Walker has called "an imaginary pilgrimage toward history."[62] Nonetheless, the symbolic restitution of a past, a culture, and a history by fictitiously placing the men, women, and nation of Arauco within the province of European historical and literary tradition—subordinating the structural components of the poem to this design—is a cardinal aspect of what may be considered one of the richest and most complex critical and literary attempts ever made to represent the entire history of the conquest of America and to reflect on its deepest meaning.

A Literary Expression of a New Consciousness

The prominence assigned to the characterization of the Araucan people in *La Araucana* and the praise expressed for their deeds are not the only things that make the poem problematical. Paralleling the development of the mythification of the natives, but in a reverse direction, is another process of characterization that contributes further to their glorification: the critical presentation of the conquistadors, who represent a systematically demythified Spanish side. The first stanza announces that the poet's song will have a twofold intention, extolling first

> el valor, los hechos, los proezas
> de aquellos españoles esforzados,
> que a la cerviz de Arauco no domada
> pusieron duro yugo por la espada.

> the courage and the glorious deeds
> of all those Spaniards who with their swords
> were the first ones to subjugate Arauco.

But it will also praise the deeds of "a people who obey no king," that is, the Araucans.

A reading of the poem quickly reveals that the priorities announced at the beginning are, to say the least, reversed: there is obviously more space devoted to portraying the Araucan characters and to describing their heroic deeds than there is space devoted to the Spaniards. The greatest contradiction between the poem and its declared purpose, however, lies not in this shift in priorities, but in the change from an explicit design of praising the Spaniards' exploits to an openly critical demythification of their characters and values. The manner in which their characterization develops not only contradicts the author's announced intent; it represents a complete break with the modes of characterization and representation first developed by the discourse of mythification.[63] It relates directly to the demythifying critical perception that began in the literature of the conquest with the narrative discourse of failure (especially the *Naufragios*), and to Las Casas's criticism of the dominant ideology that shaped the conquest. José Durand has remarked on this relation between *La Araucana* and the thinking of Las Casas, in connection with the poem's idealized, mythified native portraits: "The . . . inclination to honor certain barbarian heroes was encouraged by ideas emerging from Las Casas's great debates in regard to the humanity and dignity of the Indians and the question of the justice of the wars, which were absorbed daily in Chile, Lima, and at court."[64] Furthermore, although less apparent initially than the connection between the portrayal of the conquistador in *La Araucana* and in Las Casas's *Historia,* there is an undeniable link as well with the stark characterizations of the narrative discourse of rebellion.

In *La Araucana,* the characterization of the conquistador has two main aspects. They express the historical transformation of the warrior into a colonizer, a development associated with the first century of the conquest, as they articulate a symbolic summary of the three main stages of the literary development of the figure in the three types of narrative discourse analyzed: the model hero portrayed in the discourse of mythification; the more human, complex warrior presented in the narrative discourse of failure; and the cruel, exploitative colonizer described in the discourse of rebellion. The conquistador in *La Araucana* is an ambiguous, apparently contradictory figure precisely because in different sections of the poem, he exemplifies different instances in the historical development of the conquistador. In other words, he embodies the transformation of the heroic, courageous, messianic warrior associated with the military period of the conquest into the greedy, exploitative, unscrupulous *encomendero,* motivated by nothing but the acquisition of wealth and personal power, and typical of the emerging colonial society.

Ercilla presents the figure of the conquistador from three different angles: the representation of the collective and individual action of the Spaniards in the war against the Araucans, the comments of the narrator, and the perception the natives express through the speeches or parleys of their chieftains. The overall portrait of the conquistadors conveyed by their individual or collective action is extremely negative. In fact, reflecting as it does their cowardliness, weakness, selfishness, greed, and their complete lack of dignity or sense of honor, it is almost the complete opposite of the earlier heroic model of the warrior. Repeated incidents and images throughout the poem so dramatize the fear experienced by these degraded Spaniards that it reaches clearly grotesque proportions. As opposed to the complete control over every situation typical of the mythical conquistador in Cortés's *Letters,* the Spaniards in *La Araucana* flee from native attacks time and again in the most undignified fashion, possessed by the most agonizing panic:

> No aguardaban por esto, mas corriendo
> juegan a mucha priesa los talones
> al delantero sin parar siguiendo
> que no le alcanzarán a dos tirones
> votos, promesas entre sí haciendo
> de ayunos, romerías, oraciones,

y aún otros reservados sólo al Papa,
si Dios deste peligro los escapa.[65]

They did not wait for anything.
They only tried to outrun all those ahead of them
while they prayed to God, made vows and promises,
some of them to be made only by the Pope himself,
if only God would save them from this fearful danger.

Blind with fear, unable to face an enemy more valiant than they, the once
heroic warriors hesitate, flee, pray, and tremble. Moreover, their degradation is presented not only as a phenomenon affecting individual men but
as the manifestation of a collective state of disintegration made repeatedly
apparent by their loss of solidarity.

El hermano no escucha al caro hermano
las lástimas allí son excusadas;
quien dos pasos del otro se aventaja
por ganar otros dos muere y trabaja

. . . .

A aquel por desdicha atrás venía
ninguno, aunque sea amigo, le socorre.[66]

The brother does not listen to the brother
but struggles to move ahead of him,
if only a couple of steps

. . . .

and all ignore the friend unfortunate enough
to fall behind.

Valdivia places himself at the head of this grotesque army, so unlike the
united, exemplary corps described by Cortés. But this Valdivia is no longer
the valiant conquistador who had been the first to prevail against the
tenacious resistance of the Araucans, after the failure of numerous attempts
by others to invade their territory. He is called lazy, negligent, faithless,
remiss, careless; not a shadow is left of the earlier man who, as we are
told at the beginning of the first canto, was justly granted the first victory
over the Araucan army:

A sólo el de Valdivia esta victoria
con justa y gran razón le fue otorgada
y es bien que se celebre su memoria
pues pudo adelantar tanto su espada[67]

For this first victory
was justly and fairly granted to Valdivia.
And it is fair that to this day he be praised
for he conquered many a land with his sword.

Here he is no more than one of the members of an undignified, discredited army that is incapable of being aroused to action by either the imprecations of Doña Mencía or the harangues of Villagrán. The army's ignominy reaches its low point when, after being roundly defeated by the Araucan warriors, it flees from the Araucan women who turn out to be even more courageous and aggressive than their men:

> Mirad aquí la suerte tan trocada
> pues aquellos que el cielo no temían
> las mujeres, a quien la rueca es dada,
> con varonil esfuerzo los seguían.[68]

> Behold the reversal of roles
> as women abandoning the spinning wheel
> gave chase with male courage
> to those who til then had feared nothing
> on the face of the earth.

The reversal of roles is at its most extreme here, as the Spaniards show themselves to be inferior not only to the more able native warriors but to women, the very embodiment of weakness and vulnerability according to the military values of the code of chivalry.

Ercilla's presentation of the action of Spaniards against Araucans gradually shapes a profoundly negative characterization, whose concrete components—cowardice, dishonor, selfishness—cancel out in turn each fundamental feature of the heroic model formulated by the discourse of mythification. This devastating portrait is not presented as intrinsically or permanently accurate, however, but as the result of a process of degradation. The text neither criticizes nor denies the excellence of the heroic conquistador represented by the model in the discourse of mythification. Quite the contrary: it constantly invokes the terms of this model, not to criticize it as a mythical embodiment of the ideological values that serve to support and justify such acts of imperialistic aggression as the conquest itself, but to mark the distance that separates the model from the despicable being into which the conquistador has deteriorated: the colonizer or *encomendero*. At the same time, the text makes it unequivocally clear that the Spaniards' degradation is to be explained in terms of the historical development of the colony. Once away from the colonial context, as at San Quintín and Lepanto, the men recover their energy and glory, exhibiting none of the unworthy behavior displayed against the Araucans.

Doña Mencía's imprecations reflect an awareness of the degradation that appears to have affected the mythical figure of the conquistador once placed in an American environment and transformed into an *encomendero*:

decidme ¿qué es de quella fortaleza
que contra los que así teméis mostrasteis?
¿Qué es de aquel alto punto y la grandeza
de la inmortalidad a que aspirasteis?
¿Qué es del esfuerzo, orgullo, la braveza
y el natural valor de que os preciasteis?[69]

But, tell me. Whatever happened to the courage
that you showed earlier against the same enemies
from whom you are fleeing now?
What of the glory and immortality for which you strove?
What of the effort, the pride, and the natural courage
and daring that you used to possess?

The narrator corroborates this perception in his commentary. He provides a twofold explanation for the decadence that marks the transition from heroic warrior to petty *encomendero*. First, the conquistador has forsaken the heroic values associated with his mythical model; second, he has allowed all his ideals and high purposes, his desire for change, to be replaced by a single objective: the satisfaction of his greed. By turning away from the heroic path of military achievements and embracing the exploitative petty material interests of the *encomendero*, he has become despicable, unworthy, cowardly, and degraded. "Esto que digo y la opinión perdían por aflojar el brazo de la espada" ("In giving up their sword they surrendered all claims to dignity and fame"),[70] says Ercilla, blaming the surrender of the heroic values embodied in the sword for all the Spaniards' misfortunes and failures during their Araucan campaigns.

In the narrator's view, greed above everything else has caused the conquistador to lose his earlier values: Greed only is "ocasión de tanta guerra / y perdición total de aquesta tierra" ("the cause of these wars / and of the destruction of these lands").[71] At the end of the second canto, Ercilla symbolically synthesizes in a single stanza his perception of everything that has brought about the transformation of the conquistador into a colonizer and his view of the effect of this transformation. He is referring to Valdivia, who is on his way to join the army to do battle against Tucapel. This battle, however, which was intended to punish the chieftain, turns into a spectacular victory for the natives and a humiliating defeat for the Spaniards. After Valdivia agreed to go to the chosen site, he suddenly changed his mind:

resoluto en hacer allí de hecho
un ejemplar castigo que sonase

en todos los confines de la tierra
porque jamás moviesen otra guerra,

. . . .
Pero dejó el camino provechoso,
y, descuidado dél, torció la vía
metiéndose por otro, codicioso,
que era donde una mina de oro había,
y de ver el tributo y don hermoso
que de sus ricas venas ofrecía,
paró de la codicia embarazado,
cortando el hilo próspero del hado.[72]

He was determined to punish them
in a way that would set an example
that would deter the Araucans
from engaging in war ever again. But he abandoned
the straight and narrow path,
when irresponsibly, and moved only by greed
he went, instead,
in search of a gold mine. He was anxious to see
the golden tribute hidden in its veins
and, in his greed, he did not hesitate
to sever the propitious thread of Fortune.

Valdivia's choice contains all the main elements of the perception underlying *La Araucana*'s criticism of the conquistador. Fortune has turned against the Spaniards to punish them for an implicit change in values that has led them to abandon their heroic ways in order to pursue their own interests, a shift expressed in the poem by the prevalence of greed over all other forms of motivation. The military way is seen as unequivocally positive: it is the right way. To have abandoned it means having lost sight of "the straight and narrow path," and this change of course takes on a metaphorical significance; the motive for having left the path is greed, which muddles people's faculties of judgment and choice.[73] The result of this decision is the loss of the victorious heroic tradition—"the propitious thread"—whose continuity will here be broken, severed as a result of Valdivia's unwise choices.

The native perspective, equally harsh in regard to the two main roles played by the Spaniards (as warriors and colonizers), further confirms the already negative view of the conquistadors provided by the action and by the narrator's commentary. As warriors the men seem just as despicable to the Araucans as the events portrayed them to be or as they are described by the narrator. Rengo chases after them, insulting them and calling them infamous and vile. The stratagems of the Araucan army and the traps set by Lautaro—when for example he complains of his men's weakness and lack of food to provoke the Spaniards to aggression—are inspired by the fact that the natives know full well that the Spaniards are cowardly and have little sense of honor, and that their army is fragmented. Even the Araucan women take the unworthiness of the Spaniards for granted when, pregnant and unarmed, they chase them as they flee.[74] Their image as colonizers, on the other hand, is no more favorable. Tuconabala calls them insatiably avaricious, cruel and terrible usurpers of the common good ("insaciables avarientos," "barbudos crueles y terribles / del bien universal usurpadores"), who sow destruction and injustice wherever they go. Finally, the natives' association of all the Spaniards' actions with *destruction* is confirmed by the narrator's own evaluation when he compares them to a "swarm of locusts," razing and devouring everything along their way.[75]

Using three different viewpoints then—the action, the narrator, and the natives—Ercilla weaves a thoroughly negative characterization of the conquistador. As presented in the wars against Arauco, only two dimensions of this figure remain evident, out of the three developed throughout the narrative discourse of the conquest. The heroic model of discourse of mythification is in *La Araucana* no more than a memory alluded to in the imprecations or harangues of a Doña Mencía or a Villagrán, to stress the decadence of the conquistador and the degradation of the colonizer. The Spanish army's lack of honor, the narrator's comments—at times explicit and moralizing as in his attack on greed at the beginning of Canto 3, at others more veiled as in his denunciation of the decadence of Valdivia— and the disdain implicit in the native perspective offer a single, consistent image of the conquistador as the embodiment of highly despicable characteristics and most unworthy interests. The specific features of this characterization—cowardice, selfishness, greed, cruelty—are reminiscent of Las Casas. The ideological view expressed in the poem, however, seems to present these negative qualities not as anything necessarily intrinsic to the violence and repression that are central to the function of any conquistador, but as a temporary state that is the result of a historical process perceived as decadence. As such, this view is clearly consistent with the perception of the conquistador projected by the narrative discourse of rebellion. For Las Casas, the conquistador's moral degradation was a necessary result of his ideology, the same ideology that allowed Spain to justify a wholly unacceptable and unjust plan to exploit the natives and expropriate their dominions. But Ercilla's critique, like that of Aguirre, is founded not on a radical rejection of the right to conquer and expropriate but on his perception of the discrepancy between the mythical models of the dominant ideology and the actual corruption, exploitation, and injustice that prevailed in colonial society. Like the discourse of rebellion, *La Araucana* attributes this discrepancy to a process of degradation that it identifies with the historical transformation of the heroic warrior glorified in the discourse of mythification into a colonizer avid for power and material gain—the "maize and cassava" people so hated by Lope de Aguirre—or into the indolent *encomenderos* Ercilla punishes harshly in the poem with repeated defeat and humiliation.[76]

The apparent absence of unity or even the contradictions in Ercilla's portrayal of the Spaniards, which offers such contrary examples as the heroic army of the battle of Lepanto and the caricaturesque version of such an army at the battle of Andalicán, express his personal perception of this historical transformation. For Ercilla, as for the perception that shaped the discourse of rebellion, this transformation has occurred because a social class on the rise has exchanged the glory of warfare for the intrigue and petty material interests of the *encomendero*, losing sight of its former heroic values. The narrative discourse of rebellion and Ercilla's poem do not merely reflect the same perception of colonial reality in this regard; they both propose that this present degradation be reversed by a return to the transcendental heroic values of the past. In this sense they anticipate the nostalgic revival of the mythified values of a lost golden age, so characteristic of the Baroque period. In the poem, the recovery of these heroic values is exemplified through such episodes as the battle of Lepanto, where victory is assured, Ercilla emphasizes, by the justice of its cause.[77] On the other hand, defeat at the hands of the Araucans is presented as the harsh punishment that the Spaniards have brought upon themselves, by having abandoned the heroic philosophy of the warrior and adopted that of the rapacious *encomendero*.

In the poem, it is the Araucans, not the Spaniards, who are the true representatives of the heroic values of the model created by the discourse of mythification. It is precisely in the exemplary values and behavior of the Araucans where we find the key element that unifies in a single critical project the two antithetical processes—the glorification of the natives and the unmasking of the weaknesses of the Spaniards—that organize the two parallel modes of characterization in *La Araucana*: idealization and satire. Contrary to a tradition that presented them as beasts or objects, Ercilla's Araucans are not only human beings. They represent precisely everything the Spaniards have ceased to be, and personify every virtue the Spaniards have betrayed. Hence their superiority, the central place they occupy in the narrative, the ultimate status of role models given to them explicitly in the poem:

> Dejen de encarecer los escritores
> a los que el arte militar hallaron,
> ni más celebren ya los inventores
> que el duro acero y el metal forjaron,
> pues los últimos indios moradores
> del araucano estado así alcanzaron
> el orden de la guerra y disciplina
> que podemos tomar dellos doctrina.[78]

> Let us not sing anymore
> the praise of those who invented the art of war
> or of those who discovered the secret
> of forged steel and metal.
> Rather, it is in the superb military order
> and war discipline
> of the Araucans that we should find our models.

The clash between the Araucans and the Spaniards reflects within the text a confrontation between two conflicting philosophies. And it is precisely the Spaniards' return to their heroic values, exemplified in the battle of Lepanto and the military campaigns in the second part of the poem, that will ultimately lead them to victory over the Araucans. No doubt the exaltation of the Araucan nation was inspired by the great debates of Las Casas, as remarked on by Durand.[79] But the mythified characterization of the Native Americans has another function here, no less important than that of asserting and defending their humanity. It is designed to illustrate by simple contrast the degradation in goals and values that the poet sees as the sole cause of all the problems, abuse, injustice, and corruption of the colony. This perspective neutralizes the subversive, radical critique that the combined process of mythification of the native and denigration of the Spaniard seemed to promise. Both of these strategies are woven into a critical design in which moral judgment gradually displaces a critique that is never carried to its ultimate consequences. As far as the poem's characterization strategies are concerned, we are left with a moral condemnation that illuminates the limitations of Ercilla's denunciation. They express the vision of a moralist who, having tacitly accepted the fundamental principles of the society to which he belongs and whose values he shares and defends, is forced by his own experience of the conquest to question the effects of this very same ideology.

The critique that unfolds through the parallel development of the two antithetical characterizations appears thus to be aimed specifically at the degradation of the conquistador and the corruption of the colony—leaving the ideal conception of the conquistador and the conquest intact. Thus the contrast between a characterization that presents the Araucans as models and the Spaniards as decadent and corrupt seems to criticize the Spaniards precisely because they have forgotten the virtues of the model hero, whose excellence is thereby implicitly reaffirmed. But this reaffirmation is more illusory than real. Within the text itself the epic model will be indirectly but unequivocally challenged by the Utopian presentation of pre-Columbian America. The negative portrayal of the conquest, on the other hand, will gradually reveal a rejection of imperial aggression that sheds a new light on Ercilla's final perception of the whole enterprise.

I have already referred to the contradictory ways in which nature is portrayed in *La Araucana*.[80] Of the two central modes of presentation— idealized and realistic—the first involved an idealized transformation along the lines of representation typical of Renaissance lyrical poetry; the second continued the demythifying representation of the narrative discourses of failure and rebellion. Reacting to a trend in *criollista* criticism that has frequently maintained that nature is represented conventionally in *La Araucana*, Jaime Concha remarks emphatically on the wealth and diversity of the landscapes in the poem, which "contains all the geography of our motherland."[81] But the scope of Ercilla's representation of American nature in *La Araucana* is even broader. All the different modes of representation formulated by the different narrative discourses of the conquest are combined in a poem that, in a way, transcends them all. We find the degrading perception of America as booty, first formulated by Columbus and subsequently institutionalized through the uncontrolled greed of the conquistadors and *encomenderos*, personified by Valdivia,[82] and the landscape described in military terms in the first letter of Hernán Cortés, who chose the elements of his representation with strategic rather than aesthetic or emotional criteria in mind, thus conveying, in the words of Concha, "a military experience of the territory."[83]

But together with these two modes of instrumentalized characterization reflecting the main approaches to nature in the discourse of mythification— one used critically, while the other illustrates the continuity of the Spanish plan to control the new land by military strength—*La Araucana* also contains a presentation of nature that radically undercuts both. As in the texts of the discourse of failure and rebellion, the poem shows the character of the new land to be peculiarly and irreducibly its own, stressing its *difference* in relation to any other known land. In all the descriptions, beginning with the first cantos, and especially in the section describing the expedition to the south of Chile (in which the poet participated), America may be wild, grandiose, mysterious, hostile, or impenetrable, but it is always *different* from the way it appears in earlier reports, or from the way Europe has perceived or imagined it. As in the narrative discourse of failure, the violence and greatness of America shrink a person's stature, shatter all prior modes of perception founded on European points of reference, and give to the representation of nature in the poem a prominence that would continue in literature well into the twentieth century. It is this qualitative difference between Europe and America, a difference that invalidates European categorizations of nature, that is experienced in passages like the following one describing a tempest:

> Los cuatro poderosos elementos
> contra la flaca nave conjurados
> traspasando sus términos y asientos
> iban del todo ya desordenados

> The four elements had unleashed their power
> against the frail ship and
> crossing the boundaries of their natural territories,
> ran wild, creating chaos and destruction everywhere.

or through the mythological importance conveyed in:

> Allí con libertad soplan los vientos
> de sus cavernas cóncavas saliendo
> y furiosos, indómitos, violentos,
> todo aquel ancho mar van discurriendo
> rompiendo la prisión y mandamientos
> de Eolo su rey, el cual temiendo
> que el mundo no arruinen los encierra
> echándoles encima una gran sierra.[84]

> The winds reign sovereign in their four caves;
> there they blow and swirl, furious,
> violent, uncontrollable.
> Eolus himself has no choice but to imprison them
> under a great mountain
> lest they disobey his orders and break their chains
> running wild once again over the vast seas
> bringing destruction to the world.

The traditional division of nature into four elements no longer applies, for the attributes and limits of these are all violently transgressed, creating a state of primeval chaos, and shattering any attempt to prevail over the consequent disorder or even to classify its components. It is precisely this failure to prevail that is expressed in the second stanza by the refusal of the elements—the winds in this case—to obey reason, represented here by an Aeolus more timorous than triumphant.

American nature is characterized here by Ercilla in a way that systematically underscores its difference. And this representation, acknowledging in all its implications the natural realities of the New World, represents the final stage in a gradual process of defining American nature that began, hesitantly and inconsistently at first, in the writings of Columbus and Cortés. This representation of the new World, on the other hand, implies the final cancellation of all the myths and models formulated, elaborated upon, confirmed, and reconfirmed throughout the successive stages of a process of mythification that began with the discovery, to be later challenged more and more radically in the narrative discourses of failure and rebellion.[85] The fantastic, a fundamental structural element of the vague, fabulous accounts and mendacious tales that were spread, refashioned, and retold by Spaniards and natives alike all over the continent for an entire century, is not to be found in *La Araucana*'s representations of nature. Its absence signifies a symbolic rejection of a long tradition of representation that had, in many different ways, systematically misrepresented the reality of the New World. In its demythification of this reality, *La Araucana* shares some central aspects of the narrative discourse of failure. But in the texts of the discourse of failure, awareness was accompanied by anguish and fear. The result was a literary representation that revolved around defeat and despair. *La Araucana*, on the other hand, constitutes the first positive European approach to nature in the New World, in which difference, rather than being rejected, is magnified and extolled through its poetic representation.[86]

Although this poetic treatment of *difference*, which characterizes so many descriptions of nature in *La Araucana*, reflects an important shift in perspective, Ercilla's most radical critique of the conquest and its underlying ideology is expressed with greater clarity in the representation of pre-Columbian America found in a specific episode. The episode narrates the expedition led by Don García to the south of Chile, in which Ercilla himself participated.

Critics have remarked frequently on the idyllic quality of the episode, in contrast to the violence that dominates the action throughout most of the poem. But a closer examination of its structure and meaning will reveal that this episode conveys a personal perception of the implications of the conquest, a devastating attack against its motives and objectives, a global condemnation of the ruthless exploitation and abuse that characterized it, and, also, the elements of a possible alternative.

The episode unfolds like a condensed representation of all the events that took place throughout the century spanned by the conquest. It traces symbolically every change in perception and awareness conveyed by the texts, from the early discourse of mythification to the discourse of failure. Don García's address to his men at the beginning of Canto 35 opens a new imaginary cycle of conquests, fictitiously returning to the beginnings of a historical process now approaching its end. The declared objective of the expedition is to explore the southern strip of Chile and its adjacent islands, but in the narrative the goal becomes "another new world," a "third world" reserved by Providence for the Spaniards alone, as the New World was in the early days of discovery. In the words of Don García:

> Veis otro nuevo mundo que encubierto
> los cielos hasta agora le han tenido
> el difícil camino y paso abierto
> a sólo vuestros brazos concedido
>
> Behold yet another New World
> which the heavens had concealed until now.
> And let us follow the harsh and narrow path
> that they have revealed only to us

As in the texts of Columbus, Providence has guaranteed an enterprise that will ennoble the men and make them wealthy, and this is the sole incentive for action, summarized by Don García when he says: "siendo de tan grande empresa autores / habéis de ser sin límite señores" ("having carried out so glorious an enterprise / you will become most powerful lords").[87] After his speech defining the goal of this imaginary conquest of an illusory third world, all the main components of an archetypical representation of the progression of the conquest follow in sequence one after another. Booty is the declared objective, and the right to conquer is inseparable from plunder and expropriation:

> Sus, tomad posesión todos a una
> desas nuevas provincias y regiones
> donde os tienen los hados a la entrada
> tanta gloria y riqueza aparejada.[88]
>
> Go ahead, take possession of these lands
> which Fortune had reserved only for you.

The initial contact with the natives is disappointing: they are primitive, poor, "brutos, campestres, rústicos, salvajes / de fieras cataduras y visajes" ("rough, barbarous, and savage / frightening in expression and countenance").[89] Trinkets and gifts are bartered for information and native guides: Don García offers "cuentas de vidrio de colores / con doce cascabeles soñadores" ("colorful glass beads and bells") in exchange for "una práctica lengua y fida guía" ("reliable interpreters and guides").[90] False stories are heard from the natives, an allusion to the earlier mythical reports and legends:

> La cual nos iba siempre asegurando
> gran riqueza, ganado y poblaciones
> los ánimos estrechos ensanchando
> con falsas y engañosas relaciones.[91]

> They kept enticing us with the promise
> of ever wealthier and more civilized lands
> as they encouraged us in our despair
> with false tales and fables.

The illusory objectives promised never materialize, and when the explorers' deceitful guide disappears and they are left at the mercy of their surroundings, nature becomes the central focus of the discourse. The elements are transformed into active subjects, and the expeditionaries are now victims reduced to defending themselves against a pitiless sky, swamps that swallow their horses, and a vegetation that epitomizes the land's hostility: "Nunca con tanto estorbo a los humanos / quiso impedir el paso la natura" ("Never before had Nature been so determined / to prevent the passage of humans").[92] And finally, faced with this reality, the desire for wealth gives way to a struggle for survival; ambition, to the hope of being able to satisfy basic needs: "Así pues nuestro ejército rompiendo / de sólo la esperanza alimentado / pasaba a puros brazos" ("Thus our army survived by sheer determination / sustained only by hope").[93]

At this point, the parallel with historical events comes to an end and a Utopian alternative begins to develop in the text. For, contrary to the experience of the authors of the discourse of failure (whose defeat when their objectives failed to materialize had left them with suffering as the only possible form of redemption), Don García and his men are offered the possibility of a "happy ending," a second opportunity such as De Soto, Coronado, Narváez, Ursúa, and all the other dream seekers who had crossed the continent in almost every direction were never able to have. After seven days of torment and suffering, Don García and his followers come upon a Paradise: the archipelagos in the south of Chile. These are described in unmistakably Utopian terms that, implicitly, are made to extend to all of pre-Columbian America. The paradisiacal, idyllic appearance of the archipelagos in the poem has a very simple explanation:

Estaba retirada en esta parte
de todas nuestras tierras excluída
que la falsa cautela, engaño y arte
aún nunca habían hallado allí acogida[94]

These lands were so removed
from our conquered territories
that greed, suspicion, and deceit
have never found their way to them.

The implication is evident: these Edenic lands have retained their original nature because of their isolation from the process that turned America into "our land," all the while spreading "cunning and deceit." The design to civilize the natives and convert them to Christianity, adopted by the official ideology to justify the conquest, is implicitly unmasked and presented for what it in fact is: abuse and exploitation, which have provoked "cunning" and "deceit" among the natives. This redefinition of the real meaning of the conquest is reaffirmed when Ercilla concludes his idyllic characterization of the natives by saying:

La sincera bondad y la caricia
de la sencilla gente de estas tierras,
daban bien a entender que la cudicia
aún no había penetrado aquella sierras,
ni la maldad, el robo, la injusticia
(alimento ordinario de las guerras)
entrada en esta parte habían hallado,
ni la ley natural inficionado[95]

The sweetness and simple nature of these people
revealed without questions that greed
had not yet reached their land.
Nor had evil, violence, injustice and theft
(the usual pillars of war and conquest)
found their way into this paradise
bringing about the corruption of their natural laws.

The corrupting, destructive effect of the conquest is denounced explicitly here. But the passage also implies that the forms of its condemnation cannot be limited to the specific manner in which the initial design to civilize and convert the natives has been spoiled. The opposition between the model conquistador and the greedy *encomendero* has already been used as clear evidence of the degradation of the ideals of the conquest. However, contrary to the conception suggested by the characterization of the conquistador in *La Araucana* itself or put forward by the narrative discourse of rebellion, what is challenged here is the very notion of imperialist conquest—"the wars." Corruption is no longer perceived in isolation but as something inseparable from violence, regardless of the purpose or ideology behind it. A Utopian alternative to the model of "war" is offered by the native chieftain of the "white gesture":[96] an alternative that would mean replacing the model of imperialist conquest and exploitation with an interaction founded on the ideal of peaceful, egalitarian coexistence among different nations and cultures.

> si queréis amistad si queréis guerra
> todo con ley igual os ofrecemos:
> escoged lo mejor que, a elección mía,
> la paz y la amistad escogería[97]

> We can offer you friendship or war.
> You are free to make your choice.
> I, for my part, would rather choose
> friendship and peace.

The opportunity represented by such a solution, with its echoes of Las Casas, is missed again in *La Araucana*, however, and the text's imaginary discovery of a "third world" leads to the very same degraded reality produced by the historical conquest of America:

> Pero luego nosotros destruyendo
> todo lo que tocamos de pasada
> con la usada insolencia el paso abriendo
> les dimos lugar ancho y ancha entrada:
> y la antigua costumbre corrompiendo
> de los nuevos insultos estragada,
> plantó aquí la cudicia su estandarte
> con más seguridad que en otra parte.[98]

> But we followed our usual path
> and spread destruction further.
> With our usual insolence we sowed
> grief and destruction
> we destroyed the old harmony and made greed,
> once again, the ruler of all things.

Gone forever is any possibility of achieving the peace and harmony of pre-Columbian times, as the conquest is identified once and for all with destruction, violence, corruption, and exploitation.

This is not Ercilla's first severe critical attack against the conquest of America, for he denounces it openly and in a variety of ways throughout the poem, frequently using characterization and action to associate the conquest with oppression and native resistance with the struggle for freedom. Both the narrator's remarks and the native chieftains' speeches (Galbarino's in Canto 23, for example) expose the greed and violence beneath the ideological rhetoric used to justify the behavior of the conquistadors. Galbarino censures those "insolent, thieving adulterers" who pose as defenders of the faith and heroic, selfless agents of civilization. But up to this point it might still be claimed that the poem's negative characterization is aimed at the *specific* form the conquest has taken at the hands of the abusive adventurers in control of most of the colony at the time of Ercilla's arrival. The importance of the episode just analyzed lies precisely in its absolute and unequivocal definition of the scope of the poem's critique, which remains unchanged even after Ercilla's general statements in defense of the right to make war, added later on in Canto 37. As of the expedition to the south of Chile, this critique is no longer confined to any particular effects of the conquest of America: it encompasses all aspects, questions all conquests, challenges imperialism itself as an ideological model rather than a particular application, rejects all forms of brutality (not those solely specific to the conquest) as being inseparable from any war. The alternative the poem proposes to the degradation apparent in the colony is not then another form of conquest more faithful to the purer principles of the hero of the discourse of mythification—as ultimately proposed in the discourse of rebellion—but a just, fraternal society such as the one that would emerge if it were founded on the concepts of peaceful coexistence formulated by the chief of the natives in the south of Chile.

The coexistence within the poem of an at times profoundly radical critique of the imperialistic conquest together with an abstract glorification of the ideological and social order sustaining it, presided over by the exalted figure of Philip II; the contradictory forms of representing American nature; the parallel development of two antithetical ways of characterizing the two sides of the conflict, granting moral superiority to the Araucans but divine support and eventual victory to the Spaniards;[99] the contiguous development of on the one hand a presentation that cancels the stereotypes presented in the texts of the official discourse of "general history" that have progressively misrepresented American reality,[100] and on the other, a presentation through which structures of integration are created that profoundly undermine the very reality whose true nature the poem proposes to defend—all of these contradictory elements express, through the representation of the reality of the conquest they organize together, a profoundly divided and tormented consciousness. The ambiguity and contradictions that define this new consciousness are at the heart of the endless interplay of inconsistencies and oppositions, compromises and false solutions that shape the work's poetic material. But the key element that dramatizes, within the poem, the movement of a new consciousness split between its partial rejection of a sixteenth-century European worldview and its own inability to identify fully with an American history and culture it in part extols, in part rejects, in part ignores is the characterization and development of the narrator.

Several critics have noted this figure's importance and studied its role in the poem. Even in the nineteenth century, Manuel José Quintana declared categorically that "the most remarkable, commendable thing about *La Araucana* is the author as a character of the poem."[101] Since that time, the narrator has been analyzed from a wide variety of points of view and in connection with the most diverse issues, reflecting both the extraordinary complexity of his characterization within the poem and his crucial importance within its signifying structures.

All the central contradictions in the perception of reality apparent throughout the poem converge in the narrator, making him and his development an accurate expression of the inconsistent, ambiguous, divided consciousness mentioned above. Ercilla himself acknowledges his divided role—half poet, half soldier—saying that "at times he wields the pen, at times the lance," and critics from Valbuena Briones to Avalle Arce have approached his twofold function in a variety of ways.[102]

But the characterization of the narrator is far more complex than this dichotomy would appear to suggest. First, we are dealing not merely with two roles but with several aspects of a single figure. Second, the narrative subject's pattern of appearances and disappearances is extremely dynamic. As a result, rather than different functions (the poet versus the soldier), there are shifts in the degree of distance taken by the narrator as poet and soldier, from particular events in which he is doubly involved. The central dilemma illustrated by these variations is that there is no way of reconciling a critical perception of the conquest with an implicit allegiance to the ideological principles behind it: an allegiance made clear by the character's own participation in action that, generally speaking, he feels cómpelled to condemn.

The pronoun used in the direct presentation of the narrator is the first person singular, *I*, and if we analyze the figure of this first person narrator, we will find his thoughts to be entirely consistent with the critical consciousness that, in the poem, questions the validity of the ideological and political models underlying the conquest. Most of the action and remarks explicitly attributed to this first person narrator illustrate this coherence:

he comforts helpless heroines, protects abandoned women, defends the honor of the absent Dido, heals the wounds of the unhappy Lauca. He is a gallant gentleman, motivated by kindness, compassion, and loyalty. And this behavior is not limited to the intercalated episodes or to the narrator's relationship with women. It appears in other instances such as when he attempts to prevent the cruel hanging of Galbarino: "Yo a la sazón al señalar llegando / de la cruda sentencia condolido / salvar quise uno dellos" ("When, upon my arrival I heard of the sentence / I felt greatly distraught / and tried to save one of them"). And when he intervenes righteously and courageously to save Cariolán:

> Yo, que ver tal batalla no quisiera
> al animoso mozo aficionado
> en medio me lancé diciendo: Afuera
> caballeros, afuera, haceos a un lado!
> que no es bien que el valiente mozo muera
> antes merece ser remunerado
> y darle así la muerte ya sería
> no esfuerzo ni valor mas villanía[103]

> When I saw them
> attacking the brave youth I jumped in his support
> and ordered the soldiers to stop
> as I pointed out that the brave youth's courage
> deserved praise
> rather than the infamous death
> they were bent on inflicting upon him.

Or when he moves generously to free Cariolán so that he can join his beloved Glaura: "Amigo adiós; y lo que puedo que es daros libertad, yo os la concedo" ("Good-bye my friends. / I give you freedom, the only thing / that I am free to give").[104] The characterization of the narrator through a presentation of actions that show him to be kind, just, impartial, the very prototype of Christian chivalry, is reinforced by the poet's own commentary. Ostensibly aimed at the behavior and action of others, this commentary provides a series of veiled declarations of principle that contrast increasingly with the official ideology. One example is the narrator's absolute condemnation of Galbarino's execution, when he says:

> Con gran solemnidad y desatino
> fue el insulto y castigo injusto hecho,
> pagando allí la deuda con la vida
> en muchas opiniones no debida.[105]

> The unjust sentence was thus carried out,
> and the outrageous punishment inflicted.

And he was made to pay with his life for a crime
that to many was no crime at all.

The narrative voice in the first person singular tends to be predominant in the poem, because of its inner coherence throughout much of the work and because of its central importance within the text's structure. But this coherence is likely to make us forget that the portrait produced emphasizes only some aspects of the character, tending to eliminate or tone down as much as possible other aspects no less real that question, from within the text, its very consistency. To be more specific, it tends to downplay the implications of the poet's active role in the conquest itself. The characterization of the first person narrator reduces his participation in the conquest to a series of moving acts of justice and charity. And this is not the text's only means of neutralizing a participation that is bound to imply a measure of allegiance to the same ideology that it insistently challenges. The poet takes part explicitly in military action against the Araucans on only three occasions. On the first, the reference to his participation—"yo apercibido, sordamente / en medio del silencio y noche escura / dí sobre algunos pueblos de repente" ("I prepared myself and / in the silence of a dark night / fell upon a few villages, without warning")—is quickly neutralized in the very same stanza, by a veiled criticism of the events and a compassionate description of the natives as "helpless and unfortunate people"[106] that calls into question the validity of any conquest won through violence and aggression. On the second occasion, the poet states that he only participated in persecuting the Araucans because he was compelled to do so by Juan Remón, and neither honor nor shame would allow him to act otherwise. On the third, the narrator is forced to attack the natives in legitimate self-defense.[107] In the rest of the poem, the fundamental opposition between participating in a conquest won by war and the rejection of such an undertaking is always resolved in favor of the latter, and this resolution is reflected in the text by the intermittent appearance and disappearance of the figure of the poet whenever a military action related to the conquest is underway.

As the events involving the poet become increasingly problematical, the first person singular gradually vanishes, and other pronouns are used to represent the subject of the action. The narrative "I" is reserved for instances of irreproachable conduct motivated by honor, justice, and Christian love. It is usually replaced by "we" whenever the text describes a legitimate, necessary act of war or a collective situation that cannot easily be challenged from the poem's critical perspective. For example: "Nosotros no sin causa sospechosos / allí más de dos meses estuvimos"

("*We* had every reason to be on guard / as *we* remained there for two months"), or "cuando fue de nosotros coronada / de una gruesa muralla la montaña" ("when *we* finally managed to climb over the thick mountain wall").[108] When the action is indeed questionable, the narrator implicitly dissociates himself from it, referring to "our men" or "our people" rather than the more engaged "we." It is "our men" who pursue the Araucans without mercy after the attack against the fort is defeated and take cruel, inhuman revenge after the battle of Millarapue, tarnishing the luster of their victory; "our men" who flee miserably when they are defeated at Andalicán, leaving the city of Concepción in the hands of the enemy. Sometimes the narrator dissociates himself from such dishonorable or violent behavior by attributing it to a subject even further separated from the narrator: the third person plural, or the collective "Spaniards," or "Spanish people," no longer bearing even the weak association with the narrator implicit in the first person possessive adjective "our." And finally, the most extreme condemnation of the events is reflected by the disappearance of any subject or pronominal form whatsoever, with the action presented in the form of an impersonal construction. For example, when the Spaniards take reprisal by hanging the best Araucan warriors *en masse*, the poem reads:

> estos fueron allí constituídos
> para amenaza y miedo de la gente
> quedando por ejemplo y escarmiento
> colgados de los árboles al viento[109]

> And so they remained
> hanging from the trees and dangling in the wind
> a frightening example to other people.

There is nothing in the stanza to indicate who the responsible subject is or to link the narrator to the action. With its impersonal construction, the syntax expresses the narrator's critical distance from the event and, simultaneously, his refusal to assume any of the responsibility.

This same type of impersonal construction is used to describe the execution of Galbarino in the lines that follow: "al cuello el corredizo lazo echado / quedó en una alta rama suspendido" ("with the noose tight around his neck / he hung from a tall branch").[110] And again, when the three chieftains are brutally executed after the attack against the fort fails:

> donde trece caciques elegidos
> para ejemplar castigo y escarmiento,
> a la boca de un grueso tiro atados
> fueron, dándole fuego ajusticiados.[111]

And so thirteen caciques,
chosen as an example to all the others,
were picked and executed.

When Caupolicán is executed, there is a suicidal quality about his initial impalement that does him honor and provisionally mitigates the responsibility of the Spaniards, before his life is ended altogether by the arrows of six anonymous archers. And the distance thus created is reinforced when the explicitly critical first person narrator reappears at the end of the episode, stating that not only did he not participate, but he was not even a witness, and that furthermore: "si yo a la sazon estuviera / la cruda ejecucion se suspendiera" ("Had I been there at the time / the execution would never have been carried out").[112]

The narrator's proximity to and involvement in the action of *La Araucana*, and the censure of this action by the critical consciousness that organizes the poem, always appear in an inverse relationship to each other. Whenever the discussion concerns morality or literature, whenever the episode involves the imagination, exploration, or an Indian heroine, the "I" is at the center of the action and completely identified with it. Whenever there is military violence or brutal repression, whenever a native leader or chieftain is cruelly executed, the narrator conceals himself, using such devices as the third person or an impersonal form to describe an action from which he dissociates himself entirely. These shifts in narrative distance from the events narrated are at times very swift, occurring on occasion within a single episode, but they always conform to the inverse relationship mentioned above. The attack against the Penco fort, for example, starts out with the soldier Ercilla as "I" hastily donning his arms. But this "I" suddenly vanishes, as the rest of the episode—which occupies all of Canto 19—is described: a violent battle fought by "our people," "our men," "the Spanish people," and "they." The end of both the battle and the violence that accompanies it is marked by the return of "we," bringing us somewhat closer to the narrator. But "I" does not occupy the center of the action again until the night following the battle when, "strolling from one 'canto' to the next," the narrator reappears placing himself implicitly in opposition to the earlier violence waged by "our harquebusiers" who "on that day / had carried out such destruction." Far from being implicated in the fighting he has just described at such length, the "I" who now returns as a narrative subject in the Tegualda episode is gentle, compassionate, and generous. Other episodes—for example, the attack against the Spanish fort in Canto 31—are handled similarly. The first person singular introduces the battle at the end of Canto 31 and then disappears as soon as the fighting and destruction attributed to "them" and "our men" take over. The battle ends with the execution of the Araucan warriors, described in an impersonal narrative voice, and it is only after the army's violence has ended that the "I" reappears, first to take part in some exploration, and then to rescue and cure the unhappy Lauca.

The characterization of the first person narrator rests on actions and commentaries that constitute a clear challenge to the ideological model underlying the enterprise to conquer and exploit America. The distance that separates the narrator, both explicitly and implicitly, from all the actions considered questionable from the perspective of the "I" in the poem, calls the very process of the conquest into question, rejecting its legitimacy. Nonetheless, the "I" is not as unblemished as it may at first appear, nor is the distance taken always as systematic as in the episodes analyzed. Ercilla himself is aware of the contradictions in some of the narrator's statements, and of the occasional inconsistency of his choices and conduct. He therefore anticipates any possible criticism by defining, in Canto 37, his attitude toward the legtimate use of force and punishment:

> Quiérome declarar, que algún curioso
> dirá que aquí y allá me contradigo,
> virtud es castigar cuando es forzoso
> y necesario el público castigo[113]

> I want to make myself clear on this issue
> lest someone claim that, here and there,
> I contradict myself;
> punishment is virtue when it is warranted
> and, in such cases, public punishment
> may indeed be necessary.

Here he attempts to justify the presence in the text of two conflicting positions. The first involves a general condemnation of the violence of the conquest and a refusal to accept the presumed legitimacy of imperialistic aggression. The second, formulated explicitly in Canto 37, reflects a recognition of the necessity of war as an instrument to maintain peace, declaring it to be a basic human right as it were, a "right of the people," and stating that there are both just and unjust wars. A just war would be one fought to protect a republic, its policies, and its laws, and to preserve the peace. Anything else—that is, a war motivated by greed, ambition, hatred, or vengeance—would be an unjust war. And the imperialistic wars of conquest, represented in the poem by the campaigns against Arauco, fall by implication into this latter category.

The explanations and statements in Canto 37 allow Ercilla to reconcile ideologically two apparently contradictory attitudes at the foundation of some of the poem's most ambiguous aspects. But only ideologically, for at a literary level, that is, within the poem itself, the contradictions remain, though not always expressed by an explicit comment or a direct intrusion by the narrator. Some have to do with inconsistencies in the way the two sides are portrayed, the action is represented, and the characters and situations are described. Certainly Ercilla has created a mythified version of the Araucan people that implicitly cancels out the stereotypes put forward by the discourse of mythification and the official accounts of the conquest. But although he undeniably glorifies and mythifies the Native Americans, there is another perception that emerges from time to time alongside his highly positive portrait of the Araucan people as "freedom fighters," one that sees the natives as a "shameless people." He extols their heroic virtues and the dignity and independence of their most outstanding chieftains whom he calls "noble barbarians" or "brave barbarians." But he also speaks of one of the most worthy, heroic, invincible Araucans, the admirable Galbarino, in the most thoroughly negative terms, calling him an "infernal barbarian."[114]

These occasional flaws in the coherence of the narrator's critical consciousness are also made evident by the fact that, in some exceptional instances, his distance from certain censurable actions diminishes drastically. A case in point is the punishment of Galbarino: the narrator neither sets himself apart from this cruel, unjustified measure nor dissociates himself from it by using the third person or an impersonal construction. Rather, he makes his participation doubly clear, admitting that he was present on the occasion and did nothing to prevent the warrior's "exemplary punishment" and confessing that his anger, like that of the other men responsible, served to mitigate any pity so unwarranted an act might otherwise have inspired in him.[115]

The narrator's explanations and remarks in Canto 37 reveal how aware Ercilla in fact was of the ideological tensions in his poem and offer a theoretical means of resolving them. The last two stanzas of Canto 31, on the other hand, show the poet's awareness of his own internal contradictions and of the many ways in which they determine the ambiguities and inconsistencies we find in the poem. Ercilla's own hesitancy in relation to his material and his extremely problematical relationship with the work are also revealed in these lines:

> No sé con qué palabras, con qué gusto
> este sangriento y crudo asalto cuente,
> y la lástima justa y odio justo,

que ambas cosas concurren justamente:
el ánimo ahora humano, ahora robusto
me suspende y me tiene diferente:
que si al piadoso celo satisfago,
condeno y doy por malo lo que hago.

Si del asalto y ocasión me alejo,
dentro della y del fuerte estoy metido;
si en este punto y término lo dejo,
hago y cumplo muy mal lo prometido:
así dudoso el ánimo y perplejo,
destos juntos contrarios combatido,
lo dejo al otro canto reservado,
que de consejo estoy necesitado.[116]

What words, what emotions will suffice
to convey simultaneously the pity and the hatred
that I feel
as I narrate this cruel and bloody episode?
For pity and hatred are here inseparable
as I hesitate between compassion and harshness.
If I yield to wrath
I condemn and reject my own deeds.

But how can I distance myself from this episode
when I am part of it as I sit in that very fortress?
If I withdraw into silence
I betray my own promise
to narrate a truthful account.
And so I waiver, doubtful and confused
split between contrary emotions
as I postpone a resolution to the next canto
for the matter deserves advice and further reflection.

In both stanzas the poet's ambiguous feelings toward his subject are presented as the result of a divided consciousness. He is split by the simultaneous, contrary emotions the battle he is about to describe inspire in him, and he hesitates between two radically opposite attitudes, represented by the *humane spirit* he mentions and its opposite, the *robust* one. These opposite attitudes involve two entirely different possible ways of presenting the action, one bringing to bear a critical (or "humane") consciousness, the other, the "robust" perspective of complicity. The first stanza ends with an implicit rejection of this second mode. The second is organized around two main false alternatives, which it uses to explore and affirm the narrator's historical and aesthetic commitment. The first false alternative is whether to participate in the action or to keep out of it. The second appears to offer a choice between going on with the story or bringing it to an end. Both lead the narrator to affirm his commitment to the action, to the poem, and to carrying out his original intention, however confused, divided, and besieged he may be as a result of his internal contradictions.

These internal contradictions that split the character of the narrator and form the core of the ambiguity of the work—whose formal structure derives largely from the interplay between the critical attitude and the complicity recognized by the poet in the stanzas just quoted—express the author's gradual transformation as he finds himself forced by the reality of the Araucan wars to reappraise the myths and values of the dominant ideology in the light of his personal experience of the conquest. The depth of this transformation is reflected by the distance that separates the narrator's attitude at the beginning of the work from the radically different attitude he expresses at the end, a distance dramatically captured by the opposition between singing and weeping, between "cantar" and "llorar." In the first stanza of the poem, Ercilla announces his intention to sing— in the double sense of poetic expression and exaltation—the heroic deeds of the Spanish conquest as exemplified by the war against Arauco. But in the last stanza he concludes: "conociendo mi error de aquí adelante / será razón que llore y que no cante" ("realizing, at last, the error of my ways / from now on I will be well advised to weep rather than sing"). The distance that separates *singing* from *weeping*, the exaltation of an ideo- logical and political order—identified with "error" in the last two lines quoted—from the poet's final lament, expresses symbolically the gradual awakening of what we could call a Spanish American consciousness within the historical context of the conquest. In this context, the critique of the dominant order leads to marginalization and solitude—a solitude that Ercilla denounces bitterly in the last canto. It also results in the anguish of a double alienation: first from the dominant ideological and political order, which the narrator has felt compelled to criticize more and more radically throughout the poem, and second from the history and culture of the peoples of America. Because even though he defends and supports them with unfailing moral solidarity, the truth is that he is unable to understand them in their own terms. Only by transforming them in a way that deprives them of their specific identity, their difference, their "Amer- icanness" can he present and accept them as equals.

I have used the term Spanish American to describe the new consciousness that gradually takes shape between the lack of critical tension expressed in the beginning of the first canto and the marginalization of the lament that concludes the last. But in the historical development of this new consciousness, whose beginnings may be traced back to Bartolomé de las Casas and Alvar Núñez Cabeza de Vaca, the term Spanish American does not describe a harmonious fusion or a synthesis of the two cultures. On the contrary, it refers to the realization of the insoluble conflict between the two, and it expresses a double impossibility: on the one hand, the impossibility of allegiance to an ideological and political system that has lost all credibility through an experience of the conquest that has unmasked its real nature and implications for the narrator, alienating him and forcing him into increasing isolation, and on the other, the impossibility of ever belonging to America, a qualitatively different world whose dignity and excellence the narrator extols, but where he feels socially and culturally alien.

In exploring the dynamics of the transformation of the narrator's consciousness it becomes clear that the central meaning of *La Araucana* is twofold. The poem is no doubt an account of the conquest of America as exemplified by the Araucan campaigns. But parallel to this, we see a second signifying process unfold, a process that gradually transforms the experience of the conquest into the poet's own quest for truth. In the course of this metaphorical journey, the figure of the narrator (initially the prototype of the conquistador and the poet of his nation's glorious deeds) becomes increasingly fragmented into a series of oppositions that culminate, beginning in Canto 36, in a complete redefinition of narrator, action, and objectives. Here the narrator is characterized in terms of a single purpose, the quest for truth, while all his previous experiences appear to be implicitly subordinated to this goal. He becomes the narrator "on the lookout for signs," and he describes himself as someone who was "siempre amigo e inclinado / a inquirir y saber lo no sabido" ("always inclined / to inquire into the unknown").[117] His is not a mystical pilgrimage, however, but a search for the truth of concrete historical reality. Ercilla makes this very clear, in the first stanza of Canto 36: "digo que la verdad hallé en el suelo / por más que digan que es subida al cielo" ("although they say that truth is to be found only in the heavens / it is right here, on this land, that I discovered it").[118] Moved by his desire for knowledge, the narrator's ultimate goal is then the discovery of truth. The action traces the journey of the narrator through his experience of the conquest. And as he progresses along this path, the nature of this *truth* becomes defined with increasing clarity: it is the truth of a radical demythification of the process of conquest, which will lead the narrator to a complete rejection of it, and it is the truth of his realization of the superiority of pre-Columbian

America, expressed in the Utopian presentation of the expedition to the south. Like Ercilla the soldier, Ercilla the seeker is impelled onward toward the end of a journey, geographical in the case of the former, spiritual in the case of the latter. Both the soldier and the seeker feel driven to "go one step further" and to cross "the great expanses of troubled water"— the image of the Chacao channel that suggests other no less dangerous torrents crossed by the narrator's mind as he pursues his way toward knowledge. And when Ercilla the conquistador finally reaches the other side of the river, he is as "torn apart" as the fragmented consciousness of the narrator is when he reaches the end of his pilgrimage toward truth.

Narrating the conclusion of the poet's dual journey, all the stanzas describing the climax of the expedition to the south reveal a double meaning. This meaning is summed up in the message the narrator carves on the bark of a tree conveying the literal and symbolic outcome of his double exploration: "Aquí llegó donde otro no ha llegado / don Alonso de Ercilla" ("Only I, Don Alonso de Ercilla / was ever able to journey this far").[119] Geographically, the conquistador has come to the remotest lands ever reached in the far south of Chile. Metaphorically, Ercilla the seeker of truth has gradually developed a new consciousness of the profound significance and implications of the war against Arauco and of the enterprise of the conquest that this war represents.[120] It is from this metaphorical vantage point—the end of the poet's journey and the beginning of his poem—that *La Araucana* is composed. The poem then retraces the steps that have led through "el accidentado recorrido lleno de compensaciones y substituciones" ("a dangerous journey marked by endless compensations and substitutions")[121] to the awakening of a tormented consciousness: a Spanish American consciousness, doubly marginalized in relation to two different cultural contexts, and characterized primarily by its internal contradictions and by its critical drive.

Because of the inaccuracy of certain historical facts in the poem, the idealization of some of its characters, the clearly fictional character of novelistic or fantastic episodes intercalated in the main narrative, critics have repeatedly questioned the author's definition of his poem's meaning when he says in the first canto that *La Araucana* "es relación sin corromper sacada / de la verdad cortada a su medida" ("It is an accurate account / that conveys nothing but the truth").[122] This statement would certainly be debatable if truth were here a matter of the historical accuracy of the facts the poem describes. But if we place these apparent inconsistencies or inaccuracies within the context of the entire structure of the work, if we take into account their specific function within the main signifying processes that shape the poem as a whole, it will become clear that Ercilla's assertion, so perplexing to so many critics—and often taken to be a mere rhetorical conceit—is quite accurate. *La Araucana* contains and expresses the kind of truth claimed to be, in Canto 36, the true objective of all the poem's action and all its author's reflection. It is not a truth to be found in the historical *accuracy* of specific events narrated, at the level of the action. Rather, it concerns the tormented movement, the hesitation and transformation experienced by the narrator's consciousness, faced with those very same facts and occurrences that shape, within the poem, the representation of the actual process of the conquest. The narrator himself refers to a message *concealed* in the events he narrates, and he acknowledges the fact that his work is not part of the "general history." It is, he implies, a parallel history that expresses his own personal critique of the official history of the conquest.[123]

The demythification and questioning that shaped some of the different narrative discourses of the conquest culminate in *La Araucana*, a first Spanish American literary expression of a divided consciousness. A consciousness that through an endless series of substitutions, contradictions, and false solutions acknowledges and dramatizes the reality of its own irrevocable alienation. Bartolomé de las Casas's critique, the questioning of official ideology apparent in the texts of the discourse of failure, and the uncompromising rejection we find in the discourse of rebellion are different aspects of a single vision. They all reject or challenge the mythical representations of Columbus and Cortés, but they always focus on the discrepancies between ideological models and colonial realities. In different ways they express a similar objective: the recovery of a unity and harmony lost or disrupted by the violence, injustice, and exploitation of the conquest. Las Casas and the texts of the discourse of failure associate this restoration with a return to authentic Christian values. The discourse of rebellion seeks a nostalgic, anachronistic return to the mythified values of heroic, medieval Europe.

Ercilla takes up all these perceptions anew in *La Araucana*. He explores and develops thoroughly the implications of Las Casas's attitude and the vision of the rebels. He humanizes the natives, comparing them to the great heroes of European history, and directs a relentless critique against the philosophy and predatory behavior of the colonizers. But the resolution of the implicit ideological crisis, the restoration of a mythical harmony between the ideal principles of the conquest and its specific reality, cannot be accomplished, whether one chooses Las Casas's path or that of the rebels. Through its literary representation of the narrator's personal experience of the war and the conquest, *La Araucana* acknowledges that impossibility, tracing the poet's growing awareness of an insoluble dilemma.

The text replays all the contradictions that characterize the conquest and colonization of America and dramatizes the divisions of a consciousness whose transformation through its experience of reality and literary creation constitutes the deepest nucleus from which the work projects its meaning. Unity and harmony do not exist in the reality depicted by *La Araucana*; they exist, as Jaime Concha notes, beyond it: "For, in Ercilla's poem, peace does not belong in history but in the realm of transcendence. An eschatological transcendence in Caupolican's case, when his struggle is assimilated through martyrdom; or a spatial transcendence, like in the present situation, where we see harmony recovered, beyond the frontiers of the empire."[124] The final choice of a false transcendental solution to the contradictions of the conquest expresses very clearly the limitations of Ercilla's "metamorphosis of imperialistic consciousness."[125] But it also reveals how lucidly the poet realized his inability to resolve his own internal contradictions. The work illuminates the dynamic interplay of these contradictions through its complex poetics. And this unorthodox, problematical, and often criticized poetics shapes a literary text of fundamental ideological importance, expressing and dramatizing masterfully the movements that define an emerging Spanish American consciousness.

The composition of the poem illuminates the central ambiguities, inconsistencies, and contradictions that determine its specific literary form. And the discordant, inconsistent, or contradictory elements it contains do not express the poet's inability to follow well established literary models. They express the historical dialectics of the first century of the conquest through the literary representation of the transformation of the narrator: from an imperialistic warrior, fully identified with the dominant ideology underlying the conquest into the disillusioned and marginalized chronicler of a parallel history. It is a history that traces the gradual awakening of a critical consciousness of the discovery and conquest of America.

Reference Matter

Notes

Chapter 1

1. W. Borah and S. E. Cook, *The Indian Population of Central Mexico (1531–1610)* (Berkeley, 1960). Charles Gibson, *Los aztecas bajo el dominio español: 1519–1810* (Mexico, 1975); see esp. chap. 6 and appendix 6. Jaime Vicens Vives, *Historia social y económica de España y América* 5 vols. (Barcelona, 1977); see esp. vol. 3, pp. 324–39. Alejandro Lipschutz, *El problema racial en la conquista de América* (Mexico, 1977), pp. 210–12.

2. Pierre Chaunu, *Conquista y explotación de los nuevos mundos* (Barcelona, 1973), pp. 1–44.

3. Bartolomé de las Casas, *Historia de las Indias*, ed. Juan Perez de Tudela, 2 vols. (Madrid, 1957); also *Brevísima relación de la destrucción de las Indias*, ed. Manuel Ballesteros Gaibrois (Madrid, 1977).

4. Las Casas, *Historia*, pp. 41–43. Christopher Columbus, *Carta de Jamaica*, July 1503, in Fernández de Navarrete, *Colección de viajes y descubrimientos*, ed. Carlos Seco Serrano (Madrid, 1954), pp. 235–36. Published in English translation as "A letter written by Don Chrisopher Columbus, Viceroy and Admiral of the Indies, to the most Christian and mighty Sovereigns, the King and Queen of Spain, in which are described the events of his voyage, and the countries, provinces, cities, rivers and other marvelous matters therein discovered, as well as the places where gold and other substances of great richness and value are to be found," in *Select Letters of Christopher Columbus* (London, 1847), pp. 169–203.

5. Columbus's initial idea was to establish factories from which to organize commercial production in the new lands. On Columbus's plans for these factories and how they failed, see Richard Konetzke, *Los descubridores y conquistadores españoles* (Madrid, 1968), p. 18 and Rafael Ruiz de Lira, *Colón, el Caribe y las Antillas* (Madrid, 1980).

6. At the beginning of the discovery, Columbus was sure that he was near the outer eastern region of Asia, so fantastically described in *The Travels of Marco Polo*. S. E. Morison, *Admiral of the Ocean Sea*, 2 vols. (Boston, 1942), chap. 16.

7. Edmundo O'Gorman presents an interesting account of the geographical and philosophical aspects of the invention of the Indies in *La invención de América* (Mexico, 1947).

8. Columbus died still under the impression that Cuba was on Tierra Firme, although he assumed that Veragua and Paria were on a new continent. See Morison, *Admiral*, vol. 2.

9. Introducing the array of erudite references that he proposes to use to prove that Columbus's enterprise was rational, Las Casas says: "In the following chapters, I propose to provide certain natural reasons, and the testimony and versions of wise authorities both ancient and modern, which might very reasonably have led him to believe and even consider true the thought that he would find them in the southern and western regions of the Ocean Sea" (Las Casas, *Historia*, vol. 1, p. 27). See Las Casas's erudite arguments in defense of the above in chaps. 6–11.

10. *Imago Mundi de Pierre d'Ailly*, ed. Edmond Muron, 3 vols. (Paris, 1930), vol. 1, chap. 3.

11. Las Casas, *Historia*, vol. 1, p. 35.

12. Ibid., p. 36. Hernando Colón, *La vida del Almirante* (Madrid, 1892), pp. 50–51.

13. This is not to imply that no one had ever sailed there. The remains of shipwrecks and the theory about an unknown pilot or "protonaut" formulated several decades ago but recently defended by Juan Manzano Manzano would appear to confirm that the Atlantic had been crossed shortly before Columbus's journey. The outcome of such a venture, however, was evidently either negative or so doubtful as to provide little foundation for stating that new territories were explored during the decades before Columbus's conception of his enterprise.

14. These three scientific works, and most particularly the *Imago Mundi*, provided the main geographical foundation for Columbus's expectations as he prepared his plans.

15. Morison, *Admiral*, vol. 1, p. 120. Other authors, from Vignaud to Juan Manzano, maintain against Morison that Marco Polo's book could not have influenced the plans for the discovery because Columbus did not read it until several years after the event. I do not believe, however, that these authors have offered sufficiently convincing evidence supporting their theory. See Henri Vignaud, *Histoire critique de la Grande Entreprise de C. Colomb* (Paris, 1911); Cecil Jane, *Select Documents Illustrating the Life and Voyages of Columbus*, 2 vols. (London, 1930), vol. 1, p. 27; Emiliano Jos, *El plan y la génesis del descubrimiento colombino* (Valladolid, 1980); Juan Manzano Manzano, *Colón y sus secreto* (Madrid, 1976).

16. Ruiz de Lira, *Colón*, p. 21.

17. Ibid.

18. *The Travels of Marco Polo* (New York, 1958), p. 13.

19. Ibid., chaps. 56 (book 1) to 26 (book 2). For the description of court ritual, see esp. pp. 136–41.

20. Ibid., p. 205.

21. Pliny maintained that the distance between the Persian Gulf and the Pillars of Hercules could be covered in a few days. Aristotle claimed that there was a smallish sea lying between the outer rim of Spain and the nearest coast of India that could be sailed across in a few days.

22. *The Travels of Marco Polo*, p. 262.

23. We will return later to Columbus's messianic conception of his mission as a discoverer, which never left him and which Las Casas took pains to document

and justify on the basis of Greek and Latin sources, the Bible, and a variety of prophetical signs. See Las Casas, *Historia*, vol. 1, chap. 2.

24. See T. H. White, *Bestiary* (New York, 1980), on imaginary representations of the monstrous aspects of the New World. An early source of this bestiary was Physiologus, who took his information in turn from Herodotus, Aristotle, and Pliny.

25. S. E. Morison, *Journals and Documents of the Life and Voyages of Christopher Columbus* (New York, 1963), p. 21.

26. Las Casas, *Historia*, vol. 1, p. 45.

27. Henri Vignaud, *Toscanelli and Columbus* (London, 1902), p. 277. See also *Carta de Paolo Toscanelli físico Florentín a Cristobal Colón* in Navarrete, *Colección*, pp. 299–300. What Navarrete's text in fact reproduces under this title is Toscanelli's letter to Canon Fernan Martins, together with a brief introduction written by Toscanelli for Columbus. Toscanelli's letter to Martins is dated June 25, 1474. See also Toscanelli's second letter to Columbus, undated, reproduced by Navarrete, p. 300, and in Vignaud, pp. 279–80.

28. Second *Carta de Paolo Toscanelli a Colón*, in Navarrete, *Colección*, p. 300. See also Vignaud, *Toscanelli*, pp. 279–80.

29. See Navarrete, *Colección*, pp. 300–301; see also Vignaud, *Toscanelli*, p. 325.

30. There are three versions extant of this correspondence: (1) The reproduction of both letters in Las Casas's *Historia*. (2) The reproduction and explanation included by Ferdinand Columbus in his *Vida del Almirante*. (3) A manuscript copy attributed by some to Christopher and by others to Bartholomew Columbus, which appears on the back of a page of the *Historia Rerum* used by both brothers, now at the Biblioteca Colombina in Seville. Vignaud, with his *Toscanelli and Columbus*, heads a long list of scholars who have held this correspondence to be apocryphal; another list just as long, headed by De Lollis, maintains the opposite. Morison provides an enlightening summary of some of the main points in support of and against the authenticity of the correspondence (Morison, *Admiral*, vol. 1, pp. 56–57).

31. Las Casas, *Historia*, vol. 1, chaps. 3–16.

32. Christopher Columbus, *Diario del primer viaje*, in Navarrete, *Colección*. See also *The Journal of Christopher Columbus*, trans. Cecil Jane (London, 1968).

33. Cecil Jane examines the religiosity of the period: "In that age many were readily inclined to imagine that the Deity was both continually forming their thoughts and continually determining their actions, . . . in effect they considered themselves as so many missionaries of Heaven" (*Voyages of Columbus*, vol. 1, pp. xlix–l). The problem is that Jane uses this idea to explain many obscure, debatable aspects of Columbus's behavior, going beyond what would seem to be acceptable or provable in the light of existing documentation.

34. "The Letter of Columbus to Luis de Santángel, announcing his discovery, with extracts of his Journal," in *American History Leaflets* (New York, 1891).

35. Las Casas, *Historia*, vol. 1, p. 426.

36. "Carta de Cristóbal Colón a los Reyes," ibid., p. 425.

37. Christopher Columbus, *Lettera Rarissima*, also called *Carta de Jamaica*. Columbus wrote this letter to the king and queen on July 7, 1503, from Jamaica, where he was living in exile. Reproduced in Navarrete, *Colección*, pp. 232–40. Included by De Lollis in *Raccolta di documenti e studi publicata dalla R. Comisione Colombiana* (Rome, 1892) I, vol. 2, pp. 175–205.

38. The current names of these islands are, respectively, Wattling Island, Long

Island, Crooked Island, Cuba, Santo Domingo. See S. E. Morison, *Journals*, map of the Caribbean and islands, pp. xv–xvi.

39. Columbus, *Journal*, p. 23. 40. Ibid., pp. 30–31.

41. Ibid., pp. 40–41. 42. Ibid., p. 42.

43. The manuscript of this letter is in the Royal Archive in Aragon. It contains a formal greeting, expresses the joy of the Spanish monarchs over the interest shown by the Great Khan in the affairs of Spain, and introduces Columbus as their ambassador charged with contacting the Khan and providing him with any necessary information. Columbus took with him several copies of the letter with the name of the prince left blank, so that he might introduce himself in the same guise to any other princes he might encounter. See Las Casas's comments on this letter, *Colección*, vol. 1, p. 123, and those of Morison, *Admiral*, vol. 1, p. 142.

44. Columbus, *Journal*, p. 59.

45. Ibid., p. 137.

46. Passages quoted are translated from Pedro Mártir de Anghiera, *Décadas del Nuevo Mundo* (Buenos Aires, 1944).

47. Summary of a letter from Columbus to the king and queen, reproduced by Las Casas, *Historia*, vol. 1, p. 175. *Carta de Colón a los Reyes*, October 18, 1498, in Navarrete, *Colección*, vol. 1, p. 207. [The latter is included in *Select Letters* as "The history of a voyage which Don Christopher Columbus made the third time that he came to the Indies when he discovered terra firma, and which he sent to their Majesties from the Island of Hispaniola."—Trans.]

48. Christopher Columbus, "*Memorial* of the Second Voyage of the Admiral, Christopher Columbus, Drawn up by him for Their Highnesses King Ferdinand and Queen Isabella; and addressed to Antonio de Torres, from the city of Isabella, the 30th of January 1494," in *Select Letters*, pp. 70–71. Italics mine.

49. Juan Manzano Manzano, "Colón y su secreto," in *Raccolta* III, vol. 2, p. 515.

50. "Información y testimonio de cómo el Almirante fue a reconocer la isla de Cuba quedando persuadido de que era tierra firme." (Original in the *Archivo de Indias* in Seville, *legajo 5 del Patronato Real*.) Reproduced in Navarrete, *Colección*, vol. 1, pp. 386–87.

51. Ibid., p. 387.

52. Juan Manzano, *Colón y su secreto*, p. 565.

53. Columbus, *Carta a los reyes*, October 18, 1498, in Navarrete, *Colección*, vol. 1, p. 207. (For English version of letter, see note 47 above.)

54. D'Ailly, in *Raccolta* I, vol. 2, p. 401; the passage is based on Juan Manzano's translation, included in his "Colón y su secreto," p. 222.

55. "Letter of the Admiral to the (quondam) nurse of the Prince John, written near the end of the year 1500," in Columbus, *Select Letters*, p. 148.

56. Columbus, *Lettera Rarissima*, in Navarrete, *Colección*, vol. 1, p. 232.

57. Or with the mastic tree that Pliny had seen on the island of Chios. Columbus, *Journal*, p. 58.

58. See, for example, Columbus, *Journal*, pp. 56 and 64.

59. Navarrete, *Colección*, p. 108.

60. Columbus, *Select Letters*, pp. 77–78.

61. Quotes and references are from Columbus's "History of a voyage made . . . the third time . . ." and the "Letter of the Admiral to the (quondam) nurse . . . ," in *Select Letters*; see notes 47 and 55 above.

62. Quotes and references are from Columbus's *Lettera Rarissima* written from Jamaica on July 7, 1503. See *Select Letters*, pp. 169–203.

63. Las Casas's analysis of this paragraph refers explicitly to Martín Alonso

Pinzón, but he includes it to illustrate Columbus's case, for two reasons. First, because he attributes Pinzón's method to Columbus in the next paragraph of his *Historia*; second, because the fact that both discoverers use exactly the same approach in their interpretation of things is shown very clearly in the section that follows. Las Casas, *Historia*, vol. 1, p. 156.

64. "Carta de Michele de Cuneo a Hyeronimo Annari," *Raccolta* III, vol. 2, pp. 95–107.

65. Columbus, *Journal*, p. 24.

66. Jane, Morison, and Manzano among others discuss the mercantile component of Columbus's ideology. I believe, however, that they underestimate its importance by not perceiving it as a fundamental cause of many of Columbus's interpretations and attitudes that would otherwise seem irrational or very hard to explain, such as, for example, his obstinacy when negotiating the agreements before the first voyage.

67. "Capitulaciones de Santa Fe," April 17, 1492, in Navarrete, *Colección*, vol. 1, pp. 302, 304. Columbus obtained for himself and his heirs by this instrument five Privileges covering the most important aspects of economic and political power over the future lands. According to these, he was to (1) be appointed admiral, together with his heirs, over all the lands and islands discovered, with all the privileges pertinent thereto; (2) be named viceroy of the territories, with the right to nominate three candidates for each government position; (3) receive one tenth of each and all of the products taken from the lands and islands discovered; (4) be authorized to judge any dispute in regard to the assignment of the said products and merchandise; (5) be given the option to pay one eighth of the expenses of any fleet organized for the business involved and to retain one eighth of the profits resulting therefrom. See also "Título expedido por los reyes a Cristobal Colón" of April 30, 1492, and the "Provisiones" bearing the same date, in regard to the preparation of the fleet, in Navarrete, *Colección*, vol. 1, pp. 304–7.

68. Vicens Vives, *Historia social*, vol. 2, pp. 454–65.

69. *Diario del primer viaje*, in Navarrete, *Colección*, vol. 1, p. 100. For references to Columbus's statements see Navarrete, pp. 101, 109, 115, 125, 127. See also Columbus, *Journal*, pp. 33 and 54.

70. See Navarrete, *Colección*, vol. 1, pp. 198 and 130, respectively.

71. See Navarrete, *Colección*, vol. 1, entry for November 13, p. 112, and *Journal*, for the same day.

72. See Navarrete, *Colección*, vol. 1, entry for October 12, pp. 100–101, and *Journal*, for the same day.

73. A carrack was the largest cargo vessel known at the time of the discovery. Any port deep and wide enough to accommodate such a vessel was considered optimal for commercial purposes.

74. Columbus, *Journal*, entry for November 16, p. 64.

75. See respectively S. E. Morison, *Admiral*, pp. 231 and 233, and Columbus, *Journal*, p. 28.

76. Columbus, *Journal*, pp. 24, 36, 83–84, 111.

77. "Letter to Luis de Santángel," p. 4 (see note 34 above).

78. Columbus, *Journal*, entries for October 12 and November 6, pp. 24, 69, and 85.

79. Columbus, *Select Letters*, p. 82.

80. Columbus, *Journal*, p. 82.

81. The perception of man as merchandise must be understood within the cultural, ideological, and commercial context of the time. Trade in slaves, mainly

from Africa, was an accepted practice all over Europe. The Portuguese, Italians, and Catalonians had all been conducting a lucrative business based on the slave trade for quite some time. Thus if Columbus's discourse converted human beings into merchandise, this should not be interpreted exclusively as a consequence of his particular personality; it reflects an entire philosophy oriented toward the instrumentalization of *people* and *reality* that was characteristic of the Western culture to which he belonged. See Vicens Vives, *Historia*, vols. 1 and 2, on the tradition of slavery and the slave trade in Europe before the discovery.

82. See Las Casas, *Historia*, p. 397.

83. The idea that was to constitute the central issue in the great polemic between Bartolomé de Las Casas and Ginés de Sepúlveda, in regard to the humanity or lack thereof of the Native Americans, was formulated for the first time in this second proposal made by Columbus. The polemic—with its focus on whether or not the natives had souls—did no more than bring to the surface the broader question of the instrumentalization of human beings to the point of dehumanizing them, which neither began nor ended with the fifteenth century.

84. "Letter to Santángel," p. 5.

85. Columbus, *Select Letters*, pp. 84–86.

86. *Carta de Colón a los Reyes*, written toward the end of 1495, reproduced by Las Casas in his *Historia*, vol. 1, p. 397.

87. See "Carta de Michele de Cuneo." Also the *Carta del Dr. Chanca* to the *Cabildo* of Seville and the *Testamento de Diego Méndez*, both in Navarrete, *Colección*, vol. 1, pp. 240–48.

88. Columbus, *Select Letters*, p. 202.

Chapter 2

1. See Richard Konetzke, *Descubridores y conquistadores españoles* (Madrid, 1968), pp. 17–20.

2. Even at the beginning of Isabel and Ferdinand's reign, and as a result of civil wars preceding it, chroniclers of the period were fully aware that the royal treasure was scarce compared to that of other monarchs. See Jaime Vicens Vives, *Historia social y económica de España y America*, 5 vols. (Barcelona, 1977), vol. 2, p. 375.

3. Columbus, *Select Letters of Christopher Columbus* (London, 1847), p. 196.

4. Konetzke's estimate (*Descubridores*, p. 45) is higher: 19 tons between 1503 and 1510. According to Vicens Vives (*Historia*, vol. 2, p. 473), 14,118 kilograms were brought to Seville between 1503 and 1520.

5. Konetzke, *Descubridores*, p. 47.

6. The first cane planting experiments were conducted no earlier than 1503, and there was no cultivation of sugar that might be called acceptably successful until 1517. See Konetzke, p. 50.

7. The letter is reproduced in Las Casas, *Historia de las Indias*, 2 vols. (Madrid, 1958), vol. 1, p. 424.

8. Hernán Cortés, "Carta al Emperador Carlos V," written from Tenuxitan on October 15, 1524, in *Cartas de relación* (Mexico, 1975), pp. 209–18. See also Hernán Cortés's fourth letter in *Letters from Mexico*, tr. and ed. A. R. Pagden (New Haven, 1986).

9. Vicens Vives, *Historia*, vol. 2, p. 473. However, based on charts in E. J. Hamilton, *American Treasure and Price Revolution in Spain* (Cambridge, 1934), Pierre Chaunu claims that gold production started to decline between 1512 and 1513. See Chaunu, *Conquista y explotación de los nuevos mundos* (Barcelona, 1973), and *Seville et l'Atlantique*, 4 vols. (Paris, 1959–60).

10. Columbus, "Carta a los Reyes," reproduced in Las Casas, *Historia de las Indias*, 2 vols. (Madrid, 1958), vol. 1, p. 424.

11. "Mines and usable lands began to be assessed solely in terms of the Indians available to work them. The *encomienda* became a highly valuable possession, which was ceded, rented, bought, and sold like any other good. Absentee *encomenderos* became frequent, with their foremen and tenants exploiting the Indians and forcing them to work to the cut of a whiplash." See Vicens Vives, *Historia*, vol. 2, p. 473.

12. Ibid., p. 474. According to Las Casas, the natives numbered 1,100,000 at the time of Columbus's arrival, and 46,000 in 1510. Gonzalo Fernández de Oviedo's estimate is the same, from which Konetzke assumes that both sources were given the figure by the colonizers themselves.

13. Las Casas, *Historia*, vol. 2, p. 219.

14. Chaunu believes that there was an economic crisis already apparent in Cuba by 1516 as a direct result of the extinction of the native population, providing a decisive incentive for attempts to explore and conquer new lands. See Chaunu, *Conquista*, pp. 15–18.

15. According to the account of the expedition's first contact with the natives, provided by its chaplain, the only thing that interested Grijalva was gold. When the Aztecs offered him illustrations of the life of the Mexicas painted on cloth, Grijalva reacted by saying he "sought nothing but gold." This shows very clearly that Tierra Firme was perceived as a source of further booty, in addition to that already plundered and squandered in the Great Antilles. See *Colección de Documentos para la Historia de México* published by Joaquín Icazbalceta (Mexico, 1858). The chaplain's account is also reproduced in *Crónicas de la Conquista*, ed. Agustín Yáñez (Mexico, 1939), pp. 19–39.

16. Las Casas, *Historia*, vol. 2, p. 128.

17. Ibid., p. 130.
18. Ibid., pp. 140–41.
19. Ibid., pp. 140–42.
20. Ibid., pp. 143–45.
21. Ibid., p. 163.
22. Ibid., p. 153.
23. Ibid., p. 402.

24. Bernal Díaz del Castillo, *Historia verdadera de la conquista de Mexico* (Madrid, 1975), p. 28. Bernal Díaz's virtuous comments were made several years after the events involved, at a time when even such prestigious figures as Cortés (truly revered by Díaz) had for some time been claiming that the slave trade was not a legitimate activity.

25. See note 3 above concerning the *Lettera Rarissima*'s praise for the gold at Veragua and the list of signs indicating, according to Columbus, that the area was an extremely rich source of this metal.

26. Bernal Díaz, *Historia verdadera*, p. 29.

27. Las Casas, *Historia*, vol. 2, p. 404.

28. Bernal Díaz, *Historia verdadera*, p. 31. Besides mentioning this incident, Díaz refers constantly to any object that might indicate the presence of gold, however inferior in grade; such objects, he says, were welcomed with great joy because Peru had not yet been discovered.

29. Bernal Díaz, *Historia verdadera*, pp. 30–31 and 37.

30. Las Casas, *Historia*, vol. 2, p. 406.

31. Bernal Díaz, *Historia verdadera*, p. 37.

32. Juan Díaz, *Relación de la expedición de Juan de Grijalva*, in *Crónicas de la Conquista* (Mexico, 1939), p. 37.

33. Bernal Díaz del Castillo, *The Conquest of New Spain*, tr. J. M. Cohen (London, 1963), p. 26.

34. Las Casas, *Historia*, vol. 2. p. 445.
35. See Chap. 1, "Images of an Unknown World" above, pp. 9–20.
36. Chauna, *Seville*, vol. 8, p. 123.
37. Salvador de Madariaga, *Hernán Cortés* (Buenos Aires, 1941), p. 103.
38. Irving A. Leonard, *Books of the Brave* (Cambridge, Mass., 1949), p. 11.
39. Juan Díaz, *Relación*, pp. 24–27.
40. *Instrucciones de Diego Velázquez a Hernán Cortés*, October 23, 1518, in "Colección de documentos inéditos del Archivo de Indias," ser. 1, vol. 12, pp. 225–46. (The "Colección" will be referred to henceforth as CDIAI.)
41. Perhaps the most weighty testimony regarding the credit generally given to reports of fantastic figures or objects is to be found in Cortés's fourth letter (1525). It is hard to imagine anyone more rational, or less inclined toward imaginary lucubrations. In this document, however, when describing his organization of the systematic exploration of the territory of Mexico from his base in the conquered city of Tenochtitlan, he speaks of information heard from one of the captains he had sent to investigate certain "lords of the province of Ciguatan, who affirm that there is an island inhabited only by women, without a single man, and that at certain times men go over from the mainland and have intercourse with them; the females born to those who conceive are kept, but the males are sent away. The island is ten days' journey from this province and many of those chiefs have been there and have seen it. They also told me that it was very rich in pearls and gold. I will strive, as soon as I am equipped for it, to learn the truth and send Your Majesty a full account thereof." It should be stressed that in his characteristically rational manner, Cortés remarks that these claims have not been verified, and that only after this is done will he give them credit. But his skeptical attitude—the exception rather than the rule at the time—is what makes his caution over rejecting his captain's fantastic report particularly significant. See Cortés, *Letters from Mexico*, pp. 299–300.
42. See Chap. 1, "A Real World Disregarded" above, pp. 20–37.
43. Bernal Díaz, *The Conquest*, p. 41.
44. These instructions contain thirty clauses, which may be reduced to eight categories to analyze Velázquez's plan. Clause 10 describes the exploratory nature of the expedition, stipulating that the explorers are to survey ports and harbors and draw maps showing all the features of the coastline. Clauses 21 and 22 indicate the limits of the expedition: exploration is to be restricted to the coastal area, and the expeditionaries are expressly forbidden to go inland away from their vessels, although they may survey with caution any settlement "lying near the seacoast." Clauses 12 and 13 stipulate that the men must investigate and give Velázquez a detailed report on the customs and religion of the inhabitants of Tierra Firme. Clause 26 contains final instructions on the explorations to be done, recommending that everything possible be ascertained concerning "other lands and islands, and the presence or absence of people there," and refers to reports on Amazons and dogfaced men with large ears. Clause 25 charges Cortés with a general evaluation of the booty—the "secret" as it was termed discreetly—including "trees, fruit, plants, birds, small animals, gold, precious stones, pearls and other metals, spices and . . . since it is known that there is gold there, find out where it is obtained and how; and if you see any mines with gold and can obtain some, try to do so." Clause 20 specifies that it is an objective of the expedition to obtain "gold as well as pearls, precious stones, metals, or anything there" and advises carrying "an ark with two or three locks on it" to contain such items. Clause 11 charges Cortés with conveying to any natives encountered the basic principles of exchange under the vassalage system, emphasizing that tribute collection must be organized

immediately. Last, clauses 15, 16, 17, and 18 speak of the expedition's rescue mission, the purpose of which is to find Grijalva and any other Christians and bring them back to Cuba. See CDIAI, ser. 1, vol. 12, pp. 225–46.

45. It should be noted that even had Velázquez considered, and discussed with Cortés, the possibility and advisability of establishing settlements, he would not have been able to state this in a legal document such as the *Instrucciones* since he did not yet possess the king's authority to do so. He was not appointed *Adelantado* with the right to conquer and settle Tierra Firme until several months later (the summer of 1519). At the same time, it should be stressed that settlement was not held to be inconsistent with plunder—both activities had gone hand in hand during the disastrous exploitation of the Antilles—nor did it indicate that Velázquez's thinking was different from that of the colony itself.

46. Bernal Díaz, *The Conquest*, p. 43. Italics mine.

47. According to Bernal Díaz, it was known on the island that besides spending what he had, Cortés had to borrow funds and ask for credit: "When some merchant friends of his called Jaime Tría and Jerónimo Tría and a Pedro de Jerez heard that he had been made Captain-General, they lent him four thousand pesos in coin, and another four thousand in goods, on the security of his Indians and his estate." Bernal Díaz, *The Conquest*, p. 43.

48. Ibid., pp. 42 and 46.

49. All reports agreed that Cortés made explicit public declarations of obedience to Velázquez during the three months following his departure from Cuba, while he went about as a "gentle corsair" (as he put it years later to Las Casas), obtaining supplies as best he could for his real purpose: to conquer land and establish settlements. See Las Casas, *Historia*, vol. 2, p. 452.

50. Bernal Díaz, *The Conquest*, pp. 47 and 50–51.

51. Bernal Díaz, *Historia verdadera*, pp. 53–54. See also summary in *The Conquest*, p. 40.

52. Las Casas, *Historia*, vol. 2, p. 239.

53. Ibid., p. 449.

54. Mario Hernández Sánchez Barba uses the term "existential attitude" to refer to these early chroniclers' choice of a testimonial mode of narration instead of a more erudite one. See his *Literatura e historia en Hispano América* (Madrid, 1978).

55. Bernal Díaz, *Historia verdadera*, pp. 25 and 53, and *The Conquest*, p. 15.

56. Leonard, *Books of the Brave*, chaps. 1–3.

57. Writing about "The Chronicle of Don Roderic, with the Destruction of Spain," a fabulous chronicle the first edition of which is dated around 1511, George Ticknor says, "Most of the names throughout the work are as imaginary as those of its pretended authors; and the circumstances related are, generally, as much invented as the dialogue between its personages, which is given with a heavy minuteness of detail, alike uninteresting in itself, and false to the time it represents." See Ticknor, *History of Spanish Literature* (New York, 1965), p. 224.

58. Marcel Bataillon, *Érasme et l'Espagne* (Paris, 1937), pp. 656–58.

59. Leonard, *Books of the Brave*, p. 31.

60. For a detailed examination of this trajectory, see Edmundo O'Gorman's prologue to Oviedo's *Historia General y Natural de las Indias* (Mexico, 1939).

61. Leonard, *Books of the Brave*, chap. 4.

62. Ibid., pp. 41 and 48.

63. Despite the loss of Cortés's first letter, much of what it covers may be found in the *Letter from the Justiciary and Municipal Council* (*Carta de Justicia y Regimiento*) [referred to in *Letters from Mexico* as the "Letter sent to the Queen

Doña Juana and the Emperor, Charles V, her Son, by the Justiciary and Municipal Council of the Muy Rica Villa de la Vera Cruz on the Tenth Day of July, 1519—TRANS.]. This document was theoretically written by the *cabildo* and *regidores* of the newly founded Villa de la Vera Cruz, not by Cortés. It was clearly inspired by the latter, however, for its reasoning is extremely similar to that of the four letters extant.

64. Cortés's second letter, *Letters from Mexico*, p. 51.

65. Ibid., p. 51.

66. *Ramírez Codex* (Mexico, 1979), p. 198.

67. *Aubin Codex*, reproduced in Miguel León-Portilla, *La visión de los vencidos* (Mexico, 1976), pp. 88–89.

68. León-Portilla, *La visión de los vencidos*, pp. 81–83.

69. See Bernal Díaz, *The Conquest*, p. 244. His account is corroborated by Alvarado's own statements in response to the charges against him in his *Proceso de Residencia* (Mexico, 1847), p. 284.

70. Cited in León-Portilla, *La visión de los vencidos*, p. 90.

71. *Ramírez Codex*, pp. 199–200.

72. Bernal Díaz, *The Conquest*, p. 253.

73. He was mistaken in this regard. Once Moctezuma's brother—whom Cortés had unwittingly agreed to send as an envoy to negotiate for peace with the Aztecs—was chosen to be emperor, Moctezuma himself (who had thoroughly lost prestige in the eyes of his people as a result of his alliances with the Spaniards and his submission to them) no longer had any power or importance. See Francisco Cervantes de Salazar, *Crónica de la Nueva España* (Madrid, 1914).

74. Cortés, *Letters from Mexico*, p. 128.

75. Ibid., p. 166.

76. Bernal Díaz, *The Conquest*, p. 247.

77. Cortés's version reads: "With this I went to the fortress where, together with the great temple which was beside it, all my people were quartered. The garrison in the fortress received us with such joy it seemed we had given back to them their lives which they had deemed lost; and that day and night we passed in rejoicing, believing that all was quiet again." In *Letters from Mexico*, p. 130.

78. Ibid., p. 132.

79. Bernal Díaz is absolutely explicit in regard to Cortés's responsibility. He leaves no doubt that Cortés's last order to Moctezuma was yet another of the aggressive, inconsiderate measures characteristic of his attitude toward Moctezuma after returning to Mexico. For the change in Cortés's attitude toward Moctezuma, see Bernal Díaz, *Historia verdadera*, pp. 265–66.

80. Cortés, *Letters from Mexico*, p. 116.

81. Ibid., p. 122.

82. Ibid., p. 123.

83. Ibid., p. 125. Cortés presents Cristóbal de Tapia's arrival the same way, placing it in the same category as that of Narváez. He justifies his disobedience thereby, referring to where in his second letter he associates the intervention of anyone other than himself with *disservice* and a cause of *danger* for the land thus "disturbed." See Cortés, *Cartas de Relación* (Mexico, 1975), pp. 168–69.

84. However, in his letter to the king (*Carta de Diego de Velázquez al Rey*) dated October 12, 1519, Velázquez summarized the main political and historical points contrary to which Cortés designed his fictionalized version of his rebellion. Velázquez sets forth the historical context as a point of reference, showing the degree to which the situation is presented differently in Cortés's letters. He claims that Cortés's disobedience constitutes a threat and a crime that must be punished,

and that his punishment should serve as an example. "I have often begged your most illustrious Lordship to have such excesses and thefts severely punished whenever and however they occur. For besides the fact that so much gold has been put at risk, so much evil done, so many thefts committed (and I know not whether these evils may not have inspired others among the men who remained to imitate them), such a tumult has been caused on the island, that I assure your illustrious Lordship, aside from the effort required to pacify these bold men, Your Highness's income and interest from this island will be considerably diminished this year. God willing things will not get worse, for considering the distance between these parts and your kingdoms, if the judges and governors appointed by Your Highnesses were not very much feared and supported, and if similar excesses and thefts were not severely punished, everyone here would behave likewise and encourage others to do the same, for Spaniards are unruly and ever on the lookout for something new. Have these bad men who have caused such a commotion among your servants punished, Your Highness, so that they may provide an example for all to see" (CDIAI, ser. 1, vol. 12, pp. 246–51). The letter provides a precise description of the authority and circumstances in opposition to which Cortés drew up a fictionalized version of his expedition and design to conquer territory.

85. Bernal Díaz, *The Conquest*, p. 90. This statement is not consistent with the complete text of Velázquez's *Instrucciones*, but it may have been included in one of his letters to Cortés, handed to him with the *Instrucciones*. These letters referred far more ambiguously to the fact that booty was the expedition's primary (although not exclusive) objective.

86. Bernal Díaz, *The Conquest*, p. 88.

87. Cortés, *Letters from Mexico*, pp. 50–52.

88. "As I foresaw so clearly," says Cortés, "the harm and disservice to Your Majesty which would ensue from the above-mentioned, especially as they told me he had powerful forces with him, and brought a decree from Diego Velázquez that as soon as I and certain of my companions, whom he had singled out, were taken we should be hanged, I still determined to go to him, thinking it wise to make him recognize the great disservice which he was doing to Your Highness and to dissuade him from his evil intent. So I continued on my way." Ibid., p. 123.

89. Ibid., p. 125.

90. Ibid., p. 124.

91. Ibid., p. 53.

92. Ibid., p. 127.

93. Ibid., pp. 59–60.

94. Ibid., pp. 134 and 141–42.

95. Ibid., p. 265.

96. Las Casas, *Historia*, vol. 2, pp. 238–40. Anything problematical about Columbus's measures was caused, in Las Casas's opinion, by a "mistake," ignorance, or excessive hastiness, never by cruelty or greed. He presents Cortés, on the other hand, as a sort of embodiment of evil, of premeditated, calculated abuse. A comparison of Las Casas's characterization and those of other contemporary witnesses, such as Bernal Díaz or Andrés de Tapia, shows how prejudiced Las Casas was about Cortés, and how distorted a description of him he produced. The fragments quoted here are from Las Casas, *Historia*, vol. 2, pp. 445–46.

97. Andrés de Tapia, *Relación de la conquista de México*, in *Crónicas de la Conquista* (Mexico, 1939).

98. Bernal Díaz, *Historia verdadera*, pp. 578–81. There is abundant proof of Cortés's penchant for cards and other games, and of his having allowed them to be played despite Velázquez's explicit prohibition. One of the most curious documents concerning this is a royal warrant dated March 11, 1530, returning to Cortés and his men the money lost at cards during the campaigns to conquer Mexico. The warrant is in response to a request made by Francisco Núñez "on

behalf of the neighbors, residents, and conquerors of New Spain," claiming that "when the territory was conquered and pacified, some of the conquistadors played for gold pesos; and because it was best for them to be kept always together in case of a surprise attack and so that they could watch over the towns where they were residing, they were allowed to play cards at night and bowl during the daytime, to keep them constantly together; otherwise, and for reasons besides those already mentioned, there would have been many deaths among the Christians as well as thefts of horses and other items." Under another royal warrant bearing the same date, Cortés is reimbursed "the amount of twelve thousand pesos in gold," which he lost playing cards during the same campaigns "seven or eight years ago, causing him much injury and harm." See CDIAI, ser. 1, vol. 12, pp. 510–14.

99. Arnold Hauser traces the development of this political philosophy starting with Machiavelli's formulation of the need to separate political praxis from Christian principles and ideals, and culminating with the foundation of such an order as that of the Jesuits. "The Jesuit order," says Hauser, ". . . was to become a model of dogmatic strictness and ecclesiastical discipline and . . . became the first embodiment of the totalitarian idea. With its principle of the end justifying the means, it signifies the supreme triumph of the idea of political realism and gives the sharpest possible expression to the basic intellectual characteristic of the century." In *The Social History of Art* (New York, 1951), vol. 2, pp. 118–20.

100. Ibid., pp. 118–20.

101. Henry R. Wagner, *The Rise of Hernán Cortés* (Berkeley, 1944), p. 464.

102. Niccolò Machiavelli, *The Prince*, tr. Russell Price, ed. Quentin Skinner and Russell Price (New York, 1988), pp. 51–53. I believe Leonard, Wagner, and Madariaga considerably exaggerate the importance of the role of the *Reconquista* as a model in the development of the military conquest of Mexico. No doubt the conquest had roots going back to the Renaissance, the Spanish *Reconquista*, and the European crusades. However, this does not warrant thinking of it as simply a surviving manifestation of the "spirit of the *Reconquista*." The importance Machiavelli assigns to the science of war in *The Prince* reflects a thoroughly Renaissance view according to which weapons continued to be the basic means of transforming the political and economic reality of the European states. No governor could fail to be trained as a military man and a warrior, at a time when for even the most enlightened political philosopher, all forms of legality had to be secondary to the power of weapons. "The main foundations of all states (whether they are new, old, or mixed) are good laws and good armies. Since it is impossible to have good laws if good arms are lacking, and if there are good arms there must also be good laws, I shall leave laws aside and concentrate on arms." Machiavelli, *The Prince*, p. 42.

103. Cortés, *Letters from Mexico*, pp. 106–7.

104. Bernal Díaz, *The Conquest*, pp. 240–41.

105. Ibid., p. 241. Cortés's fictionalized version of this episode involves a transformation of his own person and behavior. In his letters he makes himself appear dignified and thoughtful, hardly raising his voice as he calmly orders the idols removed from the temple. Andrés de Tapia, who witnessed the event, describes Cortés's behavior quite differently. He bears quoting to illustrate the degree of transformation involved in Cortés's account: "before the Spaniards he had sent for arrived, angered by the words he was hearing, he took hold of an iron bar lying there and began to beat upon the idols and the precious stone work; and by my faith as a gentleman, I swear by God that I believe the Marquis's jumping about

was supernatural, as he held on to the middle of the bar and threw himself forward to hit the idol at the top of the level of its eyes." Tapia, *Relación*, p. 87.

106. Cortés, *Letters from Mexico*, pp. 59–60 and 62.

107. For example, his having fallen into a trap as a result of giving in to pressure from Alvarado and his own men to advance toward the center of the city, which caused him the loss of more than fifty men, does not mean that Cortés was lacking in foresight; it simply proves that his tactics and methods were invariably valid. The same may be said in regard to the incident involving the faulty bridges, also described in Cortés's third letter.

108. See Andrés de Tapia, *Relación*, p. 74–75; Bernal Díaz, *Historia verdadera*, pp. 164–68; and León-Portilla, *La visión de los vencidos*, pp. 43–44.

109. Andrés de Tapia, *Relación*, p. 75.

110. Bernal Díaz, *The Conquest*, p. 172. Cannibalism and sodomy, perceived as monstrous by the Europeans, constitute a recurrent obsession in Díaz's narrative, where he presents such practices as the embodiment of Evil and identifies them implicitly with the infidels.

111. Cortés, *Letters from Mexico*, pp. 73–74.

112. The letters refer openly to the use of terror and violence in connection with the characterization of their fictional hero; and although he underplayed the concrete effects of his use of repression, Cortés does not seem to have had any qualms about admitting that he was so harsh with the Cholultecas that more than 3,000 of them died. Quite the contrary: he presents the incident as evidence of his military talent, making him appear to be a man of his time rather than cruel or heartless. The hero bases his action on the very same principles formulated so clearly by Machiavelli in *The Prince* in his section on "Cruelty and mercifulness; and whether it is better to be loved or feared." We read there that "a new ruler, in particular, cannot avoid being considered harsh, since new states are full of dangers," and in discussing the choice between being loved or feared, Machiavelli formulates the same principle implicit in Cortés's transformation of terror and violence into a necessary tactic. "A controversy has risen about this: whether it is better to be loved than feared, or vice versa. My view is that it is desirable to be both loved and feared; but it is difficult to achieve both and, if one of them has to be lacking, it is much safer to be feared than loved." Cortés's behavior in Cholula and Tepeaca provides a perfect illustration of this philosophy, which is proved valid over and over again in his discourse by successful episodes that he presents, authentically or otherwise, as having been its direct result. See Machiavelli, *The Prince*, pp. 58–59.

113. Cortés, *Letters from Mexico*, p. 51.

114. Machiavelli, *The Prince*, p. 10.

115. Cortés, *Letters from Mexico*, pp. 69–70.

116. Machiavelli develops a theory based on this general principle on the appropriate use of cruelty and the political use of goodness and generosity. Cortés's relationship with his men involves a perfect combination of the two principles. He divides the troops, isolating Velázquez's followers and alternately punishing and rewarding them, killing off the most recalcitrant among them and winning the others over to his side. See Cortés's second letter in *Letters from Mexico*.

117. Wagner, *Rise of Hernan Cortés*, p. 294.

118. Madariaga, *Hernan Cortés*, p. 454.

119. Machiavelli, *The Prince*, p. 33.

120. "I had posted Spaniards in every street, so that when the people began to come out they might prevent our allies from killing those wretched people, whose number was uncountable. I also told the captains of our allies that on no account

should any of those people be slain; but they were so many that we could not prevent more than fifteen thousand being killed and sacrificed that day." Cortés, *Letters from Mexico*, p. 264.

121. Ibid., p. 323.

122. Ibid., p. 336.

123. Cortés's plan in his fourth letter, and especially in his letter of October 15, 1524, presents a political and economic model oriented toward a harmonious system of agriculture, mining, and livestock production, designed to make the region self-sufficient rather than a source of tribute for the king or the new colonizers. This change in Cortés's objectives, including the implicit role he has in mind for the natives in his new society, appears in his letter of October 15, 1524. Referring to the question of tribute demanded of the natives, Cortés states in this letter that "this should consist of neither gold nor silver, for the Indians have given away or no longer possess whatever small pieces of jewelry they had in the past. They only thing they can provide is what they are already giving to those Spaniards who own natives: maize which we use here instead of wheat; cotton with which they make their clothes; a wine they drink called *pulque*. And they can build the Spaniards' houses and raise their cattle." Cortés, "Carta de Cortés al Emperador, del 15 de Octubre de 1524," in *Cartas de Relación*, p. 212.

124. Cortés refers explicitly to this dependency to justify his disobeying Tapia and refusing to meet with him. Although less explicitly, he carefully establishes throughout the last part of the third letter and all of the fourth that he is irreplaceable in connection with the founding of New Spain.

125. There is no place in Cortés's *Letters* for anything potentially problematical, or for any note that might diverge from what needs to be said to properly characterize their fictionalized hero or describe the state he is creating. The *Letters* associate every conflict or problem with such "usurpers" and "pirates" as Tapia, Garay, and Grijalva, who, sent by Fonseca or Velázquez, might propose to undermine or share Cortés's absolute power. See Cortés, "Cuarta Cartas de Relación," in *Cartas de Relación*, p. 187.

126. It is in this context that the elements taken by Cortés from feudal forms of conduct or action should be understood, including the references to Montesinos, Roland, and other medieval heroes attributed to Cortés by Bernal Díaz. Their inclusion in his code of representation does not imply that such heroes really influenced Cortés as such, as suggested by Leonard and as was certainly true in the case of Díaz and other conquistadors. Cortés used the figures deliberately for his fictionalized portrayal of characters and actions, with a very precise political purpose in mind.

127. Cortés, "Carta al Emperador," May 15, 1522, in *Cartas de Relación*, p. 99.

128. Cortés, *Letters from Mexico*, p. 320.

129. Versus the treason the letters claim has been committed by Velázquez and his followers, who are always represented as seeking their own gain and interest, Cortés repeats over and over again that the central purpose of his plan and his action is to increase the glory and the dominions of the monarch. When, for example, he refers to the ships he is building to continue his territorial expansion toward the spice islands, he says: "I hold these ships of more importance than I can express, because I am certain that if it so please Our Lord God, they will gain for Your Caesarean Majesty more realms and dominions than those of which our country now knows . . . for I am convinced that if I do this there will then be nothing wanting to make Your Excellency monarch of the whole world." Cortés, *Letters from Mexico*, pp. 320–21.

130. Cortés not only presented all his actions as subordinate to the interests of the king, making even his most rebellious behavior appear to be the service of a good vassal; even in the exhortations addressed to his men—which he fictionalized as much as anything else—he used such concepts as *vassalage* and *service* as a maximum instrument of persuasion, thus reinforcing the importance of the ideological structure to which these terms allude. He delivered the first of such exhortations during the military campaign against the Tlaxcaltecas, and his written version of it follows: "Indeed, I heard it whispered, and almost spoken out loud, that I was a Pedro Carbonero to have led them into this place from which they could never escape . . . and I encouraged them by reminding them that they were Your Highness's vassals and that never at any time had Spaniards been found wanting, and that we were in a position to win for Your Majesty the greatest dominions and kingdoms in the world. Moreover, as Christians we were obliged to wage war against the enemies of our Faith; and thereby we would win glory in the next world, and in this, greater honor and renown than any generation before our time. They should observe that God was on our side, and to Him nothing is impossible." In his argument he gives primary importance to vassalage, presenting it as the essential motor of action; an action that is characterized implicitly as service, as the opposite of abandoning the project, which, according to the feudal code of representation he invokes, would be tantamount to treason. It is only after using the vassalage relationship as a primary argument that Cortés refers to the men's obligation to behave like Christians, and only last of all does he mention glory, honor, and renown—which in fact were the venture's main motivating factors. See Cortés, *Letters from Mexico*, p. 63.

131. Which incidentally justifies the expropriation of new lands as booty, following St. Thomas's theory, as noted by Victor Frank in his article "Imperio particular y universal en las cartas de relación de Hernán Cortés," *Cuadernos Hispanoamericanos*, 165, p. 467.

132. Henry Wagner's assessment of Cortés's choice between submitting or becoming independent is surprising. "Although Cortés was a natural born leader he was not in my opinion a great one; his judgment was not commensurate with his energy. . . . Confronted finally with the necessity to declare himself independent or returning to Spain to have his wings clipped, he tamely submitted." Wagner, *Rise of Hernán Cortés*, pp. 41–42. If Cortés's decision here not to become independent reveals anything at all, it is his perspicacity: not even all the power he achieved during the conquest made him lose sight of the political and social context of that power, which continued to have its foundation in the support afforded him by the king. Mexico was by no means a fully established absolutist state, but a dependent one in the process of constitution, which Wagner appears to have forgotten when he speaks so optimistically of the possibility of independence. The fact that Cortés had no illusions about the strength or invulnerability of his own power indicates how rational and realistic this great politician in fact was, and not—as Wagner seems to suggest—submissive, timorous, or lacking in stature and initiative.

133. Bernal Díaz, *The Conquest*, p. 185.

134. Cortés, *Letters from Mexico*, pp. 338 and 380. Italics mine.

135. It should not be forgotten that the fantastic aspects of Columbus's representation, identifying America with the fabulous or mythical kingdoms of Far East Asia, played a key role in defining the new lands as the most extraordinary reserve of spices and precious metals ever mentioned, in either the ancient texts or the travel journals of the period. See Chap. 1, "The Instrumentalization of Reality" above, pp. 37–49.

Chapter 3

1. Irving A. Leonard, *Books of the Brave* (Cambridge, Mass., 1949), p. 3. The author claims that these three elements were fundamental and gives an accurate description of the meaning of each, stressing however that they were not the only important incentives. The imaginary models in the literature of chivalry, reflecting as they did a general interest in things fantastic, no doubt constitute a fundamental element that should be taken into account (as Leonard claims), in trying to understand and evaluate the nature and development of many of the expeditions that set out to explore and conquer. See Leonard's specific analysis of the influence of this literature on these ventures, pp. 1–64.

2. Ibid., pp. 13–14.

3. See Chap. 2, above.

4. On the subject of "*el irrealismo español*," see Pierre Vilar, "El tiempo del Quijote," in *Crecimiento y desarrollo* (Barcelona, 1974).

5. Ibid., p. 342.

6. Leonard, *Books of the Brave*, p. 11. The author himself calls this general interpretation hypothetical. And although it seems likely that the points he mentions were important in creating the Spaniards' penchant for myth and fantasy, they do not of themselves explain why this phenomenon was so intense in Europe, or why Spain was so vitally inclined to prefer fantasy and myth to the facts that proved their unequivocal falsehood.

7. Enrique de Gandía notes that such potions are mentioned in Greek mythology and in Homer's references to magical rejuvenation. He also notes a reference on a 1375 Catalonian map to the kingdoms of Alexander who "cuida morir sino que Satanat lengita per la sua mort". *Historia crítica de los mitos de la conquista americana* (Buenos Aires, 1929), pp. 49–50.

8. "At the head of this forest is the city of Polumbum. Beside it is a mountain, from which the city takes its name, for the mountain is called Polumbum. At the foot of this mountain is a noble and beautiful well, whose water has a sweet taste and smell, as if of different kinds of spices. Each hour of the day the water changes its smell and taste. And whoever drinks three times of that well on an empty stomach will be healed of whatever malady he has. And therefore those who live near that well drink of it very often, and so they are never ill, but always seem young. I, John Mandeville, saw this well, and drank of it three times, and so did all my companions. Ever since that time I have felt the better and healthier, and I think I shall do so until such time as God in his grace causes me to pass out of this mortal life. Some men call that well the *fons iuuentutis*, that is, the Well of Youth; for he who drinks of it seems always young. They say this water comes from the Earthly Paradise, it is so full of goodness. Throughout this country there grows the best ginger there is anywhere; merchants come thither from distant countries to buy it." *The Travels of Sir John Mandeville*, tr. C. W. R. D. Moseley (London, 1983), p. 123.

9. "The *moriche* palm tree, which the Indians called the 'tree of life,' grew mainly along the Orinoco and . . . the tree of immortality, the *palo santo* or *lignum vitae*, and the *Xaqua*, gave their properties to the waters and rivers which came in contact with them." Gandía, *Historia crítica*, p. 54, notes 8–12.

10. Gonzalo Fernández de Oviedo, *Historia general y natural de las Indias* (Madrid, 1959), vol. 2, p. 105.

11. Ibid., vol. 4, p. 320.

12. Pietro Martire d'Anghiera, *Décadas del Nuevo Mundo* (Buenos Aires, 1944), decade 7, bk. 7, chap. 1.

13. Antonio de Herrera himself mentions that "even today there are some who

obstinately continue to seek this mystery." See Herrera's account of both versions of the myth (one involving a fountain and the other a river) in his *Historia general de los hechos de los castellanos* (1512), decade 1, bk. 9, chap. 12.

14. Ferdinand Columbus, *Historia del Almirante* (Madrid, 1892), chap. 9. See also Herrera, *Historia*, decade 1, bk. 1, chap. 2.

15. Gandía, *Historia crítica*, pp. 59–61. See also Stephen Clissold, *The Seven Cities of Cibola* (London, 1961), pp. 24–48, with its photographic reproduction of the map by Johann Ruysch.

16. Herrera refers to this episode in *Historia*, decade 1, bk. 1, chaps. 2 and 3.

17. See Clissold, *Seven Cities*, p. 26.

18. Gandía, *Historia crítica*, p. 63. The myth of Chicomoztot or of the seven caves of origin of the Nahuas is in the Annals of Cuauhtitlan.

19. Morris Bishop, *The Odyssey of Cabeza de Vaca* (London, 1933), pp. 155–56.

20. Fray Marcos de Nizza, *Relación del descubrimiento de las siete ciudades*, in "Colección de documentos inéditos del Archivo de Indias" (CDIAI), ser. 1, vol. 3, p. 344. All quotations from this account are from this version; pp. 329–50.

21. Ibid., p. 347.

22. *Instrucciones de Don Antonio de Mendoza, Visorrey de la Nueva España para Fray Marcos de Nizza*, November 20, 1538; in CDIAI.

23. Nizza, *Relación del descubrimiento*, pp. 331–32.

24. Ibid., pp. 333–34. 25. Ibid., p. 336.
26. Ibid., pp. 340–41. 27. Ibid., p. 342.
28. Ibid., pp. 347–48. 29. Ibid., p. 343.
30. Ibid., pp. 341–42.

31. Andrés's tales are recounted in Anghiera's *Décadas del Nuevo Mundo*. The information he obtained on the wonderful fountain is in the first few chapters of decade 7, bk. 7; the quotation is from the first chapter.

32. Fernández de Oviedo, *Historia general*, bk. 37, preface and chap. 1, pp. 322–25.

33. Pedro de Castañeda y Nájera, *Relación de la jornada de Cibola*. The original is in the New York Public Library. I have quoted from a transcription prepared by George Parker Winship for the 14th Annual Report of the American Bureau of Ethnology (Washington, D.C., 1896).

34. Clissold, *Seven Cities*, pp. 132–33.

35. Castañeda, *Relación de la jornada de Cibola*, p. 432.

36. Castañeda describes how "a Spaniard named Cervantes . . . solemnly swore that he had heard and seen the Turk speak with the devil in a basin of water, and that being locked up so that nobody could speak with him the Turk asked him . . . as I have said." Ibid., p. 439.

37. Ibid., p. 441.

38. The account of the arrival of the native is a summary by the Gentleman of Elvas in his *Relaçao dos trabalhos do Gobernador Don Fernando de Souto*, folio 13. The original manuscript is in the New York Public Library. The facsimile I consulted was published by James Alexander Robertson in *Publications of the Florida Historical Society* (Florida, 1933).

39. Castañeda, *Relación de la jornada de Cibola*, p. 431.

40. Elvas, *Relaçao*, folio 56.

41. Nizza, *Relación del descubrimiento*, p. 339.

42. Elvas, *Relaçao*, folios 56 and 57.

43. Columbus, *Select Letters* (London, 1847), p. 179.

44. Columbus, *Select Letters*, pp. 201–2. Fernández de Navarrete (*Colección*

de viajes y descubrimientos, Madrid, 1954) notes that the age Columbus mentions cannot have been correct.

45. Cortés, *Letters from Mexico*, tr. A. R. Pagden (New Haven, 1986), pp. 360–61.

46. Ibid., p. 386.

47. The failure of this expedition to the Hibueras was twofold. Cortés never reached his real destination, the second fabulous Culua about which he had heard so much. And the ruse lost him considerable power, together with the governorship of New Spain, which he already had, and the title of viceroy, which he expected to obtain. The commotion and struggle for power that took place during the two years of his absence, which would hardly have occurred had he remained in the city of Mexico, brought about one of his most bitter periods, for he was subject to impeachment proceedings that placed him in a very vulnerable position with all the courtiers, officials, and rivals who had been waiting for several years to take his place. See Henry R. Wagner, *The Rise of Hernán Cortés* (Berkeley, 1944); Salvador de Madariaga, *Hernán Cortés* (Buenos Aires, 1941); witness accounts of the impeachment proceedings (CDIAI, vol 12, pp. 350–58); and the correspondence between Cortés and the emperor concerning the trouble in the capital during Cortés's absence, especially Cortés's letters of May 13 and September 3, 1526, in CDIAI, ser. 1, vol. 12, pp. 367 and 480.

48. Cortés, *Letters from Mexico*, p. 422.

49. The news he had received of the struggle for power among his representatives in Mexico City who, believing him to be dead, had lost no time in going after his power and looting his home. See Cortés, *Letters from Mexico*, pp. 421–22.

50. Cortés, *Letters from Mexico*, pp. 338 and 380.

51. Ibid., pp. 355, 380, and 395. The descriptions of nature are from the fifth letter.

52. Ibid., pp. 380 and 382.

53. See notes 48 and 50 to Chapter 3.

54. *Carta de Vázquez de Coronado al Emperador*, written from Tiguez on October 20, 1541; in CDIAI, ser. 1, vol. 3, p. 363.

55. Castañeda, *Relación de la jornada de Cibola*, pp. 415–16.

56. Ibid., p. 416.

57. This is the assumption made by Winship in his edition of the annual report of the American Bureau of Ethnology, 1896.

58. Elvas, *Relaçao*, folio 22 recto.

59. *Carta de Vázquez de Coronado al Emperador*, p. 363.

60. *Relación postrera de Cibola*, reproduced by George Parker Winship in the 14th Annual Report of the Bureau of American Ethnology (Washington, D.C., 1896), p. 568.

61. Elvas, *Relaçao*, folio 47.

62. Luis Hernández de Biedma, *Relación del suceso de la jornada de Hernando de Soto*, in CDIAI, ser. 1, vol. 3, pp. 438–39.

63. Castañeda, *Relación de la jornada de Cibola*, p. 424.

64. Miguel León-Portilla, *La visión de los vencidos* (Mexico, 1976), pp. 70–71.

65. Castañeda, *Relación de la jornada de Cibola*, pp. 425 and 430.

66. Elvas, *Relaçao*, folios 47, 55, and 59.

67. Castañeda, *Relación de la jornada de Cibola*, pp. 415–16.

68. Alvar Núñez Cabeza de Vaca, *Naufragios y Comentarios acompañados de otros documentos inéditos*, ed. Serrano Sanz (Madrid, 1956) vol. 1, pp. 3 and 4.

69. Ibid., pp. 4 and 5. Italics mine.

70. See Chap. 1, above, pp. 20–37.

71. See Chap. 2, above, pp. 63–79.

72. See Chap. 2, above, pp. 80–97.

73. *The Journey of Alvar Núñez Cabeza de Vaca*, tr. Fanny Bandelier (Chicago, Rio Grande Press, 1964), pp. 23–24. The work is referred to in the body of the text as the *Naufragios*. References to chapter numbers also correspond to the Spanish text, but the English version is not divided into chapters nor does it contain the prologue. Page references to passages quoted henceforth correspond to the Bandelier translation.

74. Ibid., p. 22.

75. Ibid., p. 20.

76. Ibid., pp. 14–15.

77. Ibid., p. 41.

78. Ibid., pp. 22–23.

79. Ibid., pp. 36–37. The notion of *impossibility*, and the insistent detailed enumeration of the difficulties encountered, distinguish the two forms of discourse. In his mythified version of the action during the conquest of Mexico, Cortés systematically eliminates both aspects, and it is only in Bernal Díaz that we find a degree of realism in regard to the constant difficulties afflicting the army. Cortés now speaks of determination or will instead of achievement, generally in rather sparse, abstract terms that uphold the fictional equivalence between will and action, and thus provide a mythified impression of the development of the specific facts of the conquest.

80. *The Journey of Alvar Núñez Cabeza de Vaca*, pp. 37 and 39.

81. Ibid., pp. 50–51.

82. Cortés's *Letters from Mexico*, Díaz's *Historia verdadera de la conquista de Mexico* (Madrid, 1975), and other similar narratives contain abundant examples of incidents proving the need to subordinate one's interests to those of the community. The list of personal sacrifices undertaken for the good of the army and its mission is endless, and there are detailed descriptions in the various letters and histories that show that the military code of honor based on the notion of solidarity against the common enemy was held in very high regard. They also show, however, that this code was vulnerable—as was made evident by individual incidents described—in the face of the individualism, selfishness, and anarchy so prevalent as the conquest proceeded.

83. *The Journey of Alvar Núñez Cabeza de Vaca*, p. 89. None of the accounts of hapless adventures to be found in the narrative discourse of failure deals as obsessively with hunger as does the *Naufragios*. Núñez treats this theme with an intensity comparable to that of the picaresque novel, which in this regard he anticipates.

84. Ibid., pp. 40 and 69.

85. Ibid., p. 55. By explicitly attributing the distortion of reality to fear, Núñez reveals a problem affecting both the discourse of mythification and most of the discourse of failure: the subjective nature of perception and the effect of prejudices and emotions that transform, conceal, and distort the new reality instead of reflecting it as it truly is. Writers from Columbus to Fray Marcos de Nizza present dreams and mythical versions as if they involved objective and even confirmed truth.

86. Ibid., pp. 57–58. Italics mine.

87. Ibid., pp. 58 and 59.

88. Ibid., pp. 63 and 85.

89. Ibid., p. 64. Fernández de Oviedo, who for his *Historia General* used Núñez's *Naufragios* and the *Relación* by Castillo, Dorantes, and Núñez to the

Santo Domingo Audiencia, confirms these two episodes of cannibalism, which he describes briefly and without comment: bk. 35, vol. 4, pp. 295–97.

90. *The Journey of Alvar Núñez Cabeza de Vaca*, p. 74.

91. Ibid., pp. 108 and 137.

92. *The Journey of Alvar Núñez Cabeza de Vaca*, pp. 65–66 and 69.

93. Ibid., p. 160.

94. It should be noted that Núñez at least includes him at the end of his lists, and refers to him constantly in his text. Oviedo, who based his version of Narváez's expedition on the accounts in the *Naufragios* and the *Relación* (see note 90 above), often leaves out any mention of Esteban and refers to the *three* survivors.

95. *The Journey of Alvar Núñez Cabeza de Vaca*, p. 97. Italics mine.

96. Ibid., p. 59. This evaluation is even more revealing if we consider that the natives wept over the shipwrecked Spaniards' misfortune.

97. Ibid., p. 164.

98. For an analysis of the problems inherent in using Aristotelian theory to perceive and justify many aspects of the conquest of America, and more specifically the subjection of the *"naturales,"* see Lewis Hanke, *El prejuicio racial en el Nuevo Mundo: Aristóteles y los indios de Hispanoamérica* (Chile, 1958); and Alejandro Lipschutz, *El problema racial en la conquista de América* (Mexico, 1975).

99. Ginés de Sepúlveda, *Tratado sobre las causes de la justa guerra contra los indios* (Mexico, 1941), p. 135; quoted in Lipschutz, *El problema racial*, p. 72.

100. Sepúlveda, quoted by Lipschutz, *El problema racial*, p. 75.

101. Las Casas, *Historia de las Indias* (Madrid, 1958), vol. 2, chap. 4, p. 136.

102. Ibid., vols. 1 and 2. For an analysis of the historical significance of Las Casas's doctrines, see Marcel Bataillon, *Estudios sobre Bartolomé de las Casas* (Barcelona, 1976).

103. Marcel Bataillon, "La Vera Paz, novela e historia," in *Estudios sobre Bartolomé de las Casas*, p. 200.

104. Raquel Chang Rodríguez, *Prosa Hispanoamericana Virreinal* (Barcelona, 1978), p. 50.

105. See Chap 3, "The Narrative Discourse of Failure," above.

106. Enrique Pupo-Walker, "Sobre el discurso narrativo y sus referentes en los *Comentarios Reales* del Inca Garcilaso," in Rodriguez, *Prosa Hispanoamericana Virreinal*, pp. 30ff.

107. *The Journey of Alvar Núñez Cabeza de Vaca*, p. 190.

108. Ibid., pp. 5–6.

109. Two basic incentives seem to be stronger than any other form of inner motivation in the text, structurally complementing the "novelistic" presentation of the material. These are hunger and necessity, whose importance in keeping the action moving and developing anticipates, in a very general way, their function in the picaresque novel. I mention this extremely cautiously, however: the connection has to do with the *degree* of importance of these problems in the discourse on the conquest and in the picaresque novel, not with the *way* they operate in the respective texts nor their functions and implications within their respective contexts.

110. David Lagmanovich divides this material into four basic types: marvelous episodes, which he relates to twentieth century marvelous realism, a connection that I consider problematical at least, and strange, fantastic, and testimonial episodes. See his "Los Naufragios de Alvar Núñez como construcción narrativa," *Kentucky Romance Quarterly*, 1978. I do not believe this classification helps to clarify the true function of the intercalated episodes, which do not give the account any particularly literary dimension—a point that must be stressed. The insertion of native legends (the Bad Thing, for example), presages, premonitions, and

recognition no doubt contribute to filling out the narrative. These aspects do not make the *Naufragios* qualitatively different, however, from the many other novelistically presented chronicles typical of a long-standing tradition on the peninsula. The literary dimension of the text is related, rather, to Núñez's ability to create a double form of discourse, both denotative and connotative. The Bad Thing episode adds nothing to the understanding of the *Naufragios*'s central message, focused on the spiritual trajectory of a narrator who is shipwrecked repeatedly as he comes up against the central issue of the conquest, develops a critical consciousness, and subverts the models of the dominant ideology through his writing. Other episodes, on the other hand, that are neither intercalated additions nor, at first impression, "novelistic" (the one concerning the Bay of Horses, for example, or the one narrated in chapter 12) appear to be an extremely important part—structurally and with regard to their fundamental significance—of the work's design to present a literary presentation of the issues of the conquest.

111. *The Journey of Alvar Núñez Cabeza de Vaca*, pp.108–10.

112. Ibid., p. 110.

113. Jacques Lafaye, "Les miracles de Alvar Núñez Cabeza de Vaca," *Bulletin Hispanique*, 64 bis (1962): "Il reste a considérer l'histoire de ce temps comme un genre littéraire. Ses fins étaient celles des anciens, proposer des exemples édifiants, glorifier des personnes; et celles des modernes, exalter des valeurs spirituelles—confondues avec des intérêts nationaux ou politiques. Enfin présenter sous une forme élégante des faits excitants pour l'esprit. La notion même d'objectivité en histoire restait inaperçue; épopée en prose, œuvre de propagande, histoire naturelle, chronique familiale, l'histoire du Nouveau Monde ne peut etre utilisée par l'historien moderne que comme histoire des idées et non des faits." In the same article, Lafaye provides a very revealing and convincing indication of the use of the *miracle* as a category to give an account of how healing occurred, involving an incipient mingling of cultures similar to the one I have mentioned above in connection with the episode of the Bad Thing and Alvar Núñez's reinterpretation of it.

114. Núñez did not give his narrative the title *Naufragios*. The first edition was published in Zamora in 1542 as "La relación que dio Alvar Núñez Cabeza de Vaca de lo acaecido con los indios" (The account given by Alvar Núñez Cabeza de Vaca of what occurred with the Indians).

Chapter 4

1. See Chap. 3, "A Collective Penchant for Myth," above.

2. Leonard, *Books of the Brave* (Cambridge, Mass., 1949) pp. 54–55.

3. Demetrio Ramos Pérez refers to this connection in *El mito del Dorado: Su génesis y proceso* (Caracas, 1973). The author provides an insightful discussion of the rational and scientific foundation—consistent with the scientific knowledge of the period—underlying the mythification process, thus identifying the area reserved to the imagination proper in the complex process of formulating and reelaborating the myth of El Dorado during the conquest and exploration of the continent.

4. "Carta mensajera de los reyes al Almirante," September 5, 1493. Reproduced in Fernández de Navarrete, *Colección de viajes y descubrimientos* (Madrid, 1954) vol. 1, p. 364.

5. *Lletras reals molt notables fetas a Mossen Jaume Ferrer: e regles per el ordenades en Cosmografía y en art de Navegar, les quals XVII anys ha trobi en semps ab lo pait Sumari a tinch los mateixos originals: Coopilat per so criat*

Raphel Ferrer Coll (Barcelona, 1545), quoted in Ramos Pérez, *El mito del Dorado*, p. 22.

6. Pedro Martir de Anglería, *Décadas del Nuevo Mundo* (Buenos Aires, 1944), dec. 7, chap. 6, p. 448.

7. Padre José de Acosta, *Historia Natural y Moral de las Indias* (Madrid, 1954), bk. 4, chap. 1, pp. 88–89.

8. *The Travels of Marco Polo* (New York, 1958), p. 309.

9. Referring for example to the expeditions organized by Hernán Cortés, Leonard claims that "in all directions his lieutenants, as well as he himself, were heading expeditions with instructions to locate the Amazons and other oddities, along with gold and silver mines," in *Books of the Brave*, p. 41.

10. See Leonard, chaps. 4 and 5. On page 48, for example, speaking of the explorations undertaken from the base in New Spain, Leonard states specifically, "Chief among the latter objectives were the Amazon women, and again and again the proximity of their realm was reported."

11. See in particular Rómulo Cúneo Vidal, "Las leyendas del Perú de los Incas," *Boletín de la Real Academia de la Historia* (Madrid, 1925), on the connection between the ancient myth of the Amazons and the native accounts. Based on an etymologico-historical analysis of his material, the author discusses aspects of the society and culture of the Peruvian Incas described by the natives to the Spaniards, which served to confirm to the latter the presence in South America of their own European myths. See also Gandía's, *Historia crítica de los mitos de la conquista americana* (Buenos Aires, 1929) for an analysis of the mingling of European facts and myths with native legends that characterized the development and evolution of Greek myth in America.

12. See Gandía, *Historia crítica*, chap. 6.

13. Even as late as 1778 there is a reference by La Condamine in his *Relation Abregée d'un voyage fait dans l'intérieur de l'Amérique méridionale* to warrior women who lived without men in the lands and along the river's edge, in the region of the Amazon basin. See Gandía, *Historia crítica*, p. 87.

14. Cortés, *Letters from Mexico* tr. A. R. Pagden (New Haven, 1986), p. 298.

15. Fray Gaspar de Carvajal, *Relación del descubrimiento del río de las Amazonas* (Seville, 1894), pp. 59–60, 66–69.

16. Reproduced in Fernández de Oviedo's *Historia General y Natural de las Indias* (Madrid, 1959), bk. 26, chap. 11, p. 87.

17. Hernando de Ribera, *Relación de la expedición del río de la Plata*, published together with Núñez's *Naufragios y Comentarios* (Madrid, 1957), p. 258.

18. See "La sierra de la plata" in Gandía, *Historia crítica*, pp. 145ff.

19. The "Carta de Lebrija y Martín" contains abundant information on the objectives and development of the expeditions in search of the fabulous hinterland, especially the one led by Ximénez de Quesada. The letter is reproduced in Fernández de Oviedo, *Historia General*, pp. 83–92. It is there that reference is made to the "triangle" I mention in the next paragraph of my text.

20. Gandía, *Historia crítica*, p. 129.

21. The quotation is from Fray Pedro Simón's *Tercera Noticia* (Caracas, 1963), chap. 1. See also Gandía, *Historia crítica*, p. 112. Cúneo Vidal, moreover, relates the source of the legend of El Dorado to the Inca empire's system for collecting tribute rather than to the Guativita Lake ceremony. According to Cúneo, the Golden Indian was in fact the Inca's factor, in the ceremonies held to collect tributes of gold. "After the *manus'* gold had been collected on the *cumbi* blankets," says Cúneo, "the monarch's factor *rolled about* on it as if *taking possession* of it . . . so that his body, covered in particles of gold, shone in the sunlight like a

burning coal," in "Las leyendas del Perú de los Incas," p. 25. Gandía mentions this theory but disregards it for lack of acceptable proof, although he acknowledges it to be highly suggestive.

22. *Relación de la jornada de Omagua y el Dorado: Relación del Bachiller Francisco Vázquez que narra la expedición de Pedro de Ursúa* (Madrid, 1979), pp. 11–12.

23. Ramos Pérez examines this transformation with admirable erudition in his study, focusing specifically on the myth of El Dorado. Both analytically and from the point of view of its documentation, his work is extremely interesting and thorough.

24. Ramos Pérez, *El mito del Dorado*, p. 142.

25. Ibid., p. 153.

26. Ribera, *Relación de la expedición del río de la Plata*, pp. 256–61. Ribera's insistence on officially certifying the accuracy of his version is worth noting, precisely in view of the fantastic character of its information.

27. Ribera, *Relación de la expedición*, p. 258.

28. In *El mito del Dorado*, Ramos Pérez develops his theory according to which the increasing appearance of the lake as a symbol for concealment was based on the episode concerning the concealment of the treasure of Moctezuma. In effect, familiarity with this episode may have made it easier for the Spaniards to accept as true the native tradition according to which lakes were sacred and used as the depositories of offerings; it may likewise have contributed to making lakes an integral element of several myths.

29. Ribera, *Relación de la expedición*, p. 259.

30. Gandía, *Historia crítica*, p. 123.

31. Ribera's reference (after his first mention of a lake) to the "House of the Sun," which he takes to be the name given by the natives to the lake they describe, confirms the hypothesis that he was referring to Lake Titicaca and to the Temple of the Sun built by the Incas along its edges. Gandía summarizes the stories about lakes that were eventually all identified with a single lake deep in the unexplored hinterland: "The confusion surrounding imprecise and fabulous reports concerning Lake Titicaca, the Guativita Lake, Lake Parime, and the Lake of the Xarays, created in Peru and the River Plate the notion of an imaginary lake that was often identified with the Xarays, but also shared details in common with the other lakes." Gandía, *Historia crítica*, p. 224.

32. Ribera, *Relación de la expedición del río de la Plata*, p. 258.

33. See above note 5.

34. Ribera, *Relación de la expedición del río de la Plata*, p. 260.

35. Ladislao Gil Munilla, *El descubrimiento del Marañón* (Seville, 1954), p. 154 and pp. 192–193.

36. Fernández de Oviedo, *Historia General*, bk. 49, chap. 1.

37. Carvajal, *Relación*, pp. 3 and 5.

38. "Carta de Gonzalo Pizarro al Rey," from Tomabamba, dated September 3, 1542. The letter is transcribed by Toribio Medina in "El descubrimiento del Amazonas," a documentary appendix accompanying Fray Gaspar de Carvajal's *Relación*, pp. 85ff. The very inclusion of the search for El Dorado as an objective of the expedition makes the goal in Benalcazar's 1540 *capitulaciones* different from those in his "Carta al Emperador" written in 1542. This would appear to indicate that between 1540 and 1542 El Dorado began to be reported in Quito as being an objective at least as important as cinnamon.

39. Gonzalo Pizarro, "Carta al Rey" from Tomabamba, pp. 85ff. There is no conclusive proof, however, that cinnamon constituted a false objective from the

outset (as suggested by Gil Munilla) solely designed to disguise the true objective of Pizarro's presumed plan to find El Dorado. The only thing Pizarro's letter to the king makes clear is that the first time he reformulated his objectives was after his main design (the search for cinnamon) had failed.

40. Carvajal, *Relación*, p. 5. Italics mine.

41. Ibid., p. 15.

42. Ibid., pp. 43–44. For more on the connection with the myth of the Amazons, see pp. 67–68.

43. Ibid., pp. 67 and 70.

44. See Chap. 3, "A Collective Penchant for Myth," above.

45. Leonard, *Books of the Brave*, pp. 54–55.

46. Gil Munilla, *El descubrimiento del Marañón*, p. 152.

47. Gandía, *Historia crítica*, pp. 104 and 196.

48. Leonard, *Books of the Brave*, p. 73.

49. This is not the place to discuss in depth the nature and profound implications of the New Laws, or the degree to which they were based on the ideas of Las Casas—a task already undertaken, moreover, by a number of historians. For the purposes of this study it is important simply to point out that when these laws appeared they started a revolt that over a period of two years led to the first openly seditious movement that explicitly refused to accept Latin America's dependence on the crown.

50. Agustín de Zárate, *Historia del Perú* (Madrid, 1947), p. 508.

51. The concept of conquest expressed here—according to which discovery and occupation are viewed as a legitimate means of acquiring "averes," possessions, and a position in society—is directly connected with an entire ideology related to the *Reconquista* and to previous formulations as clear as those to be found in the *Cantar de Mío Cid*. In his summary of the possible effect of the New Laws, under which "no one would be spared from being divested of all his property," Zárate presents a thoroughly partisan version of the issues at stake and shows that he identifies completely with the class whose abusive privileges were most directly threatened by the new regulations.

52. See Marcel Bataillon, "The Pizarrist Rebellion: The Birth of Latin America," *Diogene*, Fall 1963, pp. 48 and 51.

53. Ibid., pp. 52–53.

54. Zárate, *Historia del Perú*, p. 520.

55. "So serious and weighty a negotiation as the one you have become involved in and have tried to accomplish thus far has been interpreted by his Majesty and everyone else in Spain not as rebellion or infidelity against the King, but as a means of claiming justice due you, as part of a petition put before your Prince." "Carta de Don Pedro de la Gasca a Gonzalo Pizarro," September 20, 1546, reproduced in Zárate, *Historia del Perú*, p. 547. See also "Carta del Rey a Gonzalo Pizarro," February 26, 1546, ibid.

56. Pero López, *Relación de los alzamientos de Pizarro, Castilla y Girón*, ed. Juan Friede (Madrid, 1970). The form used for the distribution of favors or rewards was not accidental. La Gasca took his orders from Prince Philip, who had ordered him to win back the rebels through generous rewards, in order to dispel their resentment and check any inclination to start a new rebellion. But the effect of this policy was predictably demoralizing and discouraging to those who had remained loyal, and it promptly became a source of active discontent.

57. Bataillon, "The Pizarrist Rebellion," p. 52.

58. Disillusionment in the face of reality was instrumental in creating a sense of critical distance, both in the northern continent and in the south. But in the first

case criticism was limited to acknowledging that the myths were not true and that the models had failed. In the south, active rebellion against the established ideological and political order (perceived as the root of a disappointing reality) soon gave rise to concrete plans to liquidate the system based on the ideological models being challenged.

59. Bataillon notes that in regard to any public definition of their plan for sedition, Pizarro's rebels went no further than adding to their flag a crown adorned at the top by the letter "P." "The Pizarrist Rebellion," p. 52.

60. See Juan Calvete y Estrella, *La vida de D. Pedro de la Gasca* (Madrid, 1965), in *Crónicas del Perú*, vol. 5, p. 99.

61. Zárate, *Historia del Perú*, p. 492.

62. "Correspondencia entre La Gasca y el Consejo de Indias," in *Documentos relativos a D. Pedro de la Gasca y Gonzalo Pizarro* (Madrid, 1964), vol. 2, letters between 1548 and 1549.

63. Demetrio Ramos Pérez, "Lope de Aguirre en Cartagena de Indias y su primera rebellión," *Revista de Indias*, nos. 73–74 (1958), p. 538.

64. Ibid., p. 539.

65. "Carta de Gonzalo Pizarro al Rey" from Tomabamba (see note 38 above), p. 90.

66. Fernández de Oviedo, *Historia General*, bk. 49, chap. 2, p. 237.

67. It appears likely that Lope de Aguirre took part in the previous rebellions led by Castilla and Hernández Girón. Basing his thesis on the documentation available, Ramos Pérez (see note 63) relates the Lope de Aguirre of the Marañón rebellion to the Lope de Aguirre who had participated earlier in the rebellion led by Martín de Guzmán after the failure of the expedition to Cenu in search of gold mines. He also mentions that this Martín de Guzmán may have been the same Martín de Guzmán who withdrew at the last minute from Pedro de Ursúa's expedition, and whose brother Fernando de Guzmán (a gentleman from Seville like the Martín de Guzmán of the Cartagena de Indias rebellion) was crowned Prince of Peru by Lope de Aguirre himself while the rebellion was underway.

68. Gonzalo de Zúñiga, *Relación de la jornada del Marañón*, "Colección de documentos del Archivo de Indias" (CDIAI), ser. 1, vol. 4, pp. 215–16.

69. Ibid., p. 217.

70. See Emiliano Jos, *Jornada de Ursúa a El Dorado* (Huesca, 1927). The *Relación Anónima* is transcribed in the documentary appendix to this work, p. 244.

71. Custodio Hernández, *Relación de la jornada de Ursúa*, transcribed in Jos, *Jornada de Ursúa a El Dorado*, p. 233.

72. Pedrarias de Almesto, *Relación de la jornada de Omagua y Dorado* (Madrid, 1979), pp. 16 and 17. Pedrarias de Almesto's account, or rather the one known generally as such (not the personal account, or *bis*, by P. de Almesto cited by Jos, which is completely different) is a copy of the original report by Francisco Vázquez. Pedrarias de Almesto added to the text a few paragraphs—almost invariably designed to justify and ennoble his role in the rebellion—together with certain minor changes in vocabulary and other details. The edition prepared by the Marquis of Fuensanta del Valle for the Sociedad de Bibliófilos Españoles reproduces the complete text of Pedrarias de Almesto's version (manuscript 3191 in the collection of the National Library in Madrid), footnoting the differences between it and Vázquez's original (manuscript 3199 in the same collection). The edition published by Miraguano in 1979, which I have used for my study and quoted from, is an exact reproduction of the Fuensanta edition. My references

henceforth are to the Vázquez version, except for fragments added to the original by Pedrarias de Almesto in regard to which I refer to the latter.

73. Vázquez, *Relación de la jornada de Omagua y Dorado*, p. 16.
74. Pedrarias de Almesto, p. 20.
75. Vázquez, p. 21n1.
76. Ibid., p. 33. Note the reference to the psychosis of revolt, mentioned earlier.
77. Custodio Hernández, *Relación de la jornada de Ursúa*, p. 235.
78. Pedrarias de Almesto, p. 28.
79. Zúñiga, *Relación de la jornada del Marañón*, p. 225.
80. Vázquez, p. 43.
81. Ibid., p. 43.
82. Ibid., pp. 49–50. Gonzalo de Zúñiga confirms the terms of the proposal and sworn statement, as does Pedrarias de Almesto, who changes nothing in Vázquez's original version regarding this point.
83. Ibid. Again the terms of Aguirre's speech are confirmed by the other reports, and all agree in claiming him to be the brains behind the design to change the expedition's objectives and proclaim a new king.
84. Zúñiga, *Relación de la jornada del Marañón*, p. 246.
85. Vázquez, p. 32.
86. Zúñiga, *Relación de la jornada del Marañón*, p. 229.
87. Vázquez, pp. 40–41.
88. *Relación Anónima*, p. 243.
89. Vázquez, pp. 41 and 32.
90. Ibid., p. 63.
91. Ibid., pp. 87–88.
92. See Chap. 3, "Demythification and Criticism in the *Naufragios*," above.
93. It is interesting to note the constant invocation of spells and incantations to describe the negative transformation of reality, the real causes of which are not understood. Vázquez is conscious of the decadence of the heroic values represented by the figure of the conquistador, and he expresses this decadence and its immediate political and ideological consequences in very effective literary terms. When he finds it necessary to refer to the causes of Ursúa's symbolic transformation, however, he feels obliged to speak of the spells wrought upon him by Inés de Atienza—just as forty years later, the "arbitrista" Cellórigo used the same image to describe the economic decadence of Spain. "It would seem," said Cellórigo, "that nothing less has been done than to attempt to reduce these kingdoms to a republic of men bewitched, living outside the natural order." And finally Cervantes—who inquired further than anyone else into the disintegration of a view of the world no longer capable of adapting to the reality that worldview itself had created—extends the substitution mechanism in Velázquez's *Relación* and uses bewitchment in *Don Quixote* to account for anything that cannot be explained rationally. See Pierre Vilar, *Crecimiento y Desarrollo*, pp. 332ff., on the historical and ideological issues of the period of *Don Quixote*.
94. Vázquez, pp. 18, 32, and 34.
95. Ibid., pp. 62 and 63.
96. Zúñiga's transcription of Aguirre's speech the day after Don Fernando was assassinated is much more explicit and detailed than Vázquez's. But although succinct Vázquez's version includes all the main points, which involve rejecting all forms of royal authority and nullifying the epic project.
97. Vázquez, pp. 64 and 65.
98. Ibid., pp. 148–49.

99. Ibid., p. 150n2, which contains a transcription of the final paragraphs of Vázquez's account not included in that of Pedrarias.

100. Marcel Bataillon, "The Pizarrist Rebellion," p. 50.

101. It should be stressed again here that this attempt at self-justification, necessarily focusing responsibility on Lope de Aguirre and virtually turning him into a scapegoat, is common to all the accounts of the expedition. The clearest and most concise version of this characterization is to be found perhaps in the short ballad included in Zúñiga's *Relación*. It is based on the use of six qualifiers in an increasingly negative progression: Biscayan-treacherous-wicked-killer-dog-rabid-diabolical. See Zúñiga, *Relación de la jornada del Marañón*, pp. 267–69.

102. See pp. 175, 187.

103. Emiliano Jos concludes, based on first-hand knowledge, that Valle Inclán was thinking of Lope de Aguirre when he created his dictator in *Tirano Banderas*. Moreover, Lope de Aguirre is the central character in many literary works by contemporary writers, among them in particular Sender, Uslar Pietri, Otero Silva, and Rosa Arciniegas; and he anticipates many aspects of the representation of the dictator and dictatorship in contemporary Latin American novels centered on a similar figure.

104. See D. Segundo de Ispizúa, *Los vascos en América, Historia de América*, vol. 5 (Madrid 1918).

105. Jos's interpretation in *Jornada de Ursúa a El Dorado*, which concludes with a categorical statement that Lope de Aguirre was mad, was responded to in 1942 by J. B. Lastres and C. A. Seguín in their historico-psychological study. To the question "Was Aguirre mad?" they reply: "Our study of his characteristics and actions inclines us to deny this. Nothing that we know about him would lead us to diagnose him as psychotic, based on our current understanding of this malady. We find no sign of an alteration in his emotional faculties that might allow us to so characterize him. Our final diagnosis is 'Abnormal personality; psychopath devoid of affect.'" See J. B. Lastres and C. A. Seguín, *Lope de Aguirre el rebelde* (Buenos Aires, 1942).

106. "Carta de Aguirre a Felipe II." I have used the Jos transcription, which indicates the differences between the Vázquez-Pedrarias transcription and the Aguilar y Córdoba transcription. The latter is in the documentary appendix to Jos, *Jornada de Ursúa a El Dorado*, p. 198.

107. "Carta de Aguirre al gobernador Collado," in the documentary appendix to Jos, *Jornada de Ursúa a El Dorado*, p. 201.

108. "Carta de Aguirre a Felipe II," p. 197.

109. See Joseph Perez, "Pour une nouvelle interprétation des 'comunidades' de Castille," *Bulletin Hispanique* 65 (1963), and José Antonio Maravall, *Las comunidades de Castilla* (Madrid, 1970), on the ideology behind the rebellion of the *comuneros*.

110. "Carta de Aguirre a Felipe II," p. 199.

111. Ibid., p. 197.

112. Ibid.

113. Speech by Lope de Aguirre transcribed by Vázquez in his *Relación*, p. 82.

114. The words and passages quoted are from "Carta de Aguirre al Provincial Montesinos" and "Carta de Aguirre a Felipe II" in the documentary appendix to Jos, *Jornada de Ursúa a El Dorado*, pp. 190 and 197–200.

115. Speeches transcribed by Zúñiga in his *Relación*, pp. 246 and 273.

116. Ibid., p. 273.

117. Speech by Lope de Aguirre transcribed by Vázquez, p. 109.

118. "Carta de Aguirre a Felipe II,", p. 197.

119. Judge Bernáldez's sentence against Lope de Aguirre, transcribed in Jos, *Jornada de Ursúa a El Dorado*, p. 104.

120. "Carta de Aguirre a Felipe II," p. 196.

121. Ibid., p. 200.

122. "Carta de Aguirre al Provincial Montesinos," in Jos, *Jornada de Ursúa a El Dorado*, p. 122.

123. "Carta de Aguirre al gobernador Collados" and "Carta al rey," in Jos, *Jornada de Ursúa a El Dorado*, pp. 201, 196, and 200.

124. José Antonio Maravall, "Un esquema conceptual de la cultura Barroca," *Cuadernos Hispanoamericanos*, 273 (1963), p. 427.

125. "Carta de Aguirre a Felipe II," p. 200. Italics mine.

126. Maravall, "Un esquema," p. 460.

127. I agree with Lastres and Seguín in disagreeing with Jos's opinion that Aguirre was "mad and resentful."

128. "Carta de Aguirre al Provincial Montesinos," in Jos, *Jornada de Ursúa a El Dorado*, p. 192.

129. Baltasar Gracián, *El discreto*. See Maravall, p. 430.

130. This is the interpretation in Jos's conclusion to *Jornada de Ursúa a El Dorado*, as well as in his later work, *Ciencia y Osadía en Lope de Aguirre el Peregrino* (Seville, 1950).

Chapter 5

1. Columbus, *Journal*, pp. 23–24.

2. See Chap. 1, "A Real World Disregarded," above, pp. 20–37.

3. Columbus's need to identify the people in America with the Asians encountered by Marco Polo is made evident by the fact that, from his first voyage on, he systematically inverts Polo's characterizations. Viewing the natives from the perspective of their possible use within the context of his commercial plans, he transforms them successively in his characterizations from men into savages, from savages into serfs, from serfs into beasts, and from beasts into merchandise. See Chap. 1, "The Instrumentalization of Reality," above, pp. 37–49.

4. Columbus's discourse made generosity an attribute of bestiality, and turned peacefulness and hospitality into cowardliness. The natives' gentle, loving disposition, to which he referred constantly in describing his contact with them, would make them good servants. Even as early as October 12, Columbus concludes from the welcome given the Spaniards by the Tainos that "they must be very good servants." And barely a month after having characterized them as savages—in his entry for October 13, where he describes them as "very beautiful" primitive people—he reduces this characterization to a single term, "heads," which marks the transformation of the savage and serf in his perception into a beast. In the last stage of his characterization, the natives are transformed from "beasts," "heads," or "pieces" in his lexicon into merchandise. Columbus formulates this explicitly for the first time in his *Memorial* to the King and Queen from Isabella, dated January 30, 1494. In this document he speaks of how to organize the transportation of slaves and how to "unload and reload their [Highnesses] vessels [of all the merchandise]"; and he refers to the caravels "that shall come over licensed for the traffic of slaves." Columbus, *Journal* (entries for October 12 and 13) and *Select Letters*, pp. 85–86.

5. See Chap. 1, "A Real World Disregarded," above, pp. 20–37, for a more detailed analysis of the appropriation of language in Columbus's texts.

6. Cortés, *Letters from Mexico*, p. 108.

7. Cortés, *Carta al Emperador*, October 15, 1524, p. 211. (Reference is to the fourth letter.)

8. Ibid. Emphasis mine.

9. Tapia, *Relación*, pp. 83–84.

10. Bernal Díaz, *The Conquest*, p. 172.

11. Ibid., p. 173.

12. See Chap. 3, "Demythification and Criticism in the *Naufragios*," above, pp. 129–51.

13. Las Casas, *Historia*, vol. 1, p. 142.

14. Ibid., p. 143.

15. Núñez, p. 160.

16. Vázquez, *Omagua y Dorado*, pp. 69–70.

17. Ibid., p. 126.

18. See J. Bautista Avalle Arce, "El poeta en su poema: El caso de Ercilla," *Revista de Occidente* 32, for an analysis of the connection between *La Araucana* and Renaissance epic forms; José Durand, "Caupolicán clave historial y épica de *La Araucana*," *Revue de Litterature comparée* 52, pp. 367–89 on the poem in relation to the *verista* tradition in Spain and the tradition of verisimilitude in Italy; Lía Schwartz, "Tradición literaria y heroínas indias en *La Araucana*," *Revista de Indias* 38 (1972), pp. 615–25, for an examination of the same question, with a focus on the characterization of female figures. For a comprehensive analysis of the poem, see especially Manuel José Quintana, "Sobre la épica castellana," *Obras completas*, vol. 1 (Madrid, 1897), pp. 545ff.; Martínez de la Rosa, "Apéndice sobre la poesía épica española in *Obras completas*," vol. 1 (Paris, 1845), p. 22; Marcelino Menéndez y Pelayo, *Antología de poetas hispanoamericanos* (Madrid, 1895), pp. 6–9; J. Ducamin, *L'Araucana* (Paris, 1900); E. Solar Correa, *Semblanzas literarias de la colonia* (Santiago, 1933); A Torres Rioseco, *La gran literatura iberoamericana* (Buenos Aires, 1945); Pedro Henríquez Ureña, *Literary Currents in Hispanic America* (Cambridge, 1945); Frank Pierce, *La poesía épica del Siglo de Oro* (Madrid, 1961); Luis Alberto Sánchez, *Historia comparada de las literaturas latinoamericanas* (Buenos Aires, 1973); J. Toribio Medina, *La Araucana*, 4 vols. (Santiago de Chile, 1913).

19. Fernando Alegría, *La poesía chilena del XVI al XIX* (Berkeley, 1945), p. 1.

20. Alonso de Ercilla, *La Araucana* (Mexico, 1975), Canto 1, p. 16. All English translations of *La Araucana* are mine and are simply meant to provide a general sense of the original text; they are not full, polished translations.

21. Ibid., pp. 22–23.

22. Elvas, *Relacao*.

23. *La Araucana*, Canto 39, pp. 403–4.

24. Ibid., Canto 8, p. 119.　　　　25. Ibid., Canto 3, p. 50.

26. Ibid., Canto 1, p. 16.　　　　27. Ibid., Canto 1, p. 17.

28. Ibid.

29. Ercilla devotes several stanzas to a detailed description of the Araucans' military tactics, their adaptation to the American environment, their attire, the construction of their fortifications, etc. See Canto 1, pp. 19–20.

30. Speaking of religion and witch doctors, Ercilla says that "estos son los que ponen en errores / . . . / Teniendo por tan cierto su locura / como nos la Evangélica Escritura." Noting their error, he nonetheless acknowledges that the Araucan faith is as valid for the natives as the Gospel is for Christians. *La Araucana*, Canto 1, p. 22.

31. *La Araucana*, Canto 2, p. 39.

32. Ibid., Canto 1, p. 23. Interpretations like the one by E. Solar Correa, for whom the Araucans were worthless savages, have absolutely no foundation in a careful reading of the poem. Such a conclusion could only be reached by attributing no importance whatsoever to the meaning of the specific elements used to characterize the natives and by disconnecting the work from its historical context and examining it in the light of values and prejudices not even current at the time the work was written.

33. Ibid., Canto 10, pp. 143–44.

34. Ibid., p. 144.

35. For further information on specific influences and literary sources involved in the characterization of the Indian heroines, see especially the article by Lía Schwartz cited in note 18 above.

36. *La Araucana*, Canto 20, p. 292.

37. Ibid., Canto 28, p. 387.

38. Ibid., p. 391.

39. Ibid., pp. 392–93.

40. This is an important point for the purpose of clarifying whether Ercilla's representation of the conquest of Chile was fundamentally historical or imaginary. It is also relevant to the issue of the poem's genre, which opposed *veristas* and "verisimilitudists" in their consideration of the true nature of Ercilla's poem. See in particular Durand's article on this topic (note 18 above), which focuses on the relationship between historical and poetic truth in the poem.

41. Schwartz, "Tradición literaria y heroinas indias," pp. 616–17.

42. Alegría, *La poesía chilena*, pp. 18 and 49. Moreover, contrary to Alegría's suggestion (pp. 49–51), Ercilla's gallantry has nothing to do with the form taken by the characterization.

43. Schwartz, "Tradición literaria y heroinas indias," p. 625.

44. *La Araucana*, Canto 8, p. 113.

45. Agustín Cueva, "Ensayo de interpretación de *La Araucana*: El espejismo heroico de la conquista," *Casa de las Américas* 110 (1978), p. 34.

46. *La Araucana*, Canto 1, p. 15.

47. Ramón Menéndez Pidal, *Los españoles en la literatura* (Buenos Aires, 1960), chap. 4.

48. Durand, "Caupolicán clave historial y épica," p. 367.

49. Voltaire, "Essai sur la poésie épique," *La Henriade* (Paris, 1853), pp. 39–43.

50. According to Martínez de la Rosa, "generally speaking, [Ercilla] discovered an appropriate mechanism for his poem." De la Rosa, *Apéndice sobre le épica española*, vol. 1, p. 24.

51. See Alegría, "Ercilla y sus críticos," in *La poesía chilena*, pp. 1–32.

52. Cuevas, "Ensayo de interpretación," p. 29.

53. *La Araucana*, Canto 15, p. 207.

54. Ibid., Canto 32, p. 445.

55. Alegría, *La poesía chilena*, pp. 46–47.

56. *La Araucana*, Canto 1, p. 21.

57. Ibid., Canto 18, p. 268.

58. Ibid., Canto 2, p. 38.

59. Ibid., Canto 7, p. 107. Ercilla narrates as follows:

> No con tanto rigor el pueblo griego
> entró por el troyano alojamiento
> sembrando frigia sangre y vivo fuego

talando hasta el último cimiento
cuando de ira, venganza y furor ciego
el bárbaro, del robo no contento,
arruina, destruye y desperdicia,
y aún no puede cumplir con su malicia.

Not even the Greeks were more ferocious
when they stormed Troy
spreading fire, spilling Frigian blood
tearing down walls, digging out foundations
than these barbarians driven by wrath,
vengeance, and blind fury
when refusing the spoils
they destroy and raze
in a vain attempt to satisfy their hatred.

60. *La Araucana*, Canto 3, p. 52.

61. Ibid., Canto 17, p. 329. The siege of Concepción is presented as a move that derived its authorization from its comparison with the Greek and Trojan sieges alluded to in note 59.

62. Enrico Pupo-Walker, "Sobre el discurso narrativo y sus referentes en los *Comentarios Reales* del Inca Garcilaso," in Raquel Chang Rodriguez, *Prosa Hispanoamericana Virreinal* (Barcelona, 1978), p. 41.

63. It should be noted that this model, which was central to the fictionalization of the conquest apparent in Cortés's *Letters from Mexico* or, from a slightly different perspective, Bernal Díaz's *The Conquest of New Spain*, was equally present, although at times less explicitly so, in the texts underlying the basic social and legal principles of colonial organization. Cortés's governmental ordinances, for example, continue the myth created in his *Letters* concerning the just, paternalistic, Christian conquistador, projecting the model beyond the sphere of the *Letters* themselves.

64. In his study on Caupolicán, Durand notes the connection between the characterization of the natives in *La Araucana* and the philosophy of Bartolomé de las Casas. In "El chapetón Ercilla y la honra Araucana," *Filología* (Buenos Aires, 1964), pp. 116–35, he discusses how familiar people were in the colony and its most important centers with the Las Casas debates. Ciriaco Pérez Bustamente likewise explores the connection between Las Casas and Ercilla in "El lascasismo en *La Araucana*," *Revista de estudios políticos* 46 (Madrid, 1952), pp. 157–68. For additional bibliography on the subject, see note 6 to Durand's "El chapetón Ercilla."

65. *La Araucana*, Canto 6, p. 97.

66. Ibid., Canto 6, pp. 97–98.

67. Ibid., Canto 1, p. 24.

68. Ibid., Canto 10, p. 143.

69. Ibid., Canto 7, p. 103.

70. Ibid., Canto 7, p. 109.

71. Ibid., Canto 3, p. 45.

72. Ibid., Canto 3, p. 45, and Canto 2, p. 44.

73. Ibid., Canto 9, p. 139, and Canto 12, pp. 173–74.

74. Ibid., Canto 10, pp. 143–44.

75. *La Araucana*, Canto 34, pp. 478–79, and Canto 35, p. 488.

76. Jaime Concha has already noted the conquistador's double role in the poem, relating it to the change in mentality inseparably associated with the conquistador's historical transformation into an *encomendero*, and explaining the fundamental

differences between Ercilla and the *encomendero* class. See "*La Araucana*, epopea della controconquista," *Materiali Critici* 2 (Genoa, 1981), pp. 93–128.

77. *La Araucana*, Canto 24, p. 336.

78. Ibid., Canto 25, p. 351.

79. Durand, "Caupolicán clave historial y épica."

80. See above pp. 240–43.

81. Concha, "*La Araucana*, epopea," p. 96.

82. The narrator specifies that Valdivia had fifty thousand vassals who offered him twelve gold marks per day, and that neither this nor even a good deal more would satisfy him. See *La Araucana*, Canto 3, p. 45. Tuconabala's speech likewise describes the same perception of America, briefly and clearly presenting the entire plan for the conquest as no more than a search for property and wealth and thus providing a summary version of the objective that was to determine the plunder of the New World throughout the conquest. See *La Araucana*, Canto 34, p. 479.

83. Concha contrasts the perception and characterization of nature from the military perspective of the conquest with what he terms the "mystical view of nature" developed later by the Jesuits. See "*La Araucana*, epopea," p. 97.

84. *La Araucana*, Canto 16, p. 230, and Canto 15, p. 216.

85. See Chap. 3, "The Narrative Discourse of Failure," above, pp. 116–29.

86. As an example of this poetic treatment and its ample register, one might recall the dramatic presentation of the sea and the sky during the tempest that connects the first and second parts of the poem, and the tenderness that infuses the stanza describing the discovery of a strawberry during the expedition to the south of Chile (Canto 35, p. 488.)

87. *La Araucana*, Canto 35, p. 482.

88. Ibid.

89. Ibid., p. 483.

90. Ibid., p. 485.

91. Ibid.

92. Ibid., p. 486.

93. Ibid., p. 487.

94. Ibid., p. 491.

95. Ibid., p. 493.

96. Concha notes the importance of this Utopian aspect of the characterization of the natives in the southern islands and observes how the emphasis given to it reveals immediately one of the poet's inner contradictions in regard to America's racial and cultural reality. "*La Araucana*, epopea," pp. 123–24.

97. *La Araucana*, Canto 36, p. 492.

98. Ibid.

99. William Melczer has already noted the deep conflict in Ercilla's ideological commitment, apparent in these contradictions: "Tormented by mixed and even contrary feelings, divided between a political allegiance to the ideals of the Spanish conquest and a moral sympathy with the Araucanian resistance, Ercilla felt committed to both sides and to neither." See "Ercilla's Divided Heroic Vision: A Reevaluation of the Epic Hero in *La Araucana*," *Hispania* 56 (April 1973).

100. Ercilla was perfectly aware that his version of the history of the conquest was concerned with precisely those aspects or processes that had been avoided by official accounts, and all through the poem, in different ways, he reaffirms his determination to speak of things that have been concealed or distorted by such versions. An example of this appears in Canto 13, which lists important events the poet intends not to describe in his poem since, as he states at the end of the section, despite their importance, they will be recorded in the general history: "No pongo su proceso en esta historia / que della general hará memoria." This statement shows that he has decided to rescue from oblivion only those things relegated there as a result of the selection made of what to include in the official version of the conquest. See *La Araucana*, Canto 13, p. 188.

101. Quintana, *Obras completas*, vol. 1, p. 545. Quintana's statement is consistent with the evaluation first made by Voltaire upon reading the poem.

102. *La Araucana*, Canto 24, p. 369. Menéndez Pelayo would also insist upon the importance of the figure of the poet in the work; Valbuena Briones drew attention to the double role of the narrator as both *narrator* and *actor*, likewise attributing greater importance to the function of the former. Avalle Arce focuses on the differences between the poetic *I* and the empirical *I* in the poem (see note 18 above). For further bibliographical references on the subject, see the critical bibliography compiled on *La Araucana* by Leonor Esquila. The division of the figure of the narrator in terms of contrary functions (military/literary/imaginary/active, etc.) is in effect based on this initial statement by Ercilla.

103. *La Araucana*, Canto 28, pp. 395 and 394.

104. *La Araucana*, Canto 26, p. 394. Mention should be made here of Carlos Albarracín Sarmiento's thorough treatment of the relationship between the use of the pronoun *I* and the diverse functions of the narrator. The author divides these functions into that of the *Character* (comprising the Protagonist, the Secondary, and the Witness) and the *Narrator* (comprising the Bard, the Moralist, and the Chronicler.) See Carlos Albarracín Sarmiento, "Pronombres de primera persona y tipos de narrador en *La Araucana*," *Boletin de la Real Academia Española* 46, no. 178, pp. 297–320.

105. *La Araucana*, Canto 26, p. 370.

106. *La Araucana*, Canto 23, p. 321.

107. Ibid., Canto 28, p. 397.

108. Ibid., Canto 17, pp. 248 and 244.

109. Ibid., Canto 26, p. 368.

110. Ibid., Canto 26, p. 371.

111. Ibid., Canto 32, p. 440.

112. *La Araucana*, Canto 36, p. 474. It is interesting to note that the suicidal aspects of Caupolicán's execution do not involve an isolated case. In Canto 26, the poet says that the natives had no hangman, and each man condemned was in charge of executing his own sentence:

> Por falta de verdugo, que no había
> quien el oficio hubiese acostumbrado
> quedó casi por uso de aquel día
> un modo de matar jamás usado:
> que a cada indio de aquella compañía
> un bastante cordel le fue entregado
> diciéndole que el árbol *eligiese*
> donde *a su voluntad* se suspendiese.

> In the absence of an executioner,
> for there was none around,
> they resorted to an unheard-of device
> when they provided each one of the indians
> with a length of rope
> and then told them to hang themselves
> in the tree of their choice.

See *La Araucana*, Canto 26, p. 371. Italics mine.

113. *La Araucana*, Canto 37, p. 505.

114. Concha has stressed the poet's hesitation and inconsistency concerning the

central issue of race during the conquest and Ercilla's inner struggle with two contradictory attitudes: one racist, which was characteristic of the colonizer; the other supporting the unity of the human race: "l'atteggiamento oscillante di Ercilla, nel quale lottano el razzismo connaturale al colonizzatore e un sentimento piu independente, forse di natura e fondo cristiani, dell'unita del genere humano." See Concha, "*La Araucana*, epopea," p. 124.

115. The stanza I refer to is in Canto 22, p. 315.

116. *La Araucana*, Canto 31, p. 435.

117. Ibid., Canto 36, p. 494.

118. Ibid., p. 491.

119. Ibid., p. 496.

120. The illumination provided by this second process of signification in Canto 36 is very plain. Diverse elements that appear throughout the poem are clearly defined here, with the result that the warrior is transformed into the embodiment of a critical consciousness of a historical process, and action is transformed into an apprenticeship in relation to the truth of this consciousness.

121. See Concha, "*La Araucana*, epopea," p. 125.

122. *La Araucana*, Canto 1, p. 15.

123. The poet tells us in the very first stanzas that there is a message hidden in the text: "pensando que pues va a vos dirigido / que debe de llevar algo escondido." See *La Araucana*, Canto 1, p. 15.

124. This "present situation" referred to by Concha concerns the expedition to the south narrated in Cantos 35 and 36. See Concha, "*La Araucana*, epopea," pp. 125ff.

125. Ibid., p. 125.

Index

In this index an "f" after a number indicates a separate reference on the next page, and an "ff" indicates separate references on the next two pages. A continuous discussion over two or more pages is indicated by a span of page numbers, e.g., "57–59." *Passim* is used for a cluster of references in close but not consecutive sequence.

Index

Index

Library of Congress Cataloging-in-Publication Data

Pastor Bodmer, Beatriz.
  [Discursos narrativos de la conquista. English]
  The armature of conquest : Spanish accounts of the discovery of
America, 1492–1589 / Beatriz Pastor Bodmer ; translated by Lydia
Longstreth Hunt.
    p.   cm.
  Translation of: Discursos narrativos de la conquista.
  Includes bibliographical references and index.
  ISBN 0-8047-1977-2
  1. Spanish American literature—To 1800—History and criticism.
2. America—Discovery and exploration—Spanish—Historiography.
3. Literature and history. 4. America in literature. 5. America—
Early accounts to 1600—History and criticism. I. Title.
PQ7081.P3413   1992   91-39494
860.9'327—dc20   CIP

∞ This book is printed on acid-free paper